The limits of law

The limits of law

The public regulation of private pollution

PETER CLEARY YEAGER

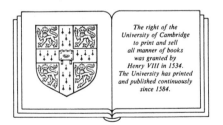

The right of the
University of Cambridge
to print and sell
all manner of books
was granted by
Henry VIII in 1534.
The University has printed
and published continuously
since 1584.

CAMBRIDGE UNIVERSITY PRESS
Cambridge
New York   *Port Chester*   *Melbourne*   *Sydney*

Published by the Press Syndicate of the University of Cambridge
The Pitt Building, Trumpington Street, Cambridge CB2 1RP
40 West 20th Street, New York, NY 10011, USA
10 Stamford Road, Oakleigh, Melbourne 3166, Australia

First published 1991

Printed in the United States of America

Library of Congress Cataloging-in-Publication Data
Yeager, Peter Cleary
The limits of law : the public regulation of private pollution /
Peter Cleary Yeager.
p. cm.
Includes bibliographical references and index.
ISBN 0-521-36535-X
1. Environmental law – United States.   2. Pollution – Law and
legislation – United States.   3. Liability for hazardous substances
pollution damages – United States.   4. Pollution – Government policy –
United States.   I. Title.
KF3775.Y4   1990
344.73′04632 – dc20
[347.3044632]   90–1997
                                                                                      CIP

British Library Cataloguing in Publication Data
Yeager, Peter Cleary
The limits of law: the public regulation of private
pollution.
I. Title
347.3044632

ISBN 0-521-36535-X hard covers

Contents

Preface

Commonly, the reasons for undertaking a lengthy social science investigation are as deeply rooted in personal commitments as they are in the problematics of any discipline. This is trivially true, but no more or less admirable, when the commitments are to the problematics themselves, as in basic science research. But the point is especially noteworthy when the commitments underlying the work are to knowledge in the ultimate service of some socially desired end. One's values provide the question and energize the long effort, while the requirements of theory and method quite literally discipline the search for answers. If this book succeeds, my hope is that it is because it contributes in some useful way to the critical quest for environmental protection and social justice while keeping faith with core analytics in social science.

As a college student twenty years ago, I was wholly dispassionate about the cause of environmentalism, even in the face of Earth Day in April 1970, which galvanized and focused the ecological concerns of millions of Americans, particularly the young on campuses across the country. Now, firmly in the grip of midlife, I find my youthful distance from the matter curious and even embarrassing. When I look out on the signs warning of the toxicity of the fish in the pretty Sudbury River near my house, my deepest sense is of injustice, and of loss. Becoming a parent has surely contributed to this sense.

The link between parental concerns and pollution was sharply dramatized to me long before my own son was born, and the episode was the first to impress me at a personal level with the force of the environmental cause. As a newspaper reporter in Minneapolis in 1972, I found myself on a small lawn in a working class neighborhood, talking with a group of residents who were being fumigated in their own homes by potent vapors emanating from the city's sewer system. The fumes were caused by the process waste being dumped into the system by a local manufacturer, and the undeniably wretched odors were wafting about from the storm drains in the streets and backing up into houses through the plumbing. This assault, by then ongoing for a year, was driving visitors away, breaking up outdoor activities, and making some residents ill, in the most poignant case sickening at least one pregnant woman to the point of vomiting. During that summer a community group began pressuring both the manufacturer and the city for an end to the hazard, and eventually some timetables for a solution were set. But with the blame being passed back and forth between the city and the company, and with the uncertainties attached to the agreements, there was reason to worry whether just results would soon be achieved. In the meanwhile, there remained the stark image of that sickened woman attempting to gestate new life.

During the same period, a much more prominent environmental drama was being played out in northern Minnesota, one that clearly portrayed the tenacious politics of delay despite substantial risks to human health. In this case, the Reserve Mining Company was dumping over 60,000 tons of mining waste each day into the pristine waters of Lake Superior from its operations in Silver Bay. By the middle of 1973, it had been demonstrated that the company's wastes included asbestos-like fibers that were contaminating the drinking water and the air of Duluth and other cities and towns on the lake. Asbestos fibers were known to be cancer-causing, and the expert inference was drawn that Reserve's wastes created unreasonable risks to the health of people in the region. Nonetheless, and against a persuasive legal case that drew national attention, the discharges continued for another several years. The federal government had initiated its enforcement effort in 1967; the dumping finally ceased in 1980.

I found these cases both intriguing and alarming. In each, it struck me that the law found it inordinately difficult to reach the right result on a timely basis. And on a more profound level, this seemed simply unjust. In sum, the origins of my research comprised equal measures of curiosity – why might law fail to achieve its stated purposes? – and indignation. Together, these motivated me to examine the operations of environmental law, and specifically its efforts to constrain industrial water pollution.

In addition to these personal motivations for the study, I found some compelling analytic reasons for undertaking it. First, my experience in a large-scale study of lawbreaking by major companies had reminded me of both the empirical and theoretical limits of officially generated data on offenses. These data are typically used as indicators of the activities of regulated parties of all sorts, from citizens to corporations. But they also register the political and legal processes of state. Therefore, not only is it necessary to understand these processes in order to interpret the data fully, but the effort to do so is rewarded by a richer understanding of the political economic relations linking the state to the society it administers. Herein lie the most fundamental questions of compliance and control, those that seek to know the structural and cultural foundations of a social system. This project is intended to illuminate these matters, if not to provide all of the answers.

Second, it is often tempting to attribute the manifest failures in regulatory law to a conspiracy in which the public interest is sacrificed to the shared, self-serving interests of government and business elites. Such arguments are made with various degrees of sophistication, and too many instances of corruption and conspiracy can be cited as examples. But these explanations miss many of the more fundamental, less visible causes of the *chronic* shortfalls in government regulation of business. The most basic limits to law's effectiveness are institutionalized in the enduring structures of social relations in a political economy, and while these limits are not permanently fixed, they are both more stable and more forceful than the periodic and fitful episodes of the corruption of law. In addition, because of the complex structuring of interests over time, there is rarely any clear identity of interests *within* the elite circles in business or government, to say nothing of *between* them. So while the identification of interests in any arena of public policy is an important starting point in research of this sort, it can never be the sum of it because interests as such are not determinative.

In this book I present an analytic history of the federal government's efforts to regulate industrial water pollution in the United States. These efforts date back one hundred years, but they gained meaningful momentum only with the passage of the Federal Water Pollution Control Act Amendments in 1972. The account focuses on the forces that produced this major piece of legislation, then on the constraints that shaped its implementation, including those that limited the Reagan administration's effort to deregulate environmental pollution in the 1980s. The story examines limits operating at the levels of both near-term instrumental politics, such as those directed at the federal Environmental Protection Agency in the 1980s, and the more enduring institutional structures that undergird American society. In the end the account is principally a structuralist one, suggesting that instrumental politics most often shapes law only within the constraints set by systemic limits. But this is not to deny the potential efficacy of organized political action in shaping the reach of law and the extent of social change. In the complex dynamics linking law and society, it happens that systemic limits themselves are subject to shifts during key historic junctures, as illustrated in this case study. Not only do social systems and political behavior shape each other, but institutions are at root the product of human action.

This last point seems especially important in the present moment. Despite two decades of significant environmental law, the nation seems to have accomplished little more than an unstable holding action against even more rapid environmental deterioration. In addition to the continuing proliferation of accounts of toxic air and water pollution that contaminates the basic substances of life, there are the newer concerns regarding the depletion of the earth's protective ozone layer and the warming of the earth's climate due to the "greenhouse effect," potentialities that are at least as threatening as the more concrete and immediate evidence of toxic wastes. And of course these serious problems transcend the bounds of national politics, implicating international relations in deeply moral questions regarding environment and economy. With the dramatic decline of communism and the rise of Green parties in politics and "green" products in markets, environmental issues are primed to take center stage in a new era of geopolitical exchange. The forthcoming discussions and debates will have to do with fundamental rights and responsibilities, fairness (as between highly developed and other nations), and ultimately survival.

The second Earth Day, in 1990, marked both the twentieth anniversary of the first one and the critical challenges yet unmet. The environmental dialogue is widening and deepening. There is both risk and opportunity in this, and the world's citizens will have to grapple with central questions of fact and value in determining the fate of the earth. This book is my attempt to chart developments in one chapter of an unfolding story whose conclusion remains much in doubt. If this effort also contributes in some small but positive way to that unfolding, I will not be disappointed.

Acknowledgments

In a piece of work spanning twelve years, one runs up an almost unconscionable account of professional and personal debts. Not only do public registers of such accounts entirely fail to repay them, but they also carry the risk of the glaring omission (thereby increasing the debt!). Nonetheless, it is important to announce these key contributions, both as a measure of my gratitude and as a reminder of my obligations.

I have enjoyed a variety of institutional supports for this research, supports manifested largely in the kindness and interest of strangers. I am especially indebted to the professionals at the Environmental Protection Agency – the lawyers, engineers, and technicians at both headquarters in Washington and the Region II offices in New York City – who not only permitted but enabled me to do my fieldwork, and even encouraged me in countless ways. Despite my reservations regarding the limits of environmental law, and the evidence of them, I was uniformly impressed by the quality and dedication of these public servants during my stays in their offices. Without their continuing efforts, both the environment and its inhabitants of every species would be all the worse. I would also like to thank officials in the Lands and Natural Resources Division, U.S. Department of Justice, for similarly giving me space and access to key legal materials, as well as the congressional representatives and their staffs who graciously made materials available to me upon request.

I have also benefited significantly from the responses of audiences to a number of manifestations of the arguments at professional conferences over the years, dating back to my first skittish effort in Dallas in 1978. That – again – kind strangers deemed that early report adequate for publishing encouraged an insecure graduate student beyond measure. (I am trusting, of course, that these ultimate results will not bring them any regrets.) In addition, I have enjoyed a number of chances to put some of these ideas and results before audiences in professional schools, including the law schools at Harvard and Yale universities and the business schools at Harvard and Boston universities.

I am also grateful for a fellowship year during 1989–90 in Harvard's Program in Ethics and the Professions, which allowed me to consider more deeply the ethical responsibilities of business and permitted me a measure of unfettered time to complete this book. Among a fine group of new colleagues in the program, I especially benefited from the exchange of ideas (and tennis shots) with two fine philosophers, Ken Winston, with whom I share an interest in questions of institutional design toward just outcomes, and Alan Wertheimer, who despite his protestations to the contrary knows plenty about the real world. Finally, I am thankful for the support, patience, and encouragement of my editors at Cambridge University Press, Colin Day, Matt Hendryx, Mary Nevader, and Cynthia Insolio Benn. In many ways, they have conspired to make this a better book. And in particular, Cynthia has worked diligently (but gently) to purge my language of its more self-destructive tendencies, and I have learned much from the almost painless process of working with her.

I am also indebted for the multifarious contributions of many other individuals, who have variously critiqued, inspired, and supported me in this work. For their readings and insightful critiques of earlier versions of this material, I thank Howard Erlanger, John DeLamater, Ronald Aminzade, David Granick, John Clark, John Braithwaite, Andy Szasz, Neal Shover, Jim Post, Gary Marx, Edwin Epstein, Michael Useem, Steven Spitzer, Bernard Phillips, Keith Hawkins, Chris Argyris, Wendell Bell, and Richard Quinney. And I should note the beyond-the-call-of-duty contributions of several individuals. Marshall B. Clinard has been both my mentor and my colleague, to say nothing of my personal link to the original inspiration of Edwin Sutherland, for whom Clinard was a research assistant in the study of white-collar crime. I am grateful to Marshall for a variety of personal and professional supports, and to Ruth Clinard as well.

Robin Stryker not only shares Hoosier roots with me, but has been an indefatigable source of support for fifteen years. Throughout that period, she has been both a stalwart friend and a sophisticated sociological critic, and the quality of her own work has been a standard for me, however imperfect my efforts to meet it. Harold Barnett is another of these rare combinations, friend and critic, who make toiling in the academic fields all the more worthwhile, almost justifying the spare material compensations for the work. Susan Eckstein has also been a fine colleague and friend, and pushed me at a propitious moment to reach for more than I believed I could grasp. Finally, Jeff Coulter has been something of a hero for me, a rare blend of keen intelligence, unimpeachable integrity, and principled compassion.

For all of their contributions, I would also like to note that the individuals just named are stout enough, individually (to say nothing of collectively), to bear responsibility for the errors and shortfalls that remain in this book. But there are strict professional norms against saying they do so, and the requirements of truth-telling also happen to forbid it, certainly in this case. So let the responsibility rest where it belongs, here.

And a last word for the deep support of my family. The phrasing " . . . without whose support . . . wouldn't have been completed . . . " by now seems trite, but most every author knows its truth. I am particularly grateful to my parents, Dorothy Cleary Yeager and Ralph Oscar Yeager, Jr., who nurtured the normative foundations that continue to guide my efforts, both personal and professional. My parents-in-law, Eleanore and Harvey Kram, have always been lion-hearted in their support, and have encouraged my work while lightening my load. And finally, my dearest support now comes from my wife and colleague, Kathy Ellen Kram, whose love, intelligence, and good humor have long sustained me in the best and worst of times, and our son, Jason William, to whose future I dedicate this project.

Many of the quantitative analyses presented in Chapter 7 were originally published as "Structural Bias in Regulatory Law Enforcement: The Case of the U.S. Environmental Protection Agency," *Social Problems*, Vol. 34, No. 4 (October 1987), pp. 330–44, © 1987 by the Society for the Study of Social Problems. I gratefully acknowledge the society for granting permission to use these materials.

CHAPTER 1

The social production of business offenses

On October 5, 1976, the U.S. government fined the large, multinational Allied Chemical Corporation $13.24 million for criminal discharges of the toxic pesticide Kepone and other chemicals into Virginia's James River. Although some observers decried the fact that the several corporate officials indicted for the offenses had been acquitted, the case nonetheless represented a high point in the growing effort to legally protect the natural environment from despoliation.[1] Not only was this single fine greater than the total fines and penalties imposed in *all* Environmental Protection Agency–initiated cases that had been previously concluded (through September 1976),[2] but merely seven years earlier neither criminal fines nor civil penalties were part of the federal government's general response to the increasingly threatening environmental degradation due to water pollution.

Seven years later the EPA's regulatory program was in disarray. Beset by deep budget cuts and overseen by a leadership eager to relieve industry of regulatory costs, the agency's enforcement efforts were in serious decline in all areas of environmental protection. This was clearly a consequence of the Reagan administration's wide-ranging policy to divest private enterprise of public regulation as part of a "supply-side" strategy to stimulate economic growth. The

---

[1] The court later reduced the fine to $5.24 million when Allied Chemical agreed to donate $8 million to a new, nonprofit corporation that would fund research projects and implement remedial activities to mitigate Kepone damage. This development had the effect of reducing the true, after-tax cost of the penalty by about $4 million, since Allied was able to claim the donation as a tax-deductible expense. The company also made a contribution to fund Kepone-related medical research and paid some of the cleanup costs, and in 1977 it faced more than twenty lawsuits for health-related damages, one of them a class action seeking more than $26 billion. For additional discussion of this noteworthy case, see Kelly (1977), Stone (1977), Reitze and Reitze (1976), and Sethi (1982).

[2] See, e.g., Environmental Protection Agency (1977a: 1).

1

results of this policy, however, proved more dramatic at EPA than in any other regulatory arena. By early 1983 the agency was awash in public scandal amid charges that its rulemaking and enforcement had become corrupted by a pattern of secret negotiations with industry representatives, exclusion of public-interest voices from policy deliberations, and improper influence exerted from the upper reaches of the Executive Branch. By April most of the president's appointees to leadership positions in the agency, including top administrator Anne Burford, had resigned under fire as the administration sought to contain the political damage occasioned by the revelations.

If the relatively aggressive prosecution of the Allied Chemical case did not represent the government's typical enforcement vigor in the 1970s (criminal prosecutions were very uncommon, multimillion-dollar fines rare indeed), neither did the administration's efforts to deregulate the economy in the 1980s signal the end of environmental protection. Instead, these two episodes suggest the policy limits within which environmental protection law can vary under present conditions of U.S. political economy. Just as the state cannot ensure environmental health and safety at the cost of economic destabilization, so is it prevented from pursuing unfettered economic growth at the expense of environmental destabilization. The Reagan administration became familiar with the latter limit when it discovered that regulatory inattention to such matters can threaten the legitimacy of government itself. The 1983 backlash to the administration's policies peaked when a bipartisan Congress, public-interest groups, and powerful media organizations sought to expose and reverse the deregulatory efforts. Although subsequent implementation of environmental laws remained at levels less rigorous than those of previous administrations, the basic structure of the law survived as the administration was forced by increasing political pressure to embrace publicly the philosophy of environmental protection, if not its rigorous application.

With the legal apparatus and broad public support for its underlying philosophy in place, contending forces will continue to struggle over where to balance the dynamic tension between economy and environment. The remarkable developments in environmental law and their partial reversals in only fifteen years suggest the volatility of any particular resolution of this contradiction. Moreover, this history provides a ripe opportunity to investigate the conditions under which the reach of law extends to define a common business practice – discharging wastes into the environment – as wrongful, thereby placing new limits on economic activity, while simultaneously being itself constrained in its regulatory efforts by countervailing pressures in social organization.

My study of the federal government's evolving efforts to regulate industrial water pollution is an attempt to make sociological sense of the dialectical relationship between these limits and constraints. This pursuit is driven by my long-standing interest in two questions: What factors promote illegal business activity, and what are the political economic limits on the law's ability to control such behavior? As I attempt to demonstrate in the next section, these questions have much to do with each other. As it happens, the study of the legal control of business not only investigates important issues in public policy, but also contributes to the analysis of the systemic relations between state and economy.

The analysis of business offenses

This study is rooted in a research tradition that, paradoxically, is long-standing but only recently developed. Social science interest in business wrongdoing dates back eighty years in the United States, to Edward A. Ross's (1907) concern with what he labeled "criminaloids" operating in the world of commerce. More than forty years would pass, however, before the sociologist Edwin H. Sutherland published his pioneering book, *White Collar Crime* (1949), which reported the first systematic analysis of large companies' violations of law. As curious as this four-decade lag may seem, even more noteworthy is that the quarter-century following Sutherland's provocative lead saw precious little research development in this area. Only a handful of studies were published in the 1950s and 1960s, and the subject had clearly failed to establish itself as a major field for research and analysis.[3]

The reasons for this failure are roughly suggested by Sutherland's experience. Although his investigation of seventy major U.S. corporations had revealed high violation rates and typically lenient federal law enforcement, it was criticized as an unjustified attack on business, and Sutherland himself was disparaged as a radical for

---

[3] Other contributions in the Sutherland era include Clinard (1946/1977, 1952), Hartung (1950/1977), Aubert (1952/1977), and Lane (1953/1977). Later analyses were published by Newman (1958/1977), Geis (1967/1977), and Leonard and Weber (1970/1977).

having challenged the integrity of the corporate world.[4] Simply put, there was little support for such work in a society that, first, was both proud and protective of its leading institutions in the economically expansionary wake of World War II and in the face of the Cold War and, second, focused on the serious domestic conflict associated with race relations and the Vietnam War. As Nicolaus (1973) has suggested, the institutional acceptance of sociology as a discipline is dependent on its usefulness to the nation's political and economic leadership, a dependency secured in large part by government and foundation control of research funds and, therefore, of research priorities. The result was that sociological criminology continued to focus almost exclusively on the politically sanctioned concern with "street" crime, concentrated primarily in the disadvantaged classes (cf., Mills, 1943; Schwendinger and Schwendinger, 1975: 128).

By the mid-1970s, however, there had been dramatic changes in the social climate. Stimulated by such developments as the Watergate episode, widespread revelations of improper corporate payments at home and abroad, and the increasing risks posed by such hazards as environmental pollution, public and governmental attention increasingly focused on the "suite crimes" of the powerful. (Important, too, was the country's military disengagement from Vietnam, which eliminated the major focus of public and news media attention of the several preceding years.) Corporate illegalities such as price fixing and pollution often came to be considered at least as serious by the public as some of the more conventionally feared crimes such as burglary and robbery, according to survey data (see, e.g., Schrager and Short, 1980; Wolfgang, 1980; Cullen, Link, and Polanzi, 1982; Cullen and Dubeck, 1985; Frank, Cullen, Travis, and Borntrager, 1989). Not surprisingly, there was a corresponding increase in scientific interest in the topic, which has by now dwarfed the volume of work earlier produced.[5] For the first

---

[4] Sutherland (1949: 247) had this to say in his *White Collar Crime*: "The persons who define business practices as undesirable or illegal are customarily called 'communists' or 'socialists' and their definitions carry little weight." Thirty years later, this sort of reaction to such research was not customary, but neither was it quite extinct. For example, in a purported review of our study of corporate illegalities (Clinard and Yeager, 1980), a writer – expressing strong disdain for both the "regulatory state" and social science (dismissed as a pseudoscience concerned *only* with morality) – wrote that "a book entitled *Corporate Crime* automatically puts us on guard to defend the corporations. . . . such a book should never have been written in the first place" (Evans, 1981: 75–6).

[5] Arguably, this new research focus was also prompted by developments in the fields

time, major federally funded research projects were begun in the generic area of "white-collar crime," most notably at the University of Wisconsin and Yale University, and a new wave of books and articles addressed many diverse questions in this fertile but vastly undercultivated field.[6]

of criminology and criminal justice. By the latter 1970s, the failure of liberal criminal justice reforms (e.g., prison rehabilitation programs, deinstitutionalization) to alleviate crime had resulted in a shift toward more punitive, "law-and-order" approaches to policy. Some leading academic criminologists became pessimistic about the discipline's contributions to social change. Simon Dinitz (1978: 234) pronounced the liberal impulse in criminology and corrections "spent," and Donald Cressey (1978: 177) charged that "the typical modern criminologist is a technical assistant to politicians bent on repressing crime, rather than a scientist seeking valid propositions stated in a causal framework."

Thus, with declining institutional support for traditional liberal concerns, the recently reidentified social problem of business lawbreaking provided an academic outlet for scientific reformers still concerned with broader issues of justice and bureaucratic wrongdoing. Indeed, this logic illuminates the liberal school's *apparently* contradictory positions on penal measures, traditionally advocating compassion and treatment for poor conventional offenders while demanding harsher penalties (more and longer periods of incarceration) for wealthy persons who violate business regulations. The latter position is in line with growing emphasis on increased control measures, while the application to elites satisfies liberal concerns for justice and fairness, and the elimination of upper level corruption. While this argument remains speculative, one could likely find supportive evidence both in the careers of many leading criminologists and in analyses of cohort differences in subfield specializations. In any event, I can attest that my own intellectual journey has passed rather in this way.

[6] The projects undertaken at the University of Wisconsin at Madison and at Yale University were both funded by the now defunct Law Enforcement Assistance Administration of the U.S. Department of Justice. Results of the former are reported in Clinard et al. (1979) and Clinard and Yeager (1980). The Yale studies include Rose-Ackerman (1978), Wheeler, Weisburd, and Bode (1982), and Shapiro (1984). Numerous other analyses of business offenses and of issues in controlling them have been published since the mid-1970s. Included are Farberman (1975), Stone (1975), Cressey (1976), Kriesberg (1976), Pearce (1976), Conklin (1977), Geis and Meier (1977), Ermann and Lundman (1978, 1982a, 1982b), Goff and Reasons (1978), Hopkins (1978, 1980), Johnson and Douglas (1978), Schrager and Short (1978, 1980), Sutton and Wild, (1978), Lauderdale, Grasmick, and Clark (1979), Needleman and Needleman (1979), Reisman (1979), Braithwaite (1980, 1982, 1984, 1985), Coffee (1980, 1981), Geis and Stotland (1980), I. Ross (1980), Barnett (1981, 1988), Fisse (1981, 1983), Cullen, Link, and Polanzi (1982), Donnelly (1982), Jones (1982), Kramer (1982, 1984), Simon and Eitzen (1982), Wickman and Dailey (1982), Calavita (1983), Clinard (1983), Fisse and Braithwaite (1983), Lynxwiler, Shover, and Clelland (1983), Vaughan (1983), Hochstedler (1984), Shapiro (1984), Curran (1984), Szasz (1984, 1986a), Coleman (1985), Szwajkowski (1985), Shover, Clelland, and Lynxwiler (1986), and Yeager (1986).

This research interest continues despite the decline in support for it at the highest levels of government and law. The interest is manifested in the many panel discussions of such topics as the "political economy of corporate crime" and "corporate crime and regulation" at professional meetings as diverse as those of the American Society of Criminology and the Academy of Management.

The limits of causal research

In general, most of the empirical work on corporate offenses has concerned the economic and organizational conditions that foster lawbreaking. In these studies, such factors as profitability, company size, and management socialization processes have been examined as potential influences (see, e.g., Burton, 1966; Staw and Szwajkowski, 1975; Asch and Seneca, 1976; Perez, 1978; Sonnenfeld and Lawrence, 1978; Clinard, Yeager, Brissette, Petrashek, and Harries, 1979). While these have proved to be important explanatory factors, this body of work has paid scant attention to another set of conditions intimately tied to business illegalities, conditions associated with the creation and implementation of law. This lopsided focus on the behavior of the *regulated* comports with the predominant research trends in mainstream criminology. In criminological research, the nature of law is typically taken as nonproblematic, and criminologists are free to investigate violations as "pure" behavioral phenomena unconfounded by the form of law or processes of its enforcement.[7]

In the study of business violations, such a focus is curious for two reasons. First, the concern with a sociology of law – particularly with the relations of power and interest that underlie legal processes – especially commends itself in the study of corporate offenses. Because law typically represents the *crystallization of (often incipient) social conflict* – in the form of legal processes that limit one set of interests in order to promote another, often contradictory set (cf., Vold, 1958: 208–9; Platt, 1975: 103; Schwendinger and Schwendinger, 1975: 124) – attempts to control powerful economic entities in capitalist societies naturally direct attention to processes of lawmaking and enforcement.[8] The underlying question is whether such

---

[7] This traditional orientation of criminology continues despite the contributions in the 1960s of the labeling perspective (e.g., Goffman, 1961; Becker, 1963; Erikson, 1964; Scheff, 1966), which underscored the role of legal institutions in the explanations of crime and deviance. The isolation of mainstream criminological thinking from broader considerations of social structure – including law and relations of power – combined with the consistent failure to reduce the burgeoning crime rates of the 1970s helped produce a perception within the discipline that criminological theory had become stagnant, that it had been infused with precious little fresh insight in recent decades (see, e.g., Dinitz, 1979: 22; Meier, 1980; see also footnote 11).

[8] Despite its lack of development, the idea that both crime and law are outcomes of processes of social conflict is not new to criminology. For example, Sellin (1938) emphasized the role of normative group conflict over fifty years ago, and Sutherland similarly underscored normative variations between groups and the role of

legal efforts are in fact constrained by the very interests they purport to regulate. As Donald Newman pointed out more than thirty years ago, "Whether he likes it or not, the criminologist finds himself involved in an analysis of prestige, power, and differential privilege when he studies upperworld crime. . . . He must be able to cast his analysis not only in the framework of those who *break* laws, but in the context of those who *make* laws as well" (1958/1977: 56; emphasis in the original).

Second, in his seminal contribution to the study of corporate offenses, Sutherland himself recognized the central importance of legal process, but failed to integrate it into his analysis. This is somewhat anomalous, because Sutherland's work in all other respects posed a head-on challenge to decades of criminological theory and research focused on the supposed personal and social pathologies of conventional offenders. It was also rooted in his philosophical opposition to perceived injustices in the "private collectivism" of big business (Cressey, 1976: 213) and to an inequitable system of law that jailed burglars and robbers while "coddling" corporate offenders with such lenient sanctions as administrative agency orders to comply and small fines. Indeed, in earlier arguing for an expanded definition of crime – to include business violations handled with civil and administrative sanctions like warnings and orders in addition to criminally punished offenses – Sutherland (1945) noted that formal legal distinctions are *politically* determined, with no necessarily logical link between the severity of the violation and the legal response. He attributed the "softer" legal definition of most corporate wrongdoing to the relative political influence of the business sector.

Nonetheless, Sutherland's classic book only suggested the importance of political and legal relations while lodging its analytic thrust in his concept of differential association. He argued that business violations, like all other types of lawbreaking, can best be explained by a learning theory: businesspeople learn the procrime or anticrime attitudes and behaviors of those with whom they most significantly associate. This social psychological explanation was premised on an underlying assumption about social organization: that normative orientations regarding law are structured in terms of competing social groups. But Sutherland only began to develop this important

conflict in legislative processes and determinations (see, e.g., Sutherland and Cressey, 1955: ch. 1). The labeling school's stream of research in the 1960s and 1970s also demonstrated the role of political power in the formulation and application of legal sanctions (see, e.g., Becker, 1963).

idea. In a short discussion at the end of his book (1949: 255–6), he introduced the concept of *differential social organization*, through which he attempted to explain his findings of high rates of business violation coupled with generally lenient legal reactions. He argued that while the business sector had reached a consensual viewpoint regarding the acceptability of law violations,[9] the public and law enforcement agencies had not organized a consensual viewpoint against such offenses; thus social control of them was weak. Sutherland hinted that the lack of public opposition to business offenses was related to "the tentacles which business throws out into government and the public for the control of those portions of society" (1949: 255). But he did not develop an analysis of the role of social structure and social relations in limiting the legal response to these offenses. Sutherland himself pointed to major shortfalls in the analysis: Differential social organization fails to explain the content of infractions and the derivation of value (group) conflicts historically (1949: 256).

Research and the role of law

That the research on business offenses has not adequately concerned itself with the analysis of sociolegal relations does not imply that its findings have been irrelevant to them. For example, studies have found significant variations in offense patterns depending on the type of law being violated. In his early study of the New England shoe industry, Lane (1953/1977) found that economic decline (as indicated by the number of employees over time) was associated with companies committing unfair trade practices such as false advertising and price fixing. Yet he found no such relationship between financial performance and violations of the labor relations laws. Similarly, the University of Wisconsin study of violations of federal laws by the large *Fortune* 500 corporations found that these firms were substantially more likely to commit violations of product safety, labor, and environmental laws than they were to violate tax, securities, and other financial laws and unfair trade laws (Clinard et al., 1979; Clinard and Yeager, 1980).

Both studies suggest that the differences reflect variations in the degree of legitimacy granted to various laws by sectors of the busi-

[9] As I discuss later, the historic evidence indicates that Sutherland was naive in attributing an ideological consensus to the business sector. Instead, the business world is often divided on political and legal issues in ways important to the understanding of the political economy of law and lawbreaking.

ness community. Lane (1953/1977: 105) suggested that financial strain may better explain violations of those laws held in higher regard by the business community, such as antitrust laws. For laws that do not accord so well with central business values, such as labor relations laws, strain may not be a necessary inducement for contravention. Impressions gathered from business journalism as well as the Wisconsin study results suggest substantial business support in principle for many of the laws established to protect the integrity of the marketplace. The antitrust and securities laws, established several decades ago as corporate capitalism asserted its control over the American economy, define the limits of acceptable behavior in competitive and ownership relations, and thereby provide relatively stable and predictable rules for what otherwise would become an unacceptably ruthless, Darwinian struggle.

There is however, more business opposition to the so-called social legislation (in contrast to the "economic" legislation mentioned previously) passed largely during the 1970s (see, e.g., P. H. Weaver, 1978; Weidenbaum, 1979). Laws designed to protect consumers, the environment, and employees restrict management autonomy at the point of production rather than simply in market relations, and can impose costly regulatory and liability requirements on companies. As Herman (1981: 185) notes, "These burdens have been especially painful to business because of their imposition at a time of accelerating international competition and structural maladjustments besetting important U.S. industries." Finally, these newer laws have often defined as illegal what had been accepted business practices and risks; the environmental laws are illustrative. As criminologists have long known, where laws lack legitimacy, violation rates are likely to be relatively high, other factors held constant.

But other factors are rarely constant, and two important considerations qualify these conclusions.[10] First, holding constant such

[10] A third consideration is the *detectability* of different offense types. Securities and antitrust offenses are often highly secret ruses in which there are no *knowing* victims; in addition, the violations are often buried in the arcane technicalities of high finance, as in the accounting concealments of improper corporate payments (see, e.g., Clinard and Yeager, 1980: chs. 7 and 8). To the extent that such offenses are more difficult and costly for government enforcement agents to detect, it is to be expected that a substantial number of them will go undetected. While such factors also hinder the enforcement of environmental-, consumer-, and employee-protection laws, they are less salient in these areas as citizens, consumers, and workers have become increasingly aware of both short- and long-term risks and their legal rights. Thus differences in *officially identified* offense levels, such as those compiled in the Wisconsin study, are to some unknown extent determined by vari-

matters as the legitimacy of law and the presumed *benefits* of infraction, offense rates are also shaped by the severity of the legal response. According to the tenets of deterrence theory, where penalties (legal *costs*) are higher, violation rates are expected to be lower. This relation appears to hold for businesses' violations of law. The Wisconsin study found that the federal government is substantially more likely to impose harsher penalties (criminal fines, sentences) for violations of the long-standing financial and unfair trade laws than for the more frequent violations of the newer environmental, product safety, and employee-protection laws (Clinard et al., 1979: 134–6).

However, while some measure of deterrence may indeed be operating to produce these results (and the reader will note that the cross-sectional data are inadequate for testing the possibility), the situation is complicated by the political economic nexus linking regulated companies and legal administration in ways typically foreign to the state's handling of conventional criminality. For example, when the state is confronted with strong opposition to legal controls from a powerful regulated constituency, as in the case of much social legislation, regulators typically proceed gingerly in order to avoid potentially disastrous (to the regulatory agency) legislative challenge or costly court battles. In this case, then, it becomes imperative to examine not simply the effects of legal sanction on compliance behavior (as suggested by the deterrence perspective), but also the "reciprocal effects" of private-sector influence on the behavior of law. Deterrence is especially likely to fail when the regulated not only question the legitimacy of law but also possess the ability to influence its administration. In sum, legal legitimacy, enforcement, and infraction are interwoven in the complex fabric of social relations that characterize the contemporary United States, as I shall attempt to demonstrate in the chapters to follow.

The second consideration complicating the regulatory scenario is that the business world is not all of a piece in these matters. Analysts from Sutherland onward have often treated commercial interests as

---

ations in detectability. The problem of estimating this effect is complicated by its contradictory relationship to identified levels of lawbreaking. On the one hand, some proportion of offenses go undetected; on the other hand, the logic of deterrence theory suggests that violation types that are difficult to detect will occur more frequently owing to the decreased *certainty* of punishment.

Although the analytic web is tangled, it seems most reasonable to conclude that variations in officially identified offense levels are the joint product of conceptions of legal legitimacy, deterrence, and detectability.

undifferentiated in their relation to law. The accumulating evidence suggests, however, that this assumption oversimplifies the dynamic relationship between law and economy. For example, sectors of business vary in ability both to comply with extant regulations and to influence their implementation. Their variations in compliance with and influence over the terms of law are, of course, closely linked. The consequence for analysis is that in order to understand fully *either* lawmaking or lawbreaking, one must study *both*.[11]

This study of the environmental regulation of business demonstrates that one cannot fully understand offense trends and enforcement patterns without analyzing the development of legislation and regulatory policy, which evolve under particular social and political conditions. In other words, observed (that is, detected) rates of business violations are the *joint production* of both business and regulatory behavior. A key implication is that, in limiting the examination of corporate wrongdoing to panels of violators *as identified by the formal, legal dispositions* of control agencies, studies of such offenses unwittingly reflect the perhaps systematic biases in law.

Rates of real as well as of discovered illegality are generated by the intersection of law and economy. Violation rates are in good part determined by the relative burden placed on businesses by legal requirements. In the same way that a ban on sleeping under bridges differentially burdens the wealthy and the homeless, so the weight of law for companies is determined in part by the differential ability of firms to absorb or pass on regulatory costs. Thus, a fully rounded explanation of business illegalities lies in dissecting the interaction of regulation and violation. Such analysis clarifies not only law's limits as a regulatory mechanism, but also its role in the reproduction

---

[11] In the face of the lack of theoretical development noted in footnote 7, the call for the revitalization of criminology has emphasized the need for the reintegration of theory. More specifically, it is now commonly argued that adequate understanding requires analyses that link crime to the nature of legal administration and that locate both in the context of prevailing social conditions (see, e.g., Taylor, Walton, and Young, 1973: 21, 1975: 54; Ball, 1978: 21; Cressey, 1978: 189; Quinney, 1979: 22; Yeager and Clinard, 1979: 64). As Durkheim (1933) and others (e.g., Hall, 1935) noted much earlier, the form that a society's law takes – and, hence, the form its crime takes – depends on the structure of social relations, especially as these are rooted in a particular mode of productive organization. To quote Aubert's (1952 [1977: 168–9]) still-necessary reminder: "It is frequently impossible to discover the sociopsychological origins and functions of criminal behavior without insight into the social processes behind the enactment of the corresponding parts of the criminal legislation. . . . The nature of the norms thus legally sanctioned may, for instance, to some extent determine whether the criminals tend to be rebels, psychopaths, or rational profit seekers."

of the prevailing social order, including patterns of business infractions (cf., Carson, 1980).

The legal regulation of industrial water pollution

The purpose of this book is to develop such an integrated explanation of regulation and infraction through an analysis of the federal government's efforts to regulate industrial water pollution in the United States. As formal state policy, these efforts are of recent origin, the first general statute having been passed by the Congress in 1948. The early regulatory attempts were tentative and unsuccessful, involving protracted negotiations with polluters, weak legal sanctions, and negligible cleanup. However, with the major shift in environmental values experienced in the 1960s and 1970s, there occurred significant legal change. Most importantly for present purposes, legislation passed in 1972 required industries to make expensive capital investments in water pollution control technology and, for the first time, established major criminal penalties for violations. In effect, the law was now forcing companies to pay, at least in part, for the use of the water resources they had traditionally considered free goods in the process of production.

The research reported here examines the evolution of this regulatory policy and the implementation of the more stringent controls during the "Environmental Decade," the 1970s. This regulatory arena reflects and reproduces fundamental conflicts in American social organization, centered on the tension between economic growth and environmental well-being. Analysis of this subject therefore provides an opportunity to examine the ways in which legal process and economic relations constrain and influence each other as the state struggles to manage its often contradictory responsibilities.

Data for this study were collected over a number of years and from a variety of sources. In 1978, at a high water mark (no pun intended) for enforcement of the 1972 Federal Water Pollution Control Act, I had the opportunity to do field research at EPA's national headquarters in Washington and at the agency's Region II headquarters in New York City. In Washington, I collected basic information on the nature and scope of the water pollution regulatory program. Agency officials graciously granted me access to all of EPA's internal policy memoranda regarding its implementation of the water law, and I interviewed enforcement attorneys, engineers, and data management personnel in an effort to disentangle the complexities of regulation in this area. I also consulted congressional documents describing the legislative history of the act and various hearings on it, as well as reports on aspects of the EPA's administration of environmental law.

At regional headquarters in New York, a research site chosen for reasons discussed in Chapter 7, I obtained systematic computer records on business violations of the 1972 law and the agency's enforcement responses. I again collected copies of the internal policy memoranda describing the region's approach to implementing the law, and interviewed attorneys and technical personnel regarding matters of enforcement and recordkeeping. At both headquarters, I sought data that would demonstrate whether and in what ways the implementation of the law varied from its stated purpose and goals, even under rather favorable social conditions for its enforcement.

In the years after the original field work, I continued to track policy in this area through a variety of sources, including government documents, news accounts, and the literature of various organizations that monitor both governmental and private-sector efforts to comply with the nation's environmental laws (the Bureau of National Affairs, the Natural Resources Defense Council, the Environmental Defense Fund, Environmental Action, and others). I also discussed developments during the "deregulatory" 1980s with experts in environmental regulation. In this phase of the work my interest was in understanding the causes and consequences of changes in policy as forces at work in American society shifted the balance point in the tension between economy and environment. Among other hunches, I suspected that these changes would produce countervailing pressures that would unsettle this most recent resolution of contradictory tendencies in state policymaking.

What follows is my effort to make sense of these data. Chapter 2 identifies social organizational constraints on effective state control of the undesirable outgrowths of private-sector production and proposes a model of linkages between state and economy that predicts a particular profile of business offenders. The next five chapters examine key arguments proposed in Chapter 2, focusing on the federal government's efforts to regulate industrial water pollution.

Chapter 3 analyzes the structure and application of the early water pollution laws in the United States. I focus on the twenty years of policy in this area in the period following World War II, a period marked by the increasing centralization of environmental policies in federal bureaucracies as the politics of pollution easily outstripped the capacities of state and local governments to respond. These early efforts were destined to fail, mainly because they lacked a broad base of support in the 1950s and 1960s. Chapter 4 turns to a discussion of the spread of environmental concern in the United States during the late 1960s and early 1970s, and of the federal government's initial scrambling efforts to respond to the new public demands for protection by creating a vast new agency to coordinate environmental regulation and by dusting off a long-forgotten nineteenth-century statute. The contradictions embedded in earlier policies and their environmental consequences had prepared the way for these dramatic changes.

Chapter 5 then examines the legislative struggle that eventuated as the Congress, the White House, and leading elements of business sought to shape new law in response to the increasingly insistent demand for it. The complex of interests and crosscurrents produced pathbreaking legislation to be sure: the Federal Water Pollution Control Act Amendments of 1972 (later, with amendments in 1977, to become known as the Clean Water Act). But while radically ambitious in its goals and stringent in its means, the legislation also necessarily contained some of the seeds of its own compromise. While the law was far from an exercise in passionate symbolism, and if it was resistant to the traditional forms of "capture" by regulated interests, by its very terms and texture this new regulatory mandate was likely to move the nation toward a cleaner, safer environment in steps quite a bit less certain and consistent than its framers had anticipated. Indeed, the risk was real that this law, and its various counterparts in other areas of environmental protection, would leave relatively undisturbed many of the deeper problems linking pollution to production and consumption.

Chapter 6 assesses the implementation of the law, those crucial stages in which legislative statements and intentions become transformed, perhaps transmogrified, into public policy. Here, in the bureaucratized relations of modern regulation, law is given effect and its impacts are determined. The often obscure and dry rhetoric of technical deliberations – whether in engineering, law, science, or simply administration – relegates their fundamentally political nature to the shadows. But these are the decisions of law that shape consequences and distribute fundamental values; political considerations are structured into them and are, in one way or another, reproduced by them. And here, the limits of law as a democratic mechanism of positive social engineering are forged, combining those from the politics of legislation with those inscribed in the bureaucratic structures of regulation, all within the constraints of the evolving political economy. In consequence, law is commonly limited in its efforts to serve broad public purposes and may reproduce systemic relations that undermine the stability of the social organism, as well as notions of equity and justice.

Chapter 7 presents an analysis of enforcement policies at EPA. These policies are examined both as formally stated and as actually applied. Despite the law's character as command and control regulation, compliance was instead commonly a matter of negotiation, often protracted long past deadlines for compliance, and arguably favoring the more powerful industrial concerns. Using quantitative data derived from EPA's enforcement records in Region II, I present results of empirical tests of the model, proposed in Chapter 2, linking business and regulatory characteristics to predict the profiles of environmental lawbreakers. Among other conclusions, the findings suggest that larger companies have specific advantages over their smaller brethren, thereby indicating that a legal structure intended to be egalitarian necessarily reproduces structural inequality, as suggested in the previous chapter. Significantly, the findings suggest that much of the advantage lies in larger companies' disproportionate access to agency decision-making procedures such that legal requirements may be modified in their favor.

Chapter 8 revisits the limits of law in light of this case study and draws on the recent history of deregulatory efforts in the 1980s to underscore some of the key dynamics shaping and constraining federal water pollution control law. The case suggests that fundamental limits underlie environmental law generally – and arguably the large body of social regulation as well – and the discussion considers some of the limits to rationality in state policymaking. Finally, I consider some of the policy implications of these results for environmental protection. Its future, and ultimately that of the quality of (ultimately the potential for) life in all its forms, depends on the careful and wise reckoning of the proper means and ends of governance.

The history examined here suggests that, just as regulation is systematically constrained within specific political and economic limits, so too are attempts to withdraw environmental controls. Once institutionalized as a recognizable state policy, and more importantly as a fundamental public *right*, pollution control is resistant to elimination when a significant public perceives a problem whose solution is beyond the voluntary capabilities of the private sector. This resistance, however, does not itself predict any one form or effectiveness of consequent policy adaptation, which depends instead on historical configurations of both political struggles and the institutional structures of lawmaking. This history indicates that law and economy maintain a complex, dialectical relationship. Rather than a legal system forever maintaining existing social structure and social relations, law and the broader institutional matrix of which it is part shape and constrain each other under particular historical conditions, suggesting that the *limits on law themselves evolve*, with various (often unpredictable) consequences for the commonweal. What is more certain is that the cumulative effects of legal change over time both shape and reflect key restructurings of the contours of political economy.

CHAPTER 2

Bringing the law back in:
an integrated approach

Like all social theory, our perspectives on law are firmly rooted in human history. It was much easier, for example, to view law as a broadly consensual, dispassionate protector of rights and arbitrator of disputes when society was characterized by a relatively decentralized market economy populated by small, competing entrepreneurs. The state's role then could be seen as simply that of ensuring the conditions under which the private entrepreneurial spirit could work its magic: creating societal progress from the competitive individual pursuit of wealth. In the main, this role meant state protection of property and contract rights and refereeing of disagreements over them.[1]

But during the past century, such a view of law became less tenable. Increasingly, the state became involved in the fundamental workings of the economy and was forced to stake out positions in the growing conflicts between capital and labor and among sectors of capital (see, e.g., Kolko, 1963; Inverarity, Lauderdale, and Feld, 1983: ch. 7). The state also necessarily developed a major role in the politics of distribution and redistribution, influencing the flow of capital and "life chances," and played an increasingly important part as purchaser of goods and producer of jobs and services. The workings of state and economy became ever more interwoven, while critical decision making in both sectors became centralized in large, powerful bureaucracies.

Thus the role of the state in economic affairs became more evident, as did the differential impacts of legal decisions on groups competing for rights and opportunities. As organized groups sought

[1] As Spitzer (1983: 324–5) points out, this laissez-faire view of the state was ideological inasmuch as it downplayed the state's increasing role in ensuring appropriate social conditions for the growth of capital: e.g., the provision of such "screening, sorting and classifying institutions" as schools and prisons. The point I make in the next paragraph is that this pristine view of the laissez-faire state became virtually impossible to sustain with the evolution of monopoly capitalism in the twentieth century.

the redistribution of social values through political action and legal reform, the resulting conflict directed attention to institutionalized biases in law.

As a result, the assumption of consensually endorsed social relations came into question and alternative theoretical perspectives on legal policy were developed. On the more benign end of the spectrum, pluralist theorists recognized intergroup conflict over the control of policy but argued that the legal apparatus itself was neutral and consensually endorsed. Thus it served to integrate a social order in which all organized interests could bring their respective causes for fair hearing. On the critical end of the spectrum, by contrast, elite or class theorists, stimulated by the work of such analysts as C. Wright Mills and Karl Marx, argued that the state in capitalist societies forged policies that served only to consolidate and reproduce the political and economic power of elites.

These qualitative changes in theory have, in the past two decades, been accompanied by a resurgence of the sociological study of law and social control (see Cohen and Scull, 1983; Hagan, 1983; Tillman and Warren, 1984). Building upon the classical traditions of Karl Marx, Emile Durkheim, and Max Weber, scholars have examined historical and contemporary control processes with a view toward understanding the institutional forces that shape them.[2] On the critical end of the theoretical spectrum, where much of the recent work has been done, efforts have generally concentrated on historically situated control policies directed at subordinate populations on behalf of elite interests, focusing on such matters as the evolution of criminal punishment and treatment of persons adjudged mentally defective.[3] This is, of course, a natural focus for perspectives that view law as a mechanism for maintaining existing patterns of domination.

The project in this chapter, in contrast, is to develop a theoretical perspective on the state's efforts to control the activities of elite in-

[2] See, for example, the recent collections offered in Cohen and Scull (1983), Black (1984a,b), and Spitzer (1986, 1987). Also see Black (1976), Nonet and Selznick (1978), Foucault (1979), Chambliss and Seidman (1982), Inverarity et al. (1983), and the fine analytic text by Pfohl (1985).

[3] See, for example, the work of Quinney (1970, 1974), Taylor, Walton, and Young (1973, 1975), Chambliss (1964, 1974, 1981), Melossi and Pavarini (1981), Greenberg (1981), Spitzer (1983), and Scull (1977). For an insightful critique of recent critical histories of incarceration, including his own, see Ignatieff (1983).

Vitality within the domain of critical perspectives is indexed by the quality of debate and the increasing sophistication in analysis. For nice examples of this intellectual fervor, see Cohen and Scull (1983).

terests. As suggested in the first chapter, such efforts are anomalous – at least in appearance – to class-based theories of law and
therefore demand a close look. Nonetheless, the project here builds
on theoretical and empirical contributions from key areas in social
science. Developments in political sociology have cast a brighter,
more penetrating light on the operations of states in capitalist societies, drawing attention to the (often contradictory) relations between government policies and the reproduction of the social order.
In addition, social scientists have begun in various ways to investigate the laws and agencies created in the 1970s to regulate the
harmful consequences of industrial production, and on these too I
gratefully draw. My intention here is to weave these analytic contributions into a theoretical template of state efforts to regulate the
undesirable products of business, against which I shall then examine
the U.S. government's attempts to control industrial water pollution.

A definition of law

Before proceeding, it is worth making explicit what has thus far
been only implicit: the definition of law intended here. Far from an
exercise in the obvious, this task is necessary because of the multi-
plicity of definitions used by social scientists for research purposes
(cf., Kidder, 1983: ch. 2). I make no claim for a "best" definition;
instead, I take the position that the adequacy of a social scientific
definition is determined by its utility in clearly delimiting a con-
struct or field of study that is widely agreed to be important to the
human condition. Definitions are never innocent in analysis – they
tell us where to look and what to look for – and so it is necessary to
alert observers as to which lens is being used to constrain the phenomenon of observation. With any good fortune at all, the chosen
definition will prove not to be entirely idiosyncratic.

For purposes of the present analysis, then, law refers to all actions
of government that seek to order the lives of a society's members,
including the rules and processes that select and constrain such actions themselves. The first half of the definition – pertaining·to social order – refers not only to the familiar efforts of law that seek to
constrain social behavior; for example, the prohibitions and requirements of criminal, civil, and administrative rules. The definition also
encompasses those actions of state that influence the distribution of
life chances in a political economy. Inasmuch as these actions are
taken in the context of formally structured government authority,

and seek to maintain particular forms of social order, they too are lawful. Thus included are such state activities as welfare, farm support, and military contract policies. The major analytic consequence of so broad a definition is that the domains of the study of law and of the state become virtually homologous.[4]

The second half of the definition emphasizes the insight of American legal realism, a century-old tradition in jurisprudence that insists upon the study of the law-in-action as well as of law-in-the-books. As legal realists – and, I suspect, average citizens – have long known, the activities of legal authorities are constrained not only by formal rules of procedure, but also by a range of extralegal factors, many unanticipated by the framers of law. The study of law is therefore not one of a closed, mechanistic process routinely turning out predictable responses. It is instead the study of a highly politicized human endeavor that reflects the pressures and constraints of the larger social system of which it is part. This contingent process is thus a constantly unfolding one, one for which the broad outlines often seem simpler to sketch than the finer details. Nonetheless, in the chapters to follow I shall attempt to link some of these details to the broader theoretical framework that occupies the remainder of this chapter.

A critical perspective on social regulation

I classify the orientation here taken to social regulation a critical perspective because of several of its guiding assumptions. First, the perspective assumes that social conflict rather than consensus underlies the regulation of business. This is not the pluralist assumption, mentioned earlier, that the state maintains societal harmony by neutrally "parceling out" individual legislative victories to various organized parties in conflict. Rather, I assume that conflict is played out through the whole of legal process, influencing not only the *terms* of legislation, but also the *execution* of law. This brings into question the neutrality of legal *procedure* as apart from the written *substance* of law. Indeed, the conflict assumption made here suggests

---

[4] This definition is most similar to that proposed by Chambliss and Seidman (1982: 3), although I exclude the actions of private (i.e., nonstate) parties in relation to law in order to conceptualize law as a relatively autonomous institutional sector upon which other social forces may act, such as social class groupings, moral reform groups, and other forms of association.

the vulnerability of the state to recurrent legitimation crises as it attempts to steer a course between the contradictory demands often made on it.

Second, the perspective seeks to identify the limits on the ability of law to achieve its publicly stated purpose. This search for limits is motivated by the observed tendency of law to maintain social hierarchies of wealth and power even in the face of recurring struggles over them. Given this, it may be expected that laws *written in* the "public interest," to the extent that they propose fundamental redistributions of social costs and benefits, confront a number of political and organizational obstacles to full implementation. The extent to which laws are in fact constrained by such barriers is, of course, an empirical one, and best understood in historical context.

Finally, I assume a dialectical relationship between state and society, such that purported legal solutions to regulatory problems tend to produce unintended, contradictory consequences. That is, in attempting to address the instant conflict or problem demanding resolution, law may unwittingly contribute to the development or deepening of other conflicts or problems. This occurs to the extent that law is constrained by forces in political economy to addressing only the symptoms of more fundamental social class conflicts, leaving undisturbed their underlying source in extant divisions of wealth and power (cf., Chambliss and Seidman, 1982: 144–9). The contradiction in policymaking is that the state is typically required to solve conflicts and crises inherent in capitalist social organization without altering its essential structures. The dialectical consequence is that such state resolutions of social instability, successful in the short term, tend ultimately to contribute to future conflict and struggle, presenting the state with recurring problems of legitimacy and stability.

To clarify the nature of these interlocking theoretical assumptions further, it is helpful to place them in the context of some earlier debates in the 1960s and 1970s regarding alternative critical theories of the state. Some of the initial arguments depicted the state as being virtually a tool of a ruling capitalist class, used directly by members or agents of that class to create laws and policies designed to reproduce the social structures that benefit it (see, e.g., Domhoff, 1967, 1970; Miliband, 1969; Quinney, 1974). From the vantage point of this *instrumentalist* perspective, laws apparently intended to control and limit capitalist interests could be simply interpreted as empty, *symbolic* gestures designed to defuse social unrest by *appearing* to address the complaints of dependent classes (see Edelman, 1964).

This position was challenged, however, by evidence that state policies – such as "nonproductive" social welfare spending and costly social regulations imposed on industry – did not always derive from the initiative of a ruling capitalist class or directly benefit it. That the state nonetheless tends to reproduce the prevailing capitalist social structure made necessary a more elaborate theoretical perspective, eventually provided by *structuralist* theories (see, e.g., O'Connor, 1973; Poulantzas, 1973; Therborn, 1978). This school of thought argues that the state (and the legal system specifically considered; see, e.g., Balbus, 1977; Beirne, 1979; Chambliss and Seidman, 1982; Jones, 1982) serves its reproductive function by being "relatively autonomous" from particular socioeconomic interests. Among other things, the perspective recognized that social classes – including the capitalist class – are less often monolithic, tightly organized entities than they are fractionated, internally divided, self-disputing groupings. Thus, the state serves to defuse social conflict by presenting itself as an arbiter in disputes not only between classes, but also between factions of the capitalist class and between various temporary alignments of different social class subgroups. While in the short term some consequent state policies prove costly to (and strongly resisted by) economic elites, structural theory argues that the state in fact organizes and implements the collective long-term interests of the capitalist class by securing the stable and predictable social and economic conditions requisite for private capital accumulation. Naturally enough, one constraint directing the state's actions to this end is its fiscal dependence on economic growth.

This perspective thus had the advantage of squaring better with important facts of political alignment and policy outcomes. In addition, the tendency of the state to reproduce capitalist social organization was posited without implausible assumptions about the far-sightedness and concerted action of a ruling class. Much like the instrumentalist theories, however, the structuralist perspective can also project a functionalist, static view of the role of state structures and policies. In both perspectives, the state can be seen as rather invariably reproducing capitalist social relations (cf., Przeworski and Wallerstein, 1982).

The structuralist perspective can be rescued from this sort of functional, teleological determinism by an appreciation of the dialectical nature of state action in society, of the often contradictory consequences of policy for social conflict. Although tending to reproduce the social stability requisite for private capital accumulation, state policies in capitalist societies also tend to reproduce division and conflict in social relations, as earlier discussed.[5] Thus the historically contingent role of *political action* must be factored into the analysis of state activity (cf., Alford and Friedland, 1985), giving a dynamic if less predictable dimension to it.

This more dynamic approach can be extrapolated from James O'Connor's (1973) work.[6] According to his analysis, the state in capitalist societies has two primary functions: ensuring the conditions for stable capital accumulation and legitimating the social order. These two functions are contradictory, however, because in maintaining the conditions for private accumulation by one social class at the expense of other classes, the state threatens to *undermine its own legitimacy* (and that of the social order) among the subordinate groups. For example, the state periodically increases the funding of social welfare programs to maintain social harmony. But its ability to do so is fiscally (and politically) restricted, because with the growth and centrality of monopoly capital (large corporations dominating highly concentrated industries), the state is also forced to socialize (in other words, pay for) more and more of the costs of accumulation (research and development, education, infrastructure) while profits continue to be privately appropriated. The resulting fiscal crisis is only exacerbated by increasing demands for social (and military) expenditures in response to severe economic dislocations (such as the corporate transfer of manufacturing to lower wage areas abroad and the loss of market to foreign competition). Alford and Friedland (1985) summarize the underlying dynamic: "Because the state can treat only the consequences and not the causes of

---

[5] In his analysis of crime control strategies, Spitzer (1983: 313) nicely and succinctly summarizes the advantages of the dialectical approach: with it, "we can investigate continuities and directions in the historical development of crime control without either missing the pattern exhibited in general historical tendencies (e.g., the decomposition of feudal structures, the centralization of control, bureaucratization, etc.), or turning those tendencies into ineluctable laws."

[6] Alford and Friedland (1985: 320–3) point to functionalist undertones in O'Connor's work. For example, they write that, "Implicit in O'Connor's position is the assumption that major developments in the state were *necessary* or even *required* by fundamental interests of monopoly capitalism" (p. 322; emphasis in the original). Nonetheless, O'Connor's logic regarding contradictions in state policymaking suggests the possibility that the functional relation between state and economy could eventually be destabilized under certain conditions of class struggle. See, for example, O'Connor's last chapter (1973: 221–56).

capitalist crisis, the internal organization of the state also becomes subject to crises of both insufficient public revenues and insufficient popular support" (pp. 284–5).

Thus the state faces not only periodic economic crises, but also recurrent political crises as it attempts to resolve the contradictory demands made of it. State activity and political struggle shape each other, such that the state's ability to maintain satisfactory social conditions for capital growth, and its own institutional legitimacy, are periodically precarious. From this perspective, the relationship between state policy and political struggle holds out the possibility of the transformation of the prevailing social order rather than its mechanistic reproduction (cf., Alford and Friedland, 1985: 285–7).

The perspective I present in the remainder of this section is congruent with this latter orientation. For want of a better term, I label the perspective *dialectical structuralism,* first to distinguish it from more static, functionalist approaches and, second, to suggest that the structuring of political action and state responses are reciprocally determining over the course of time. What should be clear, then, is that such a perspective tells us less about what we will find than it does about where to look.

It is in this light that I present the perspective in three parts, each reflecting one of the underlying assumptions described earlier. A final note before proceeding: I aim the discussion at "social" regulation, which broadly implies forms of government regulation that address the negative effects of production relations on consumers, workers, communities, and the general environment. The social science literature commonly distinguishes these forms from "economic" regulations that seek to stabilize market relations (securities, antitrust, and interstate commerce laws, for example). This distinction is quite imperfect, because economic regulations clearly affect social well-being in terms of such factors as cost of living and fully informed participation in various markets, and because social regulations can clearly affect market relations. All that I intend by my usage is that the perspective may be less relevant for those forms of regulation that serve industry interests in stabilized market relations (agencies such as the Civil Aeronautics Board and the Interstate Commerce Commission; see, e.g., Kolko, 1965),[7] if only because such

---

[7] For example, Lazarus (1973) has maintained that only two of the eleven regulatory agencies established in the 1930's were imposed on industry by the "public." He says, "The others were engineered by the industries or other affected interests

regulation has historically been attended by less widespread (or different) forms of political conflict and consequently by fewer barriers to implementation. The applicability of my categories of examination to such regulation can, of course, only be determined by empirical study.

The development of regulation

Although law is born of conflict and instabilities in a changing social system, it is by its very nature directed at the maintenance of order.[8] This conservative (in the nonideological sense of that term) orientation should not, however, be read to imply that the direction of law is generally overseen by a self-conscious and unified ruling elite. Instead, law *emerges* in historically situated contexts of systemic forces and constraints as the state seeks to manage often conflicting pressures while preserving its own legitimacy.

The development of business regulation in the United States is an aspect of the evolution of the democratic state, which itself is a regulatory mechanism that has evolved to manage the changing demands of a capitalist political economy. Steven Spitzer (1983) has pointed to the increasing centralization in the modern state of social control functions as the economy became increasingly concentrated and centralized, dominated by large, national oligopolistic corporations. The demands in such an economy for stable and predictable – that is, rationalized – social relations brought forth a growing national state, which socialized the costs of managing the manifestations of disorder and discontent associated with evolving economic relations (manifestations such as poverty, unemployment, crime; cf., O'Connor, 1973). The state assumed fiscal and managerial responsibility for these "externalities" of production processes, largely to promote economic growth in the private sector. This increased responsibility carried contradictory consequences for the state and capitalists, however, particularly in a democratic society. While the state had acted to *insulate* the private sector from the full weight of these costs, it thereby established itself as the arena in which aggrieved interests could challenge the socialization of costs and

themselves, often for the purpose of immunizing cartel practices from antitrust restraints" (pp. 216–17).

[8] This is a point on which Marx, Weber, and Durkheim could agree, although each gave a unique explanation of the relation between law and order. For useful summary discussions of their respective "sociologies of law," see Inverarity et al. (1983).

seek other constraints on corporate capital. In other words, "As capitalists become more dependent upon state authority, their power also becomes more vulnerable to democratic influence. Property and production relations are politicized" (Alford and Friedland, 1985: 433).

By the 1970s the state was under severe political pressure to *privatize* selected "externalities" of production by mandating that industry contribute heavily to their alleviation. The consequence was the creation of a number of federal agencies charged with the protection of consumer, environmental, and employee interests, including the Equal Employment Opportunity Commission (1965), the National Highway Traffic Safety Administration (1966), the Environmental Protection Agency (1970), the Occupational Safety and Health Administration (1970), and the Consumer Product Safety Commission (1972).

Historically, such pressures on the state have been mounted by various configurations of class interests under particular historical conditions. For example, the development of large corporate capitalism in the latter half of the nineteenth century set in motion social forces that produced a number of antitrust laws near the turn of the century (Kolko, 1963; Feld, 1983). As ever larger corporations came to compete in national (rather than local or regional) markets, capitalists faced the greater instability and uncertainties of heightened levels of competition. In their efforts to rationalize (render stable and predictable) their market conditions, large corporate capitalists developed a variety of anticompetitive techniques, including market allocation agreements, price-fixing conspiracies, interlocking directorates and corporate combinations, or trusts. Such efforts contributed to the development of powerful monopolies or near monopolies in a number of industries, including oil, sugar, and whiskey.

Fearing economic ruin at the hands of such corporate monoliths as Standard Oil, operators of small businesses, farmers, and elements of labor joined to oppose the power and abuses of the "robber barons," and eventually succeeded in pressing the Congress to pass the first national antitrust legislation, the Sherman Antitrust Act of 1890 (see also Clinard and Yeager, 1980: 134–6; Coleman, 1985). Similar sources of opposition to the development of monopoly capital brought about new antitrust legislation in Canada (1889), Australia (1906), and Britain (1948) (Snider, 1979; Reasons and Goff, 1980).

The early enforcement of the Sherman Act against corporate offenses was virtually nonexistent, however. No special antitrust enforcement division was established in the Department of Justice for
several years after the law's passage, nor did the Congress appropriate extra funds to Justice for its enforcement (Thorelli, 1954).
Clearly, the law was more symbolic than real, intended more to si-
phon off political discontent than to limit corporate concentration.
Indeed, in the early years following passage, the Sherman Act was
more often used against labor organizers than against violating companies (Feld, 1983: 231).

One result of nonenforcement was continuing political agitation
against concentrated corporate power by many of the same forces
responsible for the creation of the Sherman Act. In addition, following the Supreme Court's 1911 decision to uphold the first major di-
vestiture order to dissolve a monopoly – Standard Oil – while
distinguishing between "reasonable" and "unreasonable" trusts (the
former were to be held legal under that law), there was considerable
uncertainty regarding the future of antitrust enforcement. According to Gabriel Kolko's (1963) analysis, the result was that progressive
business owners, typically those at the helm of the largest corporations, themselves sought new federal legislation in this area to help
stabilize both political and economic relations. Regarding the
former, federal law would serve national corporations by protecting
against the possibility that individual states would pass more restrictive legislation, and would clarify the ambiguities in the Sherman
Act. In terms of economic relations, new law could stabilize still
troublesome competition by ruling illegal its more aggressive forms
("unfair" or "cutthroat" competition). The end result was the passage in 1914 of both the Federal Trade Commission Act, which out-
lawed unfair methods of competition, and the Clayton Act, which
made illegal such anticompetitive acts as tying and exclusive dealing
agreements that limited freedom of contracts (Feld, 1983: 236).
Kolko (1963: 268) concluded that the new laws stabilized social relations and promoted the further concentration of economic power.
Indeed, although the effects on concentration in specific markets
remain in dispute, during the two decades following passage of the
new laws there was a marked increase in *aggregate* industrial concentration as economic power and activity was increasingly centralized
in the country's largest corporations (Herman, 1981: 187–94).

A different constellation of class forces was involved in the development of federal coal mine health and safety legislation (Curran,

1984). Beginning with the first national law in 1910, legislation was passed largely in response to organized mine workers pressing for legal protection under conditions in which they had economic leverage. Workers were successful in pressing for new legislation only when coal and mining labor were in high demand; in these circumstances, the potential use of strikes threatened economic prosperity not only in the coal industry, but in other, coal-dependent sectors as well. This history again suggests, however, that under some conditions company owners themselves can come to support federal regulatory legislation. In 1910, for example, coal operators had begun to support the idea of some sort of federal legislation as a means of circumventing the patchwork of individual state laws, as trade became increasingly national in scope. Moreover, when organized labor has economic leverage, owners may support (or at least not seriously resist) the call for federal law in order to stabilize the political economic conditions in an industry. This sort of coalition between labor and capital promoted the passage of the Federal Coal Mine Safety Act of 1941 (Curran, 1984). Conversely, when labor is at an economic and political *disadvantage*, regulatory gains earlier won may be rolled back. Labor found itself at just such a disadvantage during the Reagan administration in the early 1980s; not coincidentally protections under the recently won occupational safety and health legislation were in fact rolled back (Calavita, 1983).

Finally, intraindustry competition may help spur the development of regulatory law. This was the case, for example, with the passage of the federal Meat Inspection Act of 1906 (Kolko, 1963).[9] Here, again, there was public pressure to regulate quality in the meatpacking industry, stimulated in large measure by Upton Sinclair's revelations in *The Jungle* of scandalously unsanitary conditions in the industry. It turns out, however, that the largest corporate meatpackers also sponsored stricter federal requirements. Their interests were twofold. First, the large companies called for initial federal regulation in the late nineteenth century so that meat quality could be certified to assuage the European market; several countries had imposed import restrictions on American meat because the United States did not have an inspection system that met their standards. Second, by the early years of the twentieth century the large meatpacking companies found themselves at a competitive disadvantage to smaller companies, which earlier regulatory requirements did not

[9] This brief discussion of Kolko's (1963) analysis draws from the summary prepared by Feld (1983: 241–2).

reach. The larger companies therefore supported the passage of the 1906 law, which stood not only to bring the small firms under federal regulatory control, but which also could prove more costly to the smaller companies that did not enjoy the economies of scale of the large producers. In effect, the new law became one means by which the largest companies sought to consolidate and increase their control of what had been a very competitive (hence "unstable") industry.

These examples suggest that pressures for regulatory change develop under certain socioeconomic conditions that shape class forces. Divisions within the capitalist class, in particular between large, powerful corporations and small companies, played a role in the struggle for antitrust and early product quality laws as monopoly capital came to dominate the economy, threatening smaller operators with financial ruin.

In the case of worker health and safety, the struggle is founded upon a classic clash of interests between owners and workers in industry. Even so, the coal mine safety case demonstrates that owners may themselves join the call for federal action when it best suits their economic interests to do so. This occurs when owners wish to avoid less predictable, more politically volatile or inconsistent laws in the individual states, or when they find such legislation a means of encouraging labor stability. Under particular historical conditions, then, as Neal Shover (1980: 123–4) has noted, "businessmen do not object to the criminalization of their conduct so much as they object to the inclusion of irrational or incalculable elements in criminalizing legislation. . . .Businessmen strive to eliminate sources of unpredictability in the law, or to convert them into *administrative* problems – which can later be worked out with regulators" (emphasis in the original). This suggests, of course, that the struggle for law does not cease with the passage of legislation, a fact that points to the distinction between the written law and law-in-action, the subject of the next section.

The limits of law

The failures of government regulation of business have been widely chronicled. Reports on these failures range from Bernstein's (1955) classic analysis of the "capture" of regulation by regulated businesses, through the many investigations published in the early 1970s by Ralph Nader and his associates (e.g., Fellmeth, 1970; J. S. Turner, 1970; Green, 1972, 1973; Nader and Green, 1973), to more recent

accounts of failure or demise in the newer areas of "social" regulation (e.g., Barnett, 1981; Calavita, 1983; Szasz, 1984, 1986). The
regularity with which such reports appear suggests that fundamental constraints routinely limit the application of regulatory law. The
existence of systemic constraints does not, however, justify the dis-
missal of all regulation as merely symbolic; even less so does it ne-
gate the need for their careful analysis.

Instead, the likely existence of such constraints calls for historically situated analyses of their operation on law, with a view toward
identifying the conditions under which they either limit law or are
"overcome" by it. The working assumption is that regulation ranges
from the entirely ineffective (when even its value as symbol may
evaporate) to the partially effective, in which law succeeds (at least
temporarily and to some extent) in constraining the negative externalities of production. Such variation in effectiveness may occur
across agencies at any historical moment, or may characterize the
history of a single agency – now stringently applying the law, then
paying mere lip service to the terms of legislation.[10]

Clearly, then, the operation of constraints on law is a dynamic
process, the understanding of which must be based in the study of
specific historical contexts. The purpose of this section, therefore, is
not to provide a list of factors that invariably render law impotent.
Rather, my purpose here is to outline the systemically embedded
constraints in our political economy which *tend* to limit regulatory

[10] The history of the FTC exemplifies swings in regulatory fervor. The agency was
established in 1914 to protect the free enterprise system by preventing the growth
of monopoly or other restraints on trade, and by stemming unfair or deceptive
trade practices such as false advertising. By the 1960s the FTC was being roundly
criticized for regulatory inactivity, charged with preoccupation with trivial matters
while ignoring the important matters of antitrust and deception of consumers
(see, e.g., Cox, Fellmeth, and Schultz, 1969; American Bar Association, 1969). By
the latter 1970s, however, the agency had been transformed into an activist instrument of consumer protection. With the congressional mandate of the 1974
Magnuson-Moss Act and an aggressive chairman (Michael Pertschuk, appointed by
President Carter), the FTC began to challenge abuses at the level of whole industries instead of targeting only individual predatory firms. Under the consequent
pressure from industry, however, the Congress reversed its field by 1980, going so
far as to take the unusual step of passing a legislative veto provision under which
the Congress could veto FTC regulations deemed too onerous to business. The
Congress exercised its first veto in May 1982, vacating an FTC rule that would
have required used-car dealers to notify customers of an automobile's major
known defects at the time of purchase (Tolchin and Tolchin, 1983: ch. 5; see also
Clinard and Yeager, 1980: 77–8). The explanation for such variation in regulatory
activity, and of the potential limits of variation, lies in the analysis of forces in
political economy, as already suggested.

law's effectiveness in service to the public interest. The extent to which these tendencies are realized will depend on historical configurations of social struggle and state structures.

The limits on regulatory law are all aspects of general tendencies in relations between state and economy. Furthermore, they operate at three levels of those relations: the institutional, organizational, and situational levels. By institutional, I refer to the abstract level at which state and economy are conceptualized as single entities situated in some relation to each other, whether reproductive or destabilizing. Here the relations are comprehended in terms of macrosociological theorizing. The organizational level refers to relations between organizations or between *types* of organizations, such as regulatory agencies and corporations. Theorizing at this level might be said to be of the middle range, or mezzosociological. Finally, the situational level may be conceptualized as the point at which enforcement of law occurs, the direct interchanges between regulators and the regulated in which symbolic constructions of both behavior and being are negotiated. Here we engage in microsociological analysis.

This categorization of levels of constraint should not be understood to imply their independent existence or operation. On the contrary, this schema implies the *embeddedness* of levels in which the operation of "lower" level constraints on law is most fundamentally shaped by the nature and operation of those at the "higher" levels. This should become clear in the discussion to follow.

At each of the levels of analysis, the limits on law can be conceptualized as functioning in the realms of both structures and ideology. By structures, I refer to regularly patterned relations of power and authority; included, for example, are social class structures and other hierarchically arranged authority relations, such as those within and between organizations or groups. The ideological realm, on the other hand, refers to prevailing cultural belief systems that both guide behavior and constrain the view of the possible and reasonable among members of the culture, for whom the belief system itself is largely beyond conscious reflection (it has a taken-for-granted status and surfaces most dramatically when it is challenged). It is perhaps unnecessary to emphasize here that structures of power and ideological systems tend to reinforce each other in social organization, although the degree of correspondence between them varies with historical circumstances. In the following discussion, I focus on the ways in which both structural and ideological

factors tend to constrain regulatory law and reinforce each other,
mindful of the contingent nature of these relations.

Institutional limits. The outermost constraints on regulatory law derive from the state's structural dependence on economic growth in
the private sector. Rather than engage in profitable productive activity itself, the state is dependent on tax revenues raised from profitable private accumulation (cf., O'Connor, 1973: 180; Offe, 1975;
Alford and Friedland, 1985). Herman (1981: 167–8) notes that
among Western industrial powers the United States ranks at or near
the bottom in terms of the percentage of government enterprise
that is involved in such sectors as manufacturing and mining, transportation, construction, and communications. He attributes this in
part to the absence historically in the United States of a socialist-
oriented political constituency (see, e.g., Weinstein, 1967; Kolko,
1976) likely to favor increased government enterprise, and to the
business sector's greater hostility to state ownership here as compared to Western Europe. This hostility is part of a long adversarial
relationship between state and business rooted in big business's perception – stemming from the antitrust movement of the late nineteenth century – that the state could be controlled by interests
antagonistic to forms of private commerce, and in American industry's lesser need for state support compared to foreign industrial
economies.[11] Ideologically, the separation of the state from profitmaking activities is reinforced by the primacy of private property
and individual liberty (i.e., freedom from state interference, to make
private contracts, etc.) as enshrined in constitutional, legislative and
judicial law (see, e.g., Chambliss and Seidman, 1982; Inverarity et
al., 1983: 69–71; Yeager, 1983).

Among other consequences, the state's dependence on tax revenues tends to align its interests with those of the private sector in
economic growth. Indeed, this growth historically has necessitated
expansion in the size and activity of the state, whose growing budget
therefore requires even further economic growth. Not surprisingly,

---

[11] Herman (1981: 377, fn. 24) summarizes Chandler's (1979) argument on this point:
"the rise of U.S. big business threatened small firms more severely here than
abroad, with large producers of consumer goods and railroads inflicting serious
damage on small shippers and wholesalers from an early date. This led to a hostile
government stance to big business. In England and Japan big business was more
heavily concentrated in basic industry and was export oriented. Thus big business
needed government more and threatened other indigenous businesses less." Also
see Vogel (1978).

then, the state is generally reluctant to take actions that threaten to inhibit this growth. Moreover, in the complex, tightly interwoven economies of advanced capitalist societies, the state is reliant on signals from the private sector as to the fiscal and regulatory loads the latter can or will bear before "adequate" growth is threatened. These signals are especially salient for the state given the international mobility of capital: political environments considered unfriendly to large corporate business can produce capital flight from the country, inhibiting the economy's potential for growth.

This relation of dependency suggests, therefore, that the state will tend to conservatively resolve conflicts over the externalities of production lest growth be weakened. As Gunningham (1974: 85) has noted, "any compromise solution to conflict is always resolved, not from within the full range of alternatives which represent the interests of the contending groups, but within a narrower span which favors the interests of capital" (see also Beirne, 1979: 380). The dependency can be seen in the operation of industrial advisory committees to advise the government on policy issues affecting commerce. Established by the state, these committees provided business interests with privileged access to key government decision makers, allowing them input on matters ranging from proposals for new legislation to the creation of regulatory standards implementing law. Although "sunshine" legislation passed in the 1970s formally opened participation in these committees to public interests, powerful business interests maintain privileged access to the domains of state policymaking through such instrumentalities as corporate-sponsored research and policy advisory organizations (see, e.g., Steck, 1975; Domhoff, 1978). As a result of such institutionalized influence, legislated business regulation may be constrained by insufficient penalties for infraction or a variety of exceptions and exclusions that substantially limit the reach of law.

The foregoing logic suggests, further, that the state will be especially sensitive to the political concerns of the powerful, multinational corporations that dominate the U.S. economy. It is this sector that disproportionately influences economic development, possesses the resources with which to shape politic discourse, and maintains the sort of strategic flexibility that permits the penetration of markets worldwide as economic and political conditions indicate. Thus the interests of this sector can be expected to act as a uniquely forceful (not to say always determinative) constraint on regulatory law. The salience of this constraint is only heightened by the evidence that these large firms contribute not only the lion's share of profits and wealth but also the majority of harm occasioned by violations of law (Clinard and Yeager, 1980; Barnett, 1981).

The structural fragmentation of the state also limits the legal response to regulatory conflicts (cf., Alford and Friedland, 1985: 439). The division of state authority into legislative, executive, and judicial components has a number of limiting consequences for regulatory law. No branch or unit of government has complete control over a particular policy from legislation through funding and administration. This fact tends to dampen the likelihood of significant legal change, inasmuch as opponents need only thwart change at one point in the process while supporters are required to propel reform through all its various institutional channels. It has been suggested, for example, that political reformers and mediagenic social movements have their greatest access to policy determinations in the highly visible, politically charged legislative debates, during which broad goals, (e.g., regulatory) are forged and various compromises reached (Anderson, 1980: 19; Wilson, 1980: 385; cf., Sabatier, 1975: 316–20; Handler, 1978: 16–22).

However, it is in the less visible, technically oriented implementation stage at which a new law's impacts are finally determined. This is all the more the case to the extent that the legislature – in part to avoid political damage to itself – tends to pass regulatory legislation only in broad outline (Rosenbaum, 1977: 101–2; Clinard and Yeager, 1980: 76), leaving the potentially riskier (because redistributive) implementation decisions to the agencies of the Executive Branch. This separation of legal authority poses a substantial challenge to the staying power of reform groups, which, due to limited resources, may find themselves "disenfranchised" in the process of complex and often lengthy negotiations that regularly accompany the implementation of law. At this stage, the richer business community is generally better able to present its case for limiting regulation than proregulation advocates are to argue for stringent realization of the terms of law.

Moreover, this limiting process is enhanced by the historic decline of congressional power and the corresponding concentration of state power in an increasingly "depoliticized" Executive Branch (Esping-Andersen, Friedland, and Wright, 1976).[12] This develop-

[12] This concentration of state power was part of the increasing centralization in political economy described at the outset of the chapter. Executive Branch oversight provides greater measures of efficiency and rationalization in national policymak-

ment has the effect of putting many critical policy decisions beyond the view and reach of potentially interested publics, as just described (cf., Alford and Friedland, 1985: 382–3). Therefore lacking democratic legitimacy, such executive decisions are ideologically justified on the basis of a *technocratic legitimacy* (Gold, Lo, and Wright, 1975: 50 [November]). Officials present policy determinations as rational formulations, neutrally (i.e., nonpolitically) reached through a process based on technical expertise, particularly legal and scientific knowledge beyond the ken of most citizens.

The separation of powers also limits law to the extent that different logics characterize decision making in the various units of government. For example, the courts' emphasis on proper legal reasoning when reviewing regulatory agency decisions may induce agencies to focus on *procedural* rather than on *substantive* considerations when formulating policy and making decisions, thereby giving them a more conservative cast (Mitnick, 1980: 135). Thus courts' use of rules of evidence, constitutional interpretations of due process and individual liberties, assumptions regarding liability or guilt and levels of harm, and generally time-consuming procedures (e.g., discovery) may influence the types of cases agencies decide to bring, and the conditions under which they will bring them. For example, in 1983 the Supreme Court ruled that materials developed by grand juries in criminal investigations could not be shared with civil law investigators attached to various enforcement units. Thus government agencies will have to duplicate expensive investigative efforts if they wish to develop parallel criminal and civil prosecutions of the same case, a practice that had been increasingly common in such areas as antitrust and tax enforcement. In the latter case, the result may be fewer criminal prosecutions (arguably the greatest deter-

ing than the more cumbersome (if more legitimate) devices of participatory democracy (as enacted in legislatures). In addition, Halberstam (1979: 13) has identified the confluence of the Roosevelt administration and the growing challenge posed by centralized totalitarian states overseas in the 1930s as helping to propel the shift of power from the Congress to the Executive Branch. The highly charged international environment placed a premium on familiarity with foreign affairs and efficient decision making, both more characteristic of the Executive than of the Legislative Branch. And the charismatic Franklin Roosevelt proved rather uniquely qualified to justify and reinforce this tendency by his creative use of the mass media, whose reach was by then national in scope: "He was more often than not going directly to the media rather than to the Congress with information; and he put more energy into his press relations than into his congressional ones. There was a changing institutional balance" (p. 13). Since Roosevelt, no president has been more successful in emulating this strategy of political dominance than Ronald Reagan.

rent) as the Justice Department uses its scarce resources to mount civil cases to collect taxes due (Lewin, 1983).

The disjuncture between procedural and substantive law in the regulation of business is due in good measure to the inability of the traditional categories of criminal law to comprehend the complex relations of ownership and control that characterize large, modern organizations (Jones, 1982). These traditional categories of Anglo-American law posit criminal liability in terms of demonstrable *individual* culpability, a personal blameworthiness based on knowledge or negligence that derived from and better fit simpler forms of social organization. The application of such categories to organizational misconduct limits law's effectiveness to the extent that such blameworthiness cannot be assessed.

One example of this limiting process is found in U.S. antitrust law. As written and enforced, the Sherman Antitrust Act – created to prohibit the monopolization of an industry by a single company or group of companies – has focused on demonstrable conspiracies and other clearly culpable business behavior such as price-fixing or market division agreements by companies. However, the law has not been successful in forestalling monopolistic results that stem from the structural characteristics, rather than the behavioral attributes, of an industry. In highly concentrated industries in which only a few large firms dominate, companies can (and often do) tacitly fix prices at identical levels by simply matching each other's publicly documented price changes; courts have interpreted this sort of "conscious parallelism" as beyond the reach of law even though its effects are identical to the conspiratorial agreements that are clearly prohibited (Clinard and Yeager, 1980: 136–8; also see Barnett, 1979: 176).

In more general terms, this limiting process is underscored in the difficulties associated with enforcement efforts to locate culpable individuals in corporate organizations. Given their complex divisions of labor, delegation of responsibilities, and often tacit expectations regarding performance and loyalty, large corporations tend to shroud individual culpability from legal detection.[13] As a result, regulators may often forgo such problematic criminal prosecutions in favor of more lenient, informal efforts to negotiate compliance with

---

[13] For an excellent analysis of the limits on contemporary law's penetration of the large corporation, see Christopher Stone's *Where the Law Ends: The Social Control of Corporate Behavior* (1975). Also see Clinard and Yeager, 1980: ch. 3, and Yeager, 1986.

companies (cf., Carson, 1980: 163–4), or firms may be convicted as fictitious corporate *persons,* without the parallel convictions of individual human decision makers. One likely result is lessened deterrence as top policymaking officials are left untouched by legal penalties and the associated condemnation that attaches to criminal conviction. Indeed, research clearly indicates that corporate officials are rarely prosecuted for violations of federal laws (see, e.g., Clinard et al., 1979; Clinard and Yeager, 1980).

These limits are reinforced by the logic of state budget determinations (combining legislative and executive authority), which constrain regulatory law to the extent that insufficient funds are allocated to the implementation and enforcement of new legislation.[14] Reform groups are likely to be more successful in sponsoring new regulatory legislation than they are in marshaling the necessary resources to track and influence the complex processes of budget determinations. Thus, competing fiscal needs and business opposition to large agency budgets can interact to limit agencies' resources for research, inspection and enforcement.

Under these legal and fiscal circumstances, then, major potential enforcement cases may not be brought for prosecution by resource-strained agencies facing often intractable burdens of proof regarding blameworthiness, regulatory orders and warnings to comply are not followed up, and the authorities often settle for lesser penalties to avoid costly litigation with powerful corporate opponents (Clinard and Yeager, 1980: 95–7).[15]

---

[14] The insufficient allocation of funds for regulatory tasks is the norm. For example, in the mid-1970s the federal Occupational Safety and Health Administration (OSHA) had only 400 inspectors to investigate the safety procedures of some 4 million business establishments. In addition, the National Institute of Occupational Safety and Health (NIOSH), the research unit responsible for recommending new health and safety standards to OSHA, was also greatly underfunded by the Congress. Dr. Marcus M. Key, the NIOSH director through mid-1974, noted, "Our present laboratory space isn't even adequate for any kind of research. It's substandard. . . . I don't think NIOSH is a viable organization at this time" (quoted in Calavita, 1983: 439). The story of inadequate funding in the face of wide-ranging regulatory responsibilities can be retold from agency to agency. See, e.g., Clinard and Yeager, 1980: 95–7.

[15] A *New York Times* survey in 1979 (July 15) found that the federal government rarely brought criminal cases against major corporations. A top Justice Department official said that "it's just a lot easier for us to pick on the small guy," because large firms with their complex organizations are both difficult to investigate and capable of generating major legal resistance. The department had, for example, only 60 lawyers to review approximately 2,400 potential criminal tax cases annually. Given the labor-intensive nature of this complex work, a department spokes-

Organizational limits. Theory and research in the study of *complex organizations* have also illuminated constraints that tend to limit the effectiveness of regulatory law. Much of the research on regulatory agencies has comprehended them as organizational entities mounting various survival strategies in often turbulent, uncertain, and highly politicized environments. Indeed, "the importance of studying the social control of organizational deviance at the organizational level of analysis" (Ermann and Lundman, 1978: 65) has been increasingly recognized by social scientists.

This recognition is not new, however. More than thirty years ago, Marver Bernstein (1955) published his now classic formulation of the process by which regulatory agencies are "captured" by the interests supposedly being regulated. He postulated a "natural" life cycle for regulatory agencies, in which these government bureaucracies are transformed from youthful, aggressive regulators of private enterprise to old, rigidified protectors of the formerly regulated interests. Essentially a "resource dependence" perspective on organizations (cf., Pfeffer and Salancik, 1978), capture theory emphasizes the effects on an agency's behavior of its need for sustaining political support in its institutional environment (cf. also Downs, 1967). In brief, Bernstein argued that after a reform movement's successful drive for new legislation and early enthusiasm for regulation, its active support gradually wanes as members turn their attention to other matters, satisfied that the public interest has been institutionalized in the new agency. With these changes in the vectors of political interest, leaders of the executive and legislative branches of government also turn their attention to other pressing concerns, leaving the agency with fewer and fewer political allies and financial resources. The result is that the agency finds itself facing only a single, intensely interested and powerful constituency: the oppositional interests originally targeted for increased social control. Therefore, in order to secure the minimally necessary degree of political support for its continued existence, the agency begins to accommodate and reflect the interests of the regulated in its decision making.

Aspects of Bernstein's theory have been challenged on both theoretical and empirical grounds.[16] Among other criticisms, the

person's comment that "we're missing good cases against big corporations because we lack manpower" is unsurprising.

[16] See, for example, the work of Sabatier (1975), Meier and Plumlee (1978), Plumlee and Meier (1978), and Freitag (1983).

argument does not allow for (nor account for) the rejuvenation of public-spirited regulation under particular social conditions. Rather, it posits a unidirectional decline in aggressive regulation, a position justified neither by broader conceptualizations of forces in political economy nor by historical experience, as earlier discussed. Nonetheless, Bernstein has most usefully pointed to the sorts of organizational dynamics that *tend to* vitiate regulation in the public interest.

The constraints on regulatory law are in the first instance lodged in the nature of agencies' dependencies in capitalist political economy. The primacy of private accumulation dictates that regulatory decisions not "unreasonably" infringe on the prerogatives of capitalist productivity. Several consequences follow from this. First, like all organizations regulatory agencies are sensitive to threats in their institutional environment. Thus they are concerned to avoid judicial (legal procedural), legislative, or executive reversals of agency policies that could, for example, lead to reductions in agency authority and appropriations. Indeed, agencies may be so sensitive to potential political opposition to their legal mandates that they play a game of *anticipatory politics* (Green, 1972), for example by keeping budget requests within limits perceived to be acceptable to interests concerned that regulation not be overly aggressive. In this connection, an Office of Management and Budget examiner indicated that one reason the U.S. Justice Department's Antitrust Division does not seek greater increases in its relatively small budget is because it perceives that the political climate, including business interests, "would be hostile to large increases in division activity" (S. Weaver, 1977: 141).

Second, the nature of these agency dependencies in a capitalist political economy reinforces the need for agencies to work "fairly" with powerful regulated interests; indeed, agencies are created to regulate private commercial activity, on whose continued existence the regulators' own mandate therefore rests (cf., Mitnick, 1980: 133). Third, and in consequence of the first two, regulatory agencies must carefully *justify* their actions in terms congenial to the ideologies supporting the private control of accumulation.

Agencies' sensitivity to these dependencies is heightened by another "environmental" factor: the terms of the legislation to be enforced. As mentioned earlier, the often vague or imprecise language of the law to be implemented requires interpretation and specification by the agency. Given the centrality of this task to the ultimate impact of the law on regulated interests, and the power and prestige of the latter, this requirement forces the agency essentially to bargain "in good faith" with its corporate clientele over the terms of regulation, in order to avoid provoking private-sector opposition to the agency's mandate (cf., Sabatier, 1975: 303–4). Dependence on the cooperation of the private sector increases to the extent that the legislation requires regulatory intervention in complex production processes (Anderson, 1980: 18). Under this circumstance, the agency is largely dependent on the regulated for the requisite technical information. Given companies' proprietary rights (and monopolized control) over their "trade secrets," the agency's need for technical information must be negotiated and justified.[17]

As part of the general societal process of the rationalization of social relations, agencies blunt the political opposition of powerful regulated interests by translating their legal mandates into a series of apparently neutral, technical decisions, often made under elaborate procedural rules of due process (advance notice of rule changes, predecision hearings on all relevant issues, internal adjudicative processes) (Salamon and Wamsley, 1975: 161, 183; Anderson, 1980). With critical regulatory decisions thus hinging on considerations of technological requirements and feasibility, engineering, scientific, and legal experts from industry and government often come to share a common view of regulatory "problems" as apolitical technical issues to be "reasonably" confronted on terms acceptable to the logics of their respective professions and industries.

In this decision making, regulation tends to be justified in terms of implicit or explicit costs-versus-benefits considerations. The use of this analytic framework can limit the effectiveness of law in a pair of ways. In the first place, the logic of cost–benefit analysis implicitly favors the private sector, both because it asserts the primacy of pri-

[17] The primacy of private accumulation is illustrated in the ways in which the claim of "trade secrets" has been used to constrain regulation. For example, "It was not until 1978, and after an 18-month lawsuit . . . that a federal court ordered all corporations to furnish the [Federal Trade Commission] with essential data on their product line business to aid in antitrust enforcement. The FTC order had been resisted by over 200 major corporations which refused to comply, primarily because, they claimed, competitors might obtain information through leaks from the FTC" (Clinard and Yeager, 1980: 98). In another example, the Reagan administration in 1981 revoked an OSHA rule requiring the labeling of all toxic chemicals used in the workplace so that workers would be informed. The administration was considering a new standard that would underscore companies' rights "to withhold trade secrets and to use discretion in deciding how and when to conduct the hazard evaluation research on which labeling would be based" (Calavita, 1983: 441).

vate production and because costs are typically much more easily determined than are benefits, creating the likelihood that the latter will be underassessed relative to the former. As Dickson and his colleagues have noted, "Reducing the social impact of a new technology or production process purely to quantitative measure eliminates any consideration of the moral or political dimension" (1981: 13). Second, the application of cost–benefit analysis tends to reproduce the cultural perception that legally prohibited commercial conduct is morally ambivalent, that it is only qualifiedly disapproved behavior rather than absolutely wrongful (cf., Carson, 1980; Hawkins, 1983, 1984). Such constraints on condemnation lessen the deterrent effect of law.

The rationalization of regulation just described produces another result that tends to limit the effectiveness of law. As suggested, such decision-making systems have the effect of favoring certain interests over others. Such systems are "loaded" in favor of parties possessing the financial and technical resources necessary for negotiating with agency officials (cf., Offe, 1973: 11, as quoted in Gold et al., 1975: 38 [November]; Sabatier, 1975: 308, 316). Thus, Schattschneider's (1960: 71) oft-cited comment that "organization is the mobilization of bias" applies even to intendedly egalitarian legal structures. This irony was nicely captured by Balbus (1977: 577), who noted that "the systematic application of an equal scale to systematically unequal individuals necessarily tends to reinforce systemic inequalities."[18] This statement applies as well to organizations as to individuals.

In terms of the social regulation of business, the impact of this process is twofold. First, as indicated in the previous section, a legal process oriented to technical expertise tends to disenfranchise concerned publics with too few resources to participate in the myriad decisions that in fact determine the degree of regulatory rigor. As discussed in subsequent chapters, public-interest voices have too often been excluded from debate on environmental regulation.[19]

---

[18] This process has also been identified in the prosecution of individuals in the adversary system of Anglo-American criminal law, both historically (Chambliss, 1974) and in modern times (Blumberg, 1967).

[19] In this regard, Mitnick (1980: 134) observes, "Consumers will pay higher information costs on regulatory matters, since their individual contacts with the regulated product or service, or with the regulatory agency, are only occasional. . . . For these reasons, action by industry during regulatory proceedings is likely to be better organized, funded, and informed. The regulated industry may be better able to make a case that will receive a favorable decision from the agency and survive any challenge on appeal to the courts."

Second, the regulatory process favors the larger, richer corporations over smaller, more marginal operators. Regulatory requirements can further entrench the dominant sector of large corporations because the costs of compliance are relatively higher per unit of production for smaller firms (Barnett, 1981: 13–14; Lilley and Miller, 1977: 51), thus reducing their ability to compete. This reproduction of inequality also operates within the regulatory apparatus itself. For example, due to their differential size and resources, companies are *variably* able to avail themselves of legal avenues of negotiation and appeal with regard to rules and regulations, and therefore experience greater or lesser risks of law violation. Moreover, and in recognition of these differentials, enforcement agencies tend to allocate a disproportion of their resources to the prosecution of smaller rather than larger firms in order to increase the likelihood of compiling favorable enforcement records (by more often avoiding the stiff defenses that can be raised by larger, more powerful enterprises; see, e.g., Barnett, 1979: 177; Clinard and Yeager, 1980: 92–3). In so favoring more powerful firms, regulation not only tends to distribute costs inequitably, but also tends to achieve less social protection than is economically feasible.

Situational limits. The constraints limiting law at the institutional and organizational levels of analysis can be seen operating in specific situations of enforcement, wherein law enforcement personnel seek compliance from regulated companies. Here regulation is enacted through the assumptive worlds of interacting individuals operating from their respective organizational bases. Constraints at the situational level of analysis often play themselves out in the form of *typifications* of regulated parties used by regulators to guide their use of discretion (cf., Sudnow, 1965). More generally, the enforcement process takes the form of bargaining strategies in which the reality of law is negotiated by the contending parties (Hawkins, 1983) within a particular assumptive context shaped by the contours of political economy.

One typification often used by enforcers of social regulations is that larger corporations are more likely to be socially responsible, to make good faith efforts at compliance (Hawkins, 1983; Lynxwiler et al., 1983). For example, in their study of the use of enforcement discretion in the federal Office of Surface Mining Reclamation and Enforcement, Lynxwiler and his colleagues (1983) found that inspectors operated on the basis of two assumptions: that larger mining companies were more responsive to and cooperative with regulatory demands than smaller firms, and that the former were also more likely to challenge violation citations in formal legal hearings. These assumptions were grounded in inspectors' experiences in the field, in particular their interactions with larger companies' technical experts. The knowledge of those experts rivals their own, thus eliminating the leverage of the government's regulatory expertise, and with them the inspectors could negotiate professional and technical (nonpolitical) definitions of violations and remedies. Smaller companies without such technical expertise, on the other hand, were more likely to be seen as less cooperative and less technically able to comply with their environmental responsibilities. As a result of their use of these typifications, inspectors' reports on violations tended to be less harsh for larger companies (controlling for legally relevant factors), with the consequence that smaller companies tended to be assessed higher fines.

Thus the structural biases in regulatory law noted at the organizational level of analysis are reproduced in the microsociology of interactions between inspector and company in the field. Notions of "responsiveness" and "reasonableness" in these interactions tend to reinforce economic inequalities and constrain stringent regulation, as common definitions of regulatory "problems" are negotiated in the absence of input from outside public interests.

Moreover, the negotiations of these common definitions tend to be contained within an ideological framework – shared by regulators and regulated alike – favoring the interests of private capital over competing considerations. This constraint is manifested in a shared perception that the regulated behaviors are morally ambivalent rather than abhorrent (Hawkins, 1983), and it contributes to the adoption by regulators of a technical-scientific orientation to the solution of "noncompliance problems" rather than a policing, law enforcement approach. In addition, state regulation needs to be constantly justified as reasonable to the powerful regulated interests, a need that both reflects and reinforces the notion that *regulation itself is morally ambivalent* and can at least sometimes be condemned as unreasonable and socially harmful, as when it threatens loss of profit or jobs.

Such justification can be seen in inspectors' enforcement of British factories acts (pertaining to working conditions) in the mid-nineteenth century. In his historical analysis of these laws, Carson

(1980: 167–8) notes that inspectors' enforcement strategies necessarily reflected the structure of power relations between them and the employers. He quotes an inspector's advice to his subordinates in 1835: "Your best chance of success will be by courteous and conciliatory demeanor towards the mill-owners; by impressing on their minds that the object of your visits is rather to assist them in conforming to the Act . . . rather than to fish out grounds for complaints" (p. 167). Thus warnings, persuasion, patience, and education were the strategies adopted to implement the law, strategies still commonplace in the social regulation of business. One consequence of such conciliatory approaches, as Carson suggests, is that business violations come to be more normalized than condemned by law. Thus processes of law enforcement may reproduce the very moral ambiguity of offenses that constrains their social control in the first instance.

Law and contradiction

A contradiction, as Alford and Friedland (1985: 433) note, is "a property of a system. When the conditions required by a system at the same time undermine that system and lead to its transformation, then a contradiction exists." Contradictions, therefore, are *dynamic* properties of socioeconomic systems that foster change in them. In the present context, the concept directs us to investigate the ways in which the state's attempts to resolve through law the contradictory pressures of private economic growth and public harmony can ultimately lead to further instabilities in the polity and subsequent rounds of state action.

From the standpoint of the state, the underlying contradiction is that its necessarily increasing interventions into economic relations to ensure private capital accumulation threaten its legitimacy as democratic representative of the public interest. The history of U.S. economic development is, in large part, one of growing state involvement in efforts to stabilize periodic crises and to provide the political and economic conditions requisite for growth in an increasingly centralized and international capitalist economy. This role, however, politicizes production relations by casting doubt on both the nature of the "free" enterprise system and the neutrality of the state (cf., Wright, 1977; Castells, 1980). From the standpoint of private capital, this contradiction presents itself in the form of capital's expanding need for an interventionist state that, under conditions of democratic political organization and the state's own need to maintain its legitimacy, can come to threaten the private sector's traditional prerogatives in economic relations (Alford and Friedland, 1985: 430–3). In terms of harmful business behavior, it turns out that the private sector itself needs some form of state constraint to preserve the legitimacy of production relations and to maintain satisfactory conditions for future economic expansion. It needs laws to establish product safety standards that promote marketability and working conditions that preserve the health of human capital, at least for the near term. Given the logic of competition in a free market economy, the private sector is incapable of organizing its own response to these needs. At the same time, capital seeks to maintain its fundamental autonomy in economic matters.

This central contradiction is in the near term likely to be resolved in the form of government regulation that is relatively favorable to, and at least acceptable to, the most powerful economic interests: the largest corporations that dominate the economy in terms of investment, growth, and profitability. The tendency was suggested earlier in the discussion of the historical development of regulation. However, in favoring the powerful, monopoly-sector corporations at the relative expense of smaller, competitive-sector companies (cf., O'Connor, 1973), regulatory law threatens to exacerbate the inequality between the two sectors and, indeed, to reproduce the social damage occasioned by inadequately controlled economic activity.

As I noted earlier, regulation applied evenly to businesses tends to burden the smaller companies disproportionately. That is because larger firms enjoy both "regulatory economies of scale" (increased costs are spread over larger volumes of production) and a greater ability to pass costs on to consumers due to lower levels of price competition. The disproportion is only heightened to the extent that regulators treat monopoly-sector violators more leniently than the smaller, competitive-sector companies. Thus regulation, with other factors in political economy, contributes to the strengthening of the dominant sector of large corporations and the relative weakening of the competitive sector.

This link between state regulation and increasing economic concentration can be expected eventually to contribute to destabilizing consequences that will require even more creative state responses. In the first place, the growth of the already dominant monopoly sector threatens to produce both the economic inefficiencies that often attend monopolistic economic organization, and a greater role for the state in economic affairs as large international business increasingly ties the U.S. economy to the vagaries of world trade and competition. The increasing interpenetration of state and economic relations contributes to the growing politicization of the state, as it becomes the focus of political struggles over matters ranging from government responsibility for remedying the vast employment dislocations occasioned by changing economic structures to a plethora of disputes related to the apparent loss of liberty in an increasingly centralized society. At stake, again, is the state's ability to balance its democratically based legitimation with its role in securing the conditions requisite for private capital accumulation.

A second consequence of the reproduction and deepening of economic inequality contributed by regulation is a series of contradictions central to the issue of social regulation itself. On the one hand, regulation is inefficient to the extent that it disproportionately focuses on the offenses of smaller companies and inadequately attends the more numerous infractions of more powerful corporations. In effect, regulation as typically applied proves to be regressive, with the result that the total economic costs of compliance are raised relative to the ultimate benefits achieved, a result that supports the calls of business for deregulation (Barnett: 1981: 14).

On the other hand, however, this same regulatory process reproduces the harmful corporate conduct that was the original target of law, as Harold Barnett (1981) has pointed out. Among large, monopolistic corporations, the inadequate deterrent provided by regulation raises the benefits of noncompliance relative to its costs; among smaller, competitive businesses, disproportionately targeted regulation can contribute to increased financial difficulties with the result that noncompliance may be perceived as a means of maintaining a precarious economic viability.

In addition, the productivity increases and technological development associated with economic growth can be expected to increase the potential for social harm due to business activity absent efficiently targeted social regulation. As the capacity of science to detect both long- and short-term harm increases, and as public awareness of production-related risks grows, the state is likely to face increased political pressure for regulatory protection. And this pressure is likeliest under precisely those conditions of economic growth that contribute to higher levels of risk in the first place, because conditions of economic well-being foster higher levels of public concern for and action on issues bearing on quality of life.

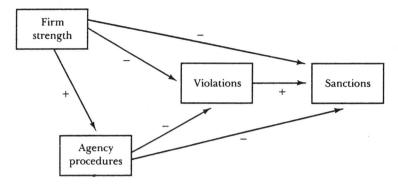

Figure 2.1. A structural model of industrial regulation.

Thus the state will be faced on one side with a system of regulatory law that produces inefficiencies in both economy and social control, and strong corporate resistance to more progressive and intrusive forms of regulation. On the other side, the state faces the prospects of greater risks to public health and safety and the declining legitimacy of government should it be perceived as inadequately protecting the commonweal. It is therefore altogether likely that the state will experience periods of intense political conflict that challenge the legitimacy of both government rule and private production relations. Ironically, these contradictory pressures may be alleviated only under conditions of economic stagnation, when issues of jobs and welfare tend to displace other items on the national agenda.

A structural model of social regulation

Taken together, the foregoing arguments suggest that structural biases are "built into" apparently neutral regulatory organizations. Figure 2.1 presents a parsimonious model of the operation of such biases. As in other studies of business offenses, it links a firm's economic strength directly to illegal behavior and also to sanctioning patterns. It elaborates on these relationships, however, by theoretically incorporating the mediating effects of regulatory agency procedures on subsequent violations and sanctioning experience. The model indicates that the economic characteristics of the company not only directly affect violation and sanctioning rates, but also indirectly influence these rates through the intervention of agency processing. Thus the model makes central (and problematic) the nature of the interpenetration of state structure and the economy in the production of corporate illegalities.

The right-hand side of the model indicates the rather straightforward relationship between violations and sanctions: firms with greater numbers of detected infractions are more likely than those with fewer to experience a higher rate of formal sanctions and more serious sanctions.[20] In addition, however, the model hypothesizes that a firm's economic strength will directly and negatively affect the number and types of sanctions received, holding constant the violations experience. This expectation is in line with the findings that suggest that enforcement agencies are often reluctant to confront powerful corporations in legal battles, preferring instead to negotiate with them and administer symbolic penalties, if any (see, e.g., Clinard and Yeager, 1980). For lack of political and economic muscle, smaller businesses are more likely to feel the full force of the law.

The model also hypothesizes that the degree of company strength is negatively related to violation rates. This assumption is derived from the argument that large, oligopolistic firms are better able than smaller, more competitive companies to both absorb and pass on regulatory costs. Therefore, the former should manifest greater compliance with the laws than the latter, because the burdens of regulations evenly applied in fact fall unevenly.

This dual advantage of more powerful corporations over their smaller brethren, regarding violations and sanctions, is only amplified by the structure of interorganizational links between firms and regulatory agencies. Here the hypothesis is that the procedures for negotiation and appeal made available by the agency are differentially available to regulated enterprises. In particular, procedural mechanisms requiring legal and technical expertise are likely to be more accessible to those interests that command the necessary resources. These are more likely to be the larger, economically more stable firms that can better afford top in-house personnel and retained expertise (cf., Curran, 1984).

---

[20] Regulatory agencies may respond to detected violations with any of a variety of informal communications directed at compliance (e.g., phone calls). In at least some agencies, violations may at times also be answered with a decision to take no action against the firm, as with EPA's Region II enforcement branch. See discussion in Chapter 7.

Therefore, it is predicted that larger companies more often approach, and have greater success with, the agency in terms of using its procedures to favorably negotiate the terms of imposed restrictions. To the extent that such terms are favorably negotiated, the benefited companies can be expected to have fewer infractions than companies less successful in procedural politics. This is because, other things being equal, the latter tend to face relatively harsher restrictions than the former, who have lobbied administratively for restraints more in line with their extant capabilities and desires to comply.

Finally, administrative procedures may similarly provide firms with indirect advantages in terms of the sanctioning experience. For example, companies appealing the terms of their federal water pollution discharge permits cannot be charged with violations of those terms while the appeal is being processed. The model hypothesizes that, again, the larger corporations disproportionately enjoy this insulation from enforcement due to their greater access to the agency's procedures.

In sum, the sector of more powerful corporate interests is expected to enjoy a number of direct and indirect regulatory advantages as compared to smaller businesses, which are more vulnerable to regulatory rigor just as they are to economic downturns (and for much the same reasons). After a discussion of Environmental Protection Agency enforcement *policies*, this hypothetical model is statistically tested with EPA data on enforcement *practices* in Chapter 7.

Conclusion

This chapter has presented a critical perspective on the social regulation of business, and has identified the types of constraints that tend to limit the effective application of such law. The remainder of this book holds the application of industrial water pollution law in the United States up to this theoretical light in order to identify the sorts of limits that have historically attended it. My analysis focuses on institutional and organizational relations that link state and economy. This choice implies nothing about the relative merits of investigating these levels rather than the situational level of business-agency relations. As the assumption of "embeddedness" suggests, there is much to be learned about the totality of social systems from examining any of their various levels. Instead, my choice implies something about my theoretical predilections when undertaking the study.[21]

[21] Such predilections may, of course, vary over time. I am conducting field research into the sociology of managerial decision making in situations posing value conflicts for corporate officials. The study is based on intensive interviews with samples of managers, and merges the organizational and situational levels of analysis.

CHAPTER 3

The politics of water: pollution policies to 1970

The attitude that law in any society will assume toward nature will be determined by the kind of value each particular culture assigns to its environment.

Earl Finbar Murphy, *Man and His Environment*

Historically, the cultural value assigned to water has varied directly with the role of this vital substance in the reproduction of human life. At the most fundamental level, of course, water consumption is necessary for the very maintenance of life, so the earliest human communities had to orient their existences around available sources. The value of water was clear to all, and unquestioned.

Nonetheless, competition over the use of scarce vital resources is inevitable. Competition over water access has occasioned wars. Indeed, the word "rival" is derived from a term in Roman law *(rivalis)* indicating individuals who shared the water of a stream or brook (Burch, 1970: 1). Thus, conflict over water has its roots in antiquity.

Water pollution itself predates antiquity. To the extent that such pollution "is taken to mean the depletion of oxygen, with consequent septic conditions, such as offensive odors, floating masses of sludge, and death of fish and other aquatic life, then pollution is undoubtedly older than recorded history," and even human communities (Benarde, 1970: 132). Even nature's own cycles can create pollution, as when leaves fall into waterways and decay.

Although of ancient origin, the pollution of water sources – and the social conflict implicit in their control and distribution – deepened radically only recently in human history, with population growth, urbanization, and industrialization. True, human beings began to engage in consequential pollution at an early point in history, after humankind distinguished itself by separating from the natural environment and seeking to manipulate it for productive (and reproductive) ends. But early societies' small populations, dispersal

51

over vast lands, and simple productive technologies rendered the damages slight. Indeed, "despite popular myth to the contrary, the average medieval town was cleaner than its successor during the eighteenth century's Age of Reason or the nineteenth century's Industrial Revolution" (Murphy, 1971: 24). By the latter period, rapidly growing populations clustered in cities, combined with the advancing technologies of production, had created major environmental problems, ranging from the stench and disease borne of human sewage to the blighting of air and water by industrial discharges.

Needless to say, in the wake of the Industrial Revolution in the West the various claims on water became more diverse and potentially conflictual. At just the time that the production and waste discharging demands on water were multiplying, the growth of concentrated human populations in urban industrial centers rendered more people vulnerable to the ill effects of despoiled environments. Ironically, then, water became simultaneously more vital to the evolving forms of social organization and more jeopardized.

The inherent contradictions presented themselves in a number of ways, the most obvious being that between the need for efficient waste disposal by the growing industrial apparatus and the need for adequately healthy populations on which to build the economic enterprise. Others include the problem that commerce itself depended on clean waterways for production and transportation.

The evolving legal systems faced something of a conundrum. It became necessary for law to stake out formal positions regarding the relative values to be placed on the seemingly contradictory demands being put to water. The pressures and constraints that shape law in this effort are the focus of this book. The purpose of this chapter is to investigate the law's historical efforts to manage this difficult responsibility, particularly in reference to the American experience. This investigation is important because it sets the context against which to assess the contemporary treatment of environmental values at law. The analysis of continuities and disjunctures in legal policy of this sort reveals much about the connections between legal relations and social organization. As it happens, modern water pollution law in the United States manifests both similarities and differences with respect to earlier control efforts, and therefore illuminates the contours of both stability and change in our political economic arrangements.

Early control efforts

Formal, legal efforts to contain environmental pollution have a long history. For example:

As early as 1307 in England a royal proclamation was issued prohibiting the burning of coal in furnaces because of the resultant acrid condition in the air above London. Admittedly most such statements of policy have gone unenforced, but at least one unfortunate found that the 1307 English edict was more than symbolic when he was executed for the offense the following year. (Wenner, 1976: 7)

Such efforts, however, were only sporadic, even fitful, responding largely to immediate local crises rather than to the systemic social forces that were beginning to threaten environmental stability. Five hundred years after the fourteenth-century edict, the British state was still unable to formulate meaningful environmental policies, even when the state itself was under unpleasant assault. In the 1830s the British Parliament "in the old palace at Westminster found the stench rising from the Thames so intense that it either had to adjourn or hang sodden canvas soaked in aromatics to cut off the vapor from the river. It was the result of the nineteenth-century decision to use water as the prime waste receptor" (Murphy, 1971: 24). Here, even the affairs of state were drowning in water pollution.

It was not until the second half of the nineteenth century that a more systematic, rational concern for environmental quality developed in the Western world (Dubos, 1968: 231). Given the Industrial Revolution's broad religiocultural injunction to dominate nature in the pursuit of material gain, environmental resources had served both as the fuel of industrialization and the unquestioned repository of its wastes. The rapid exploitation of natural resources, such as timber, permitted the more efficient development of capital despite the labor shortages that characterized the century. While "other countries might create capital from the labor of their people, . . . the American system took capital from the natural wealth" (Murphy, 1971: 21–2). At the same time, the air and waterways were considered ideal dumping sites, it being assumed that their assimilative capacities were virtually inexhaustible. In the context of rapid urbanization, however, these convenient assumptions and attitudes first failed their proponents when pollution brought serious social problems, from impeded navigation to disease and death.

The need to protect trade motivated American law's first intervention into problems of water pollution. During the nineteenth century, industry wastes ranging from pulp to animal carcasses began to choke the very waterways that were essential to the commercial transportation of products. Industry was threatening its own vitality by blocking navigational routes essential to trade. And it was not simply a matter of one industry acting at the expense of another; in some cases an industry's water pollution impeded its own transportation. Given the apparent inability of business to contain even this clearly self-destructive behavior, it was left to law to organize the collective – as apart from the separate, competitive – interests of commerce, and many jurisdictions passed statutes preventing such harmful dumping. For example:

> The dumping into rivers of lumber wastes was commonly prohibited. . . . So cheap was wood that scraps and fragments were lightly discarded into the nearest creek to be swept away by the water. These were the same streams needed to carry the logs to the mills and the lumber away from them to the railhead or market. Careless operators, heedless of the streams' capacity to bear such a burden of waste, jammed the channels with trash to the degree that, if not prevented, would have risked the life of the entire industry. (Murphy, 1971: 22)

So serious was the problem that it stimulated the first national legislation on water pollution control. During the 1890s, the Congress passed a series of laws culminating in the Rivers and Harbors Act of 1899 (known also as the Refuse Act), a criminal statute that provided for a fine of between $500 and $2,500 or imprisonment of thirty days to a year, or both, for discharges that impeded or obstructed navigation. When rail transport had replaced river transport for most commercial goods, the act became moribund.[1] But it

---

[1] The obstruction of waterways by discharged wastes remains a problem in many areas and can be quite costly despite the decline in commercial navigation on the rivers. In the early 1970s, for example, the Corps of Engineers was spending $2.8 million annually simply to clear San Francisco Bay of telephone poles and other dumped hazards to navigation (Marx, 1971: 54). Contemporary water hazards pose a variety of risks to life and property: "If the waterway passes through a lumbering area, as the Columbia River does, navigation can be made especially risky by cast-off stumps, particularly at night. Litter on the seabed as well as the surface can jeopardize property. Recently a mining company decided to mine phosphate nodules off the southern California shore. The shocked company found the marine bank littered with bombs. The bank was used as a bombing range and dump by the Navy. . . . Such explosive debris promises to booby-trap glamorous and ambitious seabed exploration projects. Oceanographic vessels are already snagging expensive trawling equipment on rocket engines, old refrigerators and other sunken debris" (Marx, 1971: 54).

remained on the books, only to be recycled decades later to serve a purpose quite at variance with the original congressional intent. In this afterlife, it also temporarily addressed serious contradictions connected to water pollution, but in a dramatically different political and cultural environment, as I later explain.

Another motivation behind early control efforts was the elimination of the water-borne bacteria and viruses associated with domestic sewage and responsible for the spread of typhoid, cholera and other diseases that commonly threatened public health. The development of the germ theory of disease in the latter 1800s was a signal event, because it demonstrated the connection between catastrophic disease and water-borne waste. The theory linked the periodic typhoid epidemics to contamination of the waterways by infected human waste (see, e.g., Marx, 1971: 37; Benarde, 1970: 31, 142). In response to this combination of disease and discovery, municipalities began to purify water by filtration, chlorination, and other methods.

The law was slower to respond to this clear health threat than to the navigational needs of industry.[2] Although such techniques as the sand filtration of water (discovered to be effective in 1829) and the exclusion of human sewage from drinking water supplies (demonstrated in 1849 to prevent cholera) had been long known, it was decades before they were widely applied in the United States. In fact, until the turn of the century, public officials who identified sources of drinking water as unsafe were as likely to be driven from office as to find a receptive audience. For example, in the late 1870s a State Committee on Water Supply was formed in Wisconsin to study the healthfulness of the state's drinking water supplies. After a state university chemistry professor refused the politically hot assignment for the committee, a brave high school chemistry teacher and principal volunteered for it and discovered that virtually all of the state's water sources were unsafe. For all his efforts, he was fired from his jobs at the school and run out of town. Not only did the findings not occasion any state action to protect water quality and the public health, but instead, the state abolished the committee, and the Board of Health, which had established it, issued a formal apology for the research and conclusions.

Into the latter quarter of the century, then, the dominant forces in political economy chose economic growth over clearly indicated

[2] The discussion of the law's delayed reaction to the public health needs for clean water is drawn from Murphy (1971: 27–9).

measures for improving citizens' health. As Murphy (1971: 27–8) put it, "The public preferred to dismiss officials who tried to act along those [preventative] lines rather than transfer scarce capital, otherwise capable of doubling itself in the normal course of investment every five years, into water and sewer projects promising slight cash return."

Ultimately, the death and disease rates from such controllable diseases rose to politically unacceptable levels. Combined with adequate economic growth, these rates produced municipal action on contaminated water. The city of Philadelphia provides an example. Between 1880 and 1906, cases of typhoid fever rose from approximately 2,000 per year to about 10,000 (Benarde, 1970: 143–4). In the latter year, the city introduced filtration of drinking water, after which the number of annual cases dropped precipitously, to about 1,000 in 1911. In 1913 the city introduced the chlorination of water, and again the cases of typhoid dropped dramatically, numbering fewer than 200 a year by 1927. Thus, when the governments finally acted, the results were impressive. It is also worth noting that the costs of these public benefits, when it became necessary to secure them, were socialized rather than assigned to the dominant economic groups the law had spent the bulk of its efforts to benefit, even to the point of long delaying clearly indicated health measures.

By the early decades of the twentieth century, the purification efforts had succeeded in radically reducing infectious diseases borne by water. Nonetheless, through the 1960s the thrust of U.S. water pollution control policy remained the socialized construction of municipal waste treatment plants to process domestic sewage. The most ambitious efforts toward this goal were made in the New Deal's public works programs, which spent millions on such construction (Davies and Davies, 1975: 11). In other words, outside of the dramatic health threats posed by sewage pollution, there was little legal recognition of other values threatened by the complex contamination of waterways. Industries were not held accountable at law for their pollution of the nation's waters, which they remained free to appropriate without cost as a means of waste removal.

Thus commerce rather than clean water goals motivated the initial use of law in this area. While inimical to certain individual business concerns, the early protection of navigation was designed to secure and maintain the *general* interests of the evolving system of production. Given industry's need for useful resources, including a relatively healthy and pacified labor force, even the early programs aimed at public health served the general interests of the dominant forces in the political economy. The costs of public health programs related to water were socialized, as were in effect the costs of most industrial water pollution, unattended as they were by law and hence passed on to present and future generations in the form of despoiled environments.

Similar processes were at work on law elsewhere. For example, in Britain, "from the beginning, the idea of pollution control was not to restrict industrial development, but to insure it" (Ridgeway, 1970: 15). The mid-nineteenth-century push for pollution control in Great Britain was spearheaded by Sir Edwin Chadwick, who had been directed in 1839 by the Poor Law Commission to study the infectious diseases, such as cholera and typhus, that plagued working class districts in the crowded cities.[3] Chadwick was a utilitarian reformer who believed that centralized state control would rationalize sanitation practices in the country, improving the health and moral character of the working classes and therefore simultaneously increasing their productivity and the social control of their behavior. In his report he quoted Villerme, the reporter of a committee of the Royal Academy of Medicine at Paris:

At Varregio in the principality of Lucca, the inhabitants, few in number, barbarous, and miserable, were annually, from time immemorial, attacked about the same period with agues; but in 1741 floodgates were constructed which permitted the escape into the sea of waters from the marshes, preventing at the same time the ingress of the ocean to these marshes both from tides and storms. This contrivance, which permanently suppressed the marsh, also expelled the fevers. In short, the canton of Varregio is at the present day one of the healthiest, most industrious, and richest on the coast of Tuscany; and a part of those families whose boorish ancestors sunk under the epidemics of the *aria cativa*, without knowledge to protect themselves, enjoy a health, a vigour, a longevity, and a moral character unknown to their ancestors. (Ridgeway, 1970: 22–8)

Chadwick's efforts resulted in the Public Health Act of 1848, establishing the principle of centralized state rationalization of public

---

[3] For example, in Liverpool in 1840, 4 percent of the population contracted fevers from cholera and typhus; the resulting deaths were concentrated among the working class, as indicated in the table (Ridgeway, 1970: 21–2):

Number of deaths	Average age of deceased (years)
137 gentry and professionals	35
1,738 tradesmen and their families	22
5,597 laborers, mechanics, and servants	15

health issues. Later, in 1876, the Parliament passed the Rivers Pollution Act, which manifested the balance of political economic values to be ensured by this series of laws:

[E]nforcement proceedings under the Rivers Pollution Act could not be initiated for two months after the alleged offender was given written notice. The court could then send around "skilled parties" to advise the offending party on the measures he might undertake to make the sewage harmless. Special exceptions were made for manufacturers. Before a sanitary authority could require a manufacturer to clean up his sewage, it needed to obtain permission from the local governing board. The local governing board was required to hold a hearing, and in giving consent to any enforcement proceeding "must have regard to the industrial interests involved in the case and to the circumstances and requirements of the locality." And the governing board ought not give its consent to proceedings by a sanitary authority of any district which is the seat of any manufacturing industry unless it is satisfied that the "means for rendering harmless the poisonous, noxious, or polluting liquids proceeding from the processes of such manufacturers are reasonably practicable . . . and that no material injury will be inflicted by such proceedings on the interests of such industry." (Ridgeway, 1970: 29)

I quote the description at length because it outlines the key elements in the law that placed primacy on the values of private production even as the state sought to control some of that production's harmful results. It was a tentative effort, designed in such a way as to guarantee regulatory failure. Occurring at the very heart of the Industrial Revolution, such tentativeness should not surprise. What is most important is that, in its emphasis on negotiation, deference to local authorities, and the primary value of industrial growth, the British law presaged the first U.S. efforts at federal water pollution controls nearly seventy-five years later.

Through roughly the first half of the twentieth century, then, the federal government continued to recognize by means of law only near term, acute crises, and governments at all levels acted only when the pollution threatened industrial activity itself or the broader social order in which the activity was sustained. What the law did not yet recognize – because of limits in both political economy and technology – was the more chronic effects of growing industrial pollution, which therefore increased unabated and would again come to jeopardize both commerce and the public health.

Eventually, too, the environmental destabilization would challenge the legitimacy of state and law, resulting in tremendous political pressures for something well beyond the symbolic assurances that government was addressing the problems of pollution. The mounting contradictions between production and pollution, and the difficulty the federal state had in managing them, ultimately became manifest in the apparent anomaly of a Republican president both creating the first national agency charged with environmental protection and not long thereafter vetoing the first substantial water pollution protection law passed by Congress. By that time, however, such political sleight-of-hand had outrun its usefulness, and the Congress overrode the veto. But those developments are for a later accounting (see Chapters 4 and 5); here it is important to understand the national government's early, tentative steps onto the new legislative terrain of controls that addressed the broader, long-term values of clean water. These steps awaited the era of postwar prosperity, and set the stage for the more effective legal controls that became law a quarter-century following the first efforts.

The politics of symbolism

The first half of the twentieth century in the United States was not congenial to systemic notions of environmental pollution and its control. The energies of the growing federal government necessarily focused on the two world wars and the economic depression of the 1930s. Despite these setbacks, however, this was a period of tremendous economic growth; by 1941 the United States was already producing about a third of the world's manufactured goods; by the end of the World War II in 1945, the nation's share of the world economy was 40 percent, "a proportion never before or since attained by a single nation" (Kennedy, 1987: 29). And it was largely this growth that the government's social and economic policies sought to foster. Notwithstanding the increasing concentration of economic assets into fewer and larger corporations operating across state and national boundaries, the governing ideology in federal policymaking highlighted the values of open competition in a free marketplace. Competition was unrestrained by any but the most urgent government controls – and these only to correct "flaws" or "imperfections" in market relations such as unfair methods of competition, the distribution of impure food products, and the relations between labor and capital. The predominant strains in social and political thought were utilitarian and optimistic in nature – the greatest good for the greatest number through unfettered market pursuits – and both policymakers and social scientists construed such matters as poverty, crime, and industrial violence to be but peripheral pathologies requiring only rather modest state efforts at amelioration (see, e.g., Shaw, 1973; Yeager, 1981: 7–38). Social control largely meant constraining the harmful behaviors and conditions that attached to individuals, especially among the poor and otherwise dispossessed; with few exceptions it was scarcely conceivable that the enterprises responsible for creating wealth and employment might also produce systemic pathologies requiring legal response.

Given the tenor of these times, it is unsurprising that any efforts at pollution control were left to the states and localities. True, the federal government had made some use of the 1899 Refuse Act, and in 1924 had passed the Federal Oil Pollution Act to prohibit oil discharges from oceangoing vessels. But the former had very limited application to problems of water pollution, and the latter proved rather ineffective even in its very narrowly delimited domain (Davies and Davies, 1975: 27). So the earliest initiatives were largely left to local and state governments, which first experienced the social costs involved in industrial and municipal water pollution, and to private victims who challenged the pollution in court.

The limits of "local options"

Municipal governments were the first to act on the problem of water pollution because of the direct threat it posed to the public health of local citizens.[4] By the early years of the twentieth century, most cities had public health ordinances designed to control the wastes of human sewage, which had been shown to spread such major diseases as typhoid fever. But the reach of municipal law was clearly limited, and there were additional water-borne threats to consider, among them forms of industrial pollution.

Most fundamentally, municipal law was limited by the integrating forces of nature. Waterways are typically shared by distinct human communities, so that the discharged wastes of upstream habitations become the inheritance of downstream locales. And so it happened that the downstream communities, needing protection from the outfalls of their upstream neighbors, pressured their respective state governments for legal intervention in the early years of the new century. Some industrialized states went so far as to enact pollution discharge permit laws to control the serious water pollution problems they were experiencing.

[4] The historical material in this section is derived from Wenner, 1976. The interpretation is mine.

The various state water pollution laws carried a number of limitations, however. They were written in such a way as to underscore the primacy of private production over environmental protection or resource conservation values. For example, in many states the laws provided for no penalties for violation; applications for pollution permits were often automatically granted to dischargers without serious questions being raised as to the burdens being imposed on the waterways. In addition, the statutes were often vaguely worded. Even such defining phrases as "pollution matter" were open to a variety of disputatious interpretations. The ambiguity had two significant results: it exposed any serious state enforcement efforts to charges of arbitrary and capricious action, just the sorts of charges that chill legal controls, and it fostered court challenges to enforcement that necessarily favored the private industrial polluters. In sum, the various state laws had little if any effect on the rising tide of water pollution, regardless of the original intentions of their framers.

There was, however, another legal mechanism by which industrial or municipal water pollution could be challenged: the courts. Where the various government authorities proved irresolute or simply resistant to the idea of regulation, private parties who felt victimized by upstream polluters could call on common law tort principles and sue dischargers for monetary damages or even cessation of the polluting. For example, a downstream farmer may find his uses of the water limited by the discharges of upstream industry.

Ultimately the courts proved as inadequate to the task of pollution control as had the legislatures. Victims' efforts to stem water pollution sharply demonstrated the inability of concepts of law derived in earlier periods of socioeconomic development to address many of the conflicts arising in more advanced stages of capitalist evolution. Principles at law that purported to hear equally the competing claims of individual disputants came inevitably to favor the purposes of larger aggregates of wealth – the corporations and other businesses – which the law formally recognized simply as other "individuals" asserting rights. This was because the industrial aggregates were so situated in the political economy that they could either pay for disproportionate use of natural resources or even justify a primary claim on them, overreaching the competing claims of others.

For example, polluters often considered damage claim litigation preferable to the installation of pollution controls, because it was generally cheaper to pay the one-time damages to one or even several plaintiffs than to rid the river of the pollution. The damages avenue, by itself, was impotent to halt the discharges of all but the most impecunious operators.

There was another avenue, however, one with potentially more clout: in an equity suit, damaged plaintiffs could seek to have the pollution enjoined. But this apparent option, too, proved to have little effect, because of the courts' typical application of a doctrine regarding the reasonable use of water by all riparian owners. Under this doctrine, the courts' decisions routinely favored the interests of municipal and industrial polluters over those of individual farmers, because the law found greater community service provided by the former in terms of employment and goods. In the transition from an agricultural to an industrial economy, then, the law came to support the increasingly organized interests of manufacturers and cities as against the rights of individual persons to fair use of natural resources. This orientation continued well into the twentieth century. Until the latter 1960s, "the general tenor of court decisions at all levels indicated that pollution of natural resources was considered a necessary evil when it occurred in conjunction with some more worthwhile acts, such as the production of goods for society" (Wenner, 1976: 9).

During the decades that saw the growth and consolidation of industrial capitalism, therefore, the institutional relations between law and economy promoted private economic growth and limited law's ability to constrain – or even to comprehend – the ever more harmful pollution attending that growth. The politics of legislation at the state level so favored the rapidly expanding forms of industrial growth that environmental control statutes were little more than exercises in futility for those few concerned with the protection of natural resources. This is, of course, unsurprising given the evolving class configurations of this period of socioeconomic transformation. The growth in the preeminence of industrialists and of the burgeoning working class that was dependent on them ensured the undervaluation of environmental considerations, whose longer term implications were well obscured by the immediate concerns of job stability, remuneration and, to some extent, safety (see Chapter 2). Such factors continue to press against environmental protection in various respects, as I discuss later. Here it is only worth noting the consequence that the more effective championing of environmental law awaited the further evolution of class structure, an evolution that, like the water pollution problem itself, turned on the economic growth of industrial capitalism.

In sum, common law concepts lodged deep in the heart of Anglo-American court law – the concepts of individual rights and equity – in this case ironically served the interests of aggregated wealth (in the form of the legally fictitious corporate "persons") over the rights of individuals, all the while purporting to hear them equally (cf., Jones, 1982). The legal balance had been weighted, and individual rights necessarily could not be equally valued at law. The courts, too, like the various state legislatures, were unable to recognize the long-term costs being accumulated in the name of short-term growth and its inherent contradictions.

Symbol and substance: the growth of federal law, 1948–1965

It would be reasonable to imagine that the federal government, situated as it is above the fray of local politics and therefore better able to assess the interdependencies linking economy and environment, first stepped into the arena of water pollution control to squarely address the limitations in state and local efforts and to rationalize this arena with a uniform set of requirements. It would also be reasonable to assume that, as is so often the case with legal initiatives, the spur to federal action was some precipitating event or environmental crisis that brought pollution control to the top of the legislative agenda.[5] Neither assumption is correct for the history of environmental law.

In truth, the major federal efforts in water pollution control before 1970 largely reproduced the limitations of the earlier state laws, reflecting deference to the political value of states' rights and the resistance of industrial polluters to aggressive federal intrusion. Dur-

---

[5] Such events and crises are often referred to as "triggering events." They may work in some combination, or singly, in motivating eventual legal action. For example, Rachel Carson's *Silent Spring* is often credited with having been an important stimulus to the environmental movement and the various laws that movement stimulated; but it is clear that the publication of that major book worked in conjunction with other social and historical factors, described in the next chapter, to produce sociopolitical pressures for environmental law. The law is sometimes prompted by specific crises, notably those that threaten the state with substantial problems of legitimation. In the late 1980s, for example, OSHA initiated a new policy prohibiting construction workers from working under prefabricated concrete slabs as they are being hoisted into place on upper floors, a practice that had been routine in the industry. The policy was initiated only three months after the collapse of a major construction project in Bridgeport, Connecticut, killed twenty-eight workers, receiving massive national publicity (Butterfield, 1987: 71).

ing the years after World War II, there was simply no public constituency inveighing against environmental pollution, whether of air or water, even in the face of deadly pollution episodes. For example, in October 1948 a deadly air inversion trapped sulfur dioxide and other pollutants in the air surrounding Donora, Pennsylvania, located thirty miles south of Pittsburgh in the heavily industrialized Monongahela River valley. At the end of the four-day episode, twenty people were dead (the normal death rate for the period was two) and 5,910 of the 12,000 residents had become ill, largely with respiratory tract infections that affected the elderly most heavily (Benarde, 1970: 183–4). Despite the seriousness of the occurrence, the town citizenry resisted aggressive air pollution control because of Donora's economic dependence on one of the major sources of the pollution, a large steel mill. As the town's local newspaper editor explained, "For almost since its founding right after the turn of the century, Donora lived of, by, and for its big steel mill. In fact, the community, you might say, was established because of the steel mill. This was bread and butter, it was the local economy, it was everything. The industry had a great deal to say about political life of the community. So that I think there was some understandable reluctance on the part of everybody to speak ill of the steel plant" (Marx, 1971: 96).

In basic respects, this reluctance in company towns was mirrored in the federal government's early water pollution control efforts. While recognizing something of the systemic nature of the growing pollution problem, and the institutional sources of it, the legislation was fundamentally deferential to industrial interests, reflecting a postwar culture that was pridefully protective of the country's leading economic institutions, especially in light of robust economic growth and Cold War antagonisms. This was, it will be remembered, precisely the national *Weltanschauung* that produced the chilly response to Edwin Sutherland's ringing indictment of corporate lawbreaking in 1949 (see Chapter 1). Thus, the federal law that evolved in the 1940s and 1950s was generated primarily by the then visionary concerns of a few legislators, combined with a natural institutional tendency toward increasing legal intervention as federal agency administrators gained experience in pollution control and sought to improve their performance and increase their authority. Absent strong public backing, federal water pollution control was largely symbolic in effect.

Once the genie of federal intervention was out of the institutional bottle, however, forces were set in motion that prepared the state for more effective regulation should the necessary political conditions evolve. After all, the New Deal had set the precedent for centralized governmental intervention to rescue the market economy; it was now certainly conceivable, if not to be expected, that the state would be called in to protect other evolving values as well. Indeed, the early, albeit weak, federal water laws established the national government as the appropriate forum for resolving social conflict over the place of environmental controls in the political economy. This was the substantive result of otherwise symbolic law.

Discretion and deference: 1948–1956. The early movement toward federal control of water pollution grew out of an alliance between midwestern Republicans and elements of the conservation movement, led by the Izaak Walton League.[6] This alliance, forged in the early years of the twentieth century, was concerned to have the nation's natural resources developed in an efficient, centrally planned fashion. Rather than environmental protection per se, however, the goal was rationally managed economic growth. Not coincidentally, the conservation movement often joined forces with large corporate interests that shared the concern for such management. For example, the conservation-minded administration of Theodore Roosevelt "aided oil prospectors in withdrawing lands from agricultural uses and reserving them for petroleum exploration [and] backed groups of commercial and manufacturing interests who were eager to build deep inland waterways which businessmen hoped would reduce the high cost of shipping by rail. Small lumber men were bitter about Roosevelt's sellout to the big lumber companies in his forest policy" (Ridgeway, 1970: 40).

Nonetheless, when the conservationists settled on the water pollution issue in the 1930s, some proposed approaches to regulation that were stringent for the times. In 1940, for example, Republican Senator Karl Mundt of South Dakota sponsored a bill that would have the federal government establish water quality standards, set minimum treatment requirements for industrial and other effluents, and enforce the law upon request of a local sanitary district or the secretary of war (the law was to be administered by the Army Corps of Engineers). But the administration of Franklin Roosevelt –

[6] This political history of the early laws draws on Ridgeway's (1970) account, as well as on those found in Davies and Davies (1975) and Wenner (1976). Again, the interpretations are mine.

including the president and his secretary of the interior, Harold Ickes – did not support aggressive federal regulation, especially of industrial pollution. Instead, Roosevelt foresaw only a limited federal role in pollution control, one in which the government promoted and coordinated education, research and enforcement, and offered grants and loans to facilitate abatement. Also lacking wide congressional support, Mundt's bill died in committee.

After the moratorium on such issues occasioned by the war effort, and after the failure of various prewar pollution control proposals, the Congress finally passed the first federal statute to broadly address water pollution: the Federal Water Pollution Control Act of 1948. Sponsored by Senators Alben Barkley and Robert A. Taft, who opposed more rigorous regulation of the sort offered by Mundt, the bill authorized only the limited federal functions earlier favored by Roosevelt. It directed the U.S. Public Health Service to provide research and technical assistance to the states and, continuing the federal role established during the New Deal, made available $22.5 million in loan funds to help finance construction of municipal waste treatment facilities. However, because of fiscal opposition to such expenditures in the Truman and Eisenhower administrations, these funds were never appropriated. In terms of enforcement, the law deferred to the states' rights issue, bowing to the resistance of state authorities to federal intrusion on their political and bureaucratic domains, and of industry groups who felt they had more influence over pollution policies at the state level. This congressional deference was made explicit in the terms of the statute:

[I]t is hereby declared to be the policy of Congress to recognize, preserve, and protect the primary responsibilities and rights of the States in preventing and controlling water pollution. (Ch. 758, 62 Stat. 1155)

The policy was made manifest in the act's enforcement provisions. The law applied only to pollution of interstate waters that endangered "the health or welfare of persons in a State other than that in which the discharge originates." In cases of such pollution, the federal government was authorized to notify the polluter and responsible state agency and recommend "reasonable and equitable" abatement measures. If compliance was not forthcoming after a "reasonable time," a second notification was authorized, which *could* be followed by a public hearing if noncompliance again continued.

Finally, if still no action was taken, the government *could* request the U.S. attorney general to bring suit in federal court, but with the crippling proviso that it could do so only with the permission of the agency or state that had presumably chosen not to act forcibly on its own.

Given these constraints, it was entirely predictable that federal enforcement would be nil. Indeed, "the House Appropriations Committee denied fiscal 1956 funds to the Public Health Service for enforcement, on the grounds that the existing law was 'almost unenforceable'" (Davies and Davies, 1975: 29). It is doubtless that some members of Congress had foreseen the failure. In response to a 1936 proposal by Barkley for a similar water pollution law, Democratic Representative Charles Faddis of Pennsylvania had argued that:

This is not an anti-pollution bill. . . . This is a bill to once more lull the forces that are working against pollution into sleep to get their minds off the subject of the real cause of pollution . . . pollution from industrial waste. There is not a member of this House but knows what is causing stream pollution. What we need is legislation with teeth in it to prevent this pollution. This is a bill for the promotion of bureaucracy. (Ridgeway, 1970: 45)

This first federal law, then, reproduced the traditional focus on municipal sewage rather than on industrial wastes, despite the fact that by 1950 American industry was consuming 77 billion gallons of water per day, fully five and a half times the municipal consumption, and most of which was returned to rivers and streams full of pollutants (Zwick and Benstock, 1971: 40). The traditional focus was manifested in the Congress's vesting of responsibility for the law in the Public Health Service, which shared the view of state public health officials that the pollution problem remained principally one of preventing infectious diseases carried by human sewage. At this historical juncture, the federal government was not inclined to challenge industrial power or risk economic growth by implementing expensive pollution controls. Indeed, the government's own power and prestige rested upon the nation's new-found industrial and military superiority in the years following World War II, a dominance rooted in the achievements of U.S. industrial capitalism. Culturally, the society placed premium value on the tide of economic growth and international supremacy, on which rode the hopes and increasing expectations of millions for the consumptive life-styles of the burgeoning middle class. Industrial water pollution might be a periodic local menace but remained far from the priorities of the national agenda.

All of which is not to say that the Congress was to sit idly by in the face of such a clearly flawed piece of legislation. Once the lawmakers had formally identified pollution as a problem of legitimate concern to the federal government, it was unlikely that the legislature could either renege on the point or abide so feeble an effort as the 1948 law. Industrial water use and pollution had grown dramatically. By 1960 industry was using 140 billion gallons per day, seven times the municipal usage (agricultural use for irrigation amounted to another 114 billion gallons daily). And it was still clear that state governments were unprepared to tackle their industrial sources of wealth on the pollution issue, and even had they been so inclined could not have dealt with the difficult matter of interstate pollution.

It only remained for interested members of Congress to activate the institutional potential that had now evolved in the federal state. As it happened, two names became prominent in the series of amendments that were eventually made to the 1948 act, and both men's political histories explain their interest in and leadership on the water pollution issue. Congressman John Blatnik represented the area surrounding Duluth, Minnesota, a region dependent on its water resources both because of the vital tourist trade attracted to the woods and waters of northern Minnesota and because of the commercial ship traffic that linked the nation's interior and its products through Duluth on the western tip of Lake Superior to the rest of the world. As a congressman, Blatnik early on took interest in developing water resources, and as a member of the House subcommittee on rivers and harbors, discovered and became concerned with the badly polluted harbors of the lower Mississippi (a river whose headwaters are in Minnesota). The other legislator was Senator Edmund Muskie of Maine, whose interest in water pollution derived from his days as governor of the state, where increasing water pollution had put at risk some of the state's major industries (see below). Both men had, therefore, experienced something of the contradictions inherent in water pollution, and sought reform through legislative action.

It was Blatnik who spearheaded the first amendments to the Federal Water Pollution Control Act (FWPCA), passed in 1956. The law was further amended seven times: 1961, 1965, 1966, 1970, 1972, 1977, and 1987. But the basic structure of the 1956 amendments shaped water pollution enforcement for the next fourteen years, and despite some improvements over its predecessor, the new law similarly failed to contain the swell of industrial pollution, principally because the law continued to express sharp deference to both state regulators and economic interests. Again, it most effectively addressed municipal sewage, authorizing $500 million over a ten-year period in matching grants for the construction of local sewage disposal plants, this time overcoming the opposition of the Eisenhower administration (Davies and Davies, 1975: 31). The new enforcement scheme, designed to step up federal pressure on industrial polluters and reluctant state regulators, ultimately could not accomplish its stated tasks.

The 1956 amendments established a three-part enforcement mechanism to address cases of interstate pollution. First, the U.S. surgeon general could call a conference of the polluters and the state and federal regulatory agencies involved in the problem, or could convene a conference "whenever requested by a State water pollution control agency or the Governor of any State." Such conferences were to develop recommendations for abatement of the water pollution. Second, if polluters did not take the recommended abatement action after at least six months' time, the secretary of the Department of Health, Education and Welfare (HEW), the parent agency of the Public Health Service, was authorized to hold a public hearing on the matter and again make recommendations for abatement, allowing a "reasonable time" for compliance, at least another six months. Finally, if polluters again failed to comply, HEW could request that the U.S. attorney general bring a civil suit to secure abatement, but only with the consent of the state water pollution control agency in the polluters' state(s) or at the written request of the downstream state(s) endangered by the pollution. In any such lawsuit, however, the act directed the courts to give "due consideration to the practicability and to the physical and economic feasibility of securing abatement of any pollution proved,"[7] a provision continued from the 1948 version and one that remained in the law until the amendments of 1972 (Wenner, 1974: 275).

The 1961 amendments to the FWPCA eliminated a couple of the obvious limitations in the law. They broadened the scope of the statute by including intrastate navigable waters in the law's purview; previously only interstate waters could be so regulated. In the case of interstate pollution, the 1961 changes also did away with the con-

---

[7] Water Pollution Control Act Amendments of 1956, Ch. 518, Sec. 8(g), 70 Stat. 505. See also Water Pollution Control Act of 1948, Ch. 758, Sec. 2, 62 Stat. 1157.

sent provision requiring permission of the state where the pollution was originating before suit could be brought, but left the proviso intact for cases of intrastate pollution. Nonetheless, the terms of the legislation produced a number of severe constraints on the law's potential as a pollution control mechanism, reflecting the federal government's continuing inability to challenge industrial wastes under the prevailing socioeconomic conditions.

That inability was, in the first instance, reproduced in the amendments' directive that the courts consider the "practicability" and "economic feasibility" of pollution abatement before ordering such changes in polluters' behavior. While this injunction appears reasonable, it tends to institutionalize a cost – benefit analysis in the courts that would generally favor the interests of polluters over those concerned with water quality.[8] The requirement formalized the old common law precept that courts consider the *reasonableness* of the uses to which water was being put, a rule that traditionally favored manufacturers' purposes. The political economy's emphasis on private-sector creation of wealth and jobs tipped judicial discretion toward industry interests, and even where meaningful pollution control could be achieved without threatening economic failure, industry control over financial and technical information could be used to present dire forecasts to forestall state-enforced pollution controls. As a practical matter, however, this limit on the 1956 pollution law's effectiveness was not actualized in federal court. Of the sixty enforcement conferences called under the law through mid-1972 (by which time other enforcement mechanisms had replaced the 1956 design), only one reached the court stage, and this case involved the city of St. Joseph, Missouri, not private industry.[9] Other constraints in the law, reflecting the institutional relationship between state and economy during this period, had inhibited the development of effective regulation at earlier stages in the enforcement process.

In important respects, these constraints were rooted in the organizational structure of the enforcement apparatus. The location of a

[8] "Like an insanity plea to a charge of murder, these clauses provided an ultimate defense for any polluter who might admit guilt concerning his activities, but might continue to pollute without abatement on the grounds that to treat his wastes would be either technically or economically not feasible" (Wenner, 1974: 275 [fn. 88]).

[9] See Zwick and Benstock (1971: appendix A) for the data on enforcement conferences called by the federal government under the 1956 FWPCA. For additional discussion of these data, see Wenner (1974: 278–80).

regulatory program in the structures of state is always an important political choice, one that typically has fateful consequences for the direction and tenor of enforcement. The 1956 amendments, as had the 1948 act, gave administrative responsibility for the law to the doctors and sanitary engineers of the Public Health Service. This choice, to be sure, reflected the traditional public and congressional concern for clean water for human consumption. In consequence of this sociopolitical logic, it also indicated that a regard for water as a general resource to be conserved had not yet evolved into a legitimate concern in the United States and therefore could not be squarely represented as such in the legislation. Most important, the assignation resulted in the dilution of federal enforcement efforts, because as the acute threat of water-borne disease due to human sewage declined, the PHS doctors began to side with the arguments of state and local public health doctors, who often no longer saw a need for substantial pollution control. Ironically, then, the federal government's own medical experts acted to undermine the efforts of the PHS attorneys charged with enforcing the water pollution law (Ridgeway, 1970: 54).

Other key aspects of the law only made it more self-limiting. In the first place, the amendments included many vital points of regulatory discretion concerning matters of both procedure and definition. For example, the outside limits of "reasonable time" periods for abatement remained undefined. Even the definition of pollution remained vague (until the 1965 amendments), with the result that enforcement proceedings were often delayed by long debate on just what was being prohibited: "In each conference considerable time and energy were spent in arguing over whether water, as defined by its chemical condition, could be said to be polluted" (Wenner, 1972: 71).

In the second place, the conference procedure emphasized negotiation and mutual agreement rather than coercion and stiff enforcement. In these meetings, the issues were typically defined as technical rather than legal, as problems to be resolved by experts rather than by adversary proceedings. An atmosphere of cooperation generally prevailed as technical experts – engineers and physicians – from the state and federal governments and the offending industries met to resolve what were often considered to be mutual problems (Wenner, 1976: 83). This mutual definition of the situation was strongly reinforced by the revolving door whereby experts changed sides from one year to the next. For example, an engineer for the federal government might the next year be a state official explaining his new employer's sluggish progress in enforcing pollution controls on industry. Similarly, a corporate expert might act on behalf of his firm one year in a conference, and be on a state's advisory board the next (Wenner, 1974: 282). Naturally enough, this pattern of interchange both reflected and reproduced a general spirit of cooperation.

And this was so despite the fact that antipollution groups could also be heard at these conferences, which were open to the public. Wenner's (1974: 282) observational research at the conferences, however, found that the regulatory authorities generally extended only formal (rather than meaningful) recognition to such groups' views, and then returned to discussing the technical and economic considerations at hand in the case. In this regulatory drama, the ecologists were typically left to communicate among themselves and with the media, in the latter case hoping to influence public opinion and politicians (Wenner, 1972: 82).

As established by the Congress, the intent of the conferences was twofold: to publicize the polluting activity and bring the weight of public opinion to bear on both the polluters and reluctant state regulators, and to reduce the political power of industrial waste dischargers by moving the regulatory forum away from their local and state spheres of influence (Wenner, 1976: 83), where private-sector threats (to relocate plants to more accommodating states for example) and persuasions had more impact. Given the climate of the times, however, public opinion was ill-suited for the role of big stick in these enforcement cases, and the federal negotiators were, at best, left to attempt to convince the previously reluctant state regulators to secure meaningful abatement from polluters. In so deferring to "states' rights," and especially in a context that emphasized cooperation and technical, rather than political, definitions of problems, the conference procedure was destined to produce more (regulatory) protraction than (environmental) protection.

The enforcement conference regarding the Raritan Bay in New Jersey illustrates the limitations inherent in this legal process (Ridgeway, 1970: 55–62). Located next to the congested New York metropolitan area beneath the New York Harbor, the bay had long been badly polluted, both by municipal sewage and severe industrial pollution, much of it carried by the Arthur Kill River, on which are situated numerous and diverse manufacturing facilities. Although the Interstate Sanitation Commission of New York and New Jersey had, in 1935, designated the Raritan to be used principally for such recreational purposes as swimming, boating, and fishing, as well as for the commercial shell-fishing industry, the states had not been able to prevent its becoming one of the most polluted bodies of water in the country.

The surgeon general initiated the first enforcement conference on the Raritan, in August 1961. From the standpoint of the federal government, the purpose was to convince state regulators and industry to forge abatement plans and schedules. But state health officials were reluctant, arguing that the current abatement programs were effective, that the bay was in good environmental condition, and that waste disposal was one of the prime purposes of the waters at issue. Ultimately, however, further federal studies of the bay discredited these disclaimers, and by the time federal regulators called a second session of the conference in May 1963 (rather than step up the proceedings to hearing status, as called for in the law), New Jersey and New York health officials were ready to announce new orders directing various municipalities and industries – largely in New Jersey – to substantially improve their pollution abatement capacities within a year. Soon after the second session, however, New Jersey officials announced that the one-year timetable was unduly burdensome for industry, and that at least two years of planning would be necessary before a timetable for compliance could be set. With this position, pollution abatement was delayed indefinitely.

In this set of proceedings, as in the others, a signal limitation was the degree of deference federal authorities gave to their state counterparts. The federal regulatory bureaucracy was split on this issue. The attorney in charge of enforcing the water law, Murray Stein, was frustrated by the PHS's own physicians in his efforts to more rigorously regulate polluters. While Stein was attempting to develop media coverage on the Raritan case, the doctors – sensitive to federal–state relations (and presumably not wishing to alienate their professional counterparts in the states' regulatory apparatuses) – were working to dampen publicity. For example, "the US Public Health Service shifted the site of the conference from the Federal courthouse at Foley Square to the offices of the Carnegie Endowment because they thought Foley Square might seem unduly oppressive from the state point of view" (Ridgeway, 1970: 61).

Given these impediments to pollution control, it is not surprising that in 1965 the federal regulators called a third session of the Raritan conference. Again the case was not elevated to the hearing stage. The session produced more plans and reports on the pollution problems, but little in the way of reform. By 1969 the government was planning yet another session and, under new leadership, New Jersey had issued new abatement orders to municipalities and industries, but with timetables for compliance that stretched into the 1970s. By this time, however, almost a decade after the federal government had initiated its enforcement action, the politics of environmental protection had changed radically, and new federal legislation in 1972 would preempt these state controls.

The frustration and delay experienced in the Raritan case were typical of the enforcement results under the conference procedure. Nationally, 60 conferences were called during the 15-year period. Of these, only 4 proceeded to the hearing stage and 1 to court (the case involving the city of St. Joseph, Missouri, mentioned earlier). Rather than proceed directly from conference to hearing, as suggested in the law, 29 of the first 51 cases (57 percent) held multiple sessions or were reconvened as of February 1971. In these 29 cases, the average length of elapsed time between the first and last meetings was 4 years. With discretion and deference the order of the day, federal enforcement was negligible and water quality showed little improvement nationwide.

Finally, the impact of the law was constrained by the limited scope of the federal government's enforcement initiative. The U.S. attorney's authority to initiate court cases to compel compliance *without* the consent of the governor of the state where the violation was occurring was limited to interstate waters, which have been estimated to include only 14 percent of the nation's rivers and streams (Zwick and Benstock, 1971: 294). In cases of intrastate pollution, such consent was still required. And the data on enforcement conferences suggest that this consent was typically too politically risky for governors whose states' industries posed serious water pollution problems. As for calling a state–federal enforcement conference, a matter less coercive than the call for a lawsuit, 8 of the 11 conferences initiated by governors for intrastate pollution were called during the incumbent's last year in office, in at least some cases to assure that "the enmity his request would create could no longer jeopardize the Governor's other programs" (Zwick and Benstock, 1971: 231). This substantial constraint, therefore, joined with the other forces of deference and discretion to completely forestall the use of aggressive court action to rein in industrial water pollution.

In sum, the 1956 amendments to the Federal Water Pollution Control Act, while representing increased federal attention to this environmental risk, nonetheless reflected the limited and limiting extent to which government was then able to challenge this aspect of production relations in the private sector. Without a strong political constituency demanding state action, and despite the increasing centralization of the affairs of state, the federal government remained dependent upon the political and economic capital generated by private industry. It was also still strongly constrained by the strictures of U.S. federalism, under which states' rights were given heavy weight absent clear cause for preemption by the central government. In so deferring to these rights in the case of water pollution control, the federal government necessarily abdicated the matter to jurisdictions ill-inclined to challenge the industrial sources of wealth and jobs.

These institutional constraints, reflected in the very terms of the legislation, predictably had effect at the organizational and situational levels of regulation. As construed by most federal officials, the only legitimate lever for federal suasion was the defense of the public against the acute risks of disease, particularly with respect to pollution problems that were interstate in nature and hence beyond the regulatory grasp of any other unit of government. So defined as an essentially medical or public health problem, it was treated as such and the responsibilities for federal regulation were initially given over to doctors, with the federal government also playing the roles of information gatherer and coordinator, and grants maker, mainly for the purposes of municipal sewers construction. Given the ultimate decline of water-borne diseases in the United States, PHS physicians not only placed lower value on enforcement but actually undercut some of the efforts of HEW enforcement attorneys. The doctors seemed more concerned to avoid embarrassing their professional peers in the various state agencies than with protecting water quality per se.

Therefore, the federal government's primary impact under the legislation came to be that of subsidizing the construction of municipal treatment works. Indeed, the initial authorization in the 1956 law for $500 million in construction grants over a ten-year period was increased during the first year of the Kennedy administration, whose support for such expenditures contrasted sharply with the

Eisenhower resistance. New legislation in 1961 authorized $80 million in 1962, $90 million in 1963, and $100 million for the next four fiscal years (Davies and Davies, 1975: 32). In addition, however, there was the influence of precedent: the evolution of pollution control regulation to this point was the "story of a gradual accretion of federal authority by means of applying the carrot of grants-in-aid rather than the stick of enforcement" (Wenner, 1974: 262). But if there should evolve a powerful coalition more interested in sticks than subsidies, the most likely focus for political pressure would be the central government. It would have to manage the contradictory pressures linking economy and environment, and the private sector polluters could be faced, for the first time, with substantial financial responsibilities for abatement. All of this, of course, was to come to pass.

The quality of water: the 1965 amendments. These changes were not to happen, however, before a small coalition of federal bureaucrats and legislators made one additional attempt to shape meaningful environmental controls for water pollution. The two major players in this coalition were Murray Stein, the PHS's beleaguered water pollution enforcement chief who was pressing for a more effective law not so deferential to state public health officials, and Senator Edmund Muskie of Maine, whose state had seen serious decline, at least in part because of pollution, in two of its major industries, fishing and shell fishing (Ridgeway, 1970: 62–5). What eventuated from their efforts was another example of state-made law (cf., Chambliss, 1974), a statute that originated in the hallways of government on the impetus of bureaucratic-professional (Stein) and narrowly construed political forces (Muskie) rather than in response to broadly based political pressures for change. Because of this, the new legislation, although on paper an improvement over the earlier versions of the FWPCA, was again fundamentally compromised by political and economic interests opposed to strong environmental controls. But while the law remained deferential to states' (and often polluters') rights, it nonetheless represented another move toward centralized governmental control of the water pollution issue.

The thrust of the Water Quality Act of 1965[10] lay in its efforts to establish water quality standards beyond which bodies of water were

[10] Pub. L. No. 89-234, 79 Stat. 903.

not to be polluted. Among other goals, such standards would be a basis by which to identify and measure pollution, thereby overcoming the problem of definitional vagueness in the 1956 amendments. Under the 1965 amendments, the individual states were to establish water quality criteria for their interstate waters by June 30, 1967, the standards to be subject to the approval of the secretary of HEW. If the states failed to create acceptable standards, the federal government was given the authority to do so on a state-by-state basis. In addition, the states were to develop implementation plans for all dischargers (municipal and industrial) so that the water quality standards were met. In important respects, then, the new law read rather like Senator Mundt's proposal for standards twenty-five years earlier.

The amendments provided a somewhat expanded enforcement authority. Under the new law, the secretary of HEW could call an enforcement conference not only in cases threatening the health and welfare of persons, but also when "substantial economic injury results from the inability to market shellfish or shellfish products in interstate commerce because of pollution."[11] Here the law made explicit the conflicts inherent in water use, often conflicts between industries, reflecting Senator Muskie's sensitivities to them. The amendments offered as well a marginally more streamlined enforcement mechanism that could be used (but need not be) in place of the sluggish conference procedures. The Water Quality Act permitted the federal government to take standards' violators to court after simply having issued a notice of violation and allowing 180 days for compliance; this waiting period cut in half the minimum allotment for compliance before the government could seek a court injunction under the old law. But given the federal authorities' record of reluctance to pursue remedies in adversarial court proceedings, stringent enforcement of the law was not necessarily to be expected, particularly in view of a national population still generally complacent about these matters.[12]

The terms of the 1965 law, forged in compromise between a more

---

[11] Pub. L. No. 89-234, Sec. 5, 79 Stat. 909.

[12] The Congress passed an additional set of amendments to the FWPCA the following year. The Clean Water Restoration Act of 1966 added several provisions to the law, including the authority for the federal government to call conferences in cases of international pollution (a provision rarely if ever used in fact), discharge reporting requirements for polluters allegedly in violation of the law, and authorization to spend $3.55 billion in federal grants to assist the construction of municipal waste treatment facilities.

activist Senate and conservative House (at least on issues of pollution control), had themselves substantially limited its potential impact.[13] For example, the new enforcement option added to the government's burden of proof should it decide to take a case to court: the federal authorities would not only have to show that the health and welfare of persons in the downstream state were being threatened (as in the original conference procedure), but they would also need to demonstrate that the polluter's discharges had caused a violation of the relevant water quality standards, *and* that the polluter was in violation of his implementation plan. If all of these facts could be demonstrated, then the government *could* issue the 180-day notice and, if compliance was still not forthcoming, *could* seek court action through the Department of Justice (which also had discretion in deciding whether to act on the case). But the law's limitations went much deeper than legal procedure.

The Water Quality Act applied only to interstate waters, representing a retreat from the scope of the conference enforcement procedure established earlier, which could be used for both interstate and intrastate water pollution. Muskie's first offering of this legislation, in 1963, had used the more inclusive "navigable waters" designation, but this was ultimately reduced to "interstate" water in the legislative deliberations. One result was to render the law less intrusive to states' rights and to many polluters on intrastate water. The language placed many of the nation's vital water resources beyond the reach of the new law.

Even for the water over which the law had jurisdiction, in many cases it may in fact have been unenforceable (cf., Glenn, 1973: 843). This was because the implementation plans intended to control individual polluters were arguably linked only coincidentally to the water quality goals they were to accomplish. The Water Quality Act was vague on the crucial issue of the implementation plans, without which the law becomes meaningless.

Senator Muskie's earlier version of the bill (1963) had provided for the establishment of effluent controls for individual polluters. With such specific limits placed on discharges, the government would have been able to take action against any violator, without having to show the pollution violated water quality criteria. The more conservative and pro-industry House Public Works Committee opposed effluent controls because they "promised to make the law

---

[13] This discussion of the limits of the 1965 amendments draws largely from Zwick and Benstock's (1971: 264–84) fine discussion, except where otherwise noted.

so much more effective against polluters" (Zwick and Benstock, 1971: 273).

Thus the final legislation denied the federal government the authority to establish effluent controls, but required it to mandate guidelines for the states to use in creating their implementation plans for dischargers, a curiously ambiguous set of injunctions. Under these terms, it was arguably allowable for the federal government to stipulate that the individual states establish effluent controls on municipalities and industries in their implementation plans. That it did not do so suggests that the Federal Water Pollution Control Administration deferred to strong industrial and state officials' opposition to this more rigorous and intrusive regulatory approach, an opposition registered most effectively in the House of Representatives. In the end the administration resolved the legal ambiguity, if not the political quagmire, by setting a uniform regulation that all states require secondary treatment, a biological process in which bacteria consume organic matter in wastewater. (A polluter could escape the requirement by demonstrating that lesser treatment allowed it to meet water standards.)

But there were two substantial limitations in this approach. The first limitation occurred because the relationship of this flat requirement to achieving states' water quality standards was questionable, with the result that the law may often have been unenforceable in court. Nonetheless, the point proved moot, as such court enforcement cases under the law were virtually nonexistent, arguably in part because of the legal obstacles imposed by this issue. The other limitation of requiring secondary treatment is that such treatment is inadequate for removing inorganic pollutants such as metals and many other toxics, an increasingly substantial component of industrial water pollution. Ironically, this failure to address an essential part of the problem would persist in various respects despite growing environmental and political attention to it in the 1970s (see Chapters 4 and 5).

What is more, the Federal Water Pollution Control Administration contradicted the law and the agency's own policy guidelines[14] when it began to approve state pollution standards that

---

[14] The agency's Policy Guideline Number 1 to the states, issued in 1966, specified that, "Water Quality standards should be designed to 'enhance the quality of water.' . . . In no case will standards providing for less than existing water quality be acceptable" (Zwick and Benstock, 1971: 270; quote taken from Hearings before the Subcommittee on Air and Water Pollution, Committee on Public Works, U.S. Senate, 89th Congress, 2nd Session, May 11, 1966, p. 431).

allowed pollution to *worsen* in various waterways. By this time, authority for control of water pollution had been transferred from HEW to the Department of the Interior (in early 1966), at the urging of both conservationists and congressional supporters of pollution control (Wenner, 1974: 264; Davies and Davies, 1975: 34). On several grounds, they believed the move would improve the quality of pollution control. First, it was argued that Interior maintained a commitment to wildlife and the preservation of natural resources, so would work to protect water in its natural state, while the PHS and HEW were more inclined to chlorinate water and temporarily close beaches to stave off pollution episodes than take a longer term view and clean up water. Second, it was felt that Interior was much less committed than PHS and HEW to working through the state agencies that had so often confounded efforts at water pollution control; Interior, it was hoped, would be less tied to the parochial interests of state governments and local industry and would therefore produce more rigorous regulation. Finally, conservationists argued that the sheer size and diversity (of programs) of HEW prevented the government from giving water pollution control its regulatory due; the smaller, more environment-focused Interior, they believed, would better prioritize this matter.

But strong advocates of pollution control were ultimately frustrated by Interior's handling of the so-called nondegradation clause. When conservation groups, including the National Wildlife Federation, found the Federal Water Pollution Control Administration approving state standards that permitted the degradation of water quality, they accused the government of issuing licenses to pollute.[15] They found an ally in Assistant Secretary of the Interior Frank DiLuzio, but were opposed by the FWPCA's own commissioner, James Quigley, who was supported in his position by a coalition of primarily Western political and economic interests in resource development (coal, oil, lumber, mining, and ranching). These interests, the customary constituency of the Interior Department, were concerned

---

[15] Zwick and Benstock (1971: 270) give the example of Illinois' water quality standards, which the federal government approved in January of 1968: "Lake Michigan's actual measured level of dissolved solids is about 155 milligrams per liter (mg/l). The Illinois standard permits the annual average of dissolved solids to go to 165 mg/l—10 mg/l higher than it is already in this polluted lake. The present level of cyanide in the lake is about 0.01 mg/l; the Illinois standard is 2½ times as high, 0.025 mg/l. In some Illinois streams there is presently no oil to be found. Yet the standards say only that oil shall not be permitted in such amounts as will create a fire hazard, coat boat hulls, or injure fish, thus implying that at least some oil is acceptable where none existed before."

that restrictive water pollution control would limit profitable economic development.

Finally, Interior Secretary Stewart Udall produced a compromise solution: state standards would carry a nondegradation clause, but with the proviso that degradation of water quality would be allowed where "such change is justifiable as a result of necessary economic and social development."[16] This phrase obviously admitted of a wide range of interpretations as well as lobbying efforts by any state authorities who wished to press the federal government for relaxed standards. In addition, the federal water pollution agency failed to demand information from the states on the current condition of their waters, so had no baseline against which to enforce nondegradation infractions.[17] The predictable result was sets of standards that greatly varied in strictness from state to state; underdeveloped states and locales had especial incentives to bypass nondegradation requirements (Wenner, 1974: 278; 1976: 84–5). Moreover, federally approved state standards were often vague. Such phrases as "suitably free of (a pollutant)" and "create a nuisance" provided wide areas of interpretation, again complicating the enforcement task (Zwick and Benstock, 1971: 280). In various respects, then, the administration of the law was compromised by the force of the contradictory pressures that coalesced in the Department of the Interior, an agency responsible for both the preservation of natural resources and their economic development by private-sector interests. To this point in the history of environmental law, the latter responsibility continued to sharply dominate the former.

The institutional relations linking state and economy were, therefore, rather clearly displayed in both the terms of the legislation and the law's administrative location in the federal bureaucracy. Entirely consistent with these constraints was the enforcement effort, which was typically lax and accomplished very little in the way of improved water resources. For example, the Federal Water Pollution Control Administration, reflecting the federal government's continued deference to states' rights, was reluctant to actively enforce the development of adequate state standards. Despite the 1967 deadline, by

[16] U.S. Department of Interior news release: "Water Quality Degradation Issue Resolved," February 8, 1968.

[17] In September 1970 the agency's regional director in Chicago noted in a statement to the Illinois Pollution Control Board that, "to our knowledge, in no areas has a baseline for non-degradation . . . been formally defined. This lack of baseline makes the non-degradation concept impossible to enforce" (Zwick and Benstock, 1971: 272).

February 1971, twenty states still had only partially approved standards; in other cases implementation was delayed when states proposed unacceptable standards. Nonetheless, the federal agency chose to negotiate with the states, rather than call its own conferences to set standards for recalcitrant states, as stipulated in the 1965 amendments. Only one such conference was ever called (in Iowa). Negotiation and persuasion were the principal means used to seek compliance (cf., Wenner, 1974: 278; 1976: 85; Zwick and Benstock, 1971: 279), techniques virtually guaranteed to ensure greater federal sensitivity to traditional state and industry interests in economic growth than to environmental values, particularly in the absence of a well-organized environmental constituency.

In addition, the federal government made precious few attempts to enforce the law against individual polluters, despite the reality that they were commonly falling behind their schedules for compliance and were therefore in violation. For example, Massachusetts was reporting that 75 percent of its industries and 70 percent of its municipalities were failing to meet their compliance deadlines (Zwick and Benstock, 1971: 281). Despite high national rates of noncompliance by 1968, the federal government did not issue its first six-month notices of violation until 1969, when it targeted five industrial polluters and one city (Toledo). The next year, only eight more notices were issued.

Enforcement activity under the 1965 act was stepped up with the establishment of the federal Environmental Protection Agency (EPA) at the end of 1970. In a favorable political climate of heightened environmental sensitivity (see next chapter), EPA had issued 143 notices of violation by December 1972 (Davies and Davies, 1975: 210). Virtually no follow-up in court yet occurred under this enforcement provision, however. Only one company, the Reserve Mining Company in Minnesota, was sued for noncompliance after protracted efforts to secure abatement of its pollution of Lake Superior. Instead, under the 1965 provisions, federal officials continued the traditional enforcement procedure of meeting in informal hearings with violators and negotiating mutually agreeable solutions (Wenner, 1974: 284). By the early 1970s, though, the federal government also was using the civil and criminal provisions of the Refuse Act of 1899, forced by increasing popular demands for environmental protection to show some aggressive action against polluters. (Those demands and the resulting governmental action are the material of the next chapter.)

In sum, the history of the early federal water pollution control efforts in the United States was one of fundamentally symbolic enforcement that accomplished very little environmental protection. These early laws, developed before the coalescence of a significant national environmental constituency, were promoted largely by a handful of legislators and bureaucrats with political or professional interests in the environment, and urged ahead by various conservationist groups. Because in the prosperous postwar era few would explicitly argue for the utility of continued despoilment of water, the Congress was able to pass a number of statutes despite the lack of fervent legislative support for them. But because economic growth in the private sector remained the principal value in the political economy, the laws were necessarily compromised. Water quality continued to deteriorate nationally as industrial (and municipal) discharges continued to be spared anything near the true costs of this resource use. Such compromise, of course, was necessary if Congress was to pass any environmental law of this type. But the federal government had clearly announced its presence in this policy area; it would forever after be the major staging area for disputes over the relative value of economic growth and environmental protection.

CHAPTER 4

Contradiction and change: environmental consciousness and the mobilization of law

In June 1969 fire and water mixed in an unlikely combination when the lower Cuyahoga River near Cleveland exploded into flame, causing extensive damage, including the near incineration of two bridges. Due largely to thousands of gallons of oil leaked from an unidentified source, one of nature's most powerful forces had come to mock one of its most vital resources – to say nothing of the nation's pollution control efforts. None of this, of course, could have happened without the intervention of humankind's evolving forms of social organization and technological achievement. Then again, without such sociotechnical evolution, neither could the species have put representatives on the moon, a widely admired feat the U.S. government first accomplished later that same summer.

Both events appeared to stretch the limits of the possible. But they tore in opposite directions, underscoring a contradictory logic embedded in social relations. The limits that had constrained environmental law manifested a fundamental tension between economic growth and environmental stability. In favoring growth, however, these limits acted to reproduce contradictory outcomes that increasingly threatened political economic stability.

Contradictions in policy and economy

The underlying contradictory logic was displayed at all levels of human action, from the interpersonal to the institutional. As the economist John Kenneth Galbraith (1958: 253) had noted in *The Affluent Society*, "They [the American family] picnic on exquisitely packaged food from a portable icebox by a polluted stream. . . . They may reflect vaguely on the curious unevenness of their blessing." At the level of institutionalized relations and ideas, it even touched the

84

evolving ecology movement, much of which maintained faith that the very scientific, technical, and industrial progress that was responsible for heavy pollution loads would also readily provide the key to their amelioration once the authorities had been properly exhorted to political action (cf., Ridgeway, 1970: 14).

Congressional proponents of this philosophy, who had steadfastly supported water pollution laws in the 1950s and 1960s, found their efforts sharply scissored between the synergistic limits imposed by public indifference and industry resistance to meaningful controls. As late as 1965, national opinion polling found that Americans typically ranked the matters of water and air pollution well below such other concerns as juvenile delinquency, unemployment, and even recreation – as if to underscore the disjointed perceptions of the ecological dimension in the public mind. For example, a September 1965 poll conducted by the Opinion Research Corporation found that while 40 percent of a national sample identified delinquency (the top vote getter) as a pressing community concern, 37 percent named unemployment, and 30 percent pointed to insufficient recreational opportunities, only 16 percent labeled water pollution as such. Even in large cities, where congestion and industrialization typically found each other, only 15 percent emphasized water pollution as troublesome.[1] As a correlate matter, and not surprisingly, survey research also found that two-thirds of the national public was unwilling to pay *anything* in increased taxes for substantial improvements in water and air pollution abatement (Benarde, 1970: 308, 318).

The American consciousness had not yet comprehended the systemic nature of pollution, including the role of consumption. The prevailing stance was inattention to the matter. At best, some citizens vaguely maintained a fragmented notion of responsibility that naively assumed that *polluters* could ultimately be made to bear the freight of cleanup (cf., Benarde, 1970: 308). Unaware of the complex socioeconomic forces that link production and consumption,

---

[1] In contrast, it should be noted, air pollution got the attention of the 31 percent of the city dwellers who said it was a major concern, as opposed to only 14 percent of the sample nation-wide (Benarde, 1970: 318). The acute effects of concentrated air pollutants in urban centers would naturally draw greater attention than the more chronic effects of industrial and municipal water pollution. By this time, recall, modern sanitation practices had rid most municipal water supplies of their acute disease-spreading potential. Moreover, river flows typically deposited water wastes downstream from population centers, while local airsheds often stubbornly detained airborne pollutants in their communities of origin (through temperature inversions).

they were unaware that costs would ultimately be shared between producers and consumers, whether through pricing or taxes, or between present and future generations. The ideology of the free marketplace, asserting the collective good to be derived from the unconstrained pursuit of commercial self-interest, obscured the interconnectedness of ecological and economic matters, highlighting instead the isolating and parallel roles of consumer and citizen.

Both business and state reinforced these perceptions. Sectors of organized business played off both of these roles in its early responses to incipient environmentalism. On the one hand, the Advertising Council, the public relations qua public interest arm of big business, sought to transform the growing environmental focus into a matter of individual citizenship responsibilities: it ran a series of ads urging a campaign against personal littering as the means of environmental protection (Rosenbaum, 1977: 86; Domhoff, 1978: 184). On the other hand, various business interests also sold the message that pollution was no more than the necessary price of the valued goods the industrial system produced. Ironically, these efforts underscored that system's very interconnections even as they sought to forestall environmental protection in the name of individual self-interest.

For example, the National Coal Association sponsored an advertisement that addressed the issue of air pollution in the following terms (Marx, 1971: 92):

If you want an instant end to air pollution . . . stop driving your car, then turn off your oil burner, brick up your fireplace, bundle your leaves, box your trash, refuse delivery of anything by truck, boycott airplanes, trains, buses, and cabs. Don't use anything which requires oil, gas, coal, or atomic energy in its manufacture – such as electricity, steel, cement, clothes, food, newspaper, babies' rattles and on and on and on and on . . . or let's face the fact that any combustion generates pollutants . . . and that any "instant end" to air pollution brakes our civilization to a halt.

In other words, the cost of substantial pollution control would be the sacrifice of the very industrial modernity on which middle class prosperity had been built.

There were business appeals, as well, to more narrowly construed and direct economic interests when circumstances so warranted. For example, after being turned away by a number of locales concerned about potential radioactive pollution, the Boston Edison utility company finally settled upon the relatively depressed Massachusetts community of Plymouth for a nuclear power plant, appropriately named after the Pilgrims who had also found first refuge there. A company official rather directly described the socioeconomic relations behind the successful site selection: "The town is sort of down on its uppers; it's sort of poor. When we announced it, they said, 'Oh, Santa Claus came.' They are a better kind of people to deal with than you'll find in some of the metropolitan areas" (quoted in Marx, 1971: 96). On those occasions when the risks of pollution are high and break through the limits of public apathy, social class differentials often produce a "better kind of people" necessarily more receptive (or at least less resistant) to socially generated hazards, a process that has historically attended the location of such institutional manifestations as prisons and waste dumping sites. Similarly, various "economic need" arguments continue to be made to justify the loosening of environmental protection restrictions, arguments that carry varying degrees of force in the arenas of law (as I indicate in subsequent chapters).

This appeal to narrow self-interested reasons – lodged in an economic culture that cast persons into disorganized, often competitive market roles as consumers and workers – was reinforced in the structures and strictures of federalism. A decentralized politics mirrored the image of a decentralized market. The result was that federal efforts to control industrial and municipal water pollution were severely diluted by their deference to states' rights of self-determination. Federal law left matters of intrastate pollution entirely to the discretion of state authorities, who generally accepted industrial pollution as one of the costs of attracting and retaining industry, not unlike the costs of state-supplied infrastructure and tax incentives. And even in the situation of interstate pollution, where conflicting state interests could hardly be resolved without the refereeing of some centralized, legitimate authority, the federal government's role was limited essentially to mediation, typically protracted negotiations that yielded minuscule pollution control. The preeminence of localized citizenship rights, retained in U.S. law and political ideology since the Revolutionary War against centralized and distant authority, stood in increasing contradiction to the centripetal forces concentrating economic power and decision making. Well through the middle of the twentieth century, law was simply unable to comprehend the policy implications of the changing contours of the political economy.

Contradictions in public policy: the reproduction of limits

The inevitable result was increasing tension between the imperatives of private markets and ecological stability. At the bottom line public policy had clearly failed, because in most respects the nation's water quality had worsened. Ultimately the failure was preordained in the federal government's constrained approach, which focused principally on the construction of improved municipal waste treatment plants, just the sort of fiscal support (in contrast to federal legal control) the states could readily endorse. A 1969 General Accounting Office (GAO) study of several rivers concluded that although "$5.4 billion had been spent at all levels of government for waste treatment plant construction during the previous 12 years, the nation's rivers were in worse shape than ever before."[2]

The logic of states' political economic interests contributed to this result, which was also fashioned by the politics of congressional financing. The GAO study found that in some cases states used the reduction of one pollution load to justify continuing and even increased discharges from other sources, particularly new industry attracted to local communities (Wenner, 1974: 273). For example, while six Louisiana cities spent $7.7 million in federal grants to reduce their Mississippi River pollution by 147,000 units on a test scale, some eighty industrial plants were discharging 2.4 million units into the same river area (Marx, 1971: 84). Congress, presumably desiring to spread the opportunity and maximize legislators' support by doing so in their often rural districts, originally limited its construction grants for waste treatment plants to $250,000 per municipality. The ceiling was subsequently raised and finally eliminated in fiscal 1968. But during the preceding twelve years, "about half of the waste-treatment facilities were built in hamlets with populations of less than 2500, and 92 percent in towns with populations under 50,000" (Bylinsky, 1970a: 34). In other words, the legislation proved more politically efficient than policy wise from the standpoint of pollution reduction.

Moreover, these constrained federal and state policies subsidized business polluters in ways that forestalled meaningful controls and

[2] U.S. General Accounting Office, *Examination into the Effectiveness of the Construction Grant Program for Abating, Controlling and Preventing Water Pollution* (1969), quoted in Freeman and Haveman (1975: 150).

maintained high levels of discharge.[3] The focus on construction grants,

by subsidizing the capital costs of municipal treatment facilities, . . . tends to reduce the sewer charges imposed on industrial, commercial, and domestic waste dischargers connected to the sewerage system. Because approximately 50 per cent of the wastes handled by municipal treatment plants are from industrial sources, the size of the subsidy to business is substantial. (Freeman and Haveman, 1975: 151)

The policy effectively transferred most of the costs of treatment from the private to the public sector for many companies that discharged their wastes into municipal treatment works. Instead of charging its clients on the basis of relative wasteloads, "under the traditional waste transfer system, the municipal plant must treat all dischargers as equals, from the fellow who flushes his toilet to the plant that flushes its industrial waste" (Marx, 1971: 84–5). Indeed, 1970 survey results suggested that in 14 percent of the country's communities, industrial dischargers were assessed nothing for sewage treatment, and in all but 13 percent of the other communities, businesses paid only a nominal flat fee or rate based on the volume of *incoming* water used, regardless of the volume of discharged wastes or the costs of treating them.[4]

Thus companies under any form of pressure, such as lawsuits, to take responsibility for their pollution loads often simply used the expedient of the local treatment works, now subsidized by federal dollars. But this expedient was destined to fail even within its limited realm of application. Municipal treatment too often proved inadequate to the loads industry was imposing, because of both their nature and volume. Typically, municipal plants provided only secondary treatment of wastes, a biological process that removes most of the oxygen-demanding organic wasteload. The problem arises in the face of industries' heavy discharges of toxic inorganic pollutants, such as chlorides, mineral wastes, and synthetic chemical compounds. Not only are these not susceptible to secondary treatment, but such toxic discharges often force the breakdown of municipal systems, during which combined industrial and domestic wastes may

[3] The discussion of the effects of the municipal grants policies draws significantly on Marx (1971: 84–5), Zwick and Benstock (1971: 37–53), and Freeman and Haveman (1975: 148–51).
[4] "Sewer Services and Charges," *Urban Data Service*, February 1970, pp. 3–5, 6, 27–30. Cited in Zwick and Benstock (1971: 41–3).

be released to rivers without benefit of any substantial treatment. Moreover, companies often tied into already overburdened municipal systems, compounding the likelihood of recurring overloads in which wastes would be discharged without treatment. By 1970 annual expenditures for municipal sewage treatment plants were – although an estimated $1.3 billion – less than half the sum ($2.8 billion) the government estimated would be needed each year between 1970 and 1974 simply to provide secondary treatment for most of the urban population in the United States. Not surprisingly, some 1,000 communities outgrew their municipal systems annually as all levels of government confronted the fiscal limits that typically attach to "nonproductive" public expenditures.[5]

Despite the availability of the "under cost" municipal alternative, most industrial wastewater was still being discharged directly into rivers, streams, and lakes, most with inadequate treatment or none at all. Industrial discharges into municipal systems accounted for less than one-tenth of business's total wastewater and less than one-quarter of its biochemical oxygen demand, or BOD, the standard unit of measure for the polluting capacity of organic wastes.[6] By the end of the 1960s, industry was contributing at minimum four to five times more water pollution than were human wastes.[7]

Federal efforts at direct subsidy of private sector pollution control failed as well to stimulate significant results. For example, the Congress's Tax Reform Act of 1969 allowed accelerated depreciation for factory waste treatment investments by companies, a roughly $120 million annual "tax expenditure." Predictably, such reforms produced little new action on the part of industry, which – given the prevailing ideological climate and more compelling market forces – typically found more profitable ways to invest its capital. In 1971 industry spent only about 4 percent of total capital expen-

---

[5] Zwick and Benstock, 1971: 38–9. The authors note that the roughly $1.3 billion spent in 1970 was less than Americans paid that year for hair sprays, tonics, and dyes, lipstick, eye makeup, and deodorant.

[6] Federal Water Quality Administration, *The Cost of Clean Water* (1968), Vol. I, p. 21, and *The Economics of Clean Water* (1970), Vol. I, p. 136. Cited in Zwick and Benstock (1971: 43).

[7] In 1968 industry was responsible for the discharge into waterways of 38.3 million pounds of BOD per day, while human populations were responsible for 8.2 million pounds per day. (Environmental Protection Agency, Cost Effectiveness and Clean Water, Annual Report to Congress, March 1971, p. 12, as cited in Zwick and Benstock, 1971: 43.) Nonetheless, this vastly underestimates the industrial contribution to water pollution, which includes great quantities of toxic inorganic wastes as well as the biodegradable organic material.

ditures on air and water pollution control (about half of this went to water pollution control), roughly the same proportion it spent in 1968 and far too little to produce meaningful reductions in pollution loads.[8]

Contradictions in economy: limiting change and changing limits

While industry's environmental uses in general remained severely undervalued, however, recognizable economic costs were accruing as decades of waste discharge and industrial growth began to corrode the distinctions between long- and short-term effects. As I have already suggested, a sharp contradiction in water use was now clearly dividing business interests, as industrial water pollution undermined such economic interests as those in fishing, agriculture, and recreation. But the contradiction embedded in this use cut even deeper, threatening to undermine the very industrial productivity responsible for much of the pollution.

By 1960 industry – comprising manufacturing, mining, and electric power – was consuming 140 billion gallons of water per day, roughly 51 percent of all water used for municipal, industrial, and agricultural purposes. By 1970 industry's share was approximately 60 percent of the total as industrial users consumed an estimated 250 billion gallons of water per day (Zwick and Benstock, 1971: 40). A decade and a half later, industry was consuming almost 500 billion gallons daily (BGD), still at least 60 percent of total national use (Rice, 1986: 17) despite the abdication to overseas sources of much production in primary industries such as steel. By this time the power industry alone was using almost 300 BGD. Other major industrial users are among the heaviest water polluters: chemical producers use approximately 75 BGD; paper, 40 BGD; steel and other primary metals firms, 34 BGD; petroleum companies, 27 BGD. Water is used for a variety of purposes in industrial production: as a cleansing agent, solvent, coolant, or ingredient. Approximately 200,000 gallons of water are required to produce a single ton of high-quality paper; 60,000 gallons for each ton of steel.

[8] For industry's pollution control expenditures, see *Business Week* (1972), Davenport (1970: 43), and Zwick and Benstock (1971: 50–1). In the *Quarterly Financial Report for Manufacturing Corporations* for the first quarter of 1970, the Federal Trade Commission and the Securities and Exchange Commission reported that manufacturing companies spent only .19 percent of their total revenues on air and water pollution control investment (Zwick and Benstock, 1971: 51).

This dependency on plentiful sources of water creates two sorts of problems for industry. First, many industrial processes require relatively clean water; substantially polluted water is of little or no use. In consequence, much of the several hundred million in sales of equipment produced by the relatively new pollution control industry in 1969 was spent by manufacturers to *purify incoming water* rather than to clean outgoing discharges.[9] Second, the contamination of sources of drinking water (whether by direct industrial discharges or landfills leaching various toxic industrial wastes), combined with periodic droughts, threatens industrial growth as water needs necessarily come to favor human consumption (including agricultural uses). By the 1980s shortages of potable water were threatening to hamper industrial growth in many areas (Rice, 1986). For example, facing severe water shortages due to contaminated supplies, several industrial towns in eastern Massachusetts considered bans on all new commercial and industrial water hookups to municipal water supplies; meanwhile the state legislature passed a Water Management Act limiting major new withdrawals.

A striking consequence of such shortages is the trafficking of fresh water itself to parched businesses. In a double irony, it has been proposed that oil tankers transport fresh water from locations rich in clean water (such as in Central America) to such industrial locations as refineries on the West Coast and the Gulf of Mexico; two former oil industry executives created International Water Resources precisely to broker fresh water in this way.[10] While water has not yet reached the status of oil as the costly fuel of industrialization, it has nonetheless been recognized as a precious lubricant now bearing cost: tanker loads of fresh water in the middle 1980s were going for $6 to $20 per 1,000 gallons (Rice, 1986: 20).[11]

---

[9] *Business Week,* October 4, 1969, p. 118. Cited in Zwick and Benstock (1971: 52).

[10] In 1986 International Water Resources cofounder James Holman reported: "We're talking to the Federal Government now about backhauling water from Panama on the supertankers that bring oil down from Alaska. Why not load up those tankers from rivers in Central America and drop the water off in San Diego or L.A.? Or we could bring water from Dominica to ports on the Gulf Coast. This sort of talk may seem bizarre, but the people we talk to aren't laughing anymore" (Rice, 1986: 21).

[11] Individual companies had also had expensive experience with water scarcity. As Rice (1986: 20) reports, New York State discovered in 1983 that the Exxon Corporation had for years been transporting Hudson River water in its own tankers to its Aruba refinery. The state defined the issue as one of unjustified diversion of its natural resources. It forced the company to cease and desist from such water hauling, and settled its civil suit against Exxon for $2 million.

The increasing value of water was already clear to American business by the dawn of the 1970s. The availability of fresh sources of water in light of growing shortages was by the middle 1960s being used to attract new business, much like tax breaks and favorable regulatory environments. For example, the Northeastern Minnesota Development Association, a business organization interested in attracting new business to the Duluth area, produced the following message in a mid-1960s brochure (quoted in Zwick and Benstock, 1971: 144):

In the past couple of years Dow Chemical, DuPont, Mallet Minerals, Hercules Powder, Union Carbide, Monsanto Chemical, Spencer Chemical, American Brake Shoe Corp., plus a dozen additional firms, are now operating taconite [a low-grade ore] related plants. But there is plenty of room for others who can envision the ramifications of a 100 million ton taconite industry in future years. . . . Much less known but nonetheless potentially highly profitable are Northeastern Minnesota's water . . . resources. *Over most of the nation good industrial water in huge amounts is becoming a scarce commodity.* Not in Northeastern Minnesota. Our watershed contains 41 million tons of water and this doesn't even include *Lake Superior representing the world's greatest single supply of fresh water.* . . . With the entire region boombound, area manufacturers are expanding operations. (Emphasis added)

Ironically, this region and mining industry were soon to become embroiled in one of the most protracted struggles between economy and environment in the history of environmental law, sharply outlining the very tension between them that made the advertisement meaningful. The case involved the Reserve Mining Company of Silver Bay, Minnesota, located about sixty miles north of Duluth on Lake Superior, one of the cleanest sources of water worldwide.[12] A joint subsidiary of Armco Steel and Republic Steel, Reserve was their principal supplier of iron ore, mining the low-grade ore known as taconite since 1955. It was also a principal employer in what had been a severely depressed region, employing more than 3,000 workers with a payroll of $31.5 million in 1969. However, the company was also depositing some 60,000 long tons of taconite waste (known as tailings) into Lake Superior each day.

When in the 1960s fishermen began reporting a drop in their catches and other evidence of pollution in the lake, the regulatory drama began. In 1967 Senator Gaylord Nelson of Wisconsin called for a federal enforcement conference, concerned about the interstate pollution migrating from the Minnesota to the Wisconsin

---

[12] Details on this case are drawn from Zwick and Benstock (1971: 140–66) and DiMento (1986: 202).

shores. The Interior Department's eventual response to such concerns was a task force investigation on Reserve's pollution load. The task force's finding, issued at the end of 1968, sharply contradicted the company's sanguine position on the discharges. The investigation found, for example, that each day Reserve's discharges included more than 2 tons of copper, over 1 ton of nickel, 3 tons of both lead and chromium, 25 tons of phosphorus, and 310 tons of manganese. And contradicting the company's argument, the task force found that much of the daily discharge of tailings was ground so fine that it remained indefinitely suspended in the water, carried by lake currents for miles each day rather than settling on the bottom. The task force concluded that the company should be given three years to find another means of disposing of its waste and to cease dumping it into Lake Superior.

What eventuated was a decade of negotiation and lawsuits involving the state and federal governments and Reserve Mining. Ultimately the central environmental issue became the potential effects of the asbestos-like fibers of the tailings on public health, particularly as these fibers had infiltrated the drinking water sources of a number of communities on Lake Superior's north shore. Finally, this salient issue drove a court order to abate the pollution, and Reserve and the state of Minnesota agreed to build a $370 million on-land disposal site for the tailings; the company also paid for filtering water for north shore cities that used Lake Superior for drinking water. Nonetheless, despite the state's agreement to underwrite some of the costs of the agreement, the company later decided to cease the taconite operations in Silver Bay entirely.

This case history again demonstrates the ability of powerful economic interests to long delay compliance with legal controls, even in the face of substantial evidence of harm to the environment and public health.[13] It also illustrates that the tensions between economic and environmental considerations manifest themselves not only at the level of broad institutional relations, but also at the level

---

[13] At one dramatic point in the lengthy court battles, a federal judge in Minneapolis ordered the company to stop its discharges entirely by the beginning of the next work week or cease operations. Reserve immediately appealed, and in a most unusual development the federal court of appeals convened in a hotel room in Springfield, Missouri, over the weekend and overturned the lower court's order. While this aspect of the case does not suggest instrumental control of the state by capitalist interests, it suggests volumes about the institutional centrality of private production in sociolegal relations, a centrality based on business's key role in employment and, as a result, in political stability both regionally and nationally.

of role conflict in single individuals especially well situated to experience them. As it happened, Reserve Mining was a major employer in the fragile economy of the congressional district of John Blatnik, the Democratic congressman who had developed a national reputation as the leading protector of water quality in the House, having authored all of the water pollution control legislation in that unit of the Congress since 1956. But in at least this case, the limits of such law seem to have cornered even this environmental advocate, who saw the taconite industry in general and Reserve in particular as vital to his district's economic stability. Thus, despite his sincere campaigns against harmful industrial pollution in the Congress, Blatnik provided early resistance to efforts to control Reserve's massive pollution of Lake Superior.[14] For example, in May 1969 Blatnik was quoted in the *Duluth News Tribune* as discrediting Interior's task force report by labeling it "completely false." He had also tried, unsuccessfully, to block a plank in the campaign platform of the Minnesota Democratic Farmer-Labor Party declaring Lake Superior to be off limits as a "dumping ground for mining or industrial wastes." His role in the early years of this conflict was to protect the interests of the taconite industry, which he had worked to attract to his state and region because of the associated employment opportunities, and of Reserve Mining, with whose president he was reported to be friendly.[15]

The faultlines of contradiction: industry shifts on environmental policy

Policymakers at various levels of government were not alone in experiencing the contradictions inherent in industrial water use; by the 1960s they were already beginning to manifest themselves in the

[14] Senator Edmund Muskie, the leading architect of water pollution control legislation in the U.S. Senate, also found himself periodically squeezed between economic and environmental impulses. For example, he supported the establishment of an oil refinery complex at Machias, Maine, despite the unusually high risks of tanker oil spills associated with the coastal geography and rough waters in the area (Ridgeway, 1970: 173). Again, immediate economic interests can cast a long shadow over longer term environmental concerns, even for legislators committed to environmental protection.

[15] Zwick and Benstock (1971: 140–66) report in some detail on Blatnik's role in the Lake Superior/Reserve Mining case. Their research suggests close ties between the congressman and the company, ties that – while perhaps most deeply rooted in the need for employment in a depressed region – undercut in this case at least the environmental sensitivities that appear to have motivated Blatnik's continued efforts to protect water nationally.

industrial sector as well. Related to many companies' need for clean incoming water was the development of a pollution control industry. Also spurred by increasing pressures in some locales to remedy acute pollution crises, industry expenditures for water pollution control had increased from $45 million in 1952 to approximately $600 million by 1969, spawning a new industry with attractive potential for profit. *Fortune* magazine reported that "on the same day that noted economists were predicting a 'serious recession' for the economy as a whole, shares of the anti-pollution companies led the stock market upward" (Davenport, 1970: 40–1). Although sales of pollution control equipment had not begun to approach the levels they would reach just five years later, they were already increasing at a rate of from 15 to 20 percent annually by the end of the 1960s.

Many of the companies developing this new niche were large and powerful diversified corporations – Monsanto, Joy Manufacturing, Koppers, W. R. Grace, Merck – some of whose own operations posed exacting pollution problems. Thus an industrial sector was emerging that stood to benefit from pressures on business to reduce air and water pollution.

If many corporate executives had by the end of the 1960s begun to sense the weight of an "environmental imperative," they appeared to experience it more as socially imposed than as a matter of real resource constraints. An interview-based survey by *Fortune* magazine of 270 chief executive officers of major U.S. corporations illustrated the complexity of their views on the new but looming issue in "corporate social responsibility" (Diamond, 1970).

The corporate chiefs now recognized environmental pollution as of "the highest priority" for public policy attention; 85 percent of them opined that environmental protection should be undertaken even if it meant reducing corporate profits. But they ranked environmental problems only fifth in overall importance, well below the matters of the Vietnam War, inflation, and law and order, a rank soon to be out of line with the general public's growing emphasis on pollution control. And in an indicator of their practical – as against ideal – sense of environmental priorities, 51 percent of the corporate leaders said their companies had committed only 3 percent or less of their 1969 capital budgets to pollution control. Notably, however, the largest of these large corporations were more likely than their smaller brethren to have committed company resources to environmental programs, not only to address present pollution problems but also for research and development. Nonetheless, the surveyed executives typically characterized the pollution control efforts of their industrial peers as less than satisfactory.

This latter view was central to the business leaders' ambivalent position on the proper role of the state in pollution control. As a group they recognized the contradiction between a voluntary corporate response to industrial pollution and the economic demands of a competitive marketplace. As a Pittsburgh executive noted, "We won't get this situation cleaned up except by laws that are enforced. If I correct my plant problems, but my competitor doesn't, that company has a competitive advantage. I have committed huge sums; they haven't. In fairness to my stockholders, therefore, I can't make that first move. I see no hope except for legislation" (Diamond, 1970: 58). The survey found the majority of executives looking for the federal government to rationalize what was becoming an uncertain and turbulent area of policy as environmental issues rose to the forefront of public consciousness. Almost three of five executives wished to see the federal government increase its regulatory activity in environmental law, and the majority of respondents favored a single national standard over a patchwork of local environmental restrictions.

At the same time, however, corporate officials were wary of the prospects of increased federal activity in this area. They were concerned that the federal government might overreact, making too expensive demands on business for immediate and total environmental cleanup. They expressed concern that conservation groups, who they thought failed to appreciate the practical issues involved, might provoke sufficient public pressure to force the state into draconian regulatory measures that would sap their companies' industrial strength and vitality. In sum, the leaders of the country's largest business enterprises saw the state as both necessary and threatening in the context of the environmental question. The need for centralized rationalization of the political economy produced the risk that such control would come on terms unfavorable to the traditional requirements of profitability and growth, a prospect enhanced by the operations of democratic political systems in which the state achieves some measure of autonomy from singular interests.

By the end of the socially and politically turbulent decade of the 1960s, therefore, faultlines had appeared in the postwar celebration of carefree economic growth in the United States. Among others, environmental limits were beginning to assert themselves, both in nature and in public sentiment and scattershot local regulations seeking to contain water pollution. Tremors of contradiction had touched both politics and business: concerned legislators could undermine their own environmental agendas in response to constituents' economic needs, and many industrialists, especially those at the head of the largest corporations that could better afford farsightedness, could nervously call for increased state regulation as they began to invest in pollution control futures. In all, the conditions for legal change were ripe at the top of the political economic hierarchies, awaiting only the crystallization of adequate pressures for change from below. These pressures, too, were prepared by longgestating developments in the American political economy.

Structure, culture, and consciousness

Despite industry's initial awakenings to environmental concerns, it is improbable that even the most farsighted of business leaders was prepared for the relatively radical shifts in public consciousness on environmental matters during the late 1960s or for the developments at law that crested on this broad wave of concern shortly thereafter. Although only a few years earlier opinion polls found little public passion for environmental issues, the period 1968–72 could be appropriately labeled "the high renaissance of ecological politics" in the United States (Rosenbaum, 1977: 6–8).

Its swift appearance notwithstanding, this remarkable cultural change had deep roots in the evolving structures of the society since the turn of the century.[16] Substantial economic growth occasioned and was occasioned by several processes that increased the prospects of conflict over environmental values. In the first place, increasing growth and centralization in the institutions of both economy and state have heightened the potential for social conflict generally. The greater social alienation inherent in systems dominated by large, distant bureaucracies increases this potential. More important, however, the centralization of power and social decision making provides a clearer focus for potential opposition, because the consequences of policy decisions ramify more widely, and because responsibility for social problems is more readily attributed in

[16] For additional assessments of the causes of the environmental movement, see for example Gunningham (1974: 30–4, 87), Mauss (1975: 556–605), and Luthans and Hodgetts (1976: 48–9).

tightly organized systems than in loosely coupled, decentralized structures. Under centralized social organization, it becomes clearer that concentrated economic and political policymaking carries greater responsibility for such problems as unemployment, prices, and official injustice than do individual attributes and simple supply and demand curves.

In commerce the twentieth century has seen the nation's industries dominated by fewer and larger corporations whose decisions, both within and between them, vitally influence employment rates and opportunities, wages and prices, product quality and safety, and environmental conditions, to name but several types of impact. And as legal scholar Christopher Stone (1977: 4) has pointed out, as large diversified companies come to dominate so much of the nation's activities, it is simply the case that "an increasing share of misconduct will originate in the corporate sector."

It is to the state that the aggrieved turned for redress. Parallel to the experience in business, and in important respects because of it, the institutions of the polity both grew and became more centralized as the focus of power shifted inexorably from the states to the federal government. Large, centralized authority was necessary to rationalize – and to cope with – the needs of increasingly international commerce and to ameliorate the numerous disputes that economic development occasioned. Citizens more frequently appealed to the federal government to resolve conflicts with industry, in areas ranging from labor relations to antitrust law, as the power of large business outstripped the resources and will of state and local governments. But its enlarged responsibilities rendered the federal government more vulnerable to recurring crises of legitimacy, whether because of failure to adequately regulate increasingly difficult socioeconomic problems (as in civil rights, fiscal policy, or foreign policy) or because of wrongdoing in the institutions of government themselves (as in the Watergate episode in the 1970s and the Iran/Contra dealings in the 1980s). In sum, the large institutions of both government and the economy became the settings of both the aspirations and the irritations of large segments of the population, bringing a precarious legitimacy and the prospects of ongoing conflicts to both. By the middle 1970s the leading institutions of both business and government had fallen into widespread disrepute in public opinion.[17]

[17] A 1978 survey found that American business had dramatically dropped in public esteem over the previous ten years (Lipset and Schneider, 1978). But the authors

In regard to environmental questions, the dynamic industrial growth in the United States following World War II produced two important results that would prove to be a politically volatile mix: dramatically increasing environmental hazards and a large and politically active middle class constituency, freed from the strains of sheer material survival, now more concerned with enhancing the *quality* of their lives. The result was growing conflict over the definition and distribution of social values.

During this postwar period, industrial pollution grew tremendously in both volume and toxicity. In the twenty-five years 1946–71, pollution increased from 200 to 2,000 percent in many industries, while production grew only 126 percent (Nader, Green, and Seligman, 1976: 18). In 1970 the president's Council on Environmental Quality (1970: 32) reported:

The more than 300,000 water-using factories in the United States discharge three to four times as much oxygen-demanding wastes as all the sewered population of the United States.[18] Moreover, many of the wastes discharged by industry are toxic. . . . The output of industrial wastes is growing several times faster than the volume of sanitary sewage.

The toxicity of industrial wastes was the newest problem and of greatest concern. It was not simply the obvious threats often posed by such toxics as heavy metals, serious as these were (mercury contamination of fish, for example, which had killed or seriously sickened more than 100 people in Japan, was found in 1970 in the United States and Canada as well [Bylinsky, 1970: 134]). There was now a more complicated and sinister public health problem, one that had remained largely unaddressed by public policy for lack of adequate recognition: "the unsolved problem of cumulative, long-term, low-level exposure to substances that may become poisonous at an undetermined threshold" (Wenner, 1976: 36). Toxic contamination by industrial products and by-products threatened human health in both water supplies and fish products, in which the toxics became greatly concentrated as they worked their way up nature's

found this to be a generalized institutional crisis of legitimacy: government and politicians were even less popular than business. Contributing to this declining prestige, of course, were the events of the Watergate episode during the Nixon administration, and the many revelations of illegal political contributions and commercial bribery, both here and abroad, by some of the country's most prominent corporations (see, e.g., Clinard and Yeager, 1980).

[18] Note that this is a more conservative estimate of the industry proportion of the pollution load than the EPA came up with a year later. See footnote 7.

food chains.[19] The threat was borne by known and suspected carcinogens, mutagens, and teratogens, and would prove all the more frightening as scientific and medical understanding of its complex contours deepened. In 1962 the publication of Rachel Carson's classic book, *Silent Spring*, first attracted broad public attention to these serious matters.[20]

The awakening of public concern was enabled by a critical factor embedded within industrial economic development itself. Advancing scientific techniques were becoming able to detect, with ever finer precision, the harmful effects of pollutants and their long-term risks for human populations. The undercurrents of social concern grew as the press reported the proliferating new findings. Hence born was a new sort of public health issue, for the first time underscoring the chronic rather than the acute effects of pollution, perhaps all the more unsettling for their uncertain future impacts in people's lives. As the political scientist James Q. Wilson (1980: 384) has noted for the establishment of the federal Environmental Protection Agency in 1970, environmentalism itself "was born not because scores of people were dying from pollution, but because the *potential* (and possibly large) effects of pollution had become a matter of concern" (emphasis in the original).

Broad-based social action on such issues awaited the conjuncture of the evolving class structure and the experience of the earlier social conflicts of the 1950s and 1960s. By the end of the 1960s the postwar era had produced in America history's largest and wealthiest middle class, highly educated and possessed of unprecedented levels of comfort, high aspirations, and, importantly, new leisure opportunities and expectations. Freed from former chronic concerns with economic scarcity, this class found common cause in higher levels of human endeavor – social and economic justice, aesthetics, environmental preservation – manifesting on the level of the social a sequential attention to collective needs analogous to Abra-

[19] For an informative discussion of some of the risks posed by toxic water pollutants, see Zwick and Benstock (1971: ch. 1).

[20] Carson's book outlined the long-range dangers of pesticides, and drew a high-level response from the chemical pesticide industry. The National Agricultural Chemical Association persuaded Congressman Jamie Whitten of Mississippi (then chairperson of House Appropriations Committee's Subcommittee on Agriculture) to write a rebuttal, eventually published as *That We May Live*. Whitten's book had been turned down by Public Affairs Press on the judgment that it was substantively weak; it "was printed only after three major pesticide manufacturers (Velsicol Corporation, Shell Oil, and Geigy Agricultural Chemicals) agreed to subsidize sales" (Zwick and Benstock, 1971: 103–4).

ham Maslow's (1954) theory of individuals' psychological "hierarchy of needs."[21]

Moreover, socioeconomic development in the United States not only had nourished this germinating consciousness of "higher" values; it had also grown a number of widening disjunctures between fact and fundamental social values. In civil rights, for example, the assurances of constitutional law and deep cultural ideals for human rights continued to run headlong against the mean realities of racial prejudice and thoroughgoing discrimination. And this discrepancy only grew more stark against a background of bountiful economic wealth: here the "American Dream" collided with an "American Dilemma," to borrow from Gunnar Myrdal's (1944) famous title. In similar logic, issues of class too became more salient as the gap between the poor and the comfortable widened to produce sharpening perceptions of relative deprivation among the former and interest in social welfare initiatives among many of the latter. For example, beginning in the 1960s both policymakers and middle class reform groups endeavored to humanize criminal justice, emphasizing decent treatment and rehabilitation. These efforts were in part a response to sharp increases in street crime, much of which was arguably due to the growth of inequality.

In all, the consequence of the disparity between espoused cultural values and bare social facts was the widespread escalation of social conflict. Beginning with the civil rights movement, through the university-based free speech and anti–Vietnam War movements, to the newer movements championing such "new" values as environmentalism, feminism, and consumer protection, the conflict embraced many areas of contradiction in social relations and at the same time undercut earlier images of consensus (or value integration) in both public and intellectual thought. For rapidly growing numbers of citizens, the social organism was neither holistically healthy nor homeostatically maintained. There was hope only in concerted social pressure against the remote institutions of power, both public and private.

The newer movements built on the foundations of the earlier ones, particularly in terms of constituencies and organizing experience. But as the 1960s shaded into the next decade, the issues in conflict subtly evolved from matters of long-enshrined cultural val-

---

[21] Maslow argued that individuals must meet their lower order needs for such things as nutrition and safety before they can attend to such higher order needs as affiliation with others and self-actualization.

ues of equality and freedom to the more derivative emphases on fairness, participation, and community in the workings of political economy. There was a growing cultural sense that in everything from foreign policy to the mass marketing of huge conglomerates the huge, distant bureaucracies of concentrated power had undermined basic notions of fairness and self-determination. The new movements were reminiscent of turn-of-the-century populism, and had similar appeal to mainstream elements of the population. But these new populists represented much of the nation's core beneficiary population, those who had benefited greatly from the strong postwar economic growth and who, when organized, wielded considerable political clout.

Activists at the heart of these incipient movements were also likely to be the young, those free from even the memories of economic vulnerability. These daughters and sons of the middle class, who combined the hopeful idealism of youth and higher education in unprecedented numbers, proved especially sensitive to the alienation and contradiction in prevailing institutional relations. And if their parents, who had first experienced the twin migrations from the Great Depression to middle class prosperity and from city to suburb, shared many of their sympathies, they did not always share their offspring's new methods of change. The activist politics of organized pressure and protest had at least vigorously supplemented, if not replaced, the staid politics of the ballot. The civil rights movement had taught the efficacy of alternative techniques of change in a democratic polity, from civil disobedience to court challenge. These lessons, too, were inherited by the new social movements.

The greening of environmentalism

By 1970 public opinion polls were finding dramatically increased concern with the problems of environmental degradation. National polls indicated that those responding that local water pollution was a serious problem had increased from 35 to 74 percent between 1965 and 1970; in large cities the increase was from 45 to 89 percent. Similarly, public concern over air pollution had increased from 28 to 69 percent, from 52 to 93 percent in the large urban areas (Erskine, 1972a). And the public was inclined to blame industry for these problems. The national percentage listing industry as among the primary causes of water pollution rose from 34 percent in 1965 to 64 percent in 1970, although it is worth noting that in-

dustrial facilities were most often mentioned in each year of the poll
(Erskine, 1972b: 265).

Moreover, citizens were supporting greater government intervention in pollution control, often even at the expense of higher taxes
and inflation. A Harris poll in 1971 found that 41 percent of the
sample chose pollution control as a problem requiring congressional
action, second only to "state of the economy" (63 percent), and
ahead of "taxes and spending" (31 percent), the Vietnam War (31
percent), and crime (28 percent) (Erskine, 1972a). Whereas in 1965
only about 1 in 3 national respondents reported willingness to
spend any money at all on pollution control, by the early 1970s polls
showed that 6 or 7 of 10 were willing to pay higher taxes and prices
to control pollution (Erskine, 1972a: 120; Benarde, 1970: 308).[22]

This percolating public sentiment began to crystallize. At the turn
of the decade, a number of media-genic events and reports
highlighted the growing environmental crisis: in 1969, the same
year that the Cuyahoga River exploded, a massive oil spill damaged
the ocean and blackened the beaches around Santa Barbara, California. Scientists had declared Lake Erie dead, and the Club of
Rome reported that the exponential growth in consumption was de-
pleting natural resources (Albrecht, 1983:541). Besides the growing
urgency of environmental degradation itself, ecology had strong potential as a unifying public issue, one that could reintegrate large
segments of the population long divided by the earlier conflicts over
civil rights and the war in Vietnam (cf., Luthans and Hodgetts,
1976: 49).

What finally brought this fast-spreading sentiment into focus for
the nation was not an environmental incident, however, nor was
it heated policy debate in the halls of Congress. Instead, it was a
one-day national celebration of the value of ecology, a coast-to-coast
manifestation of this major cultural shift. Officially proclaimed by
congressional legislation, Earth Day – April 22, 1970 – fused the
ecological concerns of traditional conservationists and radical ecologists, of naturalists, regulators, other environmental professionals,
and of suburban wage earners, and both left- and right-wing ad-
herents, who expressed their support of environmental protection

[22] The amount of tax increase used in poll questions was not large, however. The
Harris survey reported the percentages "willing to pay $14 a year more in taxes to
finance a federal program to control air pollution." On the other hand, a Roper
poll in late 1971 found that approximately two-thirds of the respondents were willing to pay 10 percent higher prices for a number of products if needed to eliminate the pollution caused by their production (Erskine, 1972a: 120).

in public demonstrations nation-wide. It tapped deeply into the youthful antagonisms toward prevailing institutional arrangements: college students around the country organized large demonstrations in support of ecological values. Massive press coverage carried the event deeper into the national consciousness, simultaneously spreading concern over despoliation and energy for the development of new environmental policies.[23]

While it is often noted as the birth of the environmental movement, Earth Day in fact built not only on public concerns, but also on developing institutional bases for the organized pressures on law that were to come.[24] Many of the old-line conservation organizations were revitalized in the 1960s with infusions of thousands of new members concerned about the decaying environment. Founded decades earlier around such upper middle class concerns as the protection of recreational resources, the preservation of species and wise resource use, such groups as the Sierra Club (founded 1892), the Audubon Society (1905), and the Izaak Walton League (1922) had become rather dormant, in part because many of the concerns had been institutionalized by absorption into the federal government (for example in the National Park Service and U.S. Forest Service) (Mauss, 1975: 585–7; Albrecht, 1977: 399). The new-found public worries over air and water pollution enlarged both the missions and the membership rolls of these formerly staid organizations. During the 1960s the membership of the Sierra Club,

[23] The press clearly played an important role in the social construction of the environment as a social movement, and as a policy issue. But the role appears reactive rather than primary. Research on the press coverage suggests that media concern was not extensive *until* legislation, accidents, and staged events such as Earth Day lent salience to the ecology issue (Schoenfeld, Meier, and Griffin, 1979). Thereafter, though, the heightened news coverage contributed to a more enduring general public interest in the issue. Indeed, the environment became a rather regular "beat" for many news organizations, and remains so today. See, for example, the fine reporting by Philip Shabecoff in *The New York Times*.

[24] Former U.S. Senator Gaylord Nelson, who penned the legislation that proclaimed Earth Day, has noted that "Earth Day did not create the interest; all it gave was an opportunity to express itself. My sole purpose was to force the issue on the politicians and to make it a part of the national dialogue." And in this, by his own account, he was most successful. When he arrived on Capitol Hill in 1963, he said, "There were not more than five broad-gauged environmentalists in the Senate: Lee Metcalf, Ed Muskie, Frank Church, Clinton Anderson, Hubert Humphrey." Today, he believes that "all one hundred senators would claim to be environmentalists, and at least fifty to sixty are very knowledgeable about one or two issues" (Borrelli, 1987: 24–5). Not coincidentally, Nelson is from Wisconsin, where environmental despoliation threatened the hunting, fishing, and camping that are central both to the state's tourism and many local citizens' life-styles.

for examle, increased from 15,000 to more than 100,000 (Albrecht, 1983: 542). In 1971 the renewed public interest organization formed the Sierra Club Legal Defense Fund, which sues corporate polluters and government agencies to force compliance with environmental statutes. This, of course, represented a radically new orientation and aggressive sphere of action for groups previously aligned with the conservationist concerns of the privileged classes.

An entirely new environmental establishment was in its formative stages at the same time. By the end of the 1960s there was a specialty nascent in environmental law, not yet so named (T. Turner, 1988). Young lawyers, some just out of law school, were attracted to it by the combination of environmental urgency, the social idealism of the age, and the excitement of forging socially responsible policies through novel uses of law. (The role of scientists in evolving environmental analyses and policymaking was similarly motivated by the attraction of participating in leading-edge research of large public importance. The dynamics of the evolution of the professions therefore periodically inform and constrain state action in interesting ways, and themselves constitute an important area for social analysis.)[25] The young lawyers seized the opportunity by establishing public interest law firms to pursue the new environmental values, organizations that today remain at the center of ecological policy and debate. Prominent among them are the Environmental Defense Fund (founded 1968), Friends of the Earth (1969), the Natural Resources Defense Council (NRDC, 1970), and Environmental Action (1970), along with the Sierra Club Legal Defense Fund. In all, a federal government study found that more than half of the country's estimated 5,000 environmental organizations were founded between 1969 and the early 1970s (Davies and Davies, 1975: 90, 95). Then, as today, the work of these organizations was supported by membership dues and donations, another indicator of the depth of public support for environmental causes. Presently, for example, the Sierra Club has a membership numbering about 400,000 and an annual budget of $23 million (Borrelli, 1987: 27).

The new environmental movement had the advantage of building upon and integrating earlier conservationist concerns but differed

---

[25] As Gunningham (1974: 32–3) has suggested, the technological and scientific advances in pollution analysis and control create an elite group of experts "in whose interests it is to define pollution as a serious and actionable social problem." In other words, growing analytic and technological capabilities may generate institutional bases for challenging some of the very properties of the social system that gave rise to these new capacities.

from its predecessor in a number of important ways. Earlier conservationism had developed no comprehensive perspective on ecological relationships, focusing instead on discrete issues, areas, or projects (blocking construction of a dam, preserving woodlands and other natural habitats, and the like). The new environmental movement embraced more comprehensive ecological concepts and policy interests. It emphasized the *interrelatedness* of environmental issues, both ecologically and geographically (as regional, national, or even global matters), and it conceived of problem solving in terms of broad social planning and long-term trends (Mauss, 1975: 591; Rosenbaum, 1977: 65). In consequence, and as a result of the logic of institutional centralization, the movement's policy efforts focused on the federal government, whereas much of the earlier movement's efforts had been local or regional in scope. In this evolving view, centralized state authority was now necessary to reverse the nation's long use of the environment as simply a tool of humankind's material progress or a convenient waste receptacle.

The new movement's primary lever of social change was litigation, which it added to the quieter lobbying and petitioning techniques of the earlier conservationist efforts. In their reliance on the courts the new environmentalists drew valuable lessons from the civil rights movement, as Borrelli (1987: 27) has pointed out:

The new environmentalists were highly legalistic and advocated clean air and water as *matters of right.* Indeed, some of the new movement's leaders such as William Futrell, a former law professor in Georgia (now president of the Environmental Law Institute in Washington, D.C.), had cut their activist teeth in the civil rights movement. A few others like John Adams, NRDC's first and only executive director, were crime fighters at the U.S. Attorney's office in Manhattan. In the context of the times, *pollution was viewed as an injustice* . . . . (Emphasis added)

Experienced in the use of confrontational legal strategies to secure rights, environmental movement lawyers were left to consider alternative tactics for effecting social change. The foundational members of the early movement did just that at a remarkable conference in 1969 in the foothills of Virginia's Shenandoah Mountains (T. Turner, 1988). There fifty conferees, some just out of law school, reflected on the law's options in ways quite telling of the evolving national perceptions of pollution. Many suggested the utility of the common law of tort, in which for example plaintiffs might establish a series of legal precedents by suing polluters for injuries done to their properties or health. Most in attendance rejected this approach as the movement's centerpiece, recognizing the inherent limits of such a case-by-case approach: it could not address the comprehensive, national, and systemic character of the pollution problem. And if it were even to dent the problem, the tort route would clog the courts and lead to a patchwork of judicial interpretations, just the sort of irrationality that could badly slow environmental protection.

Others, expressing the righteous passion of the period, argued for establishing no less than a constitutional right to a healthy environment, based on the Fourteenth Amendment's prohibition against the infringement of liberty or the taking of property without due process of law. Indeed, the notion of environmental *rights* was gaining wider currency at the turn of the decade: in 1970 in New York State, the legislature adopted and Governor Rockefeller signed an environmental bill of rights. If largely symbolic in effect, it nonetheless set out the new movement's sensibilities: "The theory was that every citizen, to borrow a hallowed phrase, was born with certain inalienable rights, among them clean air and water, protection from the assaults of industry, and the enjoyment of nature's beauty" (Borrelli, 1986: 35). This dramatic approach was not to be the environmental law movement's ultimate course of action, however. As some of the participants in the 1969 conference had predicted, the country was facing a tidal wave of forthcoming environmental legislation, the most notable of which was to be federal in origin and scope. This legislation would provide countless opportunities for public interest litigation, and the environmental law establishment soon found itself absorbed in this line of attack. As David Sive, one of the pioneers in environmental law, would note much later, "In no other political or social movement has litigation played such an important and dominant role. Not even close" (T. Turner, 1988: 27).

If the new environmental movement continued a cultural revolution emphasizing formal confrontations with the centers of entrenched power, it was also true that "beneath the euphoria of Earth Day was a strain of rationality firmly fixed in legal tradition" (Borrelli, 1986: 35). Among the leaders of the movement there was an abiding faith that the state, through law, could succeed in remedying the environmental wrongs in the context of existing institutional relations. The question of whether those relations in fact presented fundamental constraints on law's efficacy in this area remained unexamined.

Although the new movement moved far past its predecessor conservation advocates in recognizing some of the systemic properties of environmental vulnerability, it still maintained but a partial view of the matter. For example, the environmental movement drew much of its strength in numbers from the same pool of citizens, and in some cases of leadership as well, as did the consumer movement that took root around the same time in the United States. But at all appearances the dominant elements in the environmental movement failed to fully comprehend the essential relations between production, high rates of material consumption, and heavy pollution loads, and therefore to anticipate some of the thorny limits to legal rationality.

Much of this had to do with the class composition of the developing movement. It was, and remains, heavily white-collar middle class and wealthier in composition.[26] To a certain extent the movement was consciously organized to appeal to a broad, politically centrist, middle class constituency. Denis Hayes, founder and organizer of Earth Day, had this recent reflection about the original leaders' intentions:

There was a conscious decision in organizing Earth Day that [environmentalism] would not be posited in a fashion that was ideologically exclusive; there was room for middle-class housewives, business executives, radical college kids. Its capacity to reach out to an enormously broad set of constituents, and to give people a way to assimilate the values in things that they can consciously do and affect – and see consequences, have given it staying power. (Borrelli, 1987: 26)

Its constituency also ensured the movement's faith in both traditional legal mechanisms and continued material progress. It did not critically assess all the important linkages between consumption and pollution, between attitudes and behaviors deeply lodged in the capitalist culture and economic functioning. There was, and remains, the risk that the middle class – based movement would make of the environment *another consumable value,* for purposes of leisure and recreational use, and fail to comprehend the potentially contradictory relations between this and other forms of material consumption, or between the value of environmentalism and the very real

[26] Here I refer to the class nature of the *organized* environmental movement, its active participants and financial supporters. The class composition of this movement has been noted by many observers (e.g., Dunlap, 1975; Mauss, 1975: 573–80; Rosenbaum, 1977: 74). However, there is evidence to suggest that social class differences may be less marked in terms of general awareness of environmental problems and support for reform (see, e.g., Buttel and Flinn, 1978).

economic valuations (needs) of the working and lower classes. (For example, by a two-to-one margin voters in an advisory referendum in the Pittsburgh area in 1977 supported changes in federal environmental laws to save jobs in the troubled and highly polluting steel industry.)[27] Despite the sea change in the culture regarding environmental values, the movement embodied the traditional faith in material (and sociolegal) progress in which the middle classes had been reared. Therefore, there remained the real question of the extent to which the movement could free itself from deep cultural injunctions associated with the rise of industrialization, including the message in the received Judeo-Christian ethic to "fill the earth and subdue it; have dominion over the fish of the sea, over the birds of the air, and over every living thing that moves on the earth" (Genesis, 1:28).

Nonetheless, the growing environmental movement was to stimulate relatively radical changes in law, most notably at the federal level. If the evolving policies were not always fulfilled, the new legislation would prove to be something more than symbolic signposts. For the first time, there would finally be broad changes in the industrial behavior that resulted in the pollution, and the politics of the environment would take a permanent place in the national dialogue.

The mobilization of law

By the turn of the decade, the federal government's limited efforts at water pollution control had addressed only the relatively simple matters. The bulk of federal expenditures continued to go "overwhelmingly into construction of old-fashioned sewage treatment plants, which are not designed to cope with today's complex chemical pollutants" (Bylinsky, 1970b: 133). The focus had been on cleanup of organic pollutants (Freeman and Haveman, 1975: 149), the least expensive of the water pollution problems, both fiscally and politically.

But the public ground swell of environmental concern between 1968 and 1972 would alter the political equation. One close observer has argued that the surge "caught the American business community by surprise and threw it on the defensive, thereby putting a traditionally formidable sector of opposition to many environmental regulations at a disadvantage that, momentarily, disarmed it politi-

[27] *Wall Street Journal*, November 10, 1977.

cally" (Rosenbaum, 1977: 7–8). The statement rings true; as a whole the business community could not have anticipated the rapid swing in the public focus on the matter. But the business community rarely, if ever, operates as a whole, and large corporate business had begun to anticipate the pressures for regulation and would in the end participate in its formulation (see next chapter). Moreover, the state itself seemed as surprised as any sector of business, and its initial efforts at response were rather chaotic, finally collapsing into themselves as various sources of law strained at each other and the continuing limitations of political economy. Nonetheless, law began to move and a more rational legislative solution was nearly at hand.

The expansion of law: the courts

There are many nodes of law in advanced democratic systems, preventing their simple or direct control by groups of elites. The routes to and justifications for legal change are varied and complex, rendering law both sensitive to the sway of political philosophical discourse and rather unpredictable in its resolutions of conflicting forces. In the evolution of U.S. environmental law, interest groups eventually accessed all of these nodes of legal leverage, generating change in all three branches of the federal government. As so often happens, the federal courts were the first to respond to the developing public clamor for reform.

The first development, a significant one, occurred in the mid-1960s when federal appellate courts reinterpreted the law of standing, which determines the rights of citizens to sue for various forms of injury done them (T. Turner, 1988: 26–7). Traditionally, "standing to sue" had been limited at law only to those who could prove they had been or would be *economically harmed* by a decision. Economic values had displaced all others in tort law, a result fully consonant with an aggressively market-based political economy. But the moral valuation was shifting with the ascension of values around environmental aesthetics and long-term public health.

The shift at law began in 1965 in the hallmark environmental case of *Scenic Hudson Preservation Conference v. Federal Power Commission.*[28] The case involved the Consolidated Edison Company's plans to build a large hydroelectric plant on the Hudson River at Storm King Mountain near West Point in New York State. The conference joined three area towns in a lawsuit (eventually successful) to block

[28] 354 F.2d 608 (2d Cir. 1965); cert. denied, 384 U.S. 941 (1966).

the construction, arguing that the development would destroy the mountain's natural and ecological environment. Because the plaintiffs claimed no financial interest in the case, the Federal Power Commission (FPC) asked the court to dismiss it. But the U.S. Court of Appeals for the Second Circuit, in a pathbreaking departure from legal precedent, determined that the conference did have standing to sue for injunction based simply on its "aesthetic, conservational, and recreational" interests in the region. For the first time the federal courts gave prominence to environmental values, permitting them to at least approach even footing with economic considerations in the judical forum.[29] Hereafter, courts were required to weigh economic values against environmental values in such suits. Moreover, the appellate court determined that government agencies should consider all of the alternatives to proposed development projects – including the alternative of doing nothing. (The U.S. Supreme Court upheld the ruling by refusing to hear the FPC's appeal of this decision.)

In a subsequent case (1972), the Supreme Court reinforced and extended these developments in the law of standing. In *Sierra Club v. Morton*,[30] the conservation organization had sued to stop the construction of a ski development at Mineral King Valley in the Sierra Nevada. The Supreme Court ruled that to determine standing, all the club had to show was that the interests of the members, whether environmental or financial, would be harmed. The Court ruled that "once a citizen or group showed its stake in the environmental decision, the plaintiff could assert the interest of the general public as well" (Davies and Davies, 1975: 127).

In these and related cases, the federal courts had substantially broadened the scope of justiciable issues to include ecological considerations in the question of harm. By itself the approach was rather limiting in practice, dependent as it was on expensive case-by-case challenges to proposed developments, public or private.[31]

---

[29] I have qualified the effects of this conceptual equivalency at law ("*approach* even footing") because substantial financial considerations still limit the use of courts to obtain environmental protection. As Fallows (1971: 195) noted about the Storm King Mountain case, "by the time the case reached its second rehearing, the conservationists had already spent $250,000. It was not clear how much longer they could have held out, and it is certain that most nonprofit conservation groups would have had to drop out, impoverished, much earlier."

[30] 405 U.S. 727 (1972). On the facts of this specific case, however, the Court ruled that the Sierra Club lacked standing to sue because it had demonstrated no harm of any sort from the development to either itself or its members.

[31] See, e.g., footnote 29 above.

But it left an additional legacy that would prove vital to environmental protection through law: this series of cases established the rationale for the innovative citizen suits provisions that would be contained in water and air pollution legislation later passed by the Congress.[32] These provisions procedurally incorporate the environmental interests of citizens and groups as potential counterpoints to both undeterred polluters and ineffective federal enforcement (see next chapter).[33]

There was one other major court decision in the mid-1960s that both reflected shifting cultural values and laid the basis for a more aggressive federal role in water pollution control. In 1966 the Supreme Court reinterpreted the terms of the nation's seventy-year-old Refuse Act, originally passed by the Congress to keep the waterways unobstructed for commercial shipping (see Chapter 3).[34] The heart of the matter was the Court's broad construction of the law's prohibition against the discharge of "any refuse matter of any kind or description whatever"; for the first time the Court interpreted this to include discharges of industrial "pollutants" rather than simply of potential impediments to navigation. (The statute exempts municipal sewage from its coverage.)

The implications of this judgment were profound. Under its terms, unpermitted industrial pollution was now a *crime,* carrying potential fines of from $500 to $2,500 for each violation and prison sentences of up to one year. And since no more than 415 of the nation's approximately 40,000 industrial plants discharging wastes into navigable waters had obtained Refuse Act permits between 1899 and 1970, the Court's interpretation meant that 99 percent of the plants were now "committing a crime when they dump anything but pure water into our navigable waterways" (Zwick and Benstock, 1971: 286). Even though potential fines would be inconsequential

[32] See the discussion in Davies and Davies (1975: 126–8).

[33] This direction was further suggested by developments in state law. In the summer of 1970, Michigan passed the first state law that permitted ordinary citizens to sue polluters without having to demonstrate direct personal injury. Formerly, under procedures based on common law, "a complainant had to prove that a specific pollution source was caused by negligence and constituted a personal hazard to him, and he had to bolster his case with expert testimony and extensive scientific and technical evidence. The new law . . . shifts the burden of proof from the complainant to the defendant" (Holsendolph, 1970). At the time, similar laws were being considered in New York, Texas, Massachusetts, Pennsylvania, Colorado, and Tennessee.

[34] *United States v. Standard Oil,* 384 U.S. 224, 230 (1966). The Refuse Act (33 U.S.C. 407) is Section 13 of the Rivers and Harbors Act of 1899.

for many large polluters, the Court had created a dramatic new device for federal enforcement efforts, should the Executive Branch decide to use it: in addition to the risk of incarceration and the potential moral suasion of criminalization, the Court had also determined that the federal government could sue to enjoin all future discharges and to force the polluter to clean up past pollution.[35] The effects of the rulings were not immediately registered in federal pollution control policy. But given the increasing environmental clamor, by 1970 the court's opening could no longer be ignored by the federal government, which, armed with this revived statute, initiated a sweeping new program aimed at industrial polluters (see subsequent discussion). That the government did not ultimately make full and forceful use of this opportunity was a consequence of both the constricted resolve of the executive and, by 1972, updated legislation from the Congress superseding the broadened terms of the old law.

The reorganization of law: the designs of bureaucracy

The institutional locus and design of a government program are key determinants of its social impact, as well as indicators of the perceived importance and nature of the problems it ostensibly addresses. The history of the federal government's water pollution programs is instructive in this regard. Administrative responsibility for enforcement of the Federal Water Pollution Control Act has resided in four different agencies or departments – the Federal Security Agency, the Department of Health, Education, and Welfare, the Department of the Interior, and the Environmental Protection Agency – and in at least five different administrative structures over its forty-year history. In each case, the political choice of bureaucratic design shaped the tenor of the regulatory program.

As suggested in the previous chapter, the original location of administrative responsibility for the water law in the Public Health Service ensured its focus on acute water-borne diseases. In 1966, in recognition of the inadequacy of the public health approach to the deepening water pollution problems, the function was reorganized into the Department of the Interior on the assumption that the

---

[35] *United States v. Republic Steel Corp.*, 362 U.S. 482 (1960); *Wyandotte Transportation Co. v. United States*, 389 U.S. 191, 203–4, fn. 15 (1967). Cited in Zwick and Benstock (1971: 286).

department would properly prioritize the enforcement of water pollution control. But again, the anticipated results failed to eventuate, presumably because water pollution control contradicted the department's primary commitment to the economic development rather than the conservation of natural resources (see, e.g., Ridgeway, 1970: 66; Zwick and Benstock, 1971: 126; Wenner, 1974: 264–5).

By 1970 the manifest failures of federal environmental regulation stood in sharp relief against the growing public demand for authoritative action. As a result, all of the branches of government had been galvanized into action. For its part, the Congress was deliberating on major new initiatives in air and water pollution control. President Richard Nixon was also eager to show both leadership on and responsiveness to the elevated environmental expectations, among other reasons because the issue could help generate needed public support for his administration, embattled by the antagonisms associated with the war in Vietnam. By the end of that year the president had taken highly visible action on the environmental question.

With Reorganization Plan No. 3 of 1970, President Nixon created the Environmental Protection Agency (EPA), which began operations on December 2.[36] The development symbolized at the highest levels of state the importance and connectedness of environmental pollution. Indeed, this new, independent Executive Branch agency for the first time centralized the fifteen federal programs for controlling air and water pollution, environmental radiation, pesticides, and solid waste; these programs had been pulled into one agency from their diverse residences in the departments of Agriculture, Interior, and HEW. Later, offices handling noise (1971) and toxic waste (1972) were added.

This consolidation of federal environmental policy was recommended by the president's Advisory Council on Executive Reorganization (better known as the Ash Council for its head Roy L. Ash, then president of Litton Industries, a major diversified manufacturing company). In response to growing public concern about environmental protection, the president had charged the council at the end of 1969 to investigate whether federal pollution programs should be consolidated. The council quickly concluded that the federal policy was too fractured and uncoordinated to be effective (Cameron,

---

[36] This discussion of EPA's establishment draws from Zwick and Benstock (1971: 54–5), Marcus (1980: 275–7), and T. Turner (1988: 27).

1972: 130; Davies and Davies, 1975: 107–8). Ash himself favored centralizing pollution control in a new Department of Natural Resources, which would also include the federal government's timber, mineral, and energy programs, among others. Such a consolidation would, of course, have re-created the sort of structured conflict of interest that characterized the Department of Interior, subordinating environmental protection to state–industry interests in resource development. In the end, however, the council staff convinced Ash to agree to the formation of a separate environmental agency whose head would report directly to the president, and Nixon based his reorganization on the council's proposal.

The point should not be lost. The consolidation of federal environmental programs was jointly driven by public pressure for meaningful controls and by large corporate interests in the rationalization of environmental law in an increasingly turbulent political climate.

By the government's own standards, the EPA was huge from its inception. It began with almost 6,000 employees and $1.4 billion in first year appropriations; it would eventually become the largest bureaucracy in the federal government outside the military. Within the agency, primary responsibility for water pollution fell to one of the five major subdivisions, the Water Quality Office, which absorbed the responsibilities of the Interior Department's Federal Water Quality Administration.[37] As it happened, this was the largest and best-funded branch of the new agency, having 2,700 employees and a $1.1 billion annual budget. (Fully $1 billion of this first budget was targeted for sewage treatment plant construction grants to municipalities.) The second largest unit, the former National Air Pollution Control Administration from HEW, had 1,150 employees.

The reorganization reflected earlier "capture" critiques of regulation (e.g., Bernstein, 1955). The EPA was to be headed by a single administrator, more accountable to presidential authority than the alternative commission structure, and to regulate virtually all sources and types of pollution rather than simply a single industry whose perspective might over time come to dominate the culture of the agency. The organizational theory was "that fixing responsibility in one person and equipping him with authority over many different industries would minimize the chances that the EPA

---

[37] The Water Quality Office shared some water pollution control responsibilities with two of the other subdivisions, the Pesticides Office and the Radiation Office, in their special areas of responsibility. But the WQO maintained the lion's share of water regulation.

would become the tool of any single source of influence" (Marcus, 1980: 267).

As indicated, the centralization of environmental regulation was also intended to rationalize policy. In terms of environmental protection, as in other areas of public policy, such centralization can, of course, be a double-edged sword. The official rationale for creating the EPA was to improve regulation by enhancing its coordination, efficiency, and accountability. This was intended to prevent the sort of inattention or government infighting that can occur when regulatory responsibilities are subsidiary to an agency's primary mission or divided between various competing bureaucracies or philosophies of state. At the same time, however, the centralization of environmental policy in a single unit whose head is directly accountable to the president renders the agency's mission more vulnerable to the prevailing political philosophy of the executive. On this count, the familiar governmental terminology is rather ironic: the EPA is termed an *independent* federal agency precisely because it is answerable directly to the president rather than being simply a unit within an Executive department (cf., U.S. Senate, 1977b [vol. 5]: 34–6).

In a different vein, the centralization of policy proved immediately incomplete. In his statement on the reorganization, President Nixon made clear his intention that federal pollution control take a comprehensive, integrated approach to the environment:

Despite its complexity, for pollution control purposes the environment must be perceived as a single interrelated system ... a single source may pollute the air with smoke and chemicals, the land with solid wastes, and a river or lake with chemicals and other wastes. Control of the air pollution may produce more solid wastes which then pollutes the land or water. ... Control of the water may convert it into solid wastes which must be disposed of on land. ... A far more effective approach to pollution control would: identify pollutants – trace them through the entire ecological chain, observing and recording changes in form as they occur – determine the total exposure of man and his environment – examine interactions among forms of pollution and – identify where in the ecological chain interdiction would be more appropriate.[38]

But the agency's administrative organization never achieved the comprehensive system of waste management that the president's statement defined. William Ruckelshaus, the EPA's first administrator, developed a functional plan to implement the president's vision of an agency whose organizational structure and procedures would

[38] Quoted in Marcus (1980: 275–6).

mirror the ecology's interconnectedness. Under the plan, for example, EPA's diverse programs would be recombined into functional offices handling such responsibilities as research and monitoring, and standards and compliance. But the plan was never effected. Instead, for example, air pollution standards and enforcement were organized separately from those for water pollution, and the two sets of specialists had no regular exchanges with each other. In large part, this organizational failure occurred, and continues, because of the diverse statutory mandates that structure the agency's mission. The programs for control of water and air pollution, for example, were established under fundamentally different regulatory logics. As Marcus (1980: 277) has noted, the air quality goals of the Clean Air Act were based on health-and-welfare criteria, while federal water pollution control legislation defined its regulatory criteria in terms of technological capabilities. Given this, the division of labor and the attendant lack of communication between these two areas were, in the final analysis, unsurprising.

In sum, the organization of the EPA was both symbolically dramatic and ultimately consequential for environmental policy. But from the start, the rhetoric and reality of the agency had split, limiting the agency's reach and effectiveness.[39]

[39] There were two other legal developments significantly affecting the organization of environmental law, both the result of the National Environmental Policy Act of 1969 (NEPA). NEPA requires all agencies of the federal government to produce environmental impact statement (EIS) assessing the environmental risks versus benefits for all major programs proposed by the federal government (including permitting major new private developments as well as building the government's own facilities). In addition, the EIS process requires agencies to consider alternative ways of accomplishing the purpose of the proposed activity (for example, increased energy conservation rather than a new nuclear power plant). The law has resulted in numerous public interest lawsuits to compel agency compliance with the EIS process, greater bureaucratic sensitivity to the environmental hazards posed by various projects, and even the shelving of some plans determined to be seriously damaging to the environment. For example, the Army Corps of Engineers has abandoned several construction proposals for these reasons (Davies and Davies, 1975: 137). In addition, NEPA lawsuits have stalled many development projects until legislation forced their abandonment; as one example, a NEPA lawsuit delayed logging that threatened erosion in Redwood National Park until the Congress added critical areas to the park (see T. Turner, 1988: 29–30, for additional examples). NEPA had therefore become a powerful tool of environmentalism, particularly in its early years. By the latter 1970s, however, it would encounter its own limits at law.

NEPA also created the Council on Environmental Quality (CEQ), a three-member board reporting directly to the president on environmental matters. Among other responsibilities, the CEQ is charged with analyzing trends in environmental quality for the nation, coordinating all federal agencies with respect to their actions that affect the environment, and making policy recommendations to

The translation of law: new wine from old bottles?

For all of their long-range potential, by themselves the evolution of court interpretations and the development of new bureaucratic forms were insufficient responses to the surge of public expectations for federal *action* on pollution problems. The political demand was for cessation of industrial air and water pollution, and politicians from the president downward were required to recognize the newly visible (sociologically speaking) dimensions of the threats and, in principle, to support their regulation. But it was becoming clear that the procrastinating conference methods of the 1956 amendments to the FWPCA were not the political solution; with their record of minimal achievement they had been a large part of the legitimation problem now facing the federal government. What was required by current sociopolitical conditions was some show of greater executive resolve, of fresh commitment to the enforcement of environmental protection. And although new water pollution control bills were rumbling around in the Congress and between it and the Executive Branch, the political process was far too cumbersome to produce the needed short-term solution.

So it happened in 1970 that the Executive Branch found itself dusting off the venerable Refuse Act of 1899, which the Supreme Court had prepared for a refocusing only a few years before. The logical question was whether this old statute, passed in a different era for quite different purposes, could possibly be adequate to the modern demands. Ironically, the old bottle in many respects proved superior to the new wine. Because of the instant limitations to substantial legal change still inscribed in the workings of government and law, the 1899 law's potential impact on water pollution was not to be realized.

The government's application of the law was forced not by a self-conscious reading of the immediate political exigencies; left to its own workings it would arguably have continued to debate new legislative solutions as the Executive and Legislative branches contested political leadership on this hot new issue. Instead, the executive use

the president and federal agencies regarding environmental improvement (Davies and Davies, 1975: 115–6). The CEQ was thus strategically positioned to provide counsel on environmental conditions and needs to both the president and the public. As such, it could play a dramatic role in shaping federal environmental policy and, like the EPA, would be subject to the prevailing political orientations of the administration in power. By the 1980s the CEQ's role had radically diminished in the deregulation-minded Reagan administration.

of the law was forced by the threat of widespread citizens' suits against polluters based on a democratic clause in the Refuse Act's language, establishing a powerful precedent in pollution control law that would carry over into the new legislation of the 1970s.

The Refuse Act, in light of the Supreme Court's 1966 decision, provided for criminal fines of from $500 to $2,500 for each water pollution violation proven (in addition to possible incarceration of corporate officials). But it also provided that "one half of said fine . . . be paid to the person or persons giving information which shall lead to conviction."[40] This clause gave strong additional incentive for concerned citizens to report industrial water pollution to the U.S. attorneys. Even more crucially, it laid the legal foundation for *citizen suits against polluters when the government failed to prosecute*. The litigating mechanism is known as a *qui tam* action, lawsuits rooted in ancient common law that provide for citizen suits in the name of government to enforce laws.[41] Combined with the "bounty" provision of the Refuse Act, this mechanism appeared to give citizens standing to sue polluters when the government failed to enforce the law against them, because the citizens' stake in collecting part of any fine gives them direct interest in the case; earlier, the Supreme Court had in fact ruled that when a law provides for such a bounty, citizens may so sue when the government fails to do so.

By 1970 substantial public interest in this legal option had developed, stimulated in large part by Congressman Henry S. Reuss, who sponsored congressional hearings on the law's use and provided information kits to thousands of citizens interested in using the law to sue polluters.[42] Citizens filed a number of important suits in federal courts in 1970; for example, the Bass Anglers Sportsmen Society alone filed suits in three courts against 214 Alabama polluters (Zwick and Benstock, 1971; 285). As matters developed, however, the efficacy of such suits was left in doubt. In the first place, some early federal court decisions denied that citizens could file *qui tam* actions against polluters (Fallows, 1971: 206). Moreover, such pri-

[40] Rivers and Harbors Act of 1899, § 14, 33 U.S.C. § 411 (1970).
[41] For discussion of the *qui tam* logic in the context of the Refuse Act, and other matters related to the law's use in the 1970–71 period, see Fallows (1971: 204–11), Zwick and Benstock (1971: 285–301), and Wenner (1974: 255–61).
[42] Reuss himself collected some fine money by reporting polluters to the Justice Department (Zwick and Benstock, 1971: 285). Again, we have the example of a legislator from an environmentally sensitive state (Wisconsin) taking the lead in pursuing aggressive policy. This is a constant refrain in the history of U.S. environmental law, although not one without its own contradictory impulses, as I have already discussed.

vate suits would have an ad hoc character and therefore not provide for a rational, nation-wide policy on the vital matter of industrial water pollution. Nonetheless, the surge of aggressive citizen action both attracted public attention to the Refuse Act and boosted the pressure for a meaningful show of executive action. After all, virtually all industrial water polluters were now technically in criminal violation of a federal statute.

Clearly, the Nixon administration needed to show responsiveness, at one and the same time to legitimate the government's role and to forestall the grassroots surge of citizen action on the Refuse Act. But just as clearly, both widespread criminalization and cessation of water pollution, called for by increasing numbers of environmentalists and citizens on the basis of the act, remained well beyond the limits of political economic feasibility. The political and economic costs of such a policy, both real and imagined, were far too formidable to sustain it. Given the key role of industry in the nation, in everything from jobs to elections, the federal government was not about to treat business as outlaw and risk undermining the stability of both state and economy. Another drawback was the logistical nightmare of the routine enforcement of a criminal statute against the tens of thousands of regularly polluting industrial sources. The Justice Department, responsible for enforcing all federal statutes, could scarcely sustain such a burden on its quite limited resources. Moreover, in the case of large corporate polluters, this legal game would not likely prove to be worth the candle: the law's fines would be little more than a tax on the right to pollute.

Even so, the Nixon Justice Department took an especially lenient first approach to enforcement of the law despite the growing public insistence on firm action. In 1970 the department, which had responsibility for any criminal prosecutions under the law, issued policy guidance to U.S. attorneys indicating that the responsibility for controlling "pollution of a continuing nature from the ordinary operations of manufacturing plants" rested with the Interior Department under the FWPCA's generally unproductive conference negotiations, and with the states' typically ineffective water standards and enforcement proceedings. Under this new policy, the Justice Department would only bring criminal actions "to punish or prevent significant discharges, which are either accidental or infrequent, but which are not of a continuing nature."[43] In effect, this

[43] *Justice Department Guidelines for Litigation Under the Refuse Act, 1 B.N.A. Environment Reporter – Current Developments* 288 (July 17, 1970).

policy implied no real change at all; Justice had to a certain extent co-opted the use of the law by formally incorporating it into its armament, but it was only to be rolled out under those egregious conditions when pollution posed an acute danger to public or environmental health, forcing strong action. Indeed, by spring 1971 (when the administration already had another new water pollution initiative underway, described later) the Justice Department had brought only twenty-eight suits under the Refuse Act against industrial polluters, almost half of them to halt poisonous mercury contamination that had received wide publicity.

Like all previous administrations and all state governments, this administration was reluctant to force major, near term changes in industrial polluting behavior, to say nothing of criminalizing powerful businesses. To the obvious limits implied by this deep reluctance, bureaucratic politics added yet another layer of resistance to effective water pollution control. In formulating its Refuse Act enforcement guidelines, the Justice Department had been careful to consult the Federal Water Quality Administration (FWQA) in the Interior Department, which prior to the EPA had responsibility for federal water quality standards and pollution control under the FWPCA. Even this cautious deference proved too little to avoid the jealous protection of bureaucratic domains that can further weaken state policies (see, e.g., Bequai, 1977). Justice Department attorneys faced firm resistance from Interior on a number of the few cases it had considered for prosecution. According to one assistant U.S. attorney:

The one federal agency that has sophisticated technical staff and information sufficient to help us move forward against major water problems in the Northern District of Illinois had refused to give us that aid. . . . [T]he absolute refusal of the Interior Department to permit the Federal Water Pollution Control Administration [later renamed the FWQA] office to supply us *any* information or technical advice defies understanding. Our request for specific information on specified companies has gone unanswered. Our request for general advice and judgment as to which companies pose the most critical problems has gone unanswered. Our final request for just such information as would be made available to any member of the public upon request has not been complied with. . . . Facing this lack of cooperation we tried to persuade the agency to change its views. We have tried for several months to work quietly to bring about that change in attitude. Perhaps that attitude is due to the view of an Interior Department official who called me from Washington to ask why I wanted to prosecute "those nice people." Perhaps it is due to other reasons. . . . [But it] is an area too important for bureaucratic wrangling over jurisdiction or political fighting over who gets the credit. This is the public interest we are about, and if we are really a law-enforcement minded country, the pollution laws are among those which must be enforced.[44]

For its part, the FWQA took the position that the Department of Justice was too lenient in its enforcement cases, letting polluters off easily with consent agreements on future compliance. The FWQA argued that it could accomplish more with its own brand of jawboning pressure and negotiations with industry. But to investigators David Zwick and Marcy Benstock (1971: 297–8), who closely studied the agency and water pollution policy during this period, the FWQA's desire to protect customary pieces of bureaucratic turf underlay these arguments. Undercutting them, too, was the lack of any real progress in industrial water pollution control.

This duplication and division of authority over water pollution control policy had the consequence of further undermining the potential of the law, in this case by scrambling even the limited enforcement efforts of Justice attorneys seeking to respond to the joint calls of the law and the public demand for change. The Nixon administration, seeking to balance itself on the fine line between its growing legitimation needs on the environmental question and its fundamental dependence on the strength and support of industry, was assisted in the effort by the structured, if unwitting, dynamics of state organization. After all, even good faith efforts to move the ship of state would take time.

But it quickly became clear that the administration would need something more substantial than its symbolic Refuse Act policy in order to satisfy public expectations even minimally; the need was acute in light of the oncoming election year, and the president was eager to show leadership rather than simply follow whatever lead the Congress might develop.

So in December of 1970, the month he established EPA, President Nixon took what would be his last major initiative in water pollution control. With Executive Order 11574,[45] he established a federal permit program, based on the Refuse Act, requiring all industrial facilities discharging wastes into navigable waters to obtain federal permits limiting the discharges. The permits were to be issued by the Corps of Engineers with the assistance – in effect the guidance – of the new EPA. As implemented by subsequent regulations, the

---

[44] Quoted in Ridgeway (1970: 164–6).
[45] Executive Order No. 11574, 3 C.F.R. 309 (1973), 33 U.S.C. 407 (1970).

intent was to limit industrial water pollution to the extent needed to reach the water quality standards established under the 1965 FWPCA amendments, or other applicable state standards. The permits would set discharge limits and, where necessary, impose implementation schedules by which polluting facilities would reach the imposed limits. On paper, the Refuse Act permit program presented a major development in federal policy, and in fact anticipated the new legislation of the Congress that would two years later become the hallmark of the nation's modern pollution control effort. But the president's program also carried many of its own limitations. Ultimately, it would be entirely undone by one of law's internal contradictions.

In principle the plan was legally direct and simple though technically quite complex. Unlike the convoluted enforcement procedures of the FWPCA conferences, the new permit system promised a much more streamlined approach: after the government had issued a permit limiting the discharges of a plant, any violation of the limits would constitute a violation of the Refuse Act whose criminal and civil sanctions would immediately apply. Because the 1899 law addressed *all navigable waters,* the permit program extended federal authority to cover intrastate as well as interstate waters. But in contrast to the simplicity of enforcement, the EPA was required to determine the complex relationships between established water quality standards and discharge limits for countless pollutants, factories, and riverways around the country. The burden of this charge necessarily meant that program implementation would require a long lead time, years rather than months, before meaningful controls could be in place throughout the nation.

Besides this long delay in enforcing water quality standards, this technical complexity posed other substantial challenges to environmental protection goals. Most critically, the federal government was ultimately dependent on industry's good faith and expertise in accomplishing the law's core requirement: the establishment of discharge limits for industrial categories and the issuing of permits. Industry's role was prerequisite to this process, because the industrial corporations held a virtual monopoly on the key manufacturing knowledge (as to process, materials used and discharged, and other matters) necessary to the formulation of discharge standards. It is not surprising, therefore, that EPA Water Quality Office staffers told investigators (Zwick and Benstock 1971: 295) that corporate officials would be given the opportunity to participate in setting the very standards under which they would later operate. The risk to law and the public interest, of course, is that this structural dependence of the state would lead to diluted standards and weaker environmental protection than could have been, even under real economic constraints.

This is all the more likely when the public interest is underrepresented in such key deliberations, which is likely in direct proportion to the complexity of the regulatory determinations. It remained quite unclear whether and how environmental representatives could play meaningful roles in the process of implementation. For example, the initial guidelines published by the Corps of Engineers contained no mention of public participation in the permit-granting procedures (Zwick and Benstock: 1971: 292). And while a later version of the guidelines did in fact contain procedures for public notice and comment on permit applications by industry (U.S. Department of the Army, 1972),[46] a number of barriers to full public participation remained.

First, based on its monopoly of both information and expertise, industry would still be advantaged in the EPA's determination of discharge standards for classes of manufacturing, the very baselines that would determine the ultimate effectiveness of the law. Second, there remained a question as to the extent to which environmental interests would even have access to key information about industrial pollutants. As it happened, the Refuse Act permit program mandated the development of the first comprehensive inventory of industrial pollutants in the United States. This had long been successfully resisted by business interests, which argued that such information would unveil trade secrets in manufacturing. The inventory, therefore, was a substantial policy achievement; according to the Council on Environmental Quality, by the time the Refuse Act program effectively ended, in 1971, an estimated 20,000 manufacturing plants, accounting for about 90 percent of industrial water pollution, had submitted at least some data on their discharges.[47]

[46] The regulations asserted, "It is the policy of the Corps of Engineers to conduct the civil works program in an atmosphere of public understanding, trust, and mutual cooperation and in a manner responsive to the public interest" (U.S. Department of the Army, 1972: 20).

[47] Council on Environmental Quality, *Environmental Quality: Third Annual Report of the Council on Environmental Quality* (1972), p. 121. Cited in Wenner (1974: 258).

But the inventory process was long, depended on industrial cooperation, and produced complex information. Moreover, the implementing regulations of the Corps of Engineers retained protection for industry on the trade secrets logic. The regulations specified that all information related to a permit, including the nature of the plant's polluting discharges, would be available to the public "unless the applicant or permittee specifically identifies and is able to demonstrate to the satisfaction of the Secretary of the Army or his authorized representative that the disclosure of such information or data to the general public would divulge methods or processes entitled to protection as trade secrets" (U.S. Department of the Army, 1972: 27). Logical on its face in a competitive market system, the trade secrets exclusion nonetheless increased the state's dependence on industry's expertise and good faith, and forced another discretionary regulatory process that could exclude the voices of environmental interests while shaping the reach of law.

Finally, while the program's implementing regulations called for public notice and comment on permit applications, the use of any public sentiment was left to the discretion of the regulatory authorities. For example, whether or not a public hearing would be called on the basis of public concerns over the polluting facility was left entirely to the discretion of the Corps' District Engineer for the region (U.S. Department of the Army, 1972: 20–1).[48] Industry's access to the authorities was, in the nature of things, quite a bit more certain.

The complexity of the regulatory determinations was matched by the labyrinthine interorganizational relations built into the permit program. The program's implementation required the successful coordination of three major federal units – the EPA, the Army Corps of Engineers, and the Justice Department – and numerous environmental agencies of the individual states, which were to determine whether discharges on waters within states violated their own water quality standards. In considering permit applications, the Corps and the EPA were to consult both the Department of the Interior and the National Oceanic and Atmospheric Administration of the De-

---

[48] Under the interlocking terms of the FWPCA, public hearings were required if "(1) a State, other than the State of [the pollution's] origin, objects to the issuance of a permit and requests a hearing on its objections or (2) the Secretary of the Army proposes to suspend a Department of the Army permit upon notification by the certifying authority that applicable water quality standards will be violated" (U.S. Department of the Army, 1972: 22).

partment of Commerce, the two federal agencies with jurisdiction over fish and wildlife resources. If past experience was any guide, such interdepartmental relations promised limits in the implementation of law, typically only as effective as its weakest link. A couple of examples should make the point.

First in continuing to defer to individual state agencies on the pollution of intrastate waters, the new program left key determinations to authorities with poor records of pollution control and with primary jurisdiction over roughly 86 percent of the nation's river mileage (Zwick and Benstock, 1971: 292–3).

Second, while the Act now called for criminal and civil penalties for ordinary pollution violations, the government remained reluctant to use these sanctions for such offenses. Ironically, this was so even though the Justice Department, which would be responsible for bringing such cases, had loosened its restrictive enforcement policies in response to public criticism. Under guidelines set in the summer of 1971, U.S. attorneys around the country did not need to apply to their superiors in Washington for clearance to prosecute under the Refuse Act; now they were required only to seek approval from the Corps of Engineers and the EPA (Zwick and Benstock, 1971: 291). But this did not produce major change, because the EPA – which took charge of enforcement policy – essentially reproduced the policy of the earlier Justice guidelines. The new agency developed the position that litigation was to be used only as a last resort, when all efforts at negotiating voluntary compliance had failed (Glenn, 1973: 844–52). According to the agency's enforcement guidelines, criminal prosecutions were generally to be reserved for cases of isolated or instantaneous discharges that caused serious damage, and for firms that failed to file permit applications by the July 1, 1971, deadline. In such cases a lesser enforcement response would seriously challenge the legitimacy of law. Civil cases, on the other hand, were to be used to secure court-ordered treatment requirements rather than to prohibit offending discharges altogether. The EPA had argued that it was better to negotiate "voluntary" spending by firms for pollution abatement than to seek "unproductive" criminal fines (Glenn, 1973: 851–2).

Many environmentalists and congressional representatives criticized this by now familiar policy. They argued that criminal prosecutions should be more liberally used to force compliance among habitual industrial dischargers. The policy certainly seemed out of step with the nation's rising environmental consciousness. One critical congressional report on Refuse Act enforcement recommended that "the Environmental Protection Agency should abandon its restrictive litigation guidelines . . . and adopt a policy encouraging enforcement of the Refuse Act of 1899 in non-emergency, as well as emergency, cases and not engage in protracted negotiations with polluters."[49] The EPA's critics had clearly recognized the criminal law's potential to communicate both serious programmatic intent and the widespread value change regarding environment protection, and the contribution this could make to more efficient cleanup.

But the Lazarus-like government instinct to keep industrial water pollution decriminalized, asserted over many decades and governmental departments, spoke just as clearly to the political, economic, and organizational limits still shaping environmental policy. The state, with its limited resources and dependence on cooperative working relations with industry, cannot be quick to criminalize behavior that only yesterday was part of the very fabric of economic growth and the culture of production. In short, the state is reluctant to take either long or quick steps along a path that could risk forcing a showdown between democratic legitimacy and political economic viability. And in the arena of environmental law, this central constraint remains.

But it would have no further test under the terms of the Refuse Act, which prematurely expired at the end of 1971. Ironically, environmental concerns played a role in the early demise of the permit program as law came to contradict itself. In question was whether the permit-granting process came under the terms of the National Environmental Policy Act of 1969 (NEPA), which mandated that all federal agencies produce technical impact studies of the environmental risks versus the benefits of all major programs or actions they were proposing.[50] The Corps of Engineers took the position that the NEPA requirements did not cover the act of issuing discharge permits:

[Environmental impact statements] will not be required in permit cases where it is likely that the proposed discharge will not have any significant impact on the human environment. Moreover, the Council on Environmen-

---

[49] House Committee on Government Operations, Report on Enforcement of the Refuse Act of 1899, H.R. Rep. No. 92-1333, 92nd Congress, 2nd Sess. (1972). Cited in Glenn (1973: 850n).
[50] See footnote 39 for additional discussion of this important law.

tal Quality has advised that such statements will not be required where the only impact of proposed discharge or deposit will be on water quality and related water quality considerations because these matters are specifically addressed under section 21(b) and (c), the Federal Water Pollution Control Act, as amended. However, such statements shall be required in connection with proposed discharges or deposits which may have a significant environmental impact unrelated to water quality. (U.S. Department of the Army, 1972: 32)[51]

In a key case, *Kalur v. Resor*,[52] the federal district court for the District of Columbia rejected this interpretation in December 1971. In a challenge by conservationists to prevent the Corps from issuing permits to industries on an Ohio river, the court ruled that the NEPA requirements for impact statements must indeed be met before any permit issues. Immediately thereafter, the EPA announced that the decision would effectively kill the program because it was "impractical" for the government to prepare tens of thousands of impact statements in addition to its already burdensome responsibilities in pollution control (Wenner, 1974: 258–61). For the time being, the decision had created a regulatory void.

To this point, then, the complex legal structures of the advanced American state had, in rather contradictory fashion, both provided points of access for environmental interest and helped to choke off some of the early advances in law. If the apparatuses of state were too unwieldy to yield to stable elite domination, they were also rather unstable with respect to pressures for progressive change. The cause of environmentalism stood in wait of a forceful, consistent statement at law. And as it happened, the *Kalur* deadlock came on the eve of the Congress's turn at the effort. It was indeed to be a major statement, but one also constrained by certain limits in political economy.

[51] See also 33 C.F.R. 209.131(1)(2) (1973). Also Wenner (1974: 259).
[52] 335 F.Supp. 1 (D.D.C. 1971). Discussed in Wenner (1974: 258–61).

CHAPTER 5

Legislating clean water: changing conceptions of environmental rights

> The great question of the seventies is, shall we surrender our surroundings, or shall we make our peace with Nature and begin to make the reparations for the damage we have done to our air, our land, our water? . . . Clean air, clean water, open spaces – these would once again be the birthright of every American.
>
> President Richard Nixon, 1970 State of the Union Address

With this rhetorical flourish, a Republican president lent the voice of his office to the growing national chorus of the new environmental consciousness. His reference to a "birthright" suggested that the responsibilities of the present generation for the environmental well-being of future ones bore the stamp of natural law itself (cf., Borrelli, 1986). Given the climate of the times, this did not sound like hyperbole. The cause of environmental protection had come to articulate itself in terms of moral rights, for example by linking the principle of equality of opportunity to the right to a decent environment, without which opportunity is compromised (Schroeder, 1983: 16–17; also Bardach and Kagan, 1982: 13–14):

If human rights . . . are those rights which each human possesses in virtue of the fact that he is human and in virtue of the fact that those rights are essential in permitting him to live a human life (that is, . . . permitting him to fulfill his capacities as a rational and free being), then might not the right to a decent environment be properly categorized as such a human right? Might it not be conceived as a right which has emerged as a result of changing environmental conditions and the impact of those conditions on the very possibility of human life and on the possibility of the realization of other rights such as liberty and equality?[1]

Armed with this philosophy of environmental rights, all the

[1] Quoted in Schroeder (1983: 16–17). From W. Blackstone, "Ethics and Ecology," in William T. Blackstone (ed.), *Philosophy and Environmental Crisis* (Athens: University of Georgia Press, 1974).

more fascinating for its recognition of their social evolution, some environmental groups called for an "environmental bill of rights" (in this, they were not without precedent; see Chapter 8). In a concrete effort in this direction, Senator Gaylord Nelson of Wisconsin proposed a constitutional amendment to guarantee citizens an inalienable right to a decent environment. These calls for change at the very roots of American law ultimately went unheeded, but the philosophical and organizational groundwork was being laid to press for significant changes in environmental legislation. Claims properly made under the terms of such statutes would then assume the status of legally protected rights (Schroeder, 1983: 17).

The language of rights and their implementation in real terms are wholly different matters, however. Notions of right are embraced as absolutes; in practical terms environmental protection is necessarily a relative phenomenon. This is because, within the limits of foreseeable forms of social organization and technological development, environmental values continue to compete with those of economic productivity and the human aspirations culturally constructed on them, certainly at the margins. The very definition of clean water, then, is determined in the realm of *political* discourse, rather than in the purely philosophical. In his 1970 State of the Union address, the president had used the rhetoric of absolutes, itself also the stuff of political discourse. In fact, the environmental ethic reflected in his statement had reached the status of broad political demand "just when economic growth began slowing and when inflation and interest rates began rising" (McCraw, 1984: 238). So if there had been a significant shift in the morality of the culture, in the relative weightings of often competing values, both its policy implications and its permanence remained uncertain.

The politics of law, the laws of politics

From its inception, the fledgling Environmental Protection Agency and federal environmental law generally were balanced on the fine point of politics. If anything, the tensions between rhetoric and reality heightened in this early period of environmental awareness. As the political landscape began to quake along the faultlines of contradiction, politicians and administrators uncomfortably bestrode the widening gap between environment and economy as they sought to minister to the disparate demands of state. Thus as the White House issued the staunch rhetoric of ecological morality, it also served as business's refuge and hope for sound economic reasoning on the matter. In similar fashion, the federal bureaucracy in the early 1970s reached awkwardly for an accommodation of the conflicting pressures, as suggested in the previous chapter.

The awkwardness and strain in the state's policymaking apparatus is nicely illustrated in a 1970 report on water pollution in the United States by the predecessor agency to the EPA, the Federal Water Quality Administration of the Department of the Interior (1970). The FWQA recognized important aspects of the inherently contradictory relations between economic growth, evolving consumer expectations, and environmental pollution (even if shading them toward the side of consumption rather than production per se):

Higher individual incomes and expectations have led to increasing demands for food and consumer goods, for better housing and highways, for a whole range of conveniences. In most cases, production of wastes is "built in" to our technology; as industrial production increases, with attendant demands for water, so does the per capita production of wastes. The public's demand for "throw-away" containers and other convenience items, as well as the tendency toward planned obsolescence, further accelerate this trend. (Federal Water Quality Administration, 1970: 3598)[2]

Moreover, the FWQA had been quick to recognize the principal source of mounting political pressure for strong, meaningful controls: "the Nation's young people [who] have perceived – perhaps better than anyone else – that the quality of their lives in future years will depend on what we do about the environment today" (Federal Water Quality Administration, 1970: 3687). Even prior to Earth Day and the "Environmental Decade" of the 1970s, the agency had moved in 1969 to incorporate this emerging pressure group bureaucratically, forming the Student Council on Pollution and the Environment (SCOPE) to provide information exchange be-

[2] The report also recognized the serious challenge of runoff pollution, a problem twenty years later still without answer in law, which has focused on the more amenable issues of point discharges (from industrial and municipal pipes directly into waterways) and specific sources of groundwater contamination (toxic landfills and dump sites). With respect to agriculture, the report noted that "production of greater quantities of better food for American citizens has caused increasing pollution problems. Higher agricultural productivity has been based on irrigation and use of chemical fertilizers and pesticides. Runoff carries salts and chemicals, many of which are highly toxic and have long-lasting environmental effects, into streams. These diffuse waste sources are most difficult to control or treat. The possibility of irreparable and disastrous ecological consequences, particularly from persistent pesticides, has led to increasing demands for controlling or eliminating their use; no one can predict with certainty the impact of such a move on agricultural productivity" (Federal Water Quality Administration, 1970: 3599).

tween the FWQA and college and high school students concerned with environmental protection.[3] Interior Secretary Walter J. Hickel was proposing the development of a National Environmental Control Organization modeled after the Peace Corps, and the FWQA organized "Operation Clean Waters" to have teams of young men[4] clean debris from various waterways.

Even while sounding the alarm over environmental deterioration and calling for urgent action, Interior's report continued to underscore the primary regulatory role of the individual states, despite long and continuing evidence that the job far outstripped their individual and collective resolve. For example, the department was proposing that the states, rather than the federal government, be required to set effluent discharge limitations for individual polluters, thereby tying them to the patchwork of state-established water quality criteria and thus reproducing many of the limits of the 1965 FWPCA amendments (see Chapter 3). And under Interior's proposal, the traditionally reluctant states would continue to bear the primary responsibility for enforcement, the federal authorities to play but a back-up role. Of course, this support role could be important in stiffening the states' regulatory resolve. So optimistic on this score was the report that it praised the "vigorous" enforcement record of the new Nixon administration (which remained little more than a shovel against the tide; see Chapters 3 and 4).[5] Moreover, this was the same agency that some Justice Department prosecutors had accused of noncooperation in their efforts to build court cases against corporate polluters. At about the same time, the U.S. Public

[3] According to the FWQA report (1970: 3690), the value of SCOPE was that, "For the students it is an opportunity to obtain and apply governmental expertise and information to the process of formulating solutions to environmental problems and a chance to discuss their proposals for solving environmental problems with top-level government decision-makers. For the government it is a means of getting fresh viewpoints on environmental problems and solutions. Government agencies will be able to request student study and recommendations on specific points or issues."

[4] The report's reference to "young men" appears to be more than rhetorical, referring as it does to specific projects on which such individuals had worked (Federal Water Quality Administration, 1970: 3692). One may only assume that the omission of young women from the plan had not to do with their lesser environmental consciousness, but with their presumed physical limitations with respect to such "arduous" work. By the 1980s American culture had sufficiently evolved that a woman could even be appointed to do the "heavy lifting" as the EPA's administrator. That Anne Burford eventually dropped the weight handed her by President Reagan said little of her various managerial capacities, but spoke volumes of the political minefield into which she had been asked to step.

[5] On Interior's legislative proposals and assessment of the administration's enforcement record, see Federal Water Quality Administration (1970: 3622–6).

Health Service reported (in 1970) potentially harmful levels of chemicals in one-third of the nation's drinking water supply, and the president's Council on Environmental Quality concluded in 1971 that 90 percent of the country's watersheds were polluted (U.S. Senate, 1973: 99).

For his part, the president had been driven to the high rhetorical ground not only by the press of oncoming public environmental concerns, but by a complex of political pressures. He needed to show leadership on a social issue that embraced key interests at least of the politically potent middle classes, particularly given the rising chorus of opposition to the administration's policies regarding the Vietnam War. Not coincidentally, this opposition was most vociferously concentrated in precisely those segments organizing the call for major shifts in environmental policies: young, white, middle class students and recent graduates. The urgency of Nixon's political need in this regard was only amplified by the growing challenge of Democratic Senator Edmund Muskie, who had long claimed the environmental issue in the Senate and who was now riding its strong tide toward seeking Democratic nomination in the 1972 presidential campaign to challenge Nixon's quest for a second term.

The structure of strategy: the Nixon White House

In both the political and ideological spheres, the environmental cause was more a riptide, frothing in opposition to conservative sentiments more protective of economic prerogatives than of ecological stability. So quite predictably, and from the outset, the president's behavior on the issue was no match for his rhetoric. This was not a matter of simple disingenuousness. Who, after all, could seriously resist the environmental argument? But beyond the glare of popular scrutiny, the Nixon White House exhibited strong sympathy with economic interests against aggressive environmental protection, especially those of the dominant sector of large corporations. If the effects of this sympathy were themselves constrained, it was in large part because the apparatuses of state often prove unwieldy and unpredictable, even those branches of it most closely controlled by the dictates of the Executive.

To be sure, the president's actions on the matter were not limited to merely symbolic statements of leadership. He had, after all, established the EPA in 1970, and under the press of the times had signed into law the National Environmental Policy Act of 1969 (NEPA). In its early years this law fostered environmentalism as numerous public interest lawsuits successfully stalled or killed development projects that endangered species, induced soil erosion, or threatened other aspects of the environment.[6]

The president's essential caution on environmental regulation exhibited itself regularly during this period, however. Unlike his bold public statements on the issue, the political strategy he implemented was rather more subtle. He regularly worked to incorporate the concerns of business into the highest levels of government policymaking during this key and turbulent moment in environmental history. For example, in response to increasing public pressures for government action, in 1969 he established an Environmental Quality Council, which he would chair and which consisted of Cabinet members involved in environmental decisions (Marx, 1971: 155–60). Included were the secretaries of the interior, transportation, and agriculture, all prominently involved in making federal policies on national resources that often favored private development interests and entailed environmental degradation. But growing congressional sensitivities about such structured conflicts of interest resulted in a deluge of criticism that Nixon's Council couldn't be trusted to provide impartial advice to the Executive Branch. Consequently, as part of NEPA the Congress established an independent, three-member Council on Environmental Quality to advise the president and the public directly on environmental policies and trends. Even the new CEQ proved to have at best contradictory impacts on policy, here lining up behind the administration's efforts to rein in ambitious legislative proposals, there developing data suggesting the depth and reach of the environmental threat.

More significantly yet, and a powerful indicator of the convergence of state and economic interests in this policy area, in April 1970 – only three months after NEPA overrode his own version of an environmental council – the president established the National Industrial Pollution Control Council. This was an elite group of sixty-three senior officials and chief executives of many major American corporations and trade associations charged with advising the Executive Branch on evolving environmental policy. Such advisory committees, it should be noted, have been a lawful commonplace in American governance, a popular but often obscure means of linking private interests and expertise to public policymaking. By 1972, for

---

[6] For additional discussion of and references on NEPA, see Chapter 4, footnote 39.

example, a total of 1,439 advisory committees were operating in the Executive and Legislative branches, at a cost to the federal government of some $25 million (Steck, 1975: 245). These mechanisms arguably tap the expertise necessary to informed policymaking, but they have commonly served as vehicles of privileged, exclusive access to the top strata of federal rulemakers. As such nondemocratic entities, they have been the object of repeated critiques and reform efforts within government at least from the Kennedy administration through the Carter years.[7]

Indeed, the new Nixon advisory committee stood to build on a legacy of industry success at blunting the pressures for various environmental reforms. Steck (1975: 251) reports:

Advisory committees, and especially industry advisory committees, have almost routinely taken their toll over the years on the development of effective environmental policies. The successful blocking of the industrial wastes inventory for seven years by the Advisory Council on Federal Reports (now the Business Advisory Council on Federal Reports) is only one of the more notorious examples of the success of advisory committees in frustrating or redirecting information gathering efforts of pollution control agencies, distorting contracted research studies, watering down criteria reports, or otherwise influencing anti-pollution efforts in hitherto closed advisory sessions.[8]

In establishing NIPCC, the president plainly saw it as a necessary coordinating mechanism for merging public and private sector interests in environmental regulation. From its beginning, the council was intended to be a crucial voice in policymaking. Indeed, Nixon had announced that NIPCC would "help chart the route which our cooperative ventures will follow."[9] But the shape of the private sector's input was presaged in the council's structural location: the president had attached it to the Department of Commerce. So when Commerce Secretary Maurice Stans asserted at its founding that NIPCC's purpose was to obtain "the maximum input from the busi-

---

[7] See, for example, Steck (1975: 245–50), and the U.S. Senate, *Study on Federal Regulation* [Vol. 3] (1977b: 147–57).

[8] That industry has historically been able to organize to effectively frustrate government efforts to collect data for regulatory purposes has been demonstrated in a number of contexts. For example, it took an eighteen-month federal lawsuit before the Federal Trade Commission was able to collect corporate line-of-business information needed for antitrust enforcement. An earlier FTC order had been resisted by more than 200 major corporations that claimed the information might be leaked to competitors (Clinard and Yeager, 1980: 98; see also Domhoff, 1978: 38–9).

[9] The Nixon quote, and those from Commerce Secretary Stans which follow, are reported in Steck (1975: 254, 257).

ness community in coordination with the Government's effort to resolve the environmental problem," it was quite reasonable to wonder whether the problem was being construed by the Executive Branch as primarily ecological or political in nature.

That the political dimensions of the problem were driving the president's actions is further underscored by the council's membership, and by the secrecy with which it conducted its advisory business (as evidenced by closed meetings and sanitized minutes; see Steck, 1975: 247, 257–9). Secretary Stans approvingly noted that the NIPCC membership represented "a very large part of the industrial might of the country." As such, of course, the executives also represented a major proportion of the pollution-generating industries (a fact upon which the secretary presumably did not dwell, at least publicly). Included, for example, were corporate leaders from Minnesota Mining and Manufacturing, Rockwell International, General Motors, Exxon, U.S. Steel, DuPont, Ford, Procter & Gamble, and Westinghouse Electric. (In the complex web of political economy, it was not coincidental that the new EPA was referring civil and criminal cases to Justice against a number of the council's corporate members under the Refuse Act.) Importantly, the council's membership generally excluded representatives of small businesses, and was completely devoid of members from environmental groups, labor unions, consumer groups or public-interest law firms. Thus the high-level access to policy formation that NIPCC afforded was highly restricted, clearly designed to organize only the interests of elite and powerful industrial sectors, not coincidentally those increasingly the focus of public environmental concern.[10]

Given the secrecy of its operations, it is not possible to determine precisely the council's ultimate influence on environmental policy and on the evolving water pollution controls. But its sensitive location, both structurally and in time (1970–73), suggests a potent influence on the Nixon Administration's side of the legislative battle over water pollution, with important consequence for the law. The council's role remained important even after the passage of the new water pollution bill in 1972; by 1973 contacts with the EPA, defined as technical in nature, had become an important part of NIPCC's business as the agency began to translate law into regulation (cf., Steck, 1975: 256–7). Such impliedly neutral "technical" exchanges

[10] For example, the first chairman of NIPCC was Bert S. Cross, head of Minnesota Mining and Manufacturing, a firm under orders since 1967 to cease its discharges of sulfur wastes into the Mississippi River (Ridgeway, 1970: 172).

necessarily convey political meaning and pressure, particularly when they emanate from powerful sources, as suggested in Chapter 2.

Moreover, although NIPCC effectively ceased its operations in 1973,[11] congressional evidence suggests that advisory committees carrying powerful industry voices continued to have disproportionate access to environmental regulation, despite such reforms as the Federal Advisory Committee Act of 1972 (to regulate and make public the activities of such committees) and EPA's own early efforts to maintain greater balance between industry and public interest representation in such groups (see Steck, 1975: 248–53). In 1977 a U.S. Senate study of federal regulation expressed concern that thirteen of the seventeen EPA advisory committees included *"no one explicitly representing a recognized citizen, consumer, or environmental group"* (U.S. Senate, 1977b [Vol. 3]: 151–52; emphasis added). Committees without such public interest representation included the Advisory Committee on the Revision and Application of Drinking Water Standards (five members each from industry and government, plus two others), the National Air Pollution Control Techniques Advisory Committee (eight and seven, respectively, plus two), and the Environmental Radiation Exposure Advisory Committee (three and one, with six academics).

Strains and reins within the Executive: early enforcement at EPA

But all of this should not be taken to suggest that either industry or its powerful allies in government easily or always effectively control controversial policy directions. The apparatuses of state, interlinked by the complex structuring of political interests, are resistant to such simple instrumental command. This was already being suggested in the early operations of the EPA, at the same time as the Executive and Legislative branches struggled over the terms of new water pollution control law in the early 1970s. To be sure, the young agency's tactical options were severely limited, even more so its initial impacts on water pollution. But by the passage of the new legislation in

[11] NIPCC was formally terminated in January 1975. However, in 1973 the Congress refused to continue funding the council's staff for Fiscal Year 1974. Steck (1975: 280) writes that with this decision, "Congress weakened the staff infrastructure that had effectively linked the Council's members to the administrative process. . . . The Watergate atmosphere probably made it impossible for the paralyzed Nixon administration to rescue NIPCC." He dates the effective end of the council's work as 1973 (1975: 265).

1972, it had begun to demonstrate that it could displease virtually all sides of the strategy debate, including both industry and some of its own Executive Branch superiors.

To show responsiveness to the surge of environmentalism, Nixon not only formed the EPA in late 1970, but also appointed William Ruckelshaus as its first administrator. Ruckelshaus, it may be said, represented the conservationist strain in Republican philosophy. From a well-to-do and politically prominent Indiana family, he was an outdoor enthusiast with considerable appreciation for the environment. Upon graduation from the Harvard Law School in 1960, he joined the Indiana attorney general's office, where he drafted the state's air pollution control act in 1963 and prosecuted cities and industries for water pollution (Cameron, 1972: 130). In basic respects a pragmatist, he had inherited both a volatile political situation and a huge newborn agency beset with chaos. Remarkably, his early experiences at EPA would prove politically invaluable four administrations and nearly a decade and a half later, when again he was called upon to quiet a not wholly dissimilar legitimation crisis at the agency, and with some cognate consequences (Chapter 8).

Within the limits of existing environmental law and political economy, and against the background of precedent, Ruckelshaus struck a fairly aggressive stance during EPA's early years, personally lobbying industry to clean up its emissions while increasing the enforcement pressure to underscore the matter's urgency. True, the agency had determined not to rely on criminal sanctions as the policy tool of choice, preferring instead to jawbone powerful industries into a socially responsible environmentalism (see Chapter 4). And it was also the case that Ruckelshaus himself warned environmentalists that the costs of pollution control were essential to ultimate policy determinations: "We could make highways safer by enclosing them in rubber tubes," he suggested. "The reason we don't is that it costs too much. The question of what cost for what benefit is at the heart of the controversy swirling around us today, and essentially these are political questions" (quoted in Cameron, 1972: 103).

But calling prior enforcement of antipollution laws "close to a scandal," he initiated a policy under which EPA rapidly accelerated its referrals for prosecution under the Refuse Act. In contrast to the earlier, sparing use of the law, by 1973 EPA had recommended to the Justice Department lawsuits, both civil and criminal, against more than 200 corporations, including such major firms as U.S. Steel, Allied Chemical, Gulf Oil, Minnesota Mining and Manufacturing, Mobil Oil, Republic Steel, and Texaco. Ruckelshaus's enforcement stance could be construed as bolder yet in the face of the administration's freeze on wages and prices in the economy, which temporarily frustrated industries' ability to pass on pollution control costs in the form of higher prices. Moreover, there is some indication that the administrator used the swell of public opinion to achieve a degree of political insulation from White House pressures for greater moderation. According to John Quarles, EPA's first assistant administrator for enforcement, Ruckelshaus "did not seek support for his actions in the established structures of political power. He turned instead directly to the press and to public opinion, often in conflict with those very structures. In so doing, he tied the fortunes of EPA to public opinion as the only base for EPA's political support" (quoted in Marcus, 1980: 286).[12] Given the contradictory

---

[12] During the course of one of the early federal government lawsuits, in 1971, against Armco Steel for its pollution of the Houston Ship Channel, the company's general counsel sent the following, anonymous, retelling of an epic tale to the Justice Department's assistant attorney general for the Land and Natural Resources Division:

A FAIRY TALE

OR

THE LESSON FOR THE DAY

Now in the age of chivalry it came to pass that in the second year of the reign of King Arthur Milhaus [sic] Nixon a great darkness passed across the sky and the waters, causing among the people deep travail of spirit and sundry disturbances. For there was overpopulation among the dragon clans and the beasts fairly ran free in the land spewing out fire and smoke and brimstone and other noxious substances – much to the detriment of all living organisms, including the peasantry.

In Camelot – sometimes known as Naderland – King Arthur scowled across his round table at Sir Mordred Muskie of Maine and Sir Larry O'Brien, thought by some to be Merlin in disguise, who in close and evil conversation were scheming, he knew, to take care of not only the dragons but, forsooth, King Arthur as well. And among his knights there was one above all who was noted for his purity of spirit, heart and body. And he called to him Sir Galahad Ruckleshaus [sic], dressed as always in pure white and with fire in his eyes to find the Holy Grail and drink from it some purified water. And the King handed Sir Galahad the sword Excalibur and said, "Verily, Sir Knight, take my sword and all the white knights you can find, go forth and slay the dragons; how, it matters not one jot nor one tittle so long as this great travail of spirit is wafted away, and the peasantry resumes its idle feasting and drinking and dancing."

So the white knights charged off in many directions throughout the land and they slew dragons in great numbers and in short order. . . .

And at first the peasantry were overcome with joy and loudly acclaimed Sir Galahad, who paused in his quest pretty often to tell them of his victories and his future plans for dragon killing.

In certain outlying provinces, however, the peasants had trained dragons to start their fires in the morning, heat their houses, smoke their meat, fertilize their fields and otherwise contribute to their comfort and welfare. But the white knights killed any and all dragons without distinction and, despite loud and vehe-

pressures of the time, he achieved some success in this even though he failed to mollify many environmental activists.

While environmentalists were critical of EPA's limited use of the criminal sanction, the agency's new enforcement policy engendered enemies in high places, both public and private. It cleanly split the administration itself. As early as 1971 Commerce Secretary Stans, who considered Ruckelshaus's policies too aggressive, was predicting that the administrator would be out of the job by year's end. That the EPA head did not roll was at least in part a consequence of the powerful support of his mentor and original sponsor for the post, Attorney General John Mitchell.

In addition to Stans, powerful corporate petitioners also found some willing allies among the president's aides in the White House, who worked behind the scenes to blunt some of the early vigor of the EPA. For example, after an EPA official testified in support of Montana's new air pollution control standards, stiffer than the federal government's own, Anaconda Company president John B. M. Place enlisted the support of Nixon aide Peter Flanigan to combat this federal endorsement. Ultimately, Ruckelshaus took the more moderate position that the EPA would neither reject nor support state standards more stringent than the agency's (Cameron, 1972: 132).

Case study: Armco Steel Corporation

In a significant early water pollution case against a major steelmaker, White House involvement again appears to have played a part in buffering a polluter from the more dramatic force of law, this time drawing a congressional investigation of the White House role.[13] In December 1970, the Justice Department had sued the Armco Steel Corporation for toxic pollution of Houston's Ship

ment protest from the peasantry, brooked no interference. (Correspondence from William R. Bailey to Assistant Attorney General Shiro Kashiwa, May 12, 1971. In U.S. Department of Justice File No. 90-5-1-1-26, *in re United States v. Armco Steel Corporation* [C.A. No. 70-H-1535].)

This accounting creatively suggests one important view of the emerging political economics of environmental regulation. It is ironic that this lawsuit became prominently embroiled in allegations that the White House had pressed Justice and the EPA for leniency in the case. See later in text.

[13] I obtained materials on this case and controversy during field work at Justice Department headquarters in Washington in 1978 and through a follow-up Freedom of Information request to the Department. The materials are contained in the Department's File No. 90-5-1-1-26, in reference to *United States v. Armco Steel Corporation* (C.A. No. 70-H-1535).

Channel, under the authority of the 1899 Refuse Act. It was a proto-typical case of the time: it fit perfectly the federal government's emergent policy of demonstrating its new regulatory resolve by se-lective enforcement against serious polluters. Armco certainly met the profile: a large corporation, with 1969 sales of more than $1.5 billion and a net income of $95 million, its Houston steelmaking op-erations were discharging an estimated 1,015 pounds of cyanide, 414 pounds of phenol, and 11,996 pounds of ammonia into the channel each day.

After a three-week trial that produced 2,200 pages of testimony, federal district court judge Allen B. Hannay issued a precedent-setting judgment in mid-September 1971, ordering Armco to cease immediately the discharge of virtually all of the cyanide, an order that would shut down the plant's coke production and idle perhaps 300 of the operation's 4,400 employees. Almost at once corporate executives appealed the decision, but rather than through the courts

the appeal went directly to President Nixon. In correspondence dated September 28, C. William Verity, Jr., Armco's president, com-plained to the president of the government's treatment of the case:

Dear Mr. Nixon: After hearing your comments at the Detroit Economic Club on the need for a sensible balance between the environment and jobs, and after personally hearing you tell us that industry would not be a whip-ping boy in solving our environmental problems, I was shocked by the ac-tions of Mr. Ruckelshaus and the Justice Department in shutting down the blast furnace and coke ovens at our Houston Plant.

It is inconceivable to me that your Administration believes environmental problems can be solved by shutting down industry.

[Verity went on to outline the company's previous arrangements with the Texas Water Quality Board to inject the Houston wastes into deep wells; EPA had rejected the plan, fearing contamination of groundwater used for drinking, thereby setting off a dispute with the Texas environmental agency as well as with Armco.]

You should also know that this ruling of the Houston Court, if it were applied to others, would shut down not only all steel plants but also all chemical, oil and many other industries, and every Municipal Sewage Treat-ment Plant in the Country.

Armco is proud of its efforts and progress in environmental quality. In the past 6 years, more than $100,000,000 of our Shareholders' funds have been invested in Air and Water Pollution Abatement Facilities throughout the United States. We have resolved virtually all other pollution problems at Houston. We, therefore, are greatly shocked to see Representatives of your Administration pursuing such an arbitrary and ill-advised course of action.

We are bringing this to your attention, and also to the attention of the Attorney General, and the Director of the Environmental Protection Agency.

We are asking that you and the Justice Department take action to stay the Judge's decision until a sensible, satisfactory plan can be worked out to solve our Houston problem. The Company that has led the way in environmental improvement; the 300 men and women whose jobs are immediately affected; in fact, all employees of our Houston Plant deserve fairer treatment than this.

Similarly, in correspondence of September 27, Armco's director of environmental engineering, John E. Barker, wrote Nixon that the federal government had "taken such extreme steps that the industrial strength of America and the free enterprise system that has made our country so great are seriously threatened." Barker went on to suggest that if the court's ban on all such toxic discharges were applied throughout the nation, one consequence would be that "all integrated steel mills in the United States would be forced to close and the jobs of over six hundred thousand (600,000) steelworkers would be exported to Japan, or Germany, or somewhere else. . . . No, Mr. President, we do not oppose pollution control but we do oppose completely unrealistic, scientifically impossible regulations and court orders that use words such as 'all' " (emphasis in original).

According to testimony at congressional hearings on the matter in 1971 and 1972, Verity had also made phone contact in late September 1971 with Flanigan and White House aides W. John Glancy and George Crawford, who then pressed the Justice Department for "an arrangement to be worked out whereby Armco could continue operating" its complete works in Houston.[14] (News accounts also reported that Armco officers and directors had contributed $12,000 to Nixon's 1968 campaign.) Subsequently, the department and Armco agreed to a new resolution of the case in which the company could resume its cyanide and other discharges while it built a new incinerator to burn the wastes by July 1972. Judge Hannay signed the amended order November 4, 1971; Armco began incinerating the wastes at the end of the following June.

---

[14] Correspondence from Representatives Henry S. Reuss, John Conyers, Jr., and Paul N. McCloskey, Jr., of the Conservation and Natural Resources Subcommittee of the House Committee on Government Operations, to Attorney General Richard G. Kleindienst; December 29, 1972. Department of Justice File No. 90-5-1-1-26, *in re United States v. Armco Steel Corporation* (C.A. No. 70-H-1535).

144   5 Legislating clean water

This case, and the history of the early period of enforcement
generally, suggest several points that would continue to characterize
pollution control in the United States. First, the record suggests
the extent to which environmental *policy*, as against the environmental *cause* itself, split the top ranks of federal authority, in both
the Executive and Legislative branches. (The most consistently
proenvironmental protection arm of government was the judiciary
[as illustrated in the NEPA cases], which typically enjoys the greatest
short-term insularity from political pressures.) Almost as if a sort
of "law of political nature," to the extent that Ruckelshaus began
to aggressively pursue enforcement, to that extent were the ears of
his supervisors in the White House open to complaints from business regarding their version of "reason," particularly complaints emanating from powerful corporate sources, which unlike small businesses could point to their production of numerous jobs for
employees and great wealth for countless shareholders. These arguments, as employed in the Armco letters, for example, tended to ally
political economic power with the highest traditional values of capitalist democracies. And in another application of the law, if one subcommittee of Congress was outraged at the apparent White House
influence on law enforcement, another was simultaneously threatening the EPA with restricted budgets if the agency proved too asser-
tive in its regulatory mission (Cameron, 1972: 103).

At least in the Armco case it is arguable that EPA and the Justice
Department largely achieved their enforcement goal despite White
House and congressional pressures: the ultimate elimination of a
large, powerful source of toxic water pollution. Against the nation's
prior record of enforcement, this was no mean feat. Clearly, government prosecutors did not intend to seek injunctions for immediate
cessation of all major pollution sources; to do so would be to
threaten the economic life-blood of the land. But the new regulators, many themselves charged by the evolving consciousness of environmental decline and danger, sought a show of force that would
both signal their seriousness of purpose and finally begin to chip
away at the deeply embedded customs regarding the industrial consumption of the environment.

But if the specter of stiff enforcement had indeed warded off this
episode of pollution, the case remained troubling in suggesting the
distorting effects of economic power on public policy: although
Armco had originally been sued in 1955 for its pollution of the ship

channel, and ultimately fined, the company – abetted by the leniency of the Texas Water Quality Board – failed for fifteen years to propose a solution for the cyanide discharges (deep-well injection), then was able to negotiate a further reprieve of eight months with the federal government. Lengthy delays trading off short-term profitability against environmental protection would continue to characterize this policy area throughout the 1970s, particularly among the largest, most powerful polluters. Moreover, inscribed as they were in political economic relations, these delays attached not only to individual cases but also to the development of key areas of environmental *policy*, as I shall later discuss.

In general, the evidence indicates that in these early years of modern environmentalism, the leadership at EPA determined, not unreasonably, to use enforcement as both symbol and substance. The aim was to flash a signal that business, both the state's and industry's, would no longer be conducted as usual with respect to the environment. Criminal and civil cases were used not only to prosecute the most egregious polluters, but to establish the new parameters within which the government would attempt both to solve its own legitimation crisis and to negotiate with industry to ameliorate the escalating environmental threat. The agency's goal was to induce a climate of "voluntary cooperation" with industry, and toward that end its "politics of symbolism" had already demonstrated some substance, at least as indicated by the mounting resistance to EPA's neophyte efforts.

It is instructive to note the ways in which these efforts were constrained by more than powerful political resistance to cases, or the weak laws then at the agency's disposal (such as the Refuse Act of 1899 with its maximum fine of $2,500 for each violation). These were more subtle limits on law, characteristic of initial efforts at hurried reform. For one, the novel rush to prosecute highly publicized water cases in fiscal 1972 was, to some extent, undertaken at the expense of more fundamental change. That is, the EPA spent more effort making a show of filing cases for prosecution than it did preparing to ensure subsequent abatement efforts by polluters. According to John Quarles, the agency's first enforcement chief:

There was one curious feature of the early EPA enforcement program: almost the entire emphasis was placed on beginning the actions. . . . It was almost as though the mere fact of filing suit would end the problem once and for all, and if only we could sue all the polluters . . . our environmental problems would be over. The difficulties of pursuing an action through completion – achieving an actual cleanup program – seemed scarcely to be noticed, especially at first. . . .

The basic weakness of the early enforcement actions was that they were being initiated in areas where effective standards and pollution control requirements themselves had not yet been set. However aggressive the enforcement program, it could not be effective if it tried to establish these basic requirements by suing polluters one at a time. (Quoted in Boyer and Meidinger, 1985: 873–4, fn. 101, 102)

Moreover, the eagerness to finally mount a publicly impressive enforcement record may have also partially backfired because of inadequate case preparation or insufficient agreements between prosecutorial branches regarding appropriate enforcement criteria. For example, EPA came under criticism for one early episode in which it called a press conference to announce it was referring thirty-five cases against major industries for criminal prosecution by the Justice Department; the department eventually determined that only three of these cases merited prosecution (Boyer and Meidinger, 1985: 873, fn. 100). Such interorganizational differences continued to characterize water pollution enforcement even in its relatively mature stages (to be illustrated later).

The early EPA enforcement efforts against industrial water pollution served as a talisman to ward off the environmental menace. The symbols indeed had substance, but the effort was self-limiting.[15]

[15] Enforcement chief Quarles also described a form of *institutionalized* resistance to more vigorous enforcement in the context of policy change, a form inscribed in the workings of settled bureaucracies and institutional relations:

Three months after EPA was created, Ruckelshaus summoned the regional directors of the water pollution program to Washington and told them to push ahead aggressively with enforcement cases. When the months that followed produced little action, I was puzzled. Slowly I realized that the biggest factor in the delay was simply the ingrained attitude of most employees in the agency.

Prior to EPA's creation the federal pollution control programs had focused on research, planning, grants, and technical assistance, and few of the people doing that work had any taste or training for the rough and tumble of enforcement. They felt inhibited by the opposition of their state agency counterparts, who resented the intrusion of federal officials. . . . Because he knew the action would be attacked by the polluter and criticized by the state officials, he was tempted to forget the whole business. . . .

[U]ntil each regional office became experienced, the fear remained that political pressure would be used to block us and that the regional officer who had taken the initiative would be left out on a limb. (Quoted in Boyer and Meidinger, 1985: 874, fn. 103)

As I discuss in Chapter 8, Ruckelshaus again encountered similar bureaucratic resistance to enforcement at EPA when he was reappointed as agency head in 1983, once more to dispel a swirling legitimation crisis in Washington.

If the results of regulation were to endure, it would be necessary to mount a more sophisticated apparatus to effect and assess technological changes in production (cf., Boyer and Meidinger, 1985: 873–4). By 1972 both the president and the Congress were jockeying to pass legislation to do just that.

In the meantime, between 1970 and 1972 manufacturing corporations increased their pollution control research expenditures by only 12 percent; at the same time industry was spending "lavishly to advertise that business had an ecological conscience" (Rosenbaum, 1977: 16). In the private sector, symbol and substance were out of phase; in the public sector, they were approaching greater alignment.

The congressional debates: on legislating a mandate

A river is more than an amenity, it is a treasure. It offers a necessity of life that must be rationed among those who have power over it.

– Oliver Wendell Holmes

A democratic power is never likely to perish for lack of strength or of its resources, but it may very well fall because of the misdirection of its strength and the abuse of its resources.

– Alexis de Tocqueville

By 1971 power, resources, and democracy all came into complex play on the question of water pollution, as both the Congress and the Executive Branch began to debate new legislation that would greatly extend the federal government's control in this policy area. As in the enforcement of preexisting law described before, this debate both stirred and reflected the long-structured cross-currents and contradictions now becoming visible in the relations between environment and economy. In addition, the debate was only complicated by such not wholly tangential considerations as federalism, pork barrel politics, and presidential electioneering. The result was remarkable new legislation by the end of 1972, not only an election year but also one in which it might be said there was a small measure of political "space" for such concentrated attention on the environment: during the summer the last U.S. combat troops were withdrawn from Vietnam as the United States approached its final disengagement from that war, and the five Watergate burglars were arrested for breaking into the Democratic National Committee offices in Washington, setting off a chain of events that would soon dominate the national agenda and two years later lead to the resignation of President Nixon.

The roster of players in the argument was as imposing as the issues themselves: the White House, both houses of Congress, industry, the states, the newly potent public interest advocacy groups, the news media, and the public. But despite the tangle of interests attaching themselves to the question, it was clear early on that the new legislation was – for the first time in water pollution – to be formidable. Indeed, under the twin pressures of advancing environmental deterioration and growing public demand for new policy, the White House and both units of Congress had evolved some similar conclusions regarding the need. Agreement was developing that federal authority should be extended to intrastate waters, that precise effluent discharge limits should be placed on industrial polluters, and that maximum civil and criminal penalties for violation needed to be greatly increased.

Underlying these positions was the recognition that the system of water quality standards established by the 1965 law was finally inadequate for the need at hand. The standards only pertained to interstate waters, and varied in stringency from state to state (see Chapter 3). They failed to constitute a *rational* policy, because the playing field for environmental management was not only uneven but also subject to unpredictable shifts. (In addition, under the regimen of water quality standards, nature and geography could heavily shape the relative regulatory advantages of firms and therefore their market advantages: volume of water flow in the river and concentration of industry on it could influence the regulatory stringency companies faced.) Moreover, the standards were often quite difficult, in cases virtually impossible, to enforce: when many industrial sites shared a waterway, a common occurrence, determining the source of a standards violation often defied the available scientific and law enforcement technologies. Finally, on a conceptual level the 1965 approach was inadequate to the new environmental morality: the standards implied the no longer widely acceptable assumption that some level of industrial water pollution was tolerable even if the technology were available to eliminate it.[16]

---

[16] For additional discussion of the differences between the 1965 water quality approach and the eventual 1972 amendments, as well as of some of the legal issues raised by the 1972 law, see "Comment: The EPA's Power to Establish National Effluent Limitations for Existing Water Pollution Sources," *University of Pennsylvania Law Review* 125 (1976): 120–66.

Beyond this, however, there were important differences between the parties, in both kind and degree, and these differences shaped the final legislation in fateful ways. As it happened, the president was the first to name some specific alternative approaches to solving the problems of water pollution.[17] In a special message to Congress on the environment in February 1970, Nixon proposed a regimen of federally approved discharge standards for all industrial and municipal sources. He followed this with draft legislation also calling for tightened abatement schedules, greater government authority for gathering pollution data, and much higher civil penalties for polluters: $25,000 per day for first offenders and $50,000 per day for repeat violators. In his special message he had argued that "strict standards and strict enforcement are . . . necessary – not only to assure compliance, but also in fairness to those who have voluntarily assumed the often costly burden while their competitors have not. Good neighbors should not be placed at a competitive disadvantage because of their good neighborliness."[18] But this set of proposals served only as an opening, albeit an important one, and by 1971 the Congress was actively considering its own versions of amendments to the Federal Water Pollution Control Act. In the end, Nixon vetoed the new law in late 1972, only to see his veto immediately overridden by both houses of Congress.

The Senate initiative

In Congress the Senate moved first on new legislation and the House followed. Both shared the general premises noted above, and in addition were concerned to finally establish law that would not be subverted by the regulated. They were responding generally to the critiques of the "capture" theory of regulation, and to the often scathing indictments of federal pollution control law published by Ralph Nader's Center for the Study of Responsive Law: *Water Wasteland: The Report on Water Pollution* (Zwick and Benstock, 1971) and

---

[17] For descriptions of Nixon's proposals, see Zwick and Benstock (1971: 420) and Davies and Davies (1975: 40).

[18] Quoted in letter from William Ruckelshaus, EPA Administrator, to the Office of Management and Budget, October 11, 1972 [recommending presidential approval of S. 2770, The Federal Water Pollution Control Act Amendments of 1972]. Reprinted in *A Legislative History of the Water Pollution Control Act Amendments of 1972* (Congressional Research Service, Library of Congress [Serial No. 93-1], 93d Cong., 1st Sess., January 1973), p. 156. Hereafter cited as *Legislative History*.

150   5 **Legislating clean water**

*The Water Lords: The Report on Industry and Environmental Crisis in Sa-
vannah, Georgia* (Fallows, 1971).

But in the Congress, too, there were important differences on the
details of the proposed changes, differences that reflected the long-
standing distinction between the more aggressive regulatory tendency in the Senate and the more conservative, industry-sensitive
approach to water pollution controls in the House. This variation
could even be detected in the utterances of the two long-time leaders of water pollution legislation in each house as they urged their
colleagues toward new law: Edmund Muskie in the Senate and John
Blatnik in the House. For example, in arguing on the Senate floor
for the passage of what became the 1972 amendments, Muskie (then
chair of the Subcommittee on Air and Water Pollution, Senate Committee on Public Works) asked rhetorically:

Can we afford clean water? Can we afford rivers and lakes and streams
and oceans which continue to make possible life on this planet? Can we
afford life itself? Those questions were never asked as we destroyed the waters of our Nation, and they deserve no answers as we finally move to restore and renew them.

In speaking of the amendments' stated goal of eliminating all water
pollution by 1985, he continued: "These are not the pious declarations that Congress so often makes in passing its laws; on the contrary, this is literally a life or death proposition for the Nation."[19]

On the floor of the House, on the other hand, Blatnik struck a
more restrained stance in assessing the trade-offs associated with
pollution control. Speaking to the original House version of the legislation, almost as if responding directly to Muskie's absolutist tone,
he argued:

We, as Members of Congress, in considering this environmental control bill
on the floor of the House must remember that environmental control is
one of a number of competing national priorities. These other national priorities include full employment, price stabilization, rural development, social development, economic development, energy supply, a wider sharing of
an improved standard of living, retention of our foreign trade capabilities,
and protection of our natural resources. I believe the Committee on Public
Works [which Blatnik then chaired] has properly considered each of these
priorities while developing H. R. 11896 [House version of the proposed
amendments].[20]

[19] *Senate Consideration of the Report of the Conference Committee,* October 4, 1972. In
Legislative History, p. 164.
[20] *House Debate on H.R. 11896,* March 27, 1972. In *Legislative History,* p. 352.

However reasonable one might construe Blatnik's approach, however much Muskie's passionate declarations might have been fueled by the Nader critiques of his past efforts in the context of the Senator's presidential ambitions (cf., Marcus, 1980: 270–3), their differences shaded the House and Senate proposals and the final product.

The Senate bill (S. 2770), forged in Muskie's Subcommittee on Air and Water Pollution in 1971, was an aggressive statement of the new environmental ethos. At the outset, the bill decreed it a national *policy* to eliminate the discharge of *all* pollutants into the nation's navigable waters by 1985, and to thereby restore "the natural chemical, physical, and biological integrity of United States waters, and reach an interim goal of water quality for swimming and fish propagation by 1981."[21] To implement the policy, the bill erected an ambitious and intricate legislative apparatus of technical requirements for industry, tight timetables for achievement of interim and final goals for eliminating discharge, streamlined and much enhanced enforcement tools, and various provisions for public oversight of the law's implementation, including citizen suits against violators or the EPA if it failed to perform nondiscretionary duties under the law. In addition, the bill provided for $14 billion in federal funds over four years to pay for up to 70 percent of the costs of construction of publicly owned municipal treatment works (POTWs) for cities and towns. The total federal cost for the legislation would be in excess of $18 billion.

In addition to the policy of eventual elimination of water pollution, for private industry the most dramatic proposal in the bill was the requirement of new technology-forcing standards of pollution control. The bill required that all polluting companies install the "best practicable treatment technology" (BPT) by January 1, 1976; by 1981, all such discharges were to *eliminate* their water pollution or, if individual companies could demonstrate to the EPA that elim-

---

[21] *Conference Report: Federal Water Pollution Control Act Amendments of 1972* (Senate Report No. 92-1236, 92d Cong., 2d Sess.; September 28, 1972); as reprinted in *Legislative History*, p. 282.

The objective of restoring and maintaining "the chemical, physical, and biological integrity of the Nation's waters," known to Senate drafters of the bill as the Integrity Principle and contained in the final legislation passed by Congress (Sec. 101), was added to S. 2770 after George Woodwell, then of the Brookhaven National Laboratory (now director, Woods Hole Research Center and vice chairman, Natural Resources Defense Council), wrote Muskie that the bill needed a clearer statement of its objectives, and offered the phrasing: "maintenance of the chemical, physical, and biological integrity of all waters, including lakes, streams, rivers, estuaries, and the oceans" (Jorling, 1982: 36).

ination could not "be attained at a reasonable cost,"[22] to install the "best available technology" (BAT). The bill would require the EPA (not the states) to develop regulations specifying the degree of effluent reduction attainable through BPT and BAT. In essence, the agency was to define BPT and BAT for the various categories of industry, taking into account relevant factors "including the age of equipment and facilities, the process employed, and the cost of achieving such a reduction."[23]

The standards were to be enforced through a program of permits issued to all dischargers, either by the EPA or by state environmental officials if the EPA should determine that states could adequately enforce the program. The permits would specify the conditions and timetables of compliance for individual industrial sources of water pollution. Violations of the permits, including the specific pollution discharge limits therein, would bring immediate enforcement, either formal compliance orders or civil suits. For willful and negligent violations, the bill provided for a fine of up to $25,000 per day of violation and one year in jail; for repeating such violations, a fine of up to $50,000 per day and two years' incarceration.

The Senate bill represented a sharp departure from the previous regulatory philosophy at the federal level as expressed in the water quality standards approach. In essence, the very morality of pollution was now under assault. As the Senate Report on the bill described the purpose of the new, technology-driven approach:

This section [301] clearly establishes that the discharge of pollutants is unlawful. Unlike its predecessor program which permitted the discharge of certain amounts of pollutants under the conditions described above, this legislation would clearly establish that *no one has the right to pollute* – that pollution continues because of technological limits, not because of any inherent right to use the nation's waterways for the purpose of disposing of wastes.[24] (Emphasis added)

[22] *Conference Report, Legislative History*, p. 303.
[23] *Conference Report, Legislative History*, p. 307.
[24] *Senate Report: Federal Water Pollution Control Act Amendments of 1971* (Senate Committee on Public Works, Senate Report No. 92-414, 92d Cong., 1st Sess., 1971). As reprinted in *Legislative History*, p. 1460. This fundamental shift in regulatory philosophy was also noted by Thomas Jorling (1982: 36), who served as minority counsel to the Senate Committee on Public Works and participated in Muskie's subcommittee's deliberations on the new bill: "The subcommittee came to realize that it had to push for control technology and effluent limitations. The policy goal was to eliminate all discharges. To achieve it, Congress would have to guide industrial research and development as well as the general attitude toward managing material and energy. The right to pollute was repealed."

It is worth noting that technological limits were not to be defined simply by the reach of technical and scientific knowledge, but also by the costs associated with implementing such knowledge in factories.

Resistance and restraints: the House debates

The Nixon administration opposed the Senate proposal on the grounds of both fiscal conservatism and regulatory philosophy (Davies and Davies, 1975: 41; cf., Zwick and Benstock, 1971: 418–23). While the administration considered the $18 billion price tag a federal "budget buster," it also considered the regulatory provisions both too stringent and too intrusive on the states' rights to set pollution control standards. The Council on Environmental Quality prepared an analysis that purported to show that *adequate* water quality could be achieved at much less cost, and that the goal of total elimination of water pollution was not feasible. Moreover, the administration's own proposal for new legislation, forged amid continuing and exclusive exchanges with the industrial membership of NIPCC, had made EPA decisions to enforce the law discretionary rather than mandatory, and established no final deadline for compliance with the newly expanded federal water quality guidelines.

While it is difficult to gauge precisely NIPCC's role in shaping the content of the administration's resistance, the evidence available suggests it was a considerable one. For example, the initial administration proposal for new water pollution legislation, drafted at the EPA, did not contain significant "safeguards" against the potential economic impacts of mandated controls. But such impacts were the principal concern of NIPCC. In its February 1971 report to the president, for example, the advisory committee argued that "increasing public concern with the pollution consequences of our affluent society has inspired responses at some levels of government which are incompatible with the economic health of our society. Standards have been established which are unachievable with presently available technology or are unattainable at economically tolerable costs" (quoted in Steck, 1975: 272). As a consequence of such concerns, the proposal was redrafted to limit water pollution controls to those "taking into account the practicability of compliance," a sufficiently vague formulation that would permit a variety of interpretations. The day the bill was sent to Congress for its consideration, the president hosted NIPCC at a White House reception, and assured the membership that "the government – this Administration, I can assure you – is not here to beat industry over the head" (quoted in Zwick and Benstock, 1971: 421).

Clearly it was not. But here it is more interesting to note that while the president appears in these words to quite consciously differentiate his administration from the rest of the federal state – with all that seems to imply about his uncertainty regarding the final legislation to come – the more aggressive Senate bill itself contained fundamental economic constraints on the application of pollution controls, as indicated in the notions of "practicable" and "available" in BPT and BAT, respectively. Nonetheless, the administration lobbied hard against the relative regulatory stringency of the Senate proposal but failed to reshape it: the bill passed by a most compelling vote of 86–0 on November 2, 1971.

Three days after the vote NIPCC convened an "emergency" meeting with administration officials, including three White House aides; within days of the meeting the administration launched an assault on the Senate measure in the House of Representatives, which had yet to fully consider the matter (Steck, 1975: 273). It asked the House Public Works Committee to reopen its hearings on FWPCA amendments, and also "rallied industrial groups and some state officials to oppose the Senate bill" (Davies and Davies, 1975: 41).

As a unit the House had traditionally been more receptive to the complaints and concerns of business, what with representatives' much shorter election cycles and greater proximity (and political vulnerability) to the often sharp-edged economic interests of their local districts. Such considerations, too, rendered them more sympathetic to the complaints of some local and state officials regarding "improper" shifts in the balance of federalism: the threatened further encroachment of centralized federal authority on what remained of state and local control. As something of an offset for the potential loss of local autonomy, Washington's legislators could at least offer the palliative of large sums in federal monies for the construction of municipal sewage treatment plants. But given the environmental fervor of the period, it remained unclear just how Congress might alleviate the pain of regulation for industry. If the largest, most powerful constituents of corporate America wanted a more stable regulatory environment, even one that would be charted in Washington, they much more vigorously insisted that the law be "reasonable."

Under Blatnik's direction, the House Public Works Committee set out to meet this latter expectation while producing a version of amendments to the Federal Water Pollution Control Act that would also advance the cause of environmental protection. And during the winter of 1971–72, to a certain extent they succeeded in both regards. On the one hand, the committee reproduced the core logic of the Senate bill: technology-forcing standards implemented for point sources of water pollution through a system of government-enforced permits. On the other hand, the House bill, H.R. 11896, marked something of a regulatory retreat from the rigor of the Senate's proposal.[25]

The House retrenchment began with the statement of the proposed law's purpose and extended downward through some of the key regulatory provisions. Whereas in the amendments' statement of purpose the Senate bill would have established as a national *policy* the elimination of all discharges of pollution into navigable waters by 1985, the House proposal instead made this a *goal*. While legislators manifested some confusion over the implications of this terminological difference, the motivating concern in the House was that the language of "policy" would commit the state to an enforceable mandate that "zero discharge" be reached by 1985; as exhibited in other, implementing provisions of the House proposal, the representatives wished to infuse the new law with greater flexibility to take into account the economic costs of compliance with such provisions as the regulatory requirements were phased in over time.[26]

Indeed, the House bill formally structured the assessment of costs into the question of what the law would ultimately require of polluters. As had the Senate proposal, the House bill required BPT for

[25] This comparison of the House and Senate bills is based largely on the *Conference Report: Federal Water Pollution Control Act Amendments of 1972*, Senate Report No. 92-1236, 92d Cong., 2d Sess. (September 28, 1972); reprinted in the *Legislative History*, pp. 281–339. The discussion is supplemented by the commentary of legislators as contained in the *Legislative History*. For a brief summary comparison, see for example Davies and Davies (1975: 40–3).

[26] See generally, for example, the commentary on the House floor by Representatives Blatnik (*Legislative History*, pp. 354–5) and Sikes ("The Senate bill declares this to be national policy which means it is enforceable by law. The House bill declares this to be a national goal." *Legislative History*, p. 739). Interestingly, Senator Muskie was himself quoted in the House debates as having said that, in connection with the Senate proposal, "the 1985 deadline for achieving no discharge of pollutants is a policy objective. It is not locked in concrete. *It is not enforceable.* It simply establishes what the committee thinks ought to be done on the basis of present knowledge" (*Legislative History*, pp. 511–12; emphasis added).

industry by 1976 but, unlike the Senate proposal, it conditioned the 1981 requirements of either BAT or zero discharge on further research into economic feasibility and subsequent congressional action to either implement or contract the more advanced standards of clean-up. The research on which consequent congressional action was to build would be conducted by the National Academy of Sciences and the National Academy of Engineering and reported to Congress within two years of the time of the bill's passage.

This aspect of the House proposal prompted considerable debate on the floor. On the one side, many representatives were persuaded that the economic costs of such requirements were at best uncertain, at worst catastrophic. Members quoted a Council on Environmental Quality study that estimated a loss of between 50,000 and 125,000 jobs because of the 1976 BPT requirement alone.[27] Despite and to some extent because of the great uncertainty associated with all such estimates, many were concerned that complete elimination of water pollution might bring intolerable costs: if the environmental organization The Friends of the Earth was estimating a national bill of $50–$55 billion for zero discharge using land disposal techniques, the Nixon administration and EPA were projecting figures as high as $316.5 billion depending on the techniques used to achieve the goal (as against an estimated $61 billion for an 85 percent reduction in pollution).[28] (These figures do not account for the offsetting *benefits* – economic and otherwise – that might accrue to water pollution control.) There was stated concern that the Senate version of the bill might close down as much as 20 percent of the nation's industrial capacity, putting millions out of work, and that total pollution control "will have adverse effects on our international trade position, retard the growth of the real gross national product, and decrease aggregate demand for goods and services."[29] Moreover, industry representatives had complained to House members that the

[27] See, e.g., *Legislative History*, pp. 480, 523.

[28] See, e.g., the correspondence from EPA Administrator William Ruckelshaus to Representative William Harsha in *Legislative History*, pp. 436–8, and the associated floor discussion; also see, e.g., pp. 479–81.

[29] Comments of Representative Keating in *Legislative History*, p. 480. The 20 percent loss in industrial capacity was estimated by Representative Sikes (*Legislative History*, p. 740); Representative Crane noted that "even the AFL-CIO agreed that this bill may throw literally millions of Americans out of work before fully implemented. . . . We can anticipate either continuing and mounting trade deficits growing out of this legislation or a return to the economic isolationism of the McKinley era – both of which will gravely injure the American economy and American consumers" (*Legislative History*, p. 738).

Senate's requirements would put them at a competitive disadvantage
to foreign producers, forcing U.S. businesses to move their production overseas.[30]

On the other side of the argument, liberal congressmen such as
Reuss of Wisconsin and Dingell of Michigan opposed the condition-
ing of the 1981 requirements on future research and legislation as
both unnecessary and contradictory of cost-effective pollution control. These legislators argued that the 1981 requirements already
forced the consideration of costs in their implementation. As indicated by Reuss, who proposed an amendment to eliminate the study
condition in the House bill, the 1981 standard "requires all sorts of
factors to be taken into account [in its implementation], such as the
age of the equipment, the process employed, the costs, the economic, social, and environmental impact, and the impact of foreign
competition."[31] Thus, the caution of future research and lawmaking, he and others argued, was redundant. Moreover, the argument
ran, it was hypocritical to promise an insistent public stiff environmental controls in an early section of the bill, only to suspend them

[30] See, e.g., the commentary of Representative Wright (*Legislative History*, p. 513):
"Numerous representatives of industry are fearful that, if we require these objectives that we have set forth without a study of what they will cost, it might conceiv-
ably put them at a competitive disadvantage with foreign competitors to the extent
that they would have to move to other lands to conduct their business, rather than
to comply with these objectives which might be prohibitively expensive."

[31] *Legislative History*, p. 510. The section of the House bill setting forth the 1981 requirements (sec. 301[b][2][A]) read, in part, as follows: "except as provided in section 315 [conditioning the requirements on future research and legislation], [there
shall be achieved] not later than January 1, 1981, effluent limitations for point
sources, other than publicly owned treatment works, (i) which shall require the
elimination of the discharge of pollutants, unless on the basis of facts presented by
the owner or operator of any such sources, among other information, the State
under a program approved pursuant to section 402 of this Act (or, where no such
program is approved, the [EPA] Administrator) finds, that compliance is *not attainable at a reasonable cost*, in which event there shall be applied an effluent limitation
based on that degree of effluent control achievable through the application of the
best available demonstrated technology, *taking into account the cost of such controls*, as
determined in accordance with regulations issued by the Administrator pursuant
to section 304(b) of this Act, and the environmental impact . . ." (emphasis added.
See H.R. 11896, Report No. 92–911, U.S. House of Representatives, 92d Cong.,
2d Sess.; reprinted in *Legislative History*, pp. 893–1110). Section 304(b) of the
House's version of the FWPCA amendments included the requirement that "factors relating to the assessment of best available demonstrated technology shall take
into account the age of equipment and facilities involved, the process employed
(including whether batch or continuous), the engineering aspects of the application of various types of demonstrated control techniques, process changes, the cost
and the economic, social, and environmental impact of achieving such effluent
reduction, foreign competition, and such other factors as the Administrator deems
appropriate" (Sec. 304[b][2][B]).

pending further consideration and legislation in a later section. And beyond the charge of hypocrisy, Congressman Dingell suggested on the floor of the House that the proposed study was itself likely to be biased or "loaded" in favor of unjustifiably weaker controls, given its support among powerful industry representatives: "Moreover, even in providing for a study I believe it is essential that we insure a mechanism which will provide a broader based study by organizations and institutions other than just the National Academy of Sciences and the National Academy of Engineering. The study provision in the committee's bill was placed there at the insistence of the National Association of Manufacturers."[32]

Besides such charges of wasted effort, hypocrisy, and even implicit conspiracy with industry interests – the sorts of charges that often characterize legislative debates on politically "hot" and economically divisive legal initiatives – House critics of the study contingency raised a more sophisticated concern regarding the provision, a concern that would continue to bedevil water pollution control not only during the 1970s but indefinitely thereafter. This was the challenge that such piecemeal, bifurcated reform as that contained in the House bill was *fundamentally irrational from the standpoint of public policy, that it was internally contradictory and therefore ultimately self-defeating.*

More specifically, critics of the House bill suggested that divorcing the requirement of advanced technological pollution controls (BAT) and zero discharge from the first-stage BPT standard would only increase the ultimate costs of advanced pollution control, thereby rendering its achievement both politically and economically quite problematic (by helping to justify industry claims that the advanced controls were now too expensive, precisely because of companies' previous installation of the earlier generation of BPT). For example, Representatives Bella Abzug and Charles Rangel argued:

Putting off the establishment of the 1981 and 1985 [zero discharge] goals and requirements will not save money; rather it will end up costing *more* in the long run. The technology which polluters install to comply with the bill's earlier 1976 requirements may not be compatible with the better methodology they will have to use later, when the more stringent requirements go into effect. Also, research on recycling techniques which could facilitate less costly achievement of the "no discharge" goal will not begin to take place with full vigor until we make those later goals and requirements definite. Industry has a right to know what will be asked of them later on.[33]

In other words, the logic of the legislation forced industry's focus to the near term, first-generation improvements of BPT – largely extant ("practicable") technology – at the expense of the longer range development of more advanced treatment or recycling technologies. This would likely raise the cost of more advanced controls and contribute to substantial regulatory uncertainty, not only for industry but also for the state and the environment (by reducing the economic feasibility of advanced controls).

This inherently contradictory legislative logic was reinforced by the bill's focus on "end-of-pipe" treatment technology, an orientation it shared with the Senate bill. This focus survived the legislative debates to be included in the final legislation passed by the Congress later in 1972. As described in the House's consideration of the bill eventually worked out in conference with the Senate, "By the term 'control technology' [in reference to the 1976 BPT standard] the managers [of the Conference Committee] mean the treatment facilities at the end of a manufacturing, agricultural, or other process, rather than control technology within the manufacturing process itself."[34]

And if Congress provided for consideration of production process changes toward the more advanced BAT requirements, even here it was reluctant to intrude "too forcefully" into traditional managerial prerogatives in production decisions. For example, in the 1972 amendments' BAT requirements for new factories, the Conference Report first noted the possibility that these would involve consideration of new production processes, but immediately constrained the congressional intent: "This does not mean that the Administrator is to determine the kind of production processes or the technology to be used by a new source [e.g., a factory]. It does mean that the Administrator is required to establish standards of performance which reflect the levels of control achievable through improved production processes, and of process technique, etc., leaving to the individual

---

[33] "Additional Views of Hon. Bella S. Abzug and Charles B. Rangel," in *Legislative History*, p. 866. Also see the *Legislative History* for the similar critiques of Representatives Reuss (pp. 509–10), Harrington (pp. 515–16), Gude (pp. 518–19), and several cosigners of a letter to House Public Works Committee Chair John Blatnik challenging the study provision and a number of other aspects of the House bill (pp. 882–6).

[34] *House Consideration of the Report of the Conference Committee*, p. 231. In *Legislative History*, pp. 225–79.

new source the responsibility to achieve the level of performance by the application of whatever technique determined available and desirable to that individual owner or operator."[35] Thus, the state would only force the issue essentially "outside" the factory, interposing technological barriers between production processes and the environment (as in the BPT standard), engaging a new form of the "politics of circulation" (in this case, the circulation of pollutants) while continuing to maintain a safe distance from the traditionally more volatile "politics of production."

The problem of linkage between the 1976 BPT standards and the later requirements thus, in fact, transcended the House debate regarding the suspension of the 1981 controls in its version of the law, if it was nonetheless exacerbated by that suspension. In its eagerness to provide evidence of progress in the face of the public clamor for pollution control, both houses of Congress chose conventional technological approaches for first-stage BPT. Ironically, this left the matter of zero discharge not only problematic for 1981 or 1985, but indefinitely. As Representative Vander Jagt noted during the consideration of the House bill:

Having proclaimed this goal [of zero discharge by 1985], then we make the main thrust of our efforts in 1976, relying on conventional treatment and technology that have not changed for about 50 years. . . . If we rely on the conventional technology in this field, we will probably have to spend hundreds of billions of dollars, probably several trillion dollars, to achieve the goal that we have proclaimed here of zero discharge of pollutants. In other words, we will be investing in the next 2 years alone $13 billion to build [BPT] systems that we are going to have to abandon in a few years if we have any seriousness whatsoever about the 1985 goal. This is the problem that we face. . . . It is as though 10 years ago somebody said we will put a man on the moon by the end of the decade, and we raced off spending $13 billion in attempting to do that through the procedure of buying railroad tracks and railroad cars.[36]

This "you can't get there from here" characteristic of the legislation arguably constrains the reach and effectiveness of water pollution control policy to the present day.

The majority of the House was not persuaded that the legislation was self-limiting in vital respects, and Reuss's proposal to eliminate the requirement of further research before legislating BAT was defeated, 249–140.[37] As it happened, EPA Administrator Ruckelshaus

[35] *Conference Report, Legislative History*, p. 311.
[36] *Legislative History*, p. 434.
[37] *Legislative History*, p. 526.

had gone on record as favoring the study requirement,[38] while the chairman of the president's Council on Environmental Quality, Russell Train, had testified in House hearings that the goal of zero discharge would prove either too costly or ineffective in the end.[39]

Beyond these strategic considerations, the House bill also retreated from the Senate's offering in several tactical areas of regulatory implementation, including enforcement. One of the key issues involved the sensitive question of federalism: whether the individual states or the federal government would bear the primary responsibility for this regulatory apparatus. The question revolved around the matter of the permitting authority: who would have final say on the regulatory contents of individual discharge permits, which after all would determine the extent and pace of abatement. Congressional deference to the states in water pollution control had produced the series of largely ineffective laws that brought legislators to the present crisis. But sensitivities regarding the distribution of power ran wide and deep – traceable to the founding of the nation and the long-bred suspicion of centralized authority – and both houses of Congress wrestled with this tension in considering these amendments to the FWPCA.

The two resolved the balance in this tension quite differently. While both houses formally maintained that "it is the policy of the Congress to recognize, preserve, and protect the primary responsibilities and rights of States to prevent, reduce, and eliminate pollution," language that was included in the final version of the new law's statement of purpose,[40] the Senate had been concerned to overcome the inherent weaknesses in such an approach, in effect rendering the language more symbolic than real. In its version of the amendments, the Senate had provided for the transfer of the permitting and enforcement authority to individual states, but only on condition that such state regulatory programs met conditions specified by the EPA, which could also revoke such programs and reclaim control of this regulatory arena if states failed to implement and enforce the law adequately. Moreover, the EPA could veto individual permits that states might approve if the agency believed

---

[38] *Legislative History,* pp. 436–38.
[39] *Legislative History,* pp. 524–25.
[40] Federal Water Pollution Control Act Amendments of 1972, Public Law 92-500, §§ 101–518; 33 U.S.C. §§ 1251–1376. The quoted phrase is found in § 101, "Declaration of Goals and Policy." Here, as elsewhere, the reference is to the sections as numbered in P.L. 92-500.

them not to comply with the pollution control regulations devised to implement the act. The intent was to provide uniform, nation-wide requirements for pollution control, to avoid the creation of "pollution havens" in states reluctant to enforce the law or otherwise too eager to bargain regulatory stringency to keep and attract industry.

For its part, the House sought to shift the balance of federalism in the other direction, more in keeping with the formal statement of purpose. On the floor, many representatives were critical of the Senate's resolution of the issue, arguing that it "would bypass the organization, expertise, and experience of the States and would, instead, provide a full-fledged Federal bureaucracy in Washington to administer the program."[41] And, in particular, it was argued that many governors and other state representatives "deplored the duplication and second guessing that could go on if the [EPA] Administrator could unilaterally veto the State decision"; indeed, the argument was construed as the federal government's failure to trust the states.[42]

As a result, the House legislation, unlike its Senate counterpart, did not provide for EPA veto of individual permits issued by approved state programs (save in the case that a downstream state objected to the permit's issuance). While the EPA could rescind the whole state regulatory program if it were found to be inadequately enforcing the law, critics of the House bill argued with at least one governor, Wendell Anderson of Minnesota, that "the EPA Administrator should not have to veto a State's total program just to get at permits granted improperly to a couple of polluters."[43] Many felt that once individual states were given charge of the program, even under substantial violation of its terms the EPA might "find it politically distasteful to compel a State to comply with the law."[44] But an amendment offered by Reuss to provide for EPA veto of individual,

[41] Comments of Representative Sikes, *House Debate on H.R. 11896*, March 29, 1972. In *Legislative History*, p. 739.
[42] Comments of Representative Roe, *House Debate on H.R. 11896*, March 28, 1972. In *Legislative History*, pp. 578–9.
[43] In support of EPA veto rights, Anderson further testified in House hearings on the bill, "I suggest that every Governor in the country knows what is the greatest political barrier to effective pollution control. It is the threat of our worst polluters to move their factories out of any State that seriously tries to protect its environment. It is the practice of playing off one state against the other. It is the false but strident cry of the polluter that clean air and water mean fewer jobs.... My message to you today is this: the answer to threats is uniformity [of regulation]." See House Debate on H.R. 11896, March 27, 1972. In *Legislative History*, p. 452.
[44] "Additional Views of Hon. Bella S. Abzug and Charles B. Rangel," in *Legislative History*, p. 870.

state-issued permits failed on the floor of the House (154 for, 251 against). Interestingly, despite his own governor's (Anderson) strong support for it, Congressman Blatnik, long the recognized House leader on water pollution control, voted against the veto.

Finally, in a number of respects the House bill relaxed the enforcement provisions contained in the Senate amendments. First, while both bodies made *administrative* orders to correct violations mandatory upon discovery of them, the House made more consequential *civil* court enforcement of violations a discretionary matter for the EPA administrator; the Senate language had made such legal actions mandatory (e.g., when an order is violated). (Both units had provided for criminal penalties for willful or negligent violations of the law.) Second, while the Senate bill permitted the administrator to prosecute both civil and criminal cases should the Justice Department choose not to enforce EPA referrals, the House provision allowed the EPA this option only in civil cases; if Justice should choose not to pursue a criminal case referred by the agency, there could be no criminal prosecution. This limitation would become the source of substantial friction between the EPA and Justice, as later discussed. Last, the House bill restricted citizen suits (against violators or the EPA should the agency fail to carry out its nondiscretionary duties under the law) to those members of the geographic area who have a "direct interest" in the violation, or to those who have already demonstrated their interest through prior involvement in the administrative proceedings involving a case. The Senate had provided that *anyone* could bring such suits regardless of geographic location or the nature of the interest involved.[45]

[45] On these contrasts see generally the *Conference Report* in the *Legislative History*, particularly in reference to §§ 309 ("Federal Enforcement," pp. 314–15), 505 ("Citizen Suits," pp. 328–9), and 506 ("Appearance," p. 329). While the *Conference Report* indicates that both civil and criminal authority were made discretionary as against mandatory requirements in the Senate version, it appears that the change in fact only pertained to civil enforcement. The final version of the FWPCA Amendments of 1972, which adopted the House version of Section 309, states that "any person who willfully or negligently violates section 301, 302, 306, 307, or 309 of this Act, or any permit condition or limitation implementing any of such sections in a permit issued under section 402 of this Act by the Administrator or by a State, *shall* be punished by a fine of not less than $2500 nor more than $25,000 per day of violation, or by imprisonment for not more than one year, or by both" (§ 309[c][1]; emphasis added). Thus, while discretion certainly remained in the determination of willfulness or negligence, the phrasing appears to make criminal charges mandatory upon such determination. See also the discussion of the matter in *Senate Consideration of the Report of the Conference Committee*, October 4, 1972, in *Legislative History*, p. 174, which notes the difference in the House and Senate versions as pertaining only to civil enforcement.

If the House bill was less stringent in its regulatory provisions than its Senate counterpart, it was also more munificent in its provision of federal funding for the construction of municipal waste treatment plants, a most attractive feature of the bill in many representatives' districts. The House amendments provided for $18 billion in federal construction grants over a three-year period (in contrast to the Senate bill's $14 billion over four years), to cover from 60 to 75 percent (the latter if the states contribute 15 percent) of the construction costs. The total price tag of the proposed legislation was an impressive $24.7 billion, an amount unprecedented in the annals of pollution control policy. After conducting forty-four days of committee hearings, compiling 4,000 pages of testimony (more than all of the previous testimony heard by the Public Works Committee in the history of the federal water pollution program),[46] and producing a 201-page bill, the House passed the legislation by a lopsided vote of 380 to 14 on March 29, 1972.

Opposition and support: the politics of complexity

Despite the concessions made against the Senate proposal, the Nixon administration also opposed the House measure. The terms of the opposition were outlined in a letter from EPA Administrator Ruckelshaus to Blatnik in December 1971, and seconded in a letter to Blatnik from George Shultz, then director of the president's Office of Management and Budget.[47] With respect to the bill's goals and strategies, the administration objected in principle to the "across-the-board application of the 'no discharge' goal," and even to the requirement of eventual application of BAT to all industrial sources.

These objections were framed in terms of the bill's inadequate consideration of the cost – benefit trade-offs to be considered, and of the states' rights to determine the most beneficial uses of its waterways (which, by implication, include their possible use as industrial waste receptacles). In terms of regulatory procedures, the administration requested a broadening of protection of confidential corporate information beyond trade secrets (to include financial and operations information, for example), and sought procedures for administrative review of individual permits challenged by compa-

[46] *Legislative History*, p. 351.
[47] The lengthy and detailed Ruckelshaus letter is reprinted in *Legislative History*, pp. 834–58. The brief Shultz concurrence is reprinted at p. 859.

nies. (These reviews would eventually be available and, for all their rationality, would contribute to regulatory bias in the administration of the statute, as discussed more fully in Chapter 7.) Finally, the administration objected to the proposed cost of the construction grant program, arguing that its own estimated need of $6 billion over three years was more reasonable, and resisted the maximum 75 percent federal government share in projects as too high (although no alternative ceiling was proposed in the correspondence). Without explanation, the administration also opposed the bill's authorization of $800 million to the Small Business Administration for loans to small companies to assist them in acquiring the technology requisite to compliance with the new law.

In light of this high-level resistance, it might appear somewhat paradoxical that only three months later, just as the House was preparing to debate the bill on the floor in March 1972, H.R. 11896 received an endorsement from a powerful source, the National Association of Manufacturers (NAM). In a letter urging member companies to contact their congressmen to resist liberal changes to the house bill (particularly proposals to eliminate the contingency of further study and legislation before BAT requirements were levied), NAM representative M. P. Gullander wrote that, "H.R. 11896 would establish a tough, but realistic program for progress in water pollution control, whereas S. 2770 [the Senate version] could actually impede such progress through shifting and unrealistic requirements imposing tremendous costs to manufacturers. For this reason, H.R. 11896 is highly preferable to S. 2770."[48] Of course, it is likely that NAM, and large corporate business generally, recognizing the virtual certainty of substantial new legislation in the highly charged political climate, found the House compromise a tolerable burden to bear, and simply chose to ride this sure horse in an uncertain race that had to be run. It was more curious, in fact, that the administration – for all of President Nixon's early rhetoric and proposals – appeared not to see how near the finish line this race was.

The Federal Water Pollution Control Act Amendments of 1972

The momentum behind strong water pollution control legislation crested in October 1972, when both the Senate and House convened

[48] "You Must Act Now on This Water Pollution Control Bill," Letter from M. P. Gullander, National Association of Manufacturers, to U.S. companies. Reprinted in *Legislative History*, pp. 709–10.

to consider the final version of the amendments that had been worked out in conference between the two units. The Conference Report[49] itself offers no insight into the dynamics underlying the outcome of the committee's work, although the record suggests the committee experienced a particularly arduous process working out the differences in the two bills: it met thirty-nine times over a period of five months.[50] The final result was substantially more like the Senate's aggressive approach than the House's more modest proposal.

Certainly the conferees were impressed by the ever-rising public sentiment behind environmentalism; indeed, the House bill had come under considerable fire from the press for its retrenchment from the standard set by the Senate, a critique perhaps all the more salient in an election year. Then, too, there was the appeal of responding forcefully to a widespread public demand; with Big Government under increasing assault for the nation's highly divisive role in Vietnam, here was an opportunity to reclaim the image of efficacy and service for a centralized state. Some horse trading likely occurred: in exchange for more stringent regulatory measures, House members and their respective states gained the "consolation" of substantial federal resources for construction of municipal sewage treatment plants. The final version of the amendments provided for $18 billion over three fiscal years (1973–75) for construction grants to municipalities (Sec. 207), as had the House bill. This pot was sweetened beyond even the liberal terms of the House measure when the conferees agreed that the federal share of construction costs would be 75 percent in all cases; no state matching funds would be required whatsoever (Sec. 202).[51]

Whatever the precise dynamics, after nearly two years of consideration neither House nor Senate wasted much time in further deliberations on the matter. On October 4, 1972, the Senate passed the amendments with a strong sense of statement: 74–0. Given the earlier resistance, the House vote taken the same day was even more compelling: 366–11.

[49] Reprinted in *Legislative History*, pp. 281–339. For full citation, see fn. 25 above.
[50] *Senate Consideration of the Report of the Conference Committee*, October 4, 1972, in *Legislative History*, p. 161.
[51] Indeed, it has been suggested elsewhere that the *distributive* effects of the 1972 amendments – the "pork barrel" provision of large sums of federal monies for local needs – undergirded the strong congressional support for the law as much as, if not more than, the more straightforward *regulatory* aspects of the bill. See, e.g., Sabatier (1975: 331 [fn. 27]).

The 1972 amendments to the Federal Water Pollution Control Act, eighty-eight pages of legislation denoted as Public Law 92-500,[52] comprised a detailed, ambitious, and unprecedented environmental program providing for the control of both industrial and municipal water pollution, federal funding for construction and research, a radically new system of penalties for infractions, public participation in the law's administration, and "whistle blower" protection for employees reporting violations of the law, among numerous other provisions.

Mandated effluent controls at the factory. The centerpiece, of course, was the national permit program mandating technology-forcing standards of pollution control for all industrial facilities. (This discussion will leave aside those aspects of the law directed solely to municipal treatment works.) In this, the final version more resembled the Senate proposal. The law required that by July 1, 1977, all industrial plants were to achieve that level of discharge which indicates "the application of the best practicable control technology currently available" (BPT), and by July 1, 1983, that level which indicates the use of "the best available technology economically achievable" (BAT) (Sec. 301). The EPA was to require *new* industrial facilities to install BAT controls (Sec. 306), and controls more stringent than BAT could be required if necessary to meet prevailing water quality standards for a given waterway (Sec. 302). Section 307 of the law mandated pollution control limitations ("pretreatment standards") for companies discharging wastes into municipal treatment plants (where such pollutants "are determined not to be susceptible to treatment by such treatment works or . . . would interfere with the operation of such treatment works"). Finally, the legislation freed the EPA from the deadlock imposed by the *Kalur* decision (Chapter 4) by expressly exempting the process of issuing discharge permits from the complex requirements of the National Environmental Policy Act of 1969, except in the case of permits for new sources of pollution (Sec. 511 [c] [1]).

The EPA was permitted to veto individual state-issued discharge permits (Sec. 402), and the BAT requirement for 1983 was not contingent upon further study and congressional action. However, in partial concession to the House, the law called for a nonpartisan National Study Commission to report within three years of

---

[52] For the full citation, see footnote 40.

passage on the projected economic, environmental and social effects of the BAT standard (Sec. 315), and the amendments decreed the elimination by 1985 of all water pollution discharges into navigable waters to be a "national goal" rather than a matter of "policy" (Sec. 101).

Environment and economy: the uncertain costs of control. Inserted in the phrasing of BPT ("practicable") and BAT ("economically achievable") were the practical considerations of the *costs* of potential controls, including the economic ones. If polluted water had clearly become costly, so too would be the achievement of clean water. Implicit in the question of reaching the "national goal," therefore, was the notion of cost–benefit assessments of progressively stringent regulation.

The discussion of such assessments in the law and the legislative history is rather ambiguous and, at places, virtually indecipherable. The matter was left rather clearer with respect to BPT. Here, the implementing regulations (specifying discharge limits) for each industrial category were to be formulated in "consideration of the total cost of application of technology in relation to the effluent reduction benefits to be achieved"; other factors to be considered were the age and productive processes of the facilities, and the total environmental impact (including energy requirements affected) of the regulations (Sec. 304 [b] [1] [B]). In discussion of the bill on the floor of the House, the nature of this cost–benefit assessment was further defined. While on the one hand costs were to be broadly construed to include not only the financial costs to regulated companies, but also to the general economy in terms of such factors as unemployment and rural economic development,[53] on the other hand the balancing of costs and benefits was to constrain the definition of BPT only where the marginal gain in pollution control was "wholly out of proportion to the costs" of achieving it.[54] If the

[53] *House Consideration of the Report of the Conference Committee,* October 4, 1972, in *Legislative History,* p. 231.

[54] *Senate Consideration of the Report of the Conference Committee,* October 4, 1972, in *Legislative History,* p. 170. The language used to interpret this cost–benefit issue is noticeably different in tone as beween the two congressional bodies. The Senate analysis emphasizes the marginal role that such assessments should have in drawing regulations to limit pollution, while the House (see material at footnote 53) discussion is more concerned that all of the costs – micro and macro – are attended to in the end. While these are not necessarily contradictory positions, the divergence corresponds closely to the philosophical differences motivating the original bills in each unit.

key phrase lacked precision, the implication was that such "balancing tests" were themselves to be "weighted" toward the goal of progressive effluent limitations; moreover, like the regulations themselves they were to be conducted only for *whole categories of industry rather than for individual plants*: the impact of the regulations on single facilities was not to be factored into the equation.

The record is considerably less clear on the matter of determining BAT pollution controls for industry categories. In specifying the factors to be taken into account the law (Sec. 304 [b] [2] [B]) essentially replicates the terms used for BPT, except that it omits the language explicitly calling for consideration of costs "in relation to" benefits (see above). So while the section explicitly states that "the cost of achieving such effluent reduction" is to be taken into account, it remained entirely unclear how this accounting was to be made.

Nor is the legislative history helpful on the question; indeed, it further obfuscates the matter. The record from the more conservative House discussion notes that in establishing BAT regulations, "EPA must consider whether such application is economically achievable by the category or class of industries affected, and, at the same time, will result in reasonable progress toward the national goal of eliminating all water pollution."[55] And if the implications of that are less than obvious, the statement is a model of clarity compared to that of the more aggressive Senate. In expressly ruling out the requirement of a "balancing" of costs and benefits, the Senate interpretation noted that the EPA should undertake the consideration of costs through a "test of reasonableness. In this case, the reasonableness of what is 'economically achievable' should reflect an evaluation of what needs to be done to move toward the elimination of the discharge of pollutants and what is achievable through the application of available technology – *without regard to cost.*"[56] Such linguistic contortions and vagueness suggest the political effects on legislators' rationality of the fundamental contradiction between the forceful moral push toward environmental purity and the political economic pull of extant relations of production. Whatever their source, at best they promise substantial discretion for the agency; at worst, they invite protracted litigation on the law, threatening

[55] *House Consideration of the Report of the Conference Committee*, October 4, 1972, in *Legislative History*, p. 238.
[56] *Senate Consideration of the Report of the Conference Committee*, October 4, 1972, in *Legislative History*, p. 170; emphasis added.

progress whether reasonable or otherwise. In fact, much litigation was in store for EPA's regulations implementing this complex and often opaque law.

Enforcement and equity. On the matter of enforcement, the final version of the amendments retained the House's view that court action, particularly civil cases, would remain discretionary with the EPA (administrative orders for offenses would be mandatory, however) (Sec. 309), and that the Justice Department (rather than the agency) would have the final say in whether to criminally prosecute given cases (Sec. 506). Nevertheless, the bill maintained the maximum criminal penalties of $25,000 per day of violation and one year's incarceration ($50,000 and two years for repeat offenses) (Sec. 309), and defined citizens' rights to sue (violators or the EPA) in terms broader than the House's definition of standing (while more restrictive than the Senate's). The provision defined a citizen as "a person or persons having an interest which is or may be adversely affected" (Sec. 505 [g]), and the legislative history makes clear the affected interests include "aesthetic, conservational and recreational as well as economic values,"[57] a phrase drawn from the recent Supreme Court decision in *Sierra Club v. Morton*.[58]

Finally, the legislation took an interest in the equitable impacts of the bill. Despite the administration's opposition, it maintained the $800 million authorization for loans to small businesses trying to comply with the act (Sec. 8). It also mandated that industrial plants discharging their wastes into a municipal treatment plant pay user fees to cover their share of the maintenance and operation of the plant, as well as reimbursement for a proportionate share of the federal grant for its construction (Sec. 204). The latter provision was intended to eliminate much of the long-standing government subsidies of such dischargers; as later evidence would indicate, however, it failed to achieve the desired effect (see Chapter 6).

A presidential veto, and beyond

The strong congressional action on the amendments set up a final confrontation with the Nixon administration. As dramatic as it

[57] *Senate Consideration of the Report of the Conference Committee*, October 4, 1972, in *Legislative History*, pp. 220–21.
[58] 40 U.S.L.W. 4397, 3 ERC 2039, 2 ELR 20192 (1972).

proved to be, with its midnight veto and early morning roll call in the face of the election, the conflict was even more impressive in underscoring the complex political dynamics at the heart of the issue. For while the president continued to resist the legislation, his position was now being undercut by his own experts in the area: Ruckelshaus of EPA and the Council on Environmental Quality.

Certainly on the record Ruckelshaus had made a dramatic shift, indeed. Where he had earlier registered substantial objections to the relatively diluted House bill, presumably reflecting the administration's thinking, he now moved to urge the president to support the more rigorous version of the amendments finally passed by the Congress. It is not inconceivable that this drama was highly choreographed, designed in the White House to permit both the president and the EPA to "keep faith" with their strong constituencies among conservatives (fiscal and regulatory) and environmentalists, respectively, in the face of a bill virtually destined to become law. However, the record suggests instead a more structural (rather than instrumental) interpretation of this development. In this view, the EPA administrator simply read the political situation accurately and determined that it was not in the institutional interests of the nation's leading environmental agency to resist obviously needed protective legislation. If the legitimacy of the state sometimes comes into historic and analytic view as a unitary phenomenon, the precarious legitimacy of its separate and numerous component parts creates many more occasions requiring political repairs, which often defy the simple instrumental control of the executive.[59]

This interpretation is suggested by Ruckelshaus's tendency to appeal to the swell of popular support for environmentalism rather than to conventional political arrangements. It is also suggested by the extraordinarily lengthy and detailed letter he sent on October 11 urging the president to support the water pollution control

---

[59] The complexity of the state bears a contradictory relation to its periodic legitimation crises. To the extent that such complexity defies centralized, rationalized control, it creates problems of uncertainty, coordination, and contradiction that – under particular historical conditions – might come to undermine the state's legitimacy as a whole. However, an even more likely prospect is that the political damage of periodic legitimation crises is contained in part *by the very fact of this complexity*: in the labyrinthine organization of the modern democratic state, problems or crises often "appear" in one or more of the countless subunits, on which therefore popular attention and demands are typically focused (rather than on the state as a whole). But even this "solution" of the "containment of crises" remains problematic for the state, precisely to the extent that the individual solutions to such local crises defy simple rationalization and control by central authorities.

amendments.[60] By no other logic than the purely political, he appears to have simply set aside his earlier objections to the regulatory provisions and focused instead on such factors as the bill's inclusion of cost considerations in the setting of pollution control standards and that the 1985 goal of "no discharge" was not legally binding. As against his earlier opposition to BAT, even in the House measure tying it to further legislation upon additional research on its effects, he noted approvingly that such research would be conducted even though BAT would now be required by this law independent of the outcome of the study. (Congress would need to pass subsequent legislation to *remove* BAT requirements if it so decided on the basis of research or otherwise.)

In addition, the administrator now argued that the costs of the legislation, both fiscal and economic, were quite tolerable. Not only was the federal funding of municipal treatment works roughly in line with the administration's estimates of national needs, he wrote, but financial "obligations in the near-term can generally be restricted to only those projects necessary to meet the Administration's commitment to fund facilities required to achieve water quality standards"[61] (the larger expenditures coming in fiscal years 1976–81 as authorized funds are spent on actual projects), and the House had added language permitting the president flexibility in determining the actual annual expenditures.[62]

Moreover, in response to concerns over the economic impact of the regulatory provisions, he emphasized research done jointly by EPA, CEQ, and the Commerce Department suggesting quite limited effects. Not only did the research indicate that less than 0.05 percent of the nation's workforce would lose jobs due to plant closings, but Ruckelshaus went on to note that, "we expect [this] to be offset by greater demand in the control equipment and construction industries. Of the forecasted 200 to 300 plant closures caused by pollution control measures in the 1972 to 1976 time period, nearly all would have occurred by 1980 anyway because of the plants' marginal economic efficiency."[63] He also noted that the bill largely reflected the administration's own approach, that without it the administra-

---

[60] "Letter from William Ruckelshaus, Administrator of the Environmental Protection Administration [sic], To the Office of Management and Budget, October 11, 1972, Recommending Presidential Approval of S. 2770, The Federal Water Pollution Control Act Amendments of 1972." Reprinted in *Legislative History*, pp. 143–58.
[61] *Legislative History*, pp. 155–6.
[62] *Legislative History*, p. 153.
[63] *Legislative History*, p. 156.

tion's permit program (formulated originally under the Refuse Act) would die under the *Kalur* decision, thereby wasting over $100 million in industry expenditures already made in preparing permit applications and incurring the large future costs of delay, indirection, and a porous credibility.

Nonetheless, shortly before midnight on October 17, Nixon vetoed the bill, citing its "unconscionable $24 billion price tag," one that he argued was well beyond the bounds of "the strict discipline of a responsible fiscal policy – *a policy which recognizes as the highest national priority the need to protect the working men and women of America against tax increases and renewed inflation.*"[64] (While the president's message makes no mention of the regulatory characteristics of the law, his earlier resistance, in combination with his own administrator's estimates of the modest fiscal impacts to be expected, strongly suggests their relevance to his veto.) The timing of the veto resulted from a "showdown" occasioned by the Congress's original intention to adjourn on October 17 for the election recess:

> If Congress adjourned before midnight on the 17th, and the President did not sign the bill, it would not become law under the "pocket veto" provision of the Constitution. If Congress did not adjourn on the 17th, the bill would become law without the President's signature. The proponents of the water pollution bill decided they would not let Congress adjourn before midnight, believing that they had the votes to override the President if, at the last moment, he decided to veto the bill. (Davies and Davies, 1975: 43)

And so they did. At 1:30 the morning of October 18, the Senate voted 52–12 to override the veto. Later that day the House followed suit, 247–23.

The passage of law

The Congress had succeeded in passing a major, even revolutionary piece of legislation. But if the legislature in the end had responded appropriately enough to the climate of the times, the story of the law's unfolding is one that highlights the curiously contingent, contradictory, and even irrational elements in much of state policymaking as much as it suggests the rational calculation of means

---

[64] "Message from the President of the United States Returning Without Approval the Bill (S. 2770) Entitled 'The Federal Water Pollution Control Act Amendments of 1972'," October 17, 1972. Reprinted in *Legislative History*, 137–9.

to ends. The social fabric of lawmaking proved, in this case as
so frequently, to be a complex and unique weave, crafted of often
changing threads and with an uncertain durability. In hindsight
the matter stands out in even greater relief: among the legislation's supporters in 1972 were two individuals who were later leaders in an administration with a quite different attitude toward environmental regulation: Governor Ronald Reagan of California
and Representative Jack Kemp, both of whom at the time found
substantial benefits in the new law for their respective states' constituencies.[65]

For all of its contingencies and uncertainties, this episode of lawmaking broadly suggests itself as the result of a historic structuring
of forces and interests, albeit often embedded in contradictory relations to each other. Thus, for example, the role of NIPCC better
illustrates the state's structural dependence on the economic stability and goodwill of private capital than it suggests instrumental corporate control of public policy. While the president's establishment
of NIPCC surely indicates something of the administration's own
dependence on a vital constituency, it also represents the broader
reliance of both state and civil society on stable economic relations
generally. Moreover, it was a *reaction* to the structure of broad social
forces pushing for dramatic legal change; as such, it was a response
whose effects were themselves constrained within the limits of political economy. Of course, the legislature's actions were as well: absent
NIPCC and other forms of corporate and political pressure, the
Congress would nonetheless have implemented significant economic
safeguards for the private sector in the language of the new law.

The formal statements of law are, at their best, simply a com-
mencement (at worst, if uncommonly, a cynical charade), and the
complexities and uncertainties entailed in their making are typically
reproduced in their implementation. Far from the intrigue, postur-

[65] To judge from their statements, both men were attracted to the federal financial
support for cleanup in their respective states. In the context of the deliberations in
the House, a reprinted telegram from Reagan urging the California delegation to
support the House version of the law (*Legislative History*, pp. 345–6) suggests that
he found it superior to the Senate version because of its more favorable treatment
of construction grants rather than for its less stringent regulatory provisions.
Kemp, later known more for his strong support of "supply-side" economics during
the Reagan administration in the 1980s than for advocating the president's deregulatory thrust per se (although of course the two policy positions are linked),
spoke to both the fiscal (grants) and regulatory advantages of the final legislation,
specifically in connection with the troubled condition of the Great Lakes (*Legislative History*, pp. 275–6).

ing, and publicity of drafting law are the (only apparently) more prosaic facts of *applying* law. There is drama here as well, certainly politics, but it is played in more subtle forms of discourse and less visible forums of exchange. Nonetheless, it is in implementation that the law finally defines itself and the social order of which it is part.

CHAPTER 6

Controls and constraints: from law to regulation

The implementation of law is forged in the complex interplay of bureaucratic policy, court interpretations, and the forms of private compliance, a dialectic shaped by the forces evolving in the wider political economy. While true of law generally, the process of implementation is particularly dynamic and uncertain when the statutory guidance is culturally novel – threatening long-established patterns and relations – and technically complex from the standpoints of law, science, administration, or any combination of these. The complexity of law assures the vital play of discretionary judgment, while its novelty promises a key role to relations of power in the exercise of that judgment. Thus the implementation of law is inherently contingent and always problematic.

If novelty and complexity characterized much of the regulatory law drawn to control business behavior in the 1960s and 1970s, they did so nowhere more than in the 1972 amendments to the Federal Water Pollution Control Act. As I have already suggested, the Congress's vagueness regarding the ways and means of the law's "core technology" – the establishment of effluent controls for a multitude of industries and individual pollutants – meant that it was delegating key political decisions not only to the prominent office of the EPA administrator, but more important, to the less visible cadres of experts, legal, scientific and technical, down the agency's professional ranks. There, in the often arcane workings of bureaucracy, would the law finally be defined and the limits of its impact determined.

At the broadest level of social relations, the balance of institutional pressure on the agency, as originally on the Congress, was to demonstrate quick resolve and show rapid results. And focus on near term performance can contradict longer term policy aims, however impressive the immediate impact. Indeed, parallel to the concern among some in the Congress that the statute's focus on conventional technologies (particularly with respect to first-phase best practicable technology [BPT] requirements) and end-of-pipe treatment would undercut the law's more ambitious goals, the EPA quickly focused its limited energies on the regulation of conventional pollutants at the expense of controls for the substantially more alarming and resistant toxic pollutants emanating in increasing amounts from the nation's factories.

Some historic irony attended this approach: while the quite limited earlier water pollution control efforts were directed at containing the most serious health risks then posed to the growing industrial society, at the very high point of the nation's environmental consciousness and centralized state control the EPA in the 1970s appeared to address its efforts more to many secondary problems, even aesthetic ones, than to the largest hazards now posed to human health (including the gene pool) by advanced industrial processes. Moreover, in their concentration on "point sources" of water pollution such as factory and municipal discharge pipes, the law and the agency unwittingly strengthened the logic of industry's later arguments that the additional cleanup that could be provided with the "best available technology" (BAT) was often not cost-effective, perhaps not even *fair*, from a societal standpoint. How could the large marginal costs required to eliminate the last 10–15 percent of factory waste be justified in light of the government's failure even to approach a solution to the high toll exacted on the nation's waters by such nonpoint sources of waste as urban and agricultural runoff carrying pesticide residues and other toxic materials? In these ways, the nation's new water pollution program would eloquently testify to the contradictory relations that link politics and policy, success in the former often undercutting the long-term rationality of the latter.

This is not to suggest the utter failure of EPA's implementation of the 1972 amendments. Indeed, I shall make the case that in many key respects the agency's policy decisions were reasonable, given the variety of constraints involved, and that it made progress against the tide of industrial water pollution, especially when contrasted with the theoretical alternative of no new controls whatsoever. But the story of this policymaking effort nicely illustrates the types of limits that commonly constrain regulatory initiatives of this sort, even under the facilitating conditions of strong public support and sincere administrative leadership. Along the way, it suggests not only that

the analytic distinction between command-and-control and negotiated compliance regulatory strategies is more theoretical than real
(which is not to say unhelpful), but also that negotiated resolutions
often go to the heart of apparently control-oriented law and can
vitiate its intended impact. The story also suggests that the dramatic
failure of environmental law in the early 1980s was not so much a
special case of subterfuge as it was a synergistic convergence of the
various limits long structured into the apparatuses of much regulatory law.

This chapter explores EPA rulemaking under the 1972 amendments. The concern is with, first, the logic of regulation – the translation of statutory commands into more or less workable rules for
compliance – and the limits that alternately shape and constrain
that logic, and, second, with the impacts of regulation. The rulemaking period traverses EPA's history from the Nixon and Ford administrations through the Reagan administration, conservative
governments positioned on either side of the Carter administration
that directed one of the most aggressive phases in the agency's work,
especially Carter's first two years in office. As such, this rulemaking
experience contrasts the enduring, structural limits on law with the
more situational, political constraints on its reach.

As against the EPA's rulemaking policies, Chapter 7 takes up in
detail the matter of the enforcement procedures by which the
agency selected and treated industrial violators of the new pollution
control law. Chapter 8 then assesses some of the lessons of the regulatory retrenchment at EPA that, contrary to what might be the
popular view, did not originate in the Reagan administration, which
nonetheless radically accelerated it. It began, instead, in the middle
of the Carter administration as a rapidly stagnating economy
gripped the nation and increasingly threatened to make a lame
duck of the president.

The requirements of rulemaking

In its enthusiasm for a dramatic response to water pollution, the
Congress had laid at the feet of the EPA a draconian regulatory
burden. From the start it promised at least some measure of failure with respect to the law's stated goals. The EPA inherited the
impressive and complicated responsibility both for creating the
scientific and technical foundations and for developing the detailed implementing regulations and procedures for a massive

environmental program that was without precedent (cf., Rosenbaum, 1977: 125).

The scope of the assignment was immense. The statute required that the agency make the complex and politically sensitive determinations of BPT and BAT for all types of industry within a year of the law's passage, and issue water pollution control discharge permits implementing the regulations to tens of thousands of individual polluting facilities within two years.[1] Given this regulatory burden, it is not surprising that the EPA missed many of the key deadlines specified in the law.

The law itself identified twenty-eight basic industrial categories to be regulated (inorganic chemicals, iron and steel, petroleum refining, textile mills, dairy product processing, to name a few), and required EPA to revise the list, resulting in the addition of another eighteen categories (fish hatcheries, asphalt-paving, and coal mining among others). But because of the manufacturing process differences within these broad categories, and the resulting differences in pollutants, the EPA eventually developed more then 500 subcategories of industry, for each of which separate technology-based pollution control regulations had to be promulgated.[2] In addition, the law required the agency to write regulations for new sources of pollution in the various industrial categories, such as factories built after the regulations were issued. Because such facilities could more easily incorporate the most advanced techniques of pollution control, these new source standards could be more stringent than BAT: they were to require "the best available demonstrated control technology, processes, operating methods, or other alternatives, including, where practicable, a standard permitting no discharge of pollutants" (Sec. 306).

Finally, the law required the agency to establish regulations setting pretreatment standards for industrial pollutants being discharged into municipal treatment works, but which are not susceptible to, or which interfere with, such works (Sec. 304[f][1]). The 1972 amendments gave the agency four months past the act's passage to accomplish this. But the EPA only finalized its regulations in June of 1978, covering twenty-one industrial categories and

---

[1] The permit program mandated by the 1972 amendments was named the National Pollution Discharge Elimination System (NPDES). See the Federal Water Pollution Control Act Amendments of 1972, §402. The implementing regulations were published at 40 Code of Fed. Reg., Part 125 (Rev. July 1, 1977).

[2] See, e.g., the U.S. EPA booklet, *No Small Task: Establishing National Effluent Limitations Guidelines and Standards* (1976).

more than 87,000 industrial facilities discharging toxic effluents to public treatment works. At that point the agency was projecting that between 38,000 and 50,000 industrial dischargers should be in compliance with the pretreatment standards by 1983, fully ten years past the original deadline for promulgation.[3]

The pollution limits for industrial facilities making direct discharges into navigable waters had to be incorporated into massive numbers of individual permits. Not surprisingly, this job also proved too much to achieve within the statutory deadlines. For example, by February 1978 EPA and participating state agencies had received some 41,000 permit applications from nonmunicipal (largely industrial) dischargers, and had processed and issued 27,500 permits. Including municipal treatment plants and other dischargers, total applicants numbered 67,500, and almost 50,000 permits had been issued under the law.

The agency was to make all of these key policy decisions in a manner unusually open to public participation. In addition to the citizen suit provisions in the law, it required that the interested public be permitted to comment on all of the proposed effluent limitation guidelines for the many industrial categories, and even on the issuance of permits to individual polluting facilities. Beyond these deliberate procedures, there were avenues of appeal both internal and external (the courts) which were soon heavily used by both environmentalists and regulated parties. That final regulations and permit requirements for individual plants were often delayed by years, rather than merely by weeks or months, was a logical consequence of this structure of decision making, as well as of the vast numbers of complex determinations to be made.

[3] See the Bureau of National Affairs (BNA), "Costle Signs National Program for Pretreatment of Industrial Wastes," *BNA Environment Reporter – Current Developments* 9 (1978): 236–7.

The new water pollution law also required the agency to make a variety of other, often quite complex and detailed determinations within very tight time frames. For example, the EPA was to publish information within nine months on the ways and means for restoring the quality of the nation's publicly owned fresh water lakes (§ 304[i]), publish guidelines for public participation in the various phases of implementation (§ 101[e]), issue within six months guidelines on payment schedules for private sector users of public treatment works (§ 204[b][2]), and within a year water quality criteria that, among other things, reflected "the latest scientific knowledge on the kind and extent of all identifiable effects on health and welfare including, but not limited to, plankton, fish, shellfish, wildlife, plant life, shorelines, beaches, esthetics, and recreation which may be expected from the presence of pollutants in any body of water, including ground water" (§ 304[a][1][A]). As noted below, the agency had a few other statutes to interpret and enforce, as well.

Finally, despite the law's logic of a centralized, uniform policy of control, the agency in fact bestrode a much decentralized legal apparatus in implementing the terms of the water amendments. Many of the key decisions in issuing discharge permits and enforcing them were necessarily delegated to the EPA's ten regional headquarters staff, as well as to state authorities in those states authorized by the agency to administer the law under its guidance. By the end of the 1970s, thirty-two states had been granted such authority, while EPA enforced the permits in the rest.[4] Such delegation, necessary not only politically (in connection with states' rights) but fiscally, nonetheless involved the additional managerial burden of coordination and oversight, to say nothing of the potential it created for the uneven implementation of law (see the discussion of enforcement in Chapter 7).

It is worth mention that as the EPA was wrestling with this large and diverse workload, it was also vested with regulatory responsibility for the raft of other environmental laws passed during the decade, including the Clean Air Act (1970), the Noise Control Act (1972), the Federal Insecticide, Fungicide, and Rodenticide Act (amended 1972), the Safe Drinking Water Act (1974), the Resource Conservation and Recovery Act (1976), the Toxic Substances Control Act (1976), and the Comprehensive Environmental Response, Compensation, and Liability Act (1980).

During this period the agency faced a sociopolitical environment as much in need of careful management as the natural environment it was charged with protecting. A model of the "resource dependent" organization (cf., Pfeffer and Salancik, 1978), its successful functioning rested on a difficult series of exchanges with its multifarious external constituencies, in which the satisfaction of some would come at the consternation of others. From the Congress, and even from its own superiors in the Executive Branch, the EPA required substantial budgetary support and often a good measure of patience as it stumbled toward implementation of the statute. The agency required, too, the good faith cooperation of its bureaucratic partners in the effort, particularly the Justice Department and the state agencies that were to participate in enforcing the law. Wide public approval was necessary to support both budgetary levels and agency pressure on industry and municipalities. And the cooperation of industry itself was vital to the effort, both because of the

---

[4] BNA, "EPA Approves Alabama Request to Administer NPDES Program," *BNA Environment Reporter – Current Developments* 10 (1979): 1484–5.

agency's dependence on business for the key information and knowledge necessary for regulation, and because, as is true of controls generally, voluntary compliance was ultimately key to the legislation's success.

Given this delicate configuration of interests to be managed, some delay and dilution in the regulatory effort were assured. The only serious remaining question was how deep the ultimate compromises would cut, and with what consequences for stable relations between environment and economy.

Budgets, discretion, and bias

At the level of appearances, the EPA might have seemed fully up to its various responsibilities. By the middle of the decade, it was an impressive and rapidly growing bureaucracy, dwarfing most other regulatory agencies and larger even than several cabinet departments (Rosenbaum, 1977: 124). For example, by fiscal year 1974, the agency's budget was $629 million and it had some 9,200 employees,[5] up from $289 million and roughly 6,000 employees in 1971. A congressional study of government regulation found that at mid-decade, the EPA's budget was 75 percent greater than the *combined* budgets of eight other major federal regulatory agencies, including the Food and Drug Administration, the Federal Trade Commission, the Securities and Exchange Commission, and the consumer Product Safety Commission (U.S. House of Representatives, 1976: 116).[6] Total federal spending for environmental programs had increased roughly 210 percent between 1973 and 1978, while spending for all federal programs increased 79 percent. In addition, the federal government subsidized the installation of private-sector pollution controls by providing for tax-free pollution control bonds; for 1978 alone this subsidy was estimated to be $320 million.[7]

The agency's budget has always been inadequate to meet its growing regulatory responsibilities, however; the only variable over time has been the extent of its fiscal shortfalls. The congressional study

[5] BNA, "EPA Seeks More Money, Personnel, Appeals to Carter's Campaign Stands," *BNA Environment Reporter – Current Developments* 7 (1977): 1539–40.
[6] The other agencies were the Federal Communications Commission, the National Highway Traffic Safety Administration, the Interstate Commerce Commission, and the Federal Power Commission.
[7] BNA, "Special Analysis of Federal Environmental Programs from the President's Budget Request for Fiscal 1978," *BNA Environment Reporter – Current Developments* 7 (1977): 1423–4.

just mentioned made the point by noting the agency's small size relative to the industrial sector it regulates: for example, the Shell Oil Company's 1975 sales for agricultural and other chemicals alone came to more than one-quarter of EPA's 1975 budget (U.S. House of Representatives, 1976: 159).

But it is also underscored in the agency's annual difficulties in securing adequate funding authorizations from the president and the Congress. If the Republican administrations of Nixon and Ford had kept the agency on an especially short budgetary leash, and the more liberal Carter government had been more munificent, the agency was constantly strained for resources, and even more so as its statutory responsibilities leapt forward in the middle part of the decade.

This is evident in comparing the respective EPA budgets proposed for fiscal 1978 by Presidents Ford and Carter.[8] In his final budget offering, President Ford had proposed an operating budget of $803 million for EPA, up $28 million from 1977, and an increase of 130 positions, to 9,680. The proposal represented an increase for the toxic substances and solid waste programs, but much of this additional effort would come at the expense of actual cuts in other key programs, water law enforcement and research and development, to name two key ones.

For example, during this period the EPA was changing its focus from writing industry-wide water pollution control regulations and issuing the tens of thousands of individual permits, to mounting its effort to enforce against the expected permit violations. To accommodate this new workload, the agency had requested 271 additional positions for water enforcement personnel. The Ford administration's response was to ask for a *cut* of 99 positions in such personnel, suggesting a very soft approach to the ultimate matter of enforcing the law. An agency spokesperson noted at the time that, as a result,

---

[8] For discussion and analysis of these budget proposals, see the various reports in *BNA Environment Reporter – Current Developments* 7 (1977), at pp. 1395–6, 1423–9, 1539–40, 1554–7, 1587, 1590, 1629–30, and 1685; also 8 (1977), p. 788.

For Carter's EPA budgets for 1979 and 1980, see, e.g., *BNA Environment Reporter – Current Developments* 8 (1978), at pp. 1451–2, 1455, 1475–87; 9 (1978–79), pp. 1098, 1763–4, 1794–1806.

For his part, President Nixon had impounded billions of dollars of public waste treatment grant funds, a practice the Supreme Court found illegal (see 7 ERC 1497, 7 ERC 1501). Senator Muskie argued that the Ford administration had in effect continued such impoundments by restricting the EPA's personnel numbers well below those needed to manage its expanding regulatory responsibilities. See *BNA Environment Reporter – Current Developments* 7 (1977): 1539.

the EPA was considering contracting out to private firms much of the inspection and monitoring of polluting factories, an alternative he argued not only raised substantial legal questions but would increase the cost of inspections and therefore reduce their number and, in consequence, the number of enforcement actions the agency could take. In all, the president had recommended that EPA's water quality program be cut an estimated $20 million, not only vitiating the enforcement program but threatening the development of the program to control toxic water pollution, which the agency was only slowly evolving at any rate.

Ford's own EPA administrator, Russell Train, criticized the budget request as "inadequate" in testimony before the Senate Public Works Committee, and said that given the agency's growing workload its personnel shortages were "severe" and were reaching "crisis proportions."[9] At the end of January 1977, acting EPA administrator John Quarles, formerly the agency's enforcement chief, wrote to incoming President Carter's director of the Office of Management and Budget (OMB), Bert Lance, asking that the new administration reverse the "highly restrictive posture" of the Ford administration regarding EPA budgeting. Quarles wrote that, "Past decisions have seriously hampered the agency," and argued that "the present fiscal 1978 budget for EPA is not credible. Now is the ideal time to signal a change in policy and to put a Presidential priority on EPA's basic environmental missions."[10] Several days later twenty-seven members of the House of Representatives complained to Lance: "we find once again that EPA's budget is being kept at unrealistically low levels by OMB."[11]

Having campaigned in part on his pro-environment positions, Carter responded by proposing increases for the agency of $116 million ($41 million increase for the 1978 fiscal year, the remainder to be applied to the 1977 budget) and 600 positions (for a total of 10,150), to be assigned at the administrator's discretion. The budget was subsequently approved at roughly $849 million, the largest single portion – $215 million, roughly the same as in 1977 – going for water quality programs (which also drew the largest number of personnel, 3,166, compared to 1,790 for air, 1,006 for pesticides, and

[9] BNA, "Ford Proposes EPA Budget Increase, Long-term Construction Grants Funding," *BNA Environment Reporter – Current Developments* 7 (1977): 1395–6.

[10] BNA, "EPA Seeks More Money, Personnel, Appeals to Carter's Campaign Stands," *BNA Environment Reporter – Current Developments* 7 (1977): 1539–40.

[11] BNA, "Carter's Fiscal 1978 Budget Seen Boosting Funding, Staffing for EPA," *BNA Environment Reporter – Current Developments* 7 (1977): 1587.

314 for toxic substances).[12] Much of these new resources would be slated for the two new programs placed under EPA's jurisdiction by the Toxic Substances Control Act and the Resource Conservation and Recovery Act, as well as to enforcement.

But given EPA's growing workload, even this budget remained scant. Testifying before the Senate Environment and Public Works Committee, Quarles noted that while the 600-person increase in agency staff would be the largest in the EPA's history, and would permit the agency to forgo the unwanted option of contracting with private organizations for some of the vital enforcement activity, it was still a marginal budget: the agency had initially requested an additional 2,700 positions and a $350 million budget increase.[13] Thus even the 1978 supplemental appropriations of $155 million (including $94.5 million for water quality programs) and 66 new positions, bringing the annual EPA operating funds to $1.004 billion, left a still highly restrictive budget in what would soon enough come to be seen as "the best of times" for the agency in terms of resource support. Indeed, only a year later, Carter's budget for fiscal 1979 called for an increase of only $5 million for the EPA's regulatory work under the water pollution law, while Senator Muskie argued that the necessary increase was $63 million.[14]

Budgetary shortfalls necessarily shape the adequacy of regulation, among other things forcing administrators to create priorities as to which of its many regulatory programs it will emphasize, decisions that commonly respond to the shifting political winds of the time. Tight budgets not only shape the exercise of discretionary judgment, but also increase the realm of its application. As the House report on federal regulation noted, "The tighter the budget, the more important is the discretionary element" (1976: 445). Among other matters, enlarged discretion raises questions of the judiciousness with which it is exercised.

The FWPCA amendments of 1972 intentionally left key areas of discretion to the legal, technical, and scientific experts at the EPA,

[12] See BNA, "Environmental Protection Agency Tables Showing Breakdown of Budget Authority, Staff Resources in Proposed Fiscal 1979 Budget" (with comparisons to 1978), *BNA Environment Reporter – Current Developments* 8 (1978): 1486–7.

[13] BNA, "EPA Lauds Carter Budget Increases as Significant, but Just First Step," *BNA Environment Reporter – Current Developments* 7 (1977), p. 1685; also, "Ford Proposes EPA Budget Increase, Long-term Construction Grants Funding," 7 (1977): 1395–6.

[14] BNA, "Carter Asks Congress to Increase EPA's Fiscal '79 Air, Water Budgets," *BNA Environment Reporter – Current Developments* 9 (1978): 8.

the definitions of "best practicable technology" and "best available technology" just two of the important matters at stake in the implementation of the law. But given the shortages of resources and time (because of the tight timetables established by the law), and certain limiting realities in political economy, the agency with the support of the courts also pried discretion into areas of policy that the Congress had apparently foreclosed to such interpretive work (see Tennille, 1977: 50,091–50,099; U.S. House of Representatives, 1977c; but cf., Tennille, 1978 on the enforcement question).

In the case of enforcement, for example, Section 309[a][3] of the act simply states that, upon a finding of any violation of the law or of a discharge permit, the EPA administrator "*shall* issue an order requiring such person to comply . . . , or he *shall* bring a civil action . . . " (emphasis added). In other words, the section clearly indicates that, at a minimum, the EPA is to respond to water pollution violations with either formal administrative orders or a civil suit for injunctive relief or monetary penalties or both.[15] The legislative history is also unusually clear on the point. In the Senate consideration of the conference committee report, it was noted that while the Senate had deferred to the House in not making civil enforcement mandatory, "the provisions requiring the Administrator to issue an abatement order whenever there is a violation were mandatory in both the Senate bill and the House amendment, and the Conference agreement contemplates that the Administrator's duty to issue an abatement order remains a mandatory one."[16]

Nonetheless, early on the EPA had instituted its own discretionary enforcement system for the water pollution law, with the *real* options ranging from criminal and civil actions, through administrative orders, to warning letters, phone calls, and even the formal decision to take no action at all. And while federal district court decisions split on the question of whether enforcement was mandatory under the 1972 amendments (U.S. House of Representatives, 1977c: 48–50), in 1977 a federal appellate court appeared to settle the matter when it determined that enforcement was discretionary.[17]

That discretionary enforcement has not since been seriously at

---

[15] For permits enforced by states certified to manage their own regulatory programs, the law provided the EPA with the option of making thirty-day notice to the state and the violator if the state failed to act on its own. After thirty days the EPA was required to issue its own order or civil suit if the state still failed to act. See Sec. 309[a][1].

[16] *Senate Consideration of the Report of the Conference Committee*, October 4, 1972. In *Legislative History*, p. 174.

[17] *Sierra Club v. Train*, 557 F. 2d 485, 489 (5th Cir. 1977).

issue is a measure of the strength of the institutional logic that demanded it. In the first place, this use of discretion spares precious resources: issuing formal, legal orders or filing suits for each permit violation would prove to be well beyond any level of enforcement resources to be reasonably expected, even in munificent times. Discretion permits the agency to first seek compliance by simple negotiation and warning, all that may be needed and warranted in some cases. In the second place, the policy allows the agency to maintain another precious commodity: credibility. If orders or suits were used for all infractions, even the minor, isolated, or inadvertent, over time the sanctions would tend to lose their legally compelling stature, diluted by overuse. Relying on them instead only for the more serious cases maintains their symbolic force. (For additional consideration of EPA's enforcement policies and practices, see Chapter 7.)

The other side of the coin of discretion in regulatory law is the question of whether (and how) discretionary decision making becomes systematically distorted, biased in the favor of some interests over others due to structured imbalances in power and influence. In the case of enforcement, for example, regulators may be more lenient or patient with more powerful violators, which by virtue of their greater resources might raise more difficult challenges to regulation should they come to feel unfairly cornered by aggressive law enforcement. With such offenders, the agency may be more prone to take a negotiating, compromising stance toward compliance rather than a harsh legal one (cf., Novick, 1975). The natural bureaucratic and professional interest in successful prosecution records suggests that this sort of bias is not at all unlikely, despite its potential consequences for policy impact (in this case the prospect of cleaner water) and notions of justice.

The next chapter offers an extended look at such issues in the matter of enforcement. But the questions of discretion and bias pervade all of regulatory work and are intimately linked in turn to the questions of law's limits and impacts. The remainder of this chapter explores aspects of these matters in EPA's translation of the statutory mandate into specific regulatory policy, and in consideration of the law's impacts by the end of the decade.

The rigor of regulation

The question of the effectiveness of social regulation, as of any public policy, often defeats easy answers. In water pollution control law this may appear nonproblematic, because the aim seems clear: clean water. At one level, this is so: we can measure our relative progress or failures in the pollution levels of individual waterways. But the issue quickly becomes murky, even turbulent, because *the definition of clean water is a political one*, entailing trade-offs between the perceived costs and benefits of given levels of water quality. The question, "how clean is clean," remains salient because disputes continue over the nature of water's often competing beneficial uses.

In one respect, the 1972 amendments offer a straightforward measure of the law's success: the goal of discharges uncontaminated by industrial and municipal pollutants. But the law also explicitly incorporates equity considerations in its directives, the balancing of ecological and economic interests in the formation of policy, suggesting that the goal was designed to serve more as a motivator than as an end. (Given the politics of legislation, this was more likely a synthetic result than an intended one.)

Because the question of clean water is necessarily political and philosophical, there may be little agreement on the assessment of the law's impacts. In recognition of the inevitable conflict the law would occasion, the Congress attempted to design an open, democratic regulatory *process* which, to the extent it was effective, would produce "socially optimum" outcomes by accurately balancing all relevant interests through fair procedures of fact finding and negotiation. In particular, the notice and comment procedures for all regulations and the provision for citizen suits to bolster enforcement of the law were intended to ensure that the agency did not become industry's representative in environmental disputes.[18]

Thus the question of legal impact involves consideration of both process and outcomes, the former having its own import in a democratic society in addition to its role in shaping the law's impact on the environment. If the question of the statute's success defies firm answers, at least the beginnings of an answer can be found in the apparent balances struck by this new set of policies as implemented by the EPA and shaped by the courts. In its broadest terms the issue resolves itself into this: To what extent does the law protect the public interest within the context of reasonably considered economic constraints?

---

[18] Arguably, too, the citizen suits were installed at the behest of a Democratic Congress intent on avoiding the dilution of the law by conservative Republican administrations, having witnessed Nixon's rollbacks of Great Society programs (Melnick, 1983: 8).

The process of regulation

Intervention by single interest groups has changed the character of the normal relationship between the regulated and the regulator.[19]

On the basis of its language alone, it would be difficult to decipher the meaning of this assessment offered of the EPA in late 1978. While it might be interpreted as praise for the agency's independence from industry (perhaps as a result of the work of the public-interest bar), in fact it was *the complaint of industry*, offered by the Monsanto Company's group vice president for environmental policy at the annual meeting of the American Institute of Chemical Engineers. Monte Throdahl argued that the shaping of this policy had become imbalanced, in effect captured by single-minded environmental groups, especially the litigators. While such groups had their "proper place," he said, "their role should be one of a 'watchdog' to observe and comment on the regulatory product, not to inject themselves into the 'nuts and bolts' of the process." The multilayered irony in this view was surely unintended.

On the one hand, of course, this stance can only be read as genuine. By this point, industry had spent tens of billions of dollars to comply with the environmental laws of the 1970s, particularly the clean air and water acts, and the statutes were continuing to push for ever greater levels of compliance. In addition, from the perspective of business, the EPA in the 1970s took an aggressive approach to regulation. For all the constraints on its activities, the agency had succeeded in implementing significant change in both social policy and industrial behavior.

With the installation of the Carter administration in 1977, the image of aggressive regulation was enhanced. During his campaign for the presidency, Carter had criticized the agency for weak regulation. He laid the blame for much of it at the feet of Republican administrations' use of the Office of Management and Budget to constrain the EPA's effectiveness by limiting its staffing and funding and by stalling regulations through cumbersome interagency review procedures. "From the beginning," Carter argued, "the White House hamstrung EPA's operations by appointing inexperienced and 'political' people into key policy-making positions. The President's Office of Management and Budget uses the ironically titled 'quality

---

[19] BNA, "Jellinek Says Regulatory Council Will Not Undercut Environmental Protection," *BNA Environment Reporter – Current Developments* 9 (1978): 1303–4.

of life' review to slow or stall proposed EPA regulations."[20] Properly signaled by the incoming president, and in response to its own long-standing complaints against OMB interference, in January 1977 the EPA unilaterally ended the OMB review procedure for its proposed regulations after failing to come to agreement with OMB on revisions of the process.[21] Upon taking office the Carter administration appointed to leadership positions at the EPA many individuals with backgrounds in environmental protection and public interest work, including administrator Douglas Costle, deputy administrator Barbara Blum, and assistant administrator for enforcement Martin Durning.[22]

A numeric measure of industry's assessment of the EPA's implementation of the water act can be obtained from the facts that firms and their trade associations pressed more than 150 lawsuits against the regulations the EPA promulgated under the statute, and challenged individual discharge permits in approximately 2,000 individual cases (Marcus, 1980: 288).

Environmentalists could look at the same record of court action and argue that the "EPA's technology-based standards have taken a beating in the courts of appeals" (McGarity, 1983: 212). Although there was no wholesale reversal or dilution of agency BPT standards for industry groups by the courts, which upheld many key provisions toward stringent regulation, nonetheless a substantial number of regulations were remanded. Of the eighteen cases decided by the

---

[20] BNA, "Carter Sees EPA Image at Low Ebb, Calls for Less Interference by OMB," *BNA Environment Reporter – Current Developments* 7 (1976): 1024.

[21] See, e.g., BNA, "EPA Reportedly Seeking Revision of OMB's 'Quality of Life' Review," *BNA Environment Reporter – Current Developments* 7 (1976): 1197; " 'Quality of Life' Process Under Review, but OMB Rejects Two EPA Recommendations," 7 (1976): 1243–4; "EPA Ends 'Quality of Life' Review Conducted by OMB on Agency's Regulations," 7 (1977): 1443–4.

[22] Costle had worked for the Conservation Foundation, then headed Connecticut's environmental protection program; Blum had been chief lobbyist for Save America's Vital Environment in Atlanta, and Durning had been an environmental lawyer in Seattle. In addition, Charles H. Warren, considered by California environmentalists to have been one of their strongest allies in the state legislature, was appointed to head the Council on Environmental Quality; Eliot Cutler, formerly an aide to Senator Edmund Muskie, was appointed the OMB's associate director for natural resources; James Moorman, appointed the Justice Department's assistant attorney general for land and natural resources, had worked with the Sierra Club Legal Defense Fund, and Angus MacBeth, made chief of Justice's pollution control section, had earlier worked with the Natural Resources Defense Council, the leading public-interest environmental law firm. See BNA, "Environmental Group Veterans Finding Policy Jobs in Carter Administration," *BNA Environment Reporter – Current Developments* 8 (1977): 649–50.

federal courts of appeal across the country (after consolidation of many separate industry challenges), all but three resulted in court remand of the rules for further consideration by the EPA regarding one or more substantive issues (such as consideration of economic or technological feasibility; see below).[23]

In the implementation of this law, all sides would at many points attempt to shape or challenge the agency's decisions, the sort of input that the Congress intended be routinely factored into the process of policymaking. The questions then concern the patterns of these inputs and their consequences for the impact of law.

The structuring of interests at law. The nature of legislative statements shapes the legal dynamic of implementation in fundamental ways. This is obvious in the case of mandated process, where for example the statute calls for citizen suits in specified instances, or asserts that court challenges be brought in certain venues (district or appellate courts, for example). But in unintended ways the very substance of law also conditions the structuring of inputs into policymaking and the weighting of factors in decision making, in effect differentially distributing points of access to (and relative advantage in) regulation to the various interests in its outcomes. A comparison of the federal clean air and clean water laws illustrates this dynamic.[24]

---

[23] See *Consolidated Coal Co. v. Costle*, 604 F.2d 239 (4th Cir. 1979), *rev'd*, 449 U.S. 64 (1980); *National Crushed Stone Association v. Costle*, 601 F.2d 111 (4th Cir. 1979), *rev'd*, 449 U.S. 64 (1980); *BASF Wyandotte Corp. v. Costle*, 598 F.2d 637 (1st Cir. 1979); *Weyerhaeuser Co. v. Costle*, 590 F.2d 1011 (D.C. Cir. 1978); *American Iron and Steel Institute v. EPA*, 568 F.2d 284 (3rd Cir. 1977); *California & Hawaiian Sugar Co. v. EPA*, 553 F.2d 280 (2d Cir. 1977); *Marathon Oil Co. v. EPA*, 564 F.2d 1253 (9th Cir. 1977); *Appalachian Power Co. v. Train*, 545 F.2d 1351 (4th Cir. 1976); *American Paper Institute v. Train*, 543 F.2d 328 (D.C. Cir.), *cert. dismissed*, 429 U.S. 967 (1976); *National Renderers Association v. EPA*, 541 F.2d 1281 (8th Cir. 1976); *E. I. du Pont de Nemours & Co. v. Train*, 541 F.2d 1018 (4th Cir. 1976), *aff'd*, 430 U.S. 112 (1977); *CPC International, Inc. v. Train*, 540 F.2d 1329 (8th Cir. 1976); *Tanners' Council of America v. Train*, 540 F.2d 1188 (4th Cir. 1976); *American Petroleum Institute v. EPA*, 540 F.2d 1023 (10th Cir. 1976); *FMC Corp. v. Train*, 539 F.2d 973 (4th Cir. 1976); *American Frozen Food Institute v. Train*, 539 F.2d 107 (D.C. Cir. 1976); *Hooker Chemicals and Plastics v. Train*, 537 F.2d 620 (2d Cir. 1976); *CPC International, Inc. v. Train*, 515 F.2d 1032 (8th Cir. 1975).
   The three cases not resulting in remands are *Weyerhaeuser Co. v. Costle, California & Hawaiian Sugar Co. v. EPA*, and *American Paper Institute v. Train.*

[24] This analysis draws importantly from McGarity's (1983) comparisons of media-quality- and technology-based environmental standards; Melnick's (1983) detailed analysis of the implementation of the Clean Air Act (especially ch. 10); and the U.S. House of Representative's 1977 report, *Case Law Under the Federal Water Pollution Control Act Amendments of 1972.*

During the 1970s the Congress passed the Clean Air Act Amendments[25] to address the increasingly serious risks to human health and property due to air pollution. The law takes a primarily media-quality-based approach to regulation, which seeks to limit pollution levels in the affected media (air or water). It mandates that EPA set primary (health-related) and secondary (welfare-related) national standards for pollutant levels in the air, providing for an adequate margin of safety.[26] In contrast, the water amendments focus on technology-based standards, requiring polluting facilities to reach that level of pollution control made possible by specified levels of technology (BPT, BAT), regardless of water quality (although more stringent discharge standards may be set in specific cases to meet separately established water quality standards). In important respects, these alternative approaches influence both the processes and substance of regulation.

The consideration of equity matters, or the balancing of broad social interests, has been structured differently under these two statutes. For example, the federal courts have taken broadly different approaches to judicial review in these two areas of law; as a result the agency's good faith efforts to implement the law have stood up better to industry challenge and appellate court review under the Clean Air Act than under the FWPCA amendments. In contrast to the remands under the water law noted above, for example, the EPA's models for calculating pollution reduction loads to meet air quality standards have readily survived judicial review, even when industrial petitioners "have pointed to other models that appear to depend upon fewer brash assumptions" (McGarity, 1983: 216).[27] In addition, by 1983 there had been no challenges to the hazardous emission standards EPA created under section 112 of the Clean Air Act. Moreover, the courts have even gone beyond the agency in mandating stringent regulation, for example by requiring the EPA to mount a regulatory program to "prevent significant deterioration" of airsheds already well under national air quality limits. Not explicitly mandated by the Congress, the courts took as their princi-

[25] The two major sets of amendments passed in the 1970s were the Clean Air Act Amendments of 1970, Pub. L. 91-604, 84 Stat. 1676; and the Clean Air Act Amendments of 1977, Pub. L. 95-95, 91 Stat. 685, 42 U.S.C. § 7401, *et seq.*

[26] For new facilities, the law instead takes a technology-based approach, requiring the implementation of the "best available demonstrated" technology.

[27] See, e.g., *Republic Steel Corp. v. Costle*, 621 F.2d 797 (6th Cir. 1980); *Alabama Power Co. v. Costle*, 13 ERC 1993, 2032 (D.C. Cir. 1979); *Mission Industries, Inc. v. EPA*, 547 F.2d 123 (1st Cir. 1976).

pal authority for this major program the simple, broad statement of purpose in the law: "to protect and enhance the quality of the Nation's air resources."[28]

As against these "absolutist" environmental standards, under the Clean Air Act equity considerations came into play in enforcement proceedings at the district court level (Melnick: 1983: 353–55). Here, industry lawyers were often able to persuade federal judges, themselves more closely tied to local interests and conditions, to modify (reduce) requirements under the standards and to extend deadlines for compliance. Typically the courts disallowed stringent enforcement options, such as plant shutdowns (even temporary ones), that might underscore the seriousness of purpose in the law as exemplified by the standards. In effect, there remained a dynamic tension between standard setting and enforcement, one that remained beyond the forces of rationalization in law.

In contrast, such equity considerations suffused policymaking under the FWPCA amendments of 1972, potentially shaping decisions at all levels of responsibility and review. This is not to argue that water pollution standards and controls were weak; on the contrary, formal agency policy implementing the law strained toward stringent enactment of its provisions, as I discuss more fully below. But it does suggest that the dynamic tension just described was contained in all stages of implementation – standard setting, judicial review, granting of permits for individual plants, and enforcement – rather than in the split between the various phases of lawmaking. Therefore, the points at which the law's purposes might be compromised were multiplied in the case of the water amendments. Among other consequences, this "structuring" of legal process complicates the role played by representatives of the public interest in ways not anticipated by the framers of law. At the least, it stretches the always spare resources of public-interest organizations even thinner over the whole, often convoluted course of lawmaking, and denies them the hortatory support of unambiguously embraced regulatory standards at law (as in the appellate court interpretations of the Clean Air Act). (For another difficulty posed to such groups by the nature of the water law, see below.)

In the 1972 amendments to the water pollution control law, the Congress created different sets of "balancing" or equity considerations for the two levels of technology-forcing standards. For the

[28] See Melnick (1983: 71–112).

BPT requirements (to be met by mid-1977), the law provided for a balancing of costs and benefits in the establishment of industry-wide regulations, but made no provision for variances from them for individual polluting facilities.[29] The BAT requirements (to be met by 1983), on the other hand, allowed for individual facility exceptions to be made against the national standards (for permit applications filed after July 1, 1977), but provided for a reduced consideration of costs in the writing of industry-wide effluent control standards (it called for no specific balancing of costs and benefits).[30]

Despite these distinctions in the statute, the EPA administratively amended the law by inserting variance clauses in most of its BPT regulations for industry categories. Variances allowing for individual exceptions to the national rules were granted if a plant could demonstrate that its circumstances were "fundamentally different from the factors considered in the establishment of the guidelines."[31] The imprecision of these grounds left a great deal of discretion to the administrators. The court of appeals for the Second Circuit upheld this imprecise variance procedure in 1976, nonetheless, against environmentalists' challenge that it was unauthorized by the statute,[32] and the Supreme Court endorsed it the next year.[33]

Moreover, the appellate courts were often prone to insist that the EPA take greater account of cost considerations in its regulations, in some instances greater than the statute appeared to require. On the one hand, with respect to BPT regulations the agency had taken an aggressive approach to writing industry-wide rules for abatement, rules the courts upheld. For example, in a key 1976 case the 10th

[29] See Pub. L. 92-500, §§ 301[b][i][A], 304[b][i][B].
[30] See Pub. L. 92-500, §§ 301[b][2][A], 301[c], 304[b][2][B]. Individual variances from the more stringent BAT industry standards could be had if the owner or operator of a facility could show "that such modified requirements (1) will represent the maximum use of technology within the economic capability of the owner or operator, and (2) will result in reasonable further progress toward the elimination of the discharge of pollutants" (§ 301[c]).
For a discussion of the legislative uncertainty attached to the consideration of costs in establishing BAT for industry categories, see Chapter 5.
[31] See, e.g., the standards for the woven fabric finishing industry in 40 CFR (rev. July 1, 1977), § 410.42. The full specification of this imprecise phrase in the various regulations was as follows: "An individual discharger or other interested person may submit evidence to the Regional Administrator (or to the State, if the State has the authority to issue NPDES permits) that factors relating to the equipment or facilities involved, the process applied, or other such factors related to such discharger are fundamentally different from the factors considered in the establishment of the guidelines." Such language, of course, admits of wide latitude in interpretation. See discussion below.
[32] *Natural Resources Defense Council v. EPA*, 537 F.2d 642 (2nd Cir. 1976).
[33] *E. I. duPont de Nemours & Co. v. Train*, 430 U.S. 112, 128 (1977).

Circuit court rejected industry's argument that the discharge regulations must provide for a *range* of limits, within which the agency has discretion to choose specific numeric limits for individual plants. Instead, the court ruled, EPA's policy of issuing "single number" regulations to be applied to all plants (in the absence of variances) was consistent with congressional intent, which recognized that marginal plants within industries might be forced to close under the law's logic, a price worth the benefits of the anticipated cleanup; the Supreme Court upheld the EPA's "single number" approach in 1977.[34]

In addition, relying on the act's legislative history, the 10th Circuit also rejected industry's argument that EPA must carefully balance costs and benefits in establishing the BPT rules. The court ruled that the value of environmental benefits "is not capable of present-day determination" and that societal benefits are for Congress to determine, approving instead EPA's more restrictive "cost-effectiveness" standard. The courts have generally read the legislative history as indicating that "the only substantive restriction imposed on the 1977 limitations by economics would occur where the additional technology to achieve a marginal level of effluent reduction would be totally out of line with the resultant cost" (U.S. House of Representatives, 1977c: 29).

On the other hand, in contrast to the approach taken to the Clean Air Act, the appellate courts were often willing to impose on the agency a greater consideration of the costs of controls to industrial water polluters, perhaps in part because of the stringency permitted in establishing industry-wide regulations. For example, in two cases remanding regulations for the intendedly more stringent 1983 BAT discharge standards, two federal courts of appeal ruled that EPA

[34] See *American Petroleum Institute v. EPA*, 540 F.2d 1023 (10th Cir. 1976); see also EPA Headquarters Information Memorandum, "*American Petroleum Institute v. EPA* – Effluent Guidelines for Petroleum Refining," August 24, 1976. EPA's approach was upheld in the 1977 Supreme Court decision in *duPont* (see fn. 33), which resolved differences on the question among the circuit courts of appeals. In 1975 the Third Circuit had ruled that the statute required the agency to provide for ranges of discharge control in its regulations (*American Iron and Steel Institute v. EPA*, 526 F.2d 1027). In 1976, four circuits – the 10th, 4th, 2nd, and D.C. Circuits – ruled in favor of the single numbers approach (U.S. House of Representatives, 1977c: 38).

In a 1976 letter to Senator Edward Kennedy regarding a constituent company's petition for an exception to national discharge standards, Stanley Legro, the agency's assistant administrator for enforcement, noted that, "with respect to the overall impact of the legislation, Congress clearly contemplated that cleaning up the nation's waters might necessitate the closing of some marginal plants." EPA Headquarters Permits Division, July 9, 1976: correspondence regarding the request for variance by the L. S. Starrett Company, Athol, Mass.

had shown inadequate consideration of costs to industry in the record.[35] In addition, in 1976 the 4th Circuit court rejected the EPA's variance procedure for BPT regulations, not because the statute itself appeared to have ruled out the option, but because the court found that the procedure failed to adequately consider the costs to individual dischargers.[36] In two 1979 cases the 4th Circuit similarly invalidated EPA's variance regulations for inadequately considering companies' financial ability to comply; by then the 4th Circuit's series of decisions had been contradicted by the District of Columbia Circuit, which had ruled that individual companies' financial ability to comply with regulations was not pertinent to BPT considerations.[37] Industry had raised this series of challenges to EPA's policy dating to 1974, when the agency's Office of Enforcement and General Counsel had determined that economic factors were not to be considered as special circumstances under the variance option. Instead, the defining phrase in the variance rule, "factors relating to the equipment or facilities involved, the process applied, or other such factors related to the discharger," was interpreted to mean technical and engineering factors, not economic ones.[38]

The Supreme Court finally resolved the variance dispute in 1980 by reversing the 4th Circuit's two 1979 decisions and upholding EPA's more restrictive posture.[39] Nonetheless, several factors suggest that equity considerations in the variance procedure continued to be

[35] See *Hooker Chemicals & Plastics Corp. v. Train*, 537 F.2d 620 (2d Cir. 1976) (inadequate consideration of costs a factor in vacating 1983 no-discharge requirements for process waste water pollutants in the phosphate manufacturing industry); *American Petroleum Institute v. EPA*, 540 F.2d 1023 (10th Cir. 1976) (remanding 1983 standards for petroleum refineries and directing agency to more adequately consider cost factors).

[36] *Appalachian Power Co. v. Train*, 545 F.2d 1351 (4th Cir. 1976). An earlier court decision had also ruled against the variance procedure for being too inflexible; see *American Iron and Steel Institute v. EPA*, 526 F.2d 1027 (3rd Cir. 1975).

[37] The 4th Circuit cases are *National Crushed Stone Association v. Costle*, 601 F.2d 111 (4th Cir. 1979); *Consolidated Coal Co. v. Costle*, 604 F.2d 239 (4th Cir. 1979). The conflicting case is *Weyerhaueser Co. v. Costle*, 590 F.2d 1011 (D.C. Cir. 1978). See BNA, "Supreme Court Will Review BPT Case, Declines Two Other Water Act Cases," *BNA Environment Reporter – Current Developments* 10 (1980): 2037.

[38] EPA Headquarters Enforcement Memorandum, "Effluent Guidelines – Adjustment of Effluent Limitations in NPDES Permits," April 25, 1974. This and other EPA memoranda referenced in this book were collected during my field work at the agency, unless otherwise indicated. A number of the agency's internal policy memoranda are reprinted in the *BNA Environment Reporter – Current Developments*.

[39] *EPA v. National Crushed Stone Association*, 449 U.S. 64 (1980).

salient for the agency. First, while EPA policy asserted that cost factors *alone* would not justify exceptions to the BPT regulations, it is at best difficult to logically disentangle economic from technical factors, all the more so in light of the vague language delimiting the variance procedure. Second, the import of this difficulty is amplified by the context of the agency's decentralized system for issuing permits, in which often inexperienced permit writers in EPA regional offices and various state agencies issued thousands of permits against tight deadlines to often complaining businesses under a variety of legal frameworks. (For example, permits were issued under interim as well as final regulations, state water quality standards where these were stricter than actual or expected BPT regulations, and in some cases in the absence of any regulations).[40]

By the latter half of the 1970s, institutional observers from *Fortune* magazine to the Natural Resources Defense Council were criticizing the agency for administratively amending the law through too generous use of variances and exceptions.[41] (Variances can take many forms in the regulatory program, including extensions of

[40] The administrative challenges and confusion experienced under the FWPCA's tight timetables and technically demanding mandates are, of course, understandable. As only one example, many permits were issued before final regulations had been promulgated, in order to meet statutory deadlines. The analytic and policy question remains, however, to what extent was the new law given uniform, aggressive application by the federal and state agencies involved in administering it, and with what consequences for both ecology and economy. The remainder of this chapter and the next examine the data on these points.

Internal EPA memoranda indicate something of the administrative complexity and confusion that quickly attached to the implementation of the law. See, e.g., EPA Headquarters Enforcement Memorandum, "A Regional Overview of the Permit Issuing Process," [undated] ("The permit program itself is relatively young and the staff tends to be junior. . . . In most Regions, the permit issuance philosophy has been gerrymandered by various ancillary organizational entities including legal staff, Office of Water Programs, Surveillance and Analysis, and finally within itself because of its own inexperience. . . . There is an essential communications gap relative to the water quality standards area. . . . In any given case we don't know whether we have gone too far or not far enough in trying to protect the water relative to water quality standards.")

Also see Office of the EPA Administrator, "Administrator's Decision Statement No. 3: Permit Program and 303(e) Planning," January 30, 1973 (outlining permit issuance under [1] water quality standards, [2] promulgated BPT guidelines, [3] interim BPT guidance, and [4] individual facility BPT determinations for plants falling outside categories to be regulated by industry-wide rules); and EPA Headquarters Memorandum (Office of General Counsel), "Clarification of OGC Opinion No. 40," February 4, 1977 (on issuing permits to facilities when no relevant BPT regulations have been promulgated; economic impact of controls on individual dischargers to be considered).

[41] See Alexander (1976) (EPA increasingly "granting exemptions, variances, and 'extensions' "), and NRDC (1981) (noting several pending NRDC cases "contesting

deadlines in lieu of enforcement actions. See Chapter 7 for data in this study on variances of different forms.) It was perhaps not comforting to such critics that in mid-1977, fully three years after its original statement on the matter, the EPA's Office of Enforcement was disseminating its "interim procedures . . . pending possible promulgation of regulations" on the handling of variance requests from industry.[42]

The record suggests that reviewing courts and agency personnel have been more likely to constrain the reach of law under the water amendments, while the appellate courts have been more likely to uphold and even expand the agency's authorities under the Clean Air Act. These differences are shaped by the varying content of the laws themselves (McGarity, 1983: 216, 225). It may be that judges are more willing to challenge agency analysis when the terms are the more familiar ones of economics and engineering (as in technology-based standards), than they are when more abstruse and uncertain matters of toxicology and meteorology are at issue (as in the Clean Air Act's media-quality standards). But it seems likely that the aim of law's protections drives court intervention and shapes its consequences. Under the Clean Air Act, the EPA was to write regulations *to protect human health* in the context of existing, demonstrable hazards; here the courts appear on balance to have assumed the position of guardian against any agency backsliding.

Unlike implementation of the Clean Air Act, the technology-based approach of the 1972 water law largely *divorced pollution controls from considerations of impacts on human health* and even from the quality of the waters receiving pollution. Judges and administrators could more readily invoke notions of equities and balancing. They were more likely to insist on some review of the costs of controls

---

EPA's efforts to weaken uniform national treatment requirements by overly-broad application of case-by-case variances").

[42] EPA Headquarters Enforcement Memorandum, "Policy Regarding Procedures for Fundamentally Different Factors BPT Variances," August 18, 1977. (From deputy assistant administrator for water enforcement to regional administrators and directors of approved NPDES states.) The memorandum went on to again underscore headquarters' policy that such variances were rarely justified, and noted that the Office of Enforcement had recommended approval on only two requests among eleven determinations. But neither this memorandum nor other policy guidance made clear the process of review within the agency, or provided data on total variances granted, and of which types. No time frame for the eleven determinations was specified. All of which begins to suggest less than tight, centralized control on these procedures.

where the law does not explicitly concern itself with environmental risks to people. As against the abstractions of technological feasibility, the rights to conduct legitimate business and maintain employment are embodied human concerns long recognized and protected at law.[43] And as I discuss more fully in the next chapter, this characteristic of the water pollution law also shaped the prosecution of arguably criminal violations of the statute: prosecutors were often reluctant to bring criminal charges absent a showing of harm, at least to the environment, a factor contributing to the continued rarity of criminal cases, particularly against major corporate dischargers (cf., Wenner, 1982: 47–9; McGarity, 1983: 211).

The technology-based thrust of the 1972 amendments also shapes the process of lawmaking in less visible fora than those of the federal appellate courts, and for related reasons. In this case, the content of law serves to subtly bias the balance of input into regulatory decision making. Because the law concentrates on identifying and asserting the best pollution control technologies being utilized within industries, rather than on the environmental harm to receiving waters and human health,[44] debates over the terms and applica-

---

[43] The courts did not maintain consistent differences in response to these sorts of issues. The foregoing analysis has indicated important variation among the appellate circuits on the interpretation of the water amendments, often reflecting regional differences in environmental sensitivities among federal judges (like those of legislators). In her study of U.S. courts' treatment of environmental law in the 1970s, Wenner (1982) identified patterns of regional variation among the appellate circuits. In general, the eastern and northern circuits tended to rule more favorably for environmentalists' positions, the western and southern circuits for industries' concerns (cf. pp. 114–15). To some extent the difference in decisions as between the air and water laws was shaped by jurisdictional matters: appeals under the Clean Air Act were by statute directed to the D.C. Circuit, traditionally a quite favorable circuit for environmentalists, and one avoided by industry; under the FWPCA amendments of 1972, no such exclusive appellate jurisdiction was defined (Wenner, 1982: 68; also see Melnick, 1983).

In singular regard for fair play, the EPA finally took official notice of this variation and the consequent "forum shopping" engaged in by both industry and environmentalists, seeking to be first to challenge new regulations in their favorite courts of appeals and thereby establish the forum of decision. In 1979 the agency developed procedures to establish the precise time when new regulations become final ("ripe") for judicial review, so that all parties – in their "race to the courthouse" – would have equal chance to file the first suits in their preferred jurisdictions. (BNA, "Forum Shopping Plan to Be Tried When EPA Issues New NPDES Regulations," *BNA Environment Reporter – Current Developments* 10 (1979): 9–10.

[44] The appellate courts have recognized that the 1972 amendments divorced regulation from environmental impacts, instead tying standards largely to technological potentials. See, e.g., *Appalachian Power Co., et al. v. EPA*, 671 F.2d 801 (4th Cir. 1982) (ruling that discharger's impact on water quality cannot be a factor in determining whether to grant BPT variance); *Consolidated Coal Co. v. Costle*, 604 F.2d

tion of standards tend to both disproportionately attract and favor the input of industry over that of environmentalists. Couched in the dry terms of the limits of engineering technologies rather than in the environmentally and emotionally compelling language of the limits of nature, the key regulatory determinations of rule setting, permit issuance, and exceptions from the rules present themselves as purely technical, depoliticized matters that seldom evoke a sense of environmental drama in the public interest. Such regulatory exchanges necessarily favor the input of industry, which controls the technological information required for regulation in the first place, enhancing the agency's dependence on industry cooperation and providing a sort of leverage not available to environmental interests.

As McGarity (1983: 208) observes about such standards (in contrast to regulation based on media quality), "the regulated firms may feel more comfortable with a process that gives them room to bargain with the agency in low visibility proceedings that depend heavily on industry-supplied information, especially when the agency may be sympathetic toward their plight." And while the EPA took a fairly aggressive policy stance toward industrial water pollution in the 1970s, its decisions doubtlessly were shaded by the law's focus on technology rather than on harm.

The evidence on public participation in the regulation of industrial water pollution indeed suggests structured imbalances in input. At the broad levels of lawmaking, legislation, and appellate court review, environmental interests have enjoyed a rough parity with industry groups in bringing their positions to bear on policymakers' deliberations. In the actual formulation and application of the industry-wide standards to dischargers, however, the balance swings toward the regulated. For example, the most successful public-interest environmental law firm, the Natural Resources Defense Council (NRDC), has only infrequently been able to participate in the agency discussions leading to industry discharge standards. By 1977 the NRDC docket listed the Council as having fully participated in the formulation of just five of the numerous sets of regulations the EPA had written by then. Its participation included presenting expert testimony and cross-examining witnesses regarding toxic pollutants (Natural Resources Defense Council, 1977).

239 (4th Cir. 1979) (ruling EPA's variance regulations "unduly restrictive" but rejecting industry contention that quality of receiving waters should be a factor in variance determinations).

Thus, even for such professional "watchdog" groups, participation in many key decisions is limited, in this case not for lack of passion, interest, or awareness as for the lack of resources. And the narrower the decision matter, the more limited is the voice of environmentalists. An NRDC official noted that his group was rarely able to participate in such matters as EPA's adjudicatory hearings (when individual polluters challenge the terms of their discharge permits in courtlike proceedings before administrative law judges) and other permit modification proceedings. These key determinations, he said, were left largely to the deliberations of agency and industry experts. And even when his organization intervened, as in a case challenging several offshore oil permits, it was often "ill-equipped" from a resource standpoint to engage in such numerous "wars of experts."[45]

A congressional study of federal regulation has also noted this imbalance in participation in agency decision making, suggesting that the processes identified here for EPA are characteristic of regulation generally:

At agency after agency, participation by the regulated industry predominates – often overwhelmingly. Organized public interest representation accounts for a very small percentage of participation before Federal regulatory hearings. In more than half of the formal proceedings, there appears to be no such participation whatsoever, and virtually none at informal agency proceedings. In those proceedings where participation by public groups does take place, typically it is a small fraction of the participation by the regulated industry. One-tenth is not uncommon; sometimes it is even less than that. This pattern prevails in both rulemaking proceedings and adjudicatory proceedings, with an even greater imbalance occurring in adjudications than in rulemaking.

The single greatest obstacle to active public participation in regulatory proceedings is the lack of financial resources by potential participants to meet the great costs of formal participation. Lack of funds has prevented public participation in many important proceedings. (U.S. Senate, 1977b, Vol. III: vii; see also ch. 2)[46]

[45] Interview, 1981. In 1980 the Congress considered providing very limited funding for citizen participation in litigation or regulatory processes leading to EPA decisions. Such expenses as those for travel and room and board would be covered for persons otherwise unable to afford the costs of such participation. See BNA, "EPA Public Participation Proposal Sidelined by House Funds Prohibition," *BNA Environment Reporter – Current Developments* 11 (1980): 711.

[46] The congressional study of imbalances in public participation was based on information on rulemaking and adjudicatory proceedings from eight regulatory agencies, including both economic and social regulation. For no apparent reason other than simple sampling and resource constraints, this aspect of the study did not

For all their advantages over standards based on media quality, in uniformity, predictability (enhancing industry planning)[47] and enforcement, technology-based standards such as those mandated by the 1972 amendments to the FWPCA tend to shade the balance of public participation, particularly in the less visible exchanges of experts regarding the vital fine print of regulation. Moreover, in contrast to the media-quality approach, such standards are less likely to promote technological innovation due to their focus on best current practices within industry categories (and because the Congress explicitly chose not to intrude on industry's prerogatives over industrial processes). This result would limit the government's ability to control the more sophisticated and troublesome pollutants, especially the toxics, as later discussed (cf., McGarity, 1983: 205, 221–2).

Contradictions and constraints in the implementation of law

The processes and limits thus far described constrain law not only independently, but synergistically. The tendency of technology-based standards to evoke equity considerations at all stages underscores the importance of representative public input at each of them, at the same time as their highly technical nature renders such participation increasingly difficult as laws are transformed into applicable rules. Similarly, the heavy regulatory burden the water amendments placed on the agency forced it to enlarge on the law's discretionary realms, again increasing the need for wide public inputs while – because of the proliferation of decision points – making such participation more difficult to ensure and provide.

These contradictions and constraints display themselves across the broad front of regulation in industrial water pollution, and present themselves to all of the centrally involved interests: the EPA, industry, and environmentalists. But they present themselves in varying

include the EPA. Nonetheless, the report clearly suggests that the findings of imbalances in participation were generalizable across agencies of all sorts.

[47] It is likely that industry's views of the relative costs and benefits of these two approaches to pollution control are not of a piece. While in general the predictability of technology-based standards has the obvious advantage of allowing business to engage in rational planning procedures, the water-quality-based approach may have the advantage of reducing individual firms' compliance costs given the characteristics of the receiving waters (e.g., preexisting pollution levels, flow rates). By the early 1980s some industry groups were allegedly seeking greater regulatory flexibility by advocating a return to the media-quality logic. See BNA, "Water Quality Not Factor in Waivers of BPT Rules, U.S. Appeals Court Says," *BNA Environment Reporter – Current Developments* 12 (1982): 1323.

guises to each of these three major sets of players, now engaged in a typically quiet drama far from the legislative limelight, but one whose denouement always promised to be momentous.

The EPA: systemic constraints on regulatory zeal. The ambitious intent of the 1972 amendments undercut itself to a certain extent. The Congress sought fundamental change in industrial polluting behavior, and rather immediately. On paper and in principle, the law intended not only to strengthen pollution control, but to rationalize it through a set of consistently applied standards and penalties nationwide. However, the regulatory burden the legislature handed the agency ensured two other mutually reinforcing outcomes as well: delay and compromise. Moreover, the radical shift in pollution control combined with the law's due process protections to produce countless legal challenges, amplifying both delay and compromise. Therefore, despite the zeal often displayed in formal statements of policy and by environmentally inclined regulators at the agency, in practice it was permitted to operate only within the fundamental limits embedded in the substance and processes of law.

Commanded to write complex regulations for each of the many industrial categories within a year's time (by end 1973) and issue permits within two years (by December 31, 1974), the EPA immediately fell well behind the deadlines established in the law. As an initial consequence, the Natural Resources Defense Council quickly sued the agency for failing to discharge a nondiscretionary duty, and in November 1973 a federal court ordered the EPA to establish pollution control regulations for all industrial categories by November 1974. However, even this extension proved far too tight, and the original order was amended many times to extend the deadline.[48] Given the tight, logical structure of the law – permits implementing BPT and BAT to be issued on the basis of promulgated guidelines – these early delays had domino-like ramifications for all subsequent steps in the regulatory process. For example, as discussed later, many permits were issued without benefit of final regulations, resulting in considerable variation in their stringency. In addition, enforcement of permit violations was often stayed as the EPA awaited promulgation of final rules (see Chapter 7).

---

[48] EPA Headquarters, Office of Enforcement: Correspondence of Robert B. Schaffer, Director of the Permits Division, to Betty H. Olson, Ph.D., July 18, 1975 (answering queries regarding EPA's implementation of the FWPCA Amendments of 1972).

EPA's work was retarded by the sheer complexity of regulatory determinations – to identify the best control practices within industrial categories and to assess the range of economic impacts of regulation on the separate categories (impact on prices, growth, employment, and foreign trade, for example). It was also retarded by the activities of the law's (hence, the agency's) various constituencies. One of the principal participants in EPA rulemaking was the Office of Management and Budget, the Executive Branch unit responsible for managing the president's annual federal budget and ensuring that policies proposed by Executive Branch agencies conform to the budget and the president's political philosophy. OMB reviews and passes on agencies' budget requests, legislative proposals and proposed regulations. And since the establishment in 1971 of its "Quality of Life" review of social regulation (environmental, consumer protection, occupational safety and health) by then director George P. Shultz, OMB has often been charged with improper political interference in EPA's regulatory responsibilities.[49]

During the period when EPA was issuing many of its voluminous regulations under the FWPCA amendments, the years 1973–76, agency officials accused OMB of singling out the EPA for intensive oversight, subjecting its pollution control regulations to lengthy interagency reviews that had the effect of both delaying regulations and tending to reduce their stringency (Bureau of National Affairs, 1976). The delay was a two-phase result of OMB's review. There was, of course, the delay associated with the OMB review itself, which included the seeking of opinions from other federal units, many of which, like the Commerce Department, attempted to weaken EPA regulations, according to agency representatives. This external review procedure was mirrored inside the EPA, where agency officials came to give proposed regulations lengthy internal reviews (including, for example, clearance by all assistant administrators regardless of the proposals' relations to their own areas of responsibility) in especially cautious response to forthcoming external reviews.

Beyond the troublesome fact of delays, therefore, lay the specter of regulations politically shaded toward greater leniency and less environmental protection, in a process usually shielded from public

---

[49] On the role of OMB in EPA activities between 1971 and 1976, see BNA, "Special Report: Office of Management and Budget Plays Critical Part in Environmental Policymaking, Faces Little External Review," *BNA Environment Reporter – Current Developments* 7 (1976): 693–7.

participation. If the external review typically did not result in the gutting of regulations, it may well have been because the agency had engaged in a form of *anticipatory politics*, writing regulations that tend to be environmentally less aggressive in order to stave off outside political criticism and challenges, as one assistant administrator suggested (Bureau of National Affairs, 1976: 693–4).[50]

Moreover, agency officials complained that OMB often stalled the EPA's legislative proposals and testimony to Congress, giving advantages to industry and other government units, such as the Department of Commerce and the Small Business Administration, which often provided testimony in the key early stages of congressional debate on environmental matters. They worried that OMB, in its oversight role in agency testimony, might even be tampering with technical data to be submitted for legislative consideration, in effect diluting implications that more aggressive regulation was required.

Evidence of such dramatic interference did come to public light years later, when in 1989 James E. Hansen, director of the National Aeronautics and Space Administration's Goddard Institute for Space Studies, reported that OMB had altered testimony he was to give to Congress on the projections for global warming known as the greenhouse effect. OMB had changed his testimony to make more tentative his conclusions regarding the effects of systemic global warming due to atmospheric pollution by carbon dioxide and other gases. His original testimony, that such effects as drought and severe storms were well established scientifically, bolstered the position of the EPA and the State Department that urged President Bush to lead a strong international effort to forestall global warming by improving pollution control and energy measures. OMB altered the warning to suggest that the effects were quite uncertain,

[50] Such anticipatory politics appear to be a routine feature of regulatory bureaucracies with oversight responsibilities in the affairs of business, as suggested in Chapter 2 with the example of antitrust regulation (cf., Green, 1972). The OMB, of course, is a principal route of transmission for agency perceptions of restrictive political climates regarding their regulatory mandates.

An OMB official indicated in 1976 that because of their great volume, EPA's water pollution regulations were generally not given the same detailed external review as other rules, being instead subjected only to "pro forma" reviews outside the agency (BNA, 1976: 694). But given the substantial economic impacts of these rules, it seems most unlikely that they would be virtually ignored by such organizations as the Commerce Department, or that the EPA would be less cautious about these regulations because agency officials were confident they would not be carefully considered by external reviewers.

an implication in line with the president's and Energy Department's position that aggressive means, such as an international treaty to control atmospheric pollution, were not now indicated.[51]

But despite any induced conservatism in the water pollution control regulations, they were routinely subjected to appellate challenges, notably by industry groups that, regardless of outcome, often benefited from the lengthy delays associated with the appeals. For example, virtually all the water pollution control regulations were challenged by industry in the appellate courts.[52] The EPA was often sued simultaneously by both industry and environmentalists, arguing respectively that promulgated regulations were too stringent or too lenient.

In addition, individual companies mounted numerous challenges to the application of the regulations to their specific facilities through the EPA's adjudicatory hearing procedure, a formal, court-like proceeding in which the company could challenge the stringency of the limits placed on its discharges. Besides the possibility that the administrative law judge would order the permit modified in the company's interest, there was the advantage that the contested portions of the permit could not be enforced during the pendancy of the hearing.

Given the heavy caseload and the often highly technical nature of the appeals, in which companies would argue for exceptions from the industry-wide limits on the grounds that their industrial processes and discharges differed from the norm, hearings often were pending for very long periods as the backlog grew. For example, by November 1975 the agency had received more than 1,800 industry requests for hearings, of which more than 1,100 were pending. During 1975 the agency was besieged with an average of 63 new requests a month while settling an average of only 22 a month.[53] In data collected for this book and analyzed in Chapter 7, many of the hearings were found to have been pending for two and three years, and longer. More than 400 pending cases involved major dischargers (as defined by volume and content of wastewater). This huge backlog was troubling to the EPA's enforcement staff. In mid-1976

[51] See Shabecoff (1989d), p. A1.
[52] EPA Headquarters Memorandum, Office of Enforcement, "Impact of Effluent Guidelines Litigation Upon Issued NPDES Permits," December 23, 1974 (regulations for 22 of 27 industrial categories for which they have been promulgated are being challenged in court).
[53] EPA Headquarters Memorandum, Office of Enforcement, "Adjudicatory Hearing Program," November 21, 1975.

the Office of Enforcement noted that "the longer the delay in resolving these cases, the longer the polluting discharges continue unabated, thereby seriously impairing our entire national water cleanup program."[54] Such unresolved administrative appeals continued in many cases to prevent enforcement of the important July 1977 deadline for attainment of BPT by all industrial discharges.

In consequence of the complexity and delay in this regulatory schema, the rationality and uniformity anticipated by the legislators were necessarily transformed into something a good bit less orderly in the implementation of the law by the EPA. Under the law's pressure to issue tens of thousands of industrial pollution control permits in two years' time (by the end of 1974), the agency found it necessary to issue them under a number of expedient alternatives not contemplated by the statute's framers. With impressive effort the EPA was nearly able to meet the deadline Congress had set: By the end of 1974 EPA and participating state agencies had issued permits to 95 percent of the nearly 3,000 major industrial dischargers nation-wide; by the middle of 1975, the government had received 31,949 applications for permits from industrial facilities and had issued permits to 97 percent of major dischargers and 52 percent of minor polluters. However, approximately three-fifths of all permits had been issued without benefit of final regulations for the industry categories.[55]

As earlier noted, the EPA and the participating states issued permits under a variety of authorities,[56] a process that – when combined with the largely inexperienced and decentralized permit staff – promised a good deal of variation in regulatory stringency across firms, even within an industry. For example, many of the earliest permits were issued under interim technical documents of varying degrees of reliability before these were translated into formally approved regulations for industry categories. (The authority to do so is contained in Sec. 402[a][1], which expressly allows the EPA to issue discharge control permits prior to formal regulations if neces-

---

[54] EPA Headquarters Memorandum, Office of Enforcement, May 21, 1976; also EPA Headquarters Memorandum, Office of Enforcement, June 3, 1976.

[55] EPA Headquarters, Office of Enforcement: Correspondence of Robert B. Schaffer, Director of the Permits Division, to Betty H. Olson, Ph.D., July 18, 1975 (answering queries regarding EPA's implementation of the FWPCA Amendments of 1972).

[56] Regardless of authority, permits were typically issued for five-year terms and specified interim and final discharge limits, and most often a compliance schedule for installing BPT to reach the limits.

sary to accomplish the law's purposes.) A good deal of uncertainty
and discretion attached to this exercise, as illustrated in a 1973
memorandum to the regional administrators from the Office of Enforcement and General Counsel.[57] For example, in issuing permits
for the mining and milling industry, the memorandum simply ad-
vises the regions, "This [technical] guidance should only be applied
in very selected circumstances in the hard rock milling industry."
For the motor vehicle industry, it directed only that "the interim
guidance is based on fragmented data and the information base is
very limited. Hence, it must be used very selectively." And for the
cement industry, "The guidance specifies parameters for [various
indicated pollutants] but does not cover heavy metals and runoff for
storage piles. All permits issued should [nonetheless] specify limitations for heavy metals and runoff from storage piles."

In addition, permits were issued variously under proposed regulations, water quality standards, and the professional judgments of
individual permitters in the regions and states (for example, when
industrial facilities did not fall squarely within categories for which
regulations were issued). In general, under the 1972 law's severe
deadline pressures, the EPA acted to achieve near term results, even
if they came at some cost to uniformity of regulation across locales
and firms, and at least in some instances at the expense of water
quality standards.

The statutory emphasis on short-term successes led the agency to
favor best practicable technology limits over more stringent water
quality limits if necessary to meet permitting deadlines, a reversal of
the law's mandate. (Permits were to be issued on the basis of either
BPT determinations or water quality standards for the receiving waters, whichever was the more stringent.) Almost immediately following the law's passage a split developed within the EPA between the
deadline-constrained permit staff and the water quality planners.
The Office of the Administrator resolved the differences in a 1973
memorandum asserting that "even if [water quality standards]
should be the basis for the permit, the permit will issue on a BPT
basis anyway if the water quality analysis cannot be completed in
time to meet the December 31, 1974 deadline."[58]

[57] EPA Headquarters Memorandum, Office of Enforcement and General Counsel,
"Use of Interim Guidance Documents for the Issuance of Permits Prior to Formal
Promulgation of Effluent Guidelines," February 28, 1973.
[58] EPA Headquarters Memorandum, Office of the Administrator, "Water Program
Policy Issues," April 17, 1973. Also see footnote 40.

More than this, in many cases the issuance of initial permits before the EPA had finalized its industry-wide discharge regulations led to company appeals and adjudications of permit terms, at least in part owing to the uncertainty about final requirements. As a result, there was unevenness in compliance expectations across firms, even within industries. For example, regarding the heavily polluting steel industry, a survey by the American Iron and Steel Institute showed that by early 1977, "steel plants with only about 50 percent of industry capacity have permits requiring compliance with final [BPT] effluent limitations by [the] July 1, 1977 [deadline]. Plants with over 40 percent of the steel industry's capacity do not have final permits today, and therefore have not reached agreement with the authorities – EPA or State agencies – as to what are the 1977 requirements."[59]

This result bespeaks a particular dynamic in regulatory law of this sort. Complex and expensive social regulation stimulates industry challenges to its merits, both on collective bases such as court challenges to industry-wide regulations and individual bases such as company appeals of individual permits, forestalling compliance. Apart from the legal merits, the delaying effects of such challenges often bring financial benefits to firms. On the other hand, this process also "disorganizes" regulation in that its effects come to fall unequally on competitors, raising its aggregate costs relative to benefits, a result presumably not desired by business collectively but one that justifies the periodic calls for relaxed controls by various segments of industry.[60] Thus there is a tendency in these regulatory processes to undermine not only the beneficial impacts of legal control but also its fundamental logic. This is particularly true in cli-

---

[59] Testimony of Thomas C. Graham, President and Chief Executive Officer, Jones & Laughlin Steel Corporation, for the American Iron and Steel Institute, in *Hearings Before the Subcommittee on Water Resources of the Committee on Public Works and Transportation* (U.S. House of Representatives, 1977a: 322).

[60] The steel executive quoted was making the case for delayed compliance dates as the Congress considered amendments for the water law in 1977. He noted that "with the sums of money [for compliance] that are at stake here, I think that the people who assume the responsibility for the spending of that money have to have the assurance that the regulations are in fact going to fall uniformly, throughout the industry on a competitive basis, and that they're not – that an individual company is not, in fact, going to invest major funds in compliance with a rule that hasn't been tested, and subsequently be disadvantaged if that's litigated and overturned. I think that's a very real competitive problem" (U.S. House of Representatives, 1977a: 324). But he also engaged in this exchange with Representative Harsha (ibid.):

mates of scarce economic resources that demand hard choices in public policy.

Contradictory tendencies in the implementation of this law manifested themselves in other ways, as well. The statute's and the agency's focus on the installation of retrofitted, "end-of-line" (EOL) pollution control technology (rather than on changes in internal industrial processes that might reduce the polluted effluent requiring treatment [see Chapter 5]) arguably limited the beneficial impacts of law in at least three ways. First, such controls are often less cost effective than process changes, and often regressive in their impact, disproportionately costly for smaller producers and those with underutilized productive capacities because of the high fixed costs of control technology.[61] By the BPT deadline in 1977 this was a significant factor, as studies by the federal government showed that 83 percent of industry's pollution control expenditures to date had been for EOL technology (U.S. Senate, 1979: 291).

Second, the emphasis on EOL controls to meet the interim 1977 goal for BPT threatened to undermine the potential of next-stage, best available technology controls (even more so the statutory goal of zero discharge), particularly for the more complex and threatening toxic pollutants. In general, technology-forcing rules can drive industry laggards to match the standards of the pollution control leaders in their respective industries but cannot force the leaders to create new technologies (McGarity, 1983: 222). Moreover, as a number of legislators had argued during debate on the 1972 amendments, requiring the installation of conventional (BPT) technologies could effectively raise the costs of the more advanced BAT, because the two levels of controls are often incompatible. This result supported industry's petitions for delay in the deadlines and the relax-

Harsha: Mr. Graham, in all honesty, one of the problems created – or creating this area of no-return, so to speak, and the failure of the Environmental Protection Agency to promulgate the necessary rules and standards so that you know where you are, is the fact that you've been fighting the proposed rules and regulations all along, isn't that true?

Graham: I think there is clearly an element of that present.

[61] See, e.g., "Environmental Protection Agency Major Issues Agenda," memorandum by James R. Janis, acting director of the EPA Standards and Regulations Evaluation Division (no date); reprinted in *BNA Environment Reporter – Current Developments* 8 (1977): 623–37, esp. p. 631. Also see U.S. Senate (1979: 293) (citing Organization for Economic Cooperation and Development study of the costs of environmental controls in the iron and steel industry: "Fluctuations in capacity utilization will have a heavy impact upon the pollution control costs per ton of product, since a major part of the control costs is fixed and does not vary with the rate of capacity utilization").

ation of regulatory stringency,[62] both of which characterized later stages in the implementation of the water pollution law, as I illustrate in later sections.

Finally, the EPA understandably focused its scarce resources on industry's installation of BPT control technology, to the relative neglect of enforcing adequate operation and maintenance of the equipment once in place. This proved problematic for effective and equitable pollution control. An internal EPA memorandum noted in 1977 both that "there is a greater economic incentive to avoid [the expensive] O&M costs than to avoid the capital costs of installing control equipment," and that "the difficulty and cost of enforcing adequate O&M is greater than the surveillance and enforcement necessary to get greater control equipment installed." Not surprisingly, the agency found considerable evidence that "installed pollution control equipment is not achieving designed performance efficiencies."[63] Significantly, among the agency's own proposed regulatory solutions to this dilemma were two that were constrained by the terms of the law: forcing the alteration of production processes to avoid reliance on erratic EOL technologies, and administratively issued noncompliance fees (thus circumventing the need for protracted court and Justice Department intervention). Congress again rejected these proposals in the 1977 amendments, only to permit fees in a quite limited form years later in the 1987 amendments.

The Environmental Decade of the 1970s drew to a close with the contradiction that greater apparent progress had been made in industrial point discharges than in other major sources of pollution, including such nonpoint discharges as urban and rural run-off and municipal waste treatment plants. Run-off pollution carrying heavy loads of toxic and other pollutants into the nation's waterways remained virtually unaddressed in public policy.[64] And while the EPA was reporting that more than 80 percent of major industrial facto-

---

[62] In addition, the evidence reviewed previously on the role of the courts suggests that they are more likely to question the validity of such technology-based standards than they are in the case of media-quality standards (cf., McGarity, 1983: 225).

[63] "Environmental Protection Agency Major Issues Agenda," pp. 630–1.

[64] This problem was underscored, for example, in a General Accounting Office report titled, "National Water Quality Goals Cannot Be Attained Without More Attention to Pollution From Diffused or 'Nonpoint' Sources." The GAO reported that "nonpoint sources of pollution such as sediment, acid mine drainage, pesticides, and other sources of pollution carried into streams by runoff from rainstorms, currently produce more than half the pollutants entering the Nation's waterways." See U.S. Senate, 1979: 45–46.

ries were meeting the 1977 BPT discharge standards,[65] however these had ultimately been defined in individual cases, only 33 percent of the nation's almost 13,000 municipal treatment plants met the 1977 goal of secondary treatment.[66,67]

In large part this low compliance rate was due to a combination of the impoundment of some of the federal construction grant funds for municipal plants (as in the Nixon administration) and the government's difficulties in mounting efficient bureaucratic mechanisms to deliver them to the municipalities. Moreover, by 1977 EPA was proposing to limit federal sharing of construction funds to only those projects geared to achieve secondary treatment of sewage or (if more stringent) state water quality standards; if localities wanted cleaner water, the federal government wanted no part of the fiscal responsibility.[68] Under these various conditions it was increasingly difficult for the federal government to insist that industry continue to move toward zero discharge, however marginal the increments of cleanup, particularly given the escalating costs of achieving them. Given its own fiscal realities, the government was ever more receptive to business complaints of excessive environmental regulation.

Industry: irrationalities at law. Taken collectively, business's primary requirement of the state is that it provide the stable, rationalized political and macroeconomic conditions necessary for strategic planning and secure market exchange. With respect to environmental law, by the turbulent 1970s this requirement had translated into a need for a "level playing field" in regulatory constraints, one that would treat competitors alike in predictable, long-range fashion. But the nature of the 1972 law, and the legal system at large, served to confound this result.

[65] See, e.g., U.S. House of Representatives, 1977a: 339; U.S. Environmental Protection Agency, 1977b.

[66] See *The Eighth Annual Report of the Council on Environmental Quality* (Washington, D.C.: U.S. Government Printing Office, 1977), p. 36. Also U.S. Senate, 1979: 44.

[67] There was also the problem that by mid-1977 the EPA had yet to issue final pretreatment regulations governing industries' discharges into municipal treatment works. This meant that such discharges often continued to interfere with the routine operation of such facilities, resulting in large discharges of untreated sewage to waterways, or that many industrial pollutants simply passed through untreated. See *The Eighth Annual Report of the Council on Environmental Quality*, pp. 37–40.

[68] Environmental Protection Agency, "Transition Papers to Incoming Carter Administration on Areas of Agency Jurisdiction." Reprinted in *BNA Environment Reporter – Current Developments* 7 (1977): 1288.

The problem was partly the result of the uneven implementation of the law's requirements as the EPA scrambled to regulate industrial discharges under impossible deadlines. Moreover, a property-rights-based, adversarial legal system encourages time-consuming challenges to controls, even those developed in fundamental consultation with industry, as the regulated naturally seek to arrange the best possible circumstances, both collectively and individually. From the standpoint of the business system as a whole, an unintended consequence is the irregular, unpredictable tilting of the playing field of commerce which, in connection with the other forces shaping economic health, will have highly uncertain effects in the political economy. To the extent that such processes delay and frustrate effective regulation, they reinforce the potential for future demands in the political system for ever more stringent controls, especially with economic growth and the greater complexity (and toxicity) of industrial pollutants. That the 1972 amendments tended to promote the best of extant technologies, rather than to extend their frontiers, only enlarged the likelihood that pollution loads would ultimately outstrip the new controls, and in that way contribute to subsequent demands for greater regulation.

Other inequitable impacts were structured into the very terms of the law, embedded in the logic of the technology-based standards. Such technology design standards have a regressive character, because they tend to impose relatively equal costs on all firms so that unit costs are higher for the smaller companies (and those with underutilized productive capacity), placing them at additional competitive disadvantage. This has two salient consequences. First, it again has the effect of raising the aggregate costs of regulation relative to a given level of environmental benefits (Barnett, 1981), contributing to near term pressures for deregulation from some sectors of industry. But any such deregulation was virtually guaranteed to be both politically and environmentally destabilizing, as ultimately manifested in the deregulatory policies of the Reagan administration in the 1980s.

Second, to the extent that environmental law shares this regressive characteristic with much of public policy (including, for example, tax law), it may contribute to (but not alone cause) the further concentration of the economy (cf., Lilley and Miller, 1977: 51) into fewer and larger industrial organizations, particularly those operating on a multinational basis. The potential costs include reduced economic efficiencies (depending on the market structures in various industries, for example), reduced innovation (because smaller firms disproportionately contribute to research and development), and fewer employment opportunities in many localities. Ironically, they also include greater public pressures for government regulation of business in general, as citizens have historically borne greater distrust and animosity toward larger, more distant organizations than toward smaller, locally rooted ones. One close observer has argued:

> In general, the American people are overwhelmingly pro-capitalist and anti-regulation; but their attitudes toward small business are consistently higher than those toward big business, and their attitudes toward regulation of particular industries seem to be closely related to the degree of social contact between the business and individual consumers. . . . In this light, those concerned about regulation would do well to go beyond consideration of abstract property rights and consider *what forms of private property* stir greatest passions in their defense, as well as what means of communication and social interaction will maximize social contact. (Chickering, 1978: 226–7; emphasis in the original)

If this argument has limited applicability to such producer goods industries as the steel and chemical, and to regulatory matters involving fundamental matters of human health and safety, it nonetheless underscores a key dynamic validated in the history of social movements in regulatory law.

The 1972 amendments also called for the application of more stringent pollution control standards for new industrial facilities on which construction was to begin after the publication of the relevant regulations.[69] They did so on the reasoning that more advanced controls can be more cost effectively installed in new construction than in the retrofitting of existing plants. But in placing the regulatory burden disproportionately on facilities not yet built (which, by the way, are less able to negotiate their interests than extant ones), the law may create disincentives for industrial expansion and innovation, the result being that some companies may abandon or delay their expansion plans and stay longer with outmoded, inefficient, and more heavily polluting facilities (especially to the extent that firms have successfully argued for reductions in

[69] See Pub. L. 92-500, § 306. This section addresses standards for new facilities, calling for controls that reflect "the greatest degree of effluent reduction which the Administrator determines to be achievable through application of the best available demonstrated control technology, processes, operating methods, or other alternatives, including, where practicable, a standard permitting no discharge of pollutants."

standards in the courts and with the EPA), as Melnick (1983: 385–6) and others have suggested. To the extent that this result obtains, the costs are accounted against both the environment and the economy. (On the other side of this matter, this issue may be used to increase the leverage of industry arguments against stricter standards for new facilities, regardless of their ultimate affordability under the requirement of more advanced controls. In many cases, the EPA has set its "new source performance standards" equal to those for existing facilities, presumably in response to industry objections; see below.)

Environmentalists: the public interest at law. To a large extent, the contradictions facing the organized environmental movement, particularly as represented by the public-interest bar, parallel those experienced by the EPA in its efforts to reduce industrial pollution. But there are in addition two other types of problems that the 1972 law poses to environmental activists, worth brief mention here.

I have already noted the tendency for environmental interests to be disenfranchised in many of the numerous, key point decisions involved in the implementation of the water pollution law. Despite the Congress's careful insistence in the amendments that all key regulatory decisions be fully accessible to all sides, the necessarily complex implementation of the law often placed impossible resource demands on public-interest groups, particularly in respect of financial and informational resources. But it is worth adding that this problem is greatly aggravated by the technology-based nature of the law, which creates a large knowledge advantage for the regulated industries that disproportionately control the available information. As McGarity (1983: 225) has pointed out, "Under the [alternative, but largely eschewed] media-quality-based approach, which focuses more on toxicology than technology, the sides are more evenly matched."

Second, the law locked the public-interest advocacy of environmental groups into existing technology, both regulatory and industrial. The terms of the statute and the structure of the legal apparatus together channeled the energies of the environmental movement largely into demands that industry implement the better (BPT) and best (BAT) of existing technologies, however inefficient these might be in both the short and long terms, both environmentally and economically. The efforts of the public-interest bar were necessarily directed at the implementation and enforcement of these amendments, and precisely to that extent reproduced the limitations inherent in them. This is not to say that the efforts were wasted, because indeed the 1972 law offered the first real opportunity for some significant restraints on industrial pollution. But as a result of these tendencies in law, the frontiers of technology were neither adequately pushed nor questioned, and the potential for a comfortable accommodation between environment and economy therefore remains uncertain.

Of science, politics, and law: the regulation of toxics

Technology
I used to hope
for a break-through.
Now I wonder
What into?
  – Wendell Berry[70]

At the core of industrialization have been the advances of technology. But the blessings of technical progress have not been unmixed. Sigmund Freud, for example, "once wrote about the wondrous benefits of modern technology that permitted him to speak to his children hundreds of miles away. On second thought, he noted, it was the damn modern railroad that took them so far away in the first place" (Bazelon, 1981: 210). Indeed, the ambivalent effects of technology are distributed over time, place, and populations, often concentrating benefits here and costs there, raising fundamental philosophical questions about the peculiar nature of progress, its wisdom and justice. A jurist with long experience and a large role in key environmental law matters, Senior Circuit Judge David L. Bazelon of the U.S. Court of Appeals for the District of Columbia Circuit, has nicely illustrated the sorts of dilemmas that have often bedeviled both philosophy and law:

The chemicals in safety windshields, which protect drivers, may cause cancer in auto workers. Chlorinated water may protect against some diseases, but cause others. Nuclear energy may reduce nationwide cancer caused by burning fossil fuels. But it may increase risks to those living near the reactor and create an uncertain hazard to future generations because of radioactive wastes. Each of these developments affects the economy, which in turn affects the amount of poverty in the country. And poverty is related to risks of disease, mental illness, suicide, crime, even war. (1981: 213–14)

[70] Quoted in Bazelon (1981: 209).

Despite the great technical developments of the twentieth century, and in fact in large measure because of them, the wild card of a large measure of uncertainty – both scientific and philosophical – continues to characterize many of the vital deliberations of public policy. By now the key questions are as familiar as they are recurring: What risks (especially chronic risks) inhere in the use of new technologies? How large are they? And how should they be traded off against the potential benefits of new products and processes? Such uncertainties would humble Solomon.

They have commonly humbled regulatory law, particularly in combination with the opaque probabilities of politics.[71] Such uncertainty, like statutory vagueness, is often the open door through which regulatory politics most confidently walks. In the legal history of industrial water pollution, nowhere have the politics of uncertainty (and the uncertainties of politics) been more manifest than in the relatively recent, but long frustrated, efforts to regulate toxic discharges, first addressed in serious fashion by the 1972 amendments. Given the seriousness of the environmental impacts often involved, and the complexities of the numerous determinations to be made, these efforts more than any others test both the limits and potentials of regulatory law of this sort. And they again underscore the lesson that such limits and potentials typically run far deeper than those attributed to the instrumental politics of the moment (such as the Reagan administration's policies to greatly deregulate the environment). Rather, they are most fundamentally inscribed in the basic structures and processes of political economy, where science, politics, and law all intersect.

Aggressive law, tentative regulation

At the level of statement, in the 1972 amendments to the Federal Water Pollution Control Act the Congress took an uncompromising stand on toxic pollutants. The law clearly addressed toxics as a regulatory matter of a different sort from more conventional pollutants, one to be handled with an aggressive regimen of controls. The

---

[71] Regarding the uncertainties in risk assessments, Judge Bazelon (1981: 212) has noted that "risk estimates may depend on future contingencies of human behavior or other highly complex and unpredictable variables. . . . The best risk estimates are subject to an unknown degree of residual uncertainty and may thus overstate or understate the dangers involved. Indeed, many times [a regulatory] agency must act in circumstances that make a crap game look as certain as death and taxes."

rationale for so doing was indicated clearly enough in the statute's definition of toxics (however turgid the legal prose):

The term "toxic pollutant" means those pollutants, or combinations of pollutants, including disease-causing agents, which after discharge and upon exposure, ingestion, inhalation or assimilation into any organism, either directly from the environment or indirectly by ingestion through food chains, will, on the basis of information available to the Administrator, cause death, disease, behavioral abnormalities, cancer, genetic mutations, physiological malfunctions (including malfunctions in reproduction) or physical deformations, in such organisms or their offspring.[72]

The seriousness of the Congress's regulatory purpose was made clear at the outset, in the statement of the law's policy and goals, where it wrote that "it is the national policy that the discharge of toxic pollutants in toxic amounts *be prohibited*."[73] This statement of *policy* stood in contrast to the law's general *goal* of the elimination of all pollutants by 1985, given the Congress's internal debates on the latter statement, as illustrated in the previous chapter. In addition, the law distinguished the regulatory logic for toxics from that to be applied to conventional pollutants. Instead of the technology-based (and cost-constrained) standards to be applied to the more traditional pollutants, the 1972 amendments sought to regulate toxic discharges not on the basis of technological potentials, but on the more stringent criteria of their broad environmental effects on water and water-based organisms, and up the food chain to human health, making no mention of the limits of extant control technologies or costs.[74]

Here, then, was the law's strongest statement on water pollution, one fully consonant not only with unbridled notions of fundamental *human* rights (to health and procreation) that all legitimate governments must seek to insure, but also with the emergent view that fundamental *environmental* rights attached to all living organisms, the protection of which would now similarly test the legitimacy of rule. And to underscore the Congress's sense of the matter's urgency (likely both to the environment and governmental legitimacy), it

[72] Pub. L. 92-500, § 502[13].

[73] Pub. L. 92-500, § 101[a][3]; emphasis added.

[74] The law authorized the EPA to promulgate toxic effluent standards that "shall take into account the toxicity of the pollutant, its persistence, degradability, the usual or potential presence of the affected organisms in any waters, the importance of the affected organisms and the nature and extent of the effect of the toxic pollutant on such organisms," § 307[a][2]; unlike the statements for establishing BPT and BAT, no mention at all is made of the costs of controls (cf., Schroeder, 1983: 27–8).

mandated very tight timetables for compliance: within 15 months of
the law's passage the EPA was to publish a list of toxic pollutants
(both singly and in toxic combinations, a large task indeed) and to
finalize the multitude of discharge regulations controlling them
"with an ample margin of safety" to protect the environment. Industrial firms directly discharging such toxics into the nation's waters
were to be in compliance with the new limits no more than one year
after their promulgation.[75] The statute called for similar regulations
for companies discharging their effluents into municipal waste treatment plants.[76]

But the law-in-action quickly became something quite different.
By 1989, fully sixteen years after the law's passage, key regulations
were still not yet in place, to say nothing of widespread industrial
compliance. Ultimately, the limits of law had as much to do with the
techniques (and politics) of regulation as with the technologies of
industry.

Complexity, uncertainty, and delay. The limits of toxics regulation are
rooted in the vast complexities and uncertainties that characterize
much of modern chemical science and production. The limits are
more vexing to the extent that these uncertainties and complexities
are subject to periodic manipulation by regulated parties seeking to
constrain the reach of law. And even in the face of good faith efforts
from manufacturers, the combined limits of law and science synergistically constrain the impacts of public policy.

Some 65,000 chemicals are manufactured in the United States every year, and for many there is little knowledge of their toxic effects,
either alone or in their myriad combinations (Schneider, 1985: 15;
Conservation Foundation, 1982: 119–22). Moreover, by 1977 the
EPA's Toxicological Assessment Branch was estimating that the nation's drinking water contained between 3,000 and 5,000 different
chemicals, and the waterways some several hundred thousand chemical compounds; the agency also noted that the ability even to iden-

---

[75] Pub. L. 92-500, §§ 307[a][1, 2, 4, 5, 6].
[76] Pub. L. 92-500, § 307[b]. My discussion focuses on the regulation of plants dis-
    charging pollutants directly into receiving waters ("direct dischargers") rather than
    on the "indirect dischargers" whose effluent is sent to municipal treatment plants.
    This decision reflects nothing about the relative importance (in public policy) of
    these two types. Instead, I focus on direct dischargers to avoid the analytic (and
    regulatory) complications involved in considering the compliance roles of munici-
    pal treatment works, which were, among other things, importantly shaped by the
    bureaucratic and budgetary politics of federal funding for their construction.

tify such compounds was far outstripping scientists' ability to determine their toxic effects (for humans and other organisms) and at what levels of concentration they occur (U.S. House of Representatives, 1977b: 24). This knowledge gap has at best remained constant since then, as the proliferation of new chemical compounds in industry challenges improvements in science's abilities to assess them.[77]

The knowledge gap was exacerbated in EPA's regulatory environment. Given the high costs, difficulties, and uncertainties attached to monitoring and assessing toxic pollutants, it was predictable that the agency would pursue a regulatory course more likely to produce fast results for the environment (and consequent political benefits for the EPA), regulating long-familiar conventional pollutants that could be substantially limited with existing technologies (controlling biochemical oxygen demand [BOD], total suspended solids [TSS], and pH for example). Understandable in theory, it was nonetheless ironic from a public policy standpoint that the agency immediately gave its most important water pollution control mandate a clearly second class status.

This status was clear in the EPA's earliest efforts to implement the 1972 amendments. By 1977, *two years after the statutory deadline for industry compliance with the new toxic regulations,* EPA's own personnel testified in congressional hearings that its permit system implementing the 1972 amendments had produced very little information on the types and loads of toxic chemicals being discharged by industry.[78] The lack of baselines was the joint product of the EPA's general inattention to the regulation of toxics to that point and industry's disinterest in volunteering such information (surely reinforced by the agency's signals). Intentionally or otherwise companies often withheld or even misrepresented their toxics data, fre-

---

[77] During the 1980s a number of important studies confirmed the continuing existence of a large gap in the accumulated knowledge on toxics (Schneider, 1985). For example, in 1984 a National Academy of Sciences study reported that regulatory agency files did not contain sufficiently accurate data to determine the safety of most of the 65,000 chemicals on the market. According to the report, "Of tens of thousands of commercially important chemicals, only a few have been subjected to extensive toxicity testing, and most have scarcely been tested at all" (quoted in Schneider, 1985: 15). The gap is due to a combination of high costs of testing, the inability of extant scientific technologies to measure many types of effects, misrepresentation of data and inadequate agency oversight. See footnote 79.

[78] R. G. Tardiff, chief of EPA's Toxicological Assessment Branch, testified, "At present, the permit system only yields very nebulous information that is useful for health hazard evaluations. It really does not give us a good profile of the types of chemicals that are being discharged" (U.S. House of Representatives, 1977b: 18).

quently to the later surprise of the agency.[79] The high costs of monitoring individual plants (EPA was sampling only about 1,000 facilities per year) and ambient water quality in rivers and streams broadened the knowledge gap (see U.S. House of Representatives, 1977b: 19–23).

In light of such constraints, it is less surprising that the first round of EPA's five-year pollution discharge permits regulated virtually none of the toxic pollutants (such as organic chemicals and metals). Moreover, the writing of specific regulations for toxics got off to an extraordinarily slow start, owing to the uncertainties and costs of formulating them in a political environment demanding an immediate show of at least *some* results. Adding to the weight of these scientific and regulatory uncertainties was the agency's need to create a *defensible regulatory record,* one that could withstand the inevitable court challenges to the rules. While reviewing courts were unlikely to challenge specific expert determinations and judgments, they often remanded regulations on the charge that the EPA had not produced an adequate record of decision making. During a number of the final rulemaking procedures for toxic water pollution in the 1980s, the EPA voluntarily withdrew proposed regulations under industry challenges to the record, anticipating that the courts would force such a decision in the absence of agency reconsideration.[80]

[79] In the congressional hearings, the case of the FMC Corporation's permit was used to illustrate the ineffectiveness of the permit system for monitoring toxics (U.S. House of Representatives, 1977b: 19). In its original permit application, the company first listed a carbon tetrachloride discharge of 71 pounds a day, later increasing its report to 800 pounds. In spring 1977 before a congressional hearing, however, the company submitted that it was discharging between 2,000 and 4,000 pounds of the material per day. An official of West Virginia's Division of Water Resources, which with the EPA had co-issued the discharge permit to FMC, said the new report "came as quite a surprise to us, as well as to EPA . . . it was a shocker."

Evidence from related regulatory arenas also suggests that data on industrial chemicals are often unreliable because of either inadequate and falsified industry tests, inadequate agency oversight of such chemicals and private-sector testing, or a combination of the two. Such problems have been identified, for example, in connection with the federal Food and Drug Administration's new drug approval process, the EPA's testing of pesticide ingredients, and the National Cancer Institute's cancer testing system. See, e.g., Schneider (1985).

[80] For example, the EPA relaxed its proposed rules for pretreatment of discharges to municipal treatment plants by electroplating facilities in an out-of-court settlement with the National Association of Metal Finishers (45 Fed. Reg. 45322), which had filed suit against them (*BNA Environment Reporter – Current Developments* 11 [1980]: 385). Similarly, in late 1986 the agency voluntarily withdrew its BAT regulations for the pesticide industry for reconsideration (*BNA Environment Reporter – Current*

In consequence of such difficulties, by late 1973 the EPA had listed only nine toxic substances for regulation,[81] and by 1976 had still failed to produce regulations on even these, because the agency believed the analytic record developed at its public hearings on the nine would not withstand judicial review.[82] As a result, three environmental groups sued the EPA for failure to perform nondiscretionary duties, and in 1976 the federal district court for the District of Columbia approved a consent decree (known as the Flannery Decree after the presiding judge) establishing a new regulatory framework and timetable for compliance. The court ordered that regulations be finalized no later than the end of 1979, with industry to achieve compliance no later than June 30, 1983 (*Natural Resources Defense Council v. Train* [D.D.C. 1976; 8 ERC 2120]). The decree required the EPA to regulate sixty-five "priority" toxic pollutants and classes of pollutants in twenty-one industrial categories, and its basic terms were endorsed by the Congress in the Clean Water Act of 1977 (amending the 1972 law).[83] But as it happened many additional extensions became necessary, and the decree was modified by the court in 1979, 1982, 1983, 1984 (twice), 1985, 1986, and 1987.[84] Finally, when Congress again amended the water pollution law in 1987, the final deadline for industrial compliance was set at March 31, 1989.[85] But even at fourteen years past the original compliance deadline, this too proved optimistic.

The limits of technology

The daunting uncertainties inherent in the statute's mandate for toxics – scientific/technical, administrative, and ultimately political – drove the EPA to administratively amend the 1972 law, with the imprimatur of the federal courts and environmentalists via the Flannery decree. The decree largely transformed the regulatory ap-

Developments 17 [1986]: 1,419), and in 1987 voluntarily proposed modifications in the rules for the leather tanning and finishing industry to settle a court challenge to the proposed ones (*BNA Environment Reporter – Current Developments* 17 [1987]: 1617–18).

[81] The nine were aldrin/dieldrin, benzidine, cadmium, cyanide, DDT (DDE, DDD), endrin, polychlorinated biphenyls, mercury, and toxaphene.
[82] See *Natural Resources Defense Council v. Train* (D.D.C. 1976; 8 ERC 2120, 2123).
[83] Pub. L. 95-217; see 33 U.S.C. 1251 *et seq.* (1982 ed.). Also see U.S. Senate (1977a).
[84] See, e.g., 52 Fed. Reg. 42522 (establishing toxic regulations for the Organic Chemicals and Plastics and Synthetic Fibers industrial category; reviewing history of legal authority).
[85] Pub. L. 100-4; see 33 U.S.C. 1251 *et seq.* (Supp. V 1987). For a summary overview of the changes wrought by the 1987 amendments, see Garrett (1987).

proach from the stringent, absolutist toxic effects considerations ordered by the Congress to the cost – and technology – constrained application of "best available technology" for industry categories. (The decree left the more stringent approach in place for four highly toxic pesticides, plus benzidine and polychlorinated biphenyls [PCBs].)[86] This reorientation at law allowed the agency to proceed sure-footedly on the basis of real technologies rather than on its highly suspect abilities to penetrate the obscure mysteries of nature. As the EPA had noted in proposed toxic regulations in 1976, in connection with the notion of an "ample margin of safety":

In any case where a discharge is allowed, on a spectrum ranging from certain safety (a prohibition) to that uncertain point where harmful effects are caused and safety ends, a logical break point is struck where the very best that control technology can do is required.[87]

This transformation represented a retreat from the rights-based approach mandated by the Congress (cf., Schroeder, 1983: 36–8), and it clearly bespoke the fundamental limits on this regulatory enterprise. For many toxics science could not adequately determine safe levels of exposure, but any consequent argument for zero discharge ran headlong against the realities of political economy. The uncertainties of science confronted the realpolitik of such matters as jobs and inflation: How to justify large risks in either for uncertain environmental benefits? The focus on technology put into play other dynamics that shape the reach of environmental law, including a certain place for instrumental politics. But these dynamics cut both ways, both limiting law and ensuring some degree of control over toxic pollutants. If instrumental attempts to limit regulation (as by the Reagan administration in the 1980s) helped stall it in the near term, such attempts themselves were constrained by longer term forces in both law and public demands on policy.

The logics of technology. By the time the EPA began to implement the terms of the Flannery Decree, some close expert observers of the process were critiquing its technology dependency much as some congressional representatives had in prospect years earlier (see

[86] See 42 Fed. Reg. 2613 (Jan. 12, 1977); 40 Code of Fed. Reg., Part 129 (Rev. July 1, 1977).
[87] Proposed Toxic Pollutant Effluent Standards, 41 Fed. Reg. 12576 (1976). (Quoted in McGarity [1983: 207].) The federal courts approved this departure from the statutory directive regarding an "ample margin of safety" in *Environmental Defense Fund v. EPA*, 598 F.2d 62 (D.C. Cir. 1978), and in *Hercules, Inc. v. EPA*, 598 F.2d 91 (D.C. Cir. 1978).

Chapter 5). The combination of the earlier requirement of first-stage BPT for conventional pollutants, with insufficient governmental expenditures for research and development on new pollution control technologies, threatened to constrain the effectiveness – even the requirement – of second-stage BAT for the more complicated pollutants. For example, from his analysis of the water law Tripp (1977: 245) concluded:

> The commitment of very large sums of money to waste treatment techniques that are designed to control "traditional" pollutants may be locking in both industries and municipalities so that when toxic substances with adverse public health effects are subsequently identified, there will be no economically feasible method of meeting the effluent standards established for the toxins.[88]

In theory, under the 1972 amendments the EPA could establish BAT on the basis of model plants privately or publicly funded, or the single best plant in an industry. But as a practical matter, the agency did not do so, instead basing its regulations for toxics on the controls that the technologically more advanced firms in industry categories had in place, or (less stringent yet) on the dominant industry practices. For a number of categories, the EPA rejected BAT altogether, settling for the less stringent BPT. For example, after initially proposing BAT for the leather tanning industry, in response to industry criticisms the agency issued a final rule in 1982 setting controls at BPT because, it said, *the proposed BAT controls had not yet been demonstrated in the industry and were not economically achievable.* The same year the EPA revoked proposed BAT for the petroleum refining industry and promulgated final regulations setting the controls on toxics as BPT.[89] That powerful industry successfully resisted the agency's original proposal that greatly restricted the flow of wastes by mandating recycling and reuse of waste streams, controls that – unlike typically end-of-pipe and less effective BPT – apparently intruded too forcefully on the industry's traditional production practices.

Such constraints inhere in regulatory approaches emphasizing extant technologies, even "leading" ones. This is especially true where the state, whether for fiscal, political, or philosophical reasons, is largely divorced from the development of the technical means of production, leaving them to the private sector. From the standpoint

---

[88] Cf., McGarity (1983: 205): "The technology-based approach in practice can bias pollution control in favor of capital-intensive 'white elephant' technologies which may be ineffective in the long run."

[89] See Bureau of National Affairs (1983).

of legal administration, the technology-based approach carries a number of advantages (see, e.g., McGarity, 1983: 206–9), including reduced public arousal regarding (and therefore fewer conflicting political pressures on) the agency's various regulatory decisions. This is because they are couched in the dry, abstract, and depoliticized language of technological potentials, rather than in the impassioned terms of basic human rights and fundamental questions of morality (such as risks to human health) that the toxic effects (or water-quality-based) approach elicits. As such, the regulatory decision-making process bends toward technical exchanges between EPA and industry experts, and tends to exclude those environmentalist interests lacking the appropriate scientific and engineering expertise. In consequence, the public interest tends to be resolved conservatively (shaded toward economic interests) rather than aggressively (toward environmental values). According to one public-interest litigator who helped shape the agency's implementation of toxics regulations in the 1980s, the rules are conservative because the EPA is "risk averse," fearing industry challenges to more aggressive alternatives.[90] Such challenges naturally carry a "bite," given industries' near monopoly on technological process information and the courts' insistence on an adequate regulatory record.

The orientation toward technology-based controls was virtually total at the EPA by the latter half of the 1970s. As a result, the consideration of the human health effects of toxic pollutants, to say nothing of the effects on other important organisms, became clearly subordinated to the concerns of agency specialists in engineering and technologies. In 1977 there were only some fifteen physicians on EPA's (relatively) large professional staff, and EPA Administrator Douglas Costle suggested in congressional hearings that the agency's research on the health effects of toxics was quite limited. Other congressional testimony indicated that EPA experts tended to deal more with cities' and towns' treatment facilities' managers than with their public-health officials, again underscoring the engineering emphasis, and that within EPA there was poor coordination between the dominant engineering component and the health effects researchers.[91]

With respect to the regulation of toxics, there was no small irony in this. Indeed, the regulatory wheel had turned fully through time. In its earliest manifestations, public-health interests had had to

[90] Interview with Robert Adler, director of Clean Water Program, Natural Resources Defense Council, June 28, 1989.
[91] See U.S. House of Representatives (1977b: 4, 9, 34).

wrest water policy from sole concern with commercial transportation matters to the broader issues of human health. Later, the U.S. Public Health Service came to impede regulatory progress against industrial pollutants not obviously connected to human health (see Chapter 3). Now again, near the close of the twentieth century, the matter of the chronic effects of toxics found health criteria in the shadows of public policy. Whatever else, a common denominator in the limits of law has been its tendency over time to address acute rather than chronic crises and effects, but with increasingly hazardous potentials at each turn. If in the earlier era the needs of commerce appeared prior to those of public health, in the later era the nature of industrial technology to some extent obscured the polity's view of the public-health consequences of toxics.

Finally, the technology-based approach had the effect of setting different discharge limitations for the same toxic pollutants, the levels of control depending on the production processes in the various industry categories. Moreover, limits were set without regard to the effects of specific pollutants on specific waterways (the questionable possibility that more stringent water quality standards might be applied notwithstanding), which vary widely in terms of their vulnerability to toxic effects. This approach to controls thus risks underachieving benefits relative to aggregate regulatory costs, debiting both ecology and economy in the process.

The logics of politics. The regulatory logic just described, rooted in basic facts of political economy (such as concern for costs and the privatization of technology) and constrained by the limits of knowledge, shaped the reach of instrumental politics. Near term political pressures for more or less stringent environmental regulation are themselves shaped by prevailing ideological leanings, both in the broader culture and in the governmental apparatuses, and by economic conditions whether munificent or troubled. Such pressures have always acted on environmental law with varying effects on its impacts. But whether the politics of regulation invoke the often abstruse arguments and methods of economic analysis or involve less sophisticated cloakroom dealings with regulated parties (as alleged during the Reagan administration), their reach is commonly constrained as well by countervailing forces in law less subject to instrumental control. Thus while environmental regulation has certainly been responsive to political pressures and constraints, it resists full subordination to them. From the philosophical standpoint urging more aggressive, rights-based pollution controls, the barriers in political economy to full implementation of such policies are substantial. But so are those barriers to the implementation of the opposing stance of deregulation, the most powerful of which are the real facts of environmental deterioration..

Other, more prosaic forces are at work as well. I shall illustrate some of these with examples from the Reagan administration's environmental policies regarding regulation of toxic water pollution. (See the final chapter for discussion of related issues, including those related to cost–benefit assessments.)

The Reagan administration took office in 1981 amid a deepening economic recession and widespread popular dissatisfaction with government policies on the economy and foreign affairs. Given its own ideological leanings, the administration translated these signals into a mandate to "deregulate" the economy, freeing commerce from costly legal controls as part of a so-called supply-side strategy to stimulate economic growth. (One of the leading architects of this strategy was Congressman Jack Kemp, previously a supporter of much of the logic of the 1972 amendments, as earlier noted.)

Executive Order 12291, issued by President Reagan shortly after he took office in 1981,[92] mandated that EPA and other agencies conduct benefit – cost analyses ("regulatory impact analyses") of all major new regulations, defined as those that impose an annual cost of $100 million or more on the economy, significantly increase prices and unemployment, or meet other, related criteria. The order requires that economic efficiency (maximizing aggregate net benefits) be the basis for evaluating these regulations, and that agencies submit their analyses to the president's Office of Management and Budget for approval prior to the publication of proposed rules.[93]

The effect of the order – and its aggressive, arguably extralegal implementation by the Reagan executive team [94] – was to delay, dilute, and in some cases indefinitely bury regulations, particularly

[92] See 46 Fed. Reg. 13193 (Feb. 19, 1981).
[93] For a useful discussion of many of the issues and uncertainties associated with Executive Order 12291, see Smith (1984).
[94] A report prepared by the Congressional Research Service for the House Subcommittee on Oversight and Investigations, Committee on Energy and Commerce, concluded that OMB was exceeding its legal authority in hosting *secret* meetings between private, largely corporate interests and top White House officials regarding proposed regulations, and that the executive order violated the Administrative Procedure Act of 1946 in subordinating expert agency decision making to the judgment of the OMB (Tolchin and Tolchin, 1983: 67–9).

those social regulations on industry that addressed questions of public health and safety.[95] The Reagan policy gave industrial interests especial hearing at the highest levels of the Executive Branch, for example through private, *ex parte* meetings with OMB officials well before proposed regulations were published (see, e.g., Tolchin and Tolchin, 1983: 39–71). The policy also sent a clear message to the agencies that thereafter regulatory policy would concern itself first with private-sector costs rather than principally with public-sector benefits.[96] This message was underscored by the formation of the aptly titled Presidential Task Force on Regulatory Relief, designed to coordinate the president's deregulatory efforts and headed by Vice President George Bush (who later, in 1988, found it necessary to campaign as a proenvironment candidate in a successful bid for the presidency). The policy was especially aimed at the EPA, which had produced some of the nation's most expensive regulations to date. The message was reinforced by large cuts in the agency's budget (and, not incidentally, in its research budget) just as it was gearing up a number of major regulatory initiatives to control toxics in water and hazardous waste disposal, and by the appointment as EPA administrator of Anne (Gorsuch) Burford, who took the deregulatory mission of her chief executive quite seriously indeed.

In her first budget request to the OMB, Burford recommended a 39 percent budget reduction (in real dollars, controlling for inflation) from the fiscal 1981 budget of the Carter administration to the 1983 Reagan budget. EPA research programs were to be cut between 15 and 54 percent, and large reductions were planned as well for water quality programs and water pollution enforcement, and grants for the states' environmental programs (the Reagan adminis-

---

[95] The early effects of the order were dramatic indeed. During the first five months of its implementation, the volume of proposed rulemaking by federal agencies declined by 50 percent compared with the same period in 1980 (although at least some portion of this change was presumably due to the natural lag to be expected during transitions between administrations). Vice President George Bush also announced that 180 regulations had been either withdrawn, delayed, or modified, saving $6 billion a year; businesses, he said, would in total save some $18 billion in forestalled equipment purchases as a result (Tolchin and Tolchin, 1983: 70).

[96] At one point in 1983, House Energy Committee chairman John Dingell complained that executives of some thirty companies had been given access to internal EPA files while many of their companies were targets of agency enforcement actions. The executives were reviewing EPA's operations as members of the President's Private Sector Survey on Cost Control, and worked for such large corporations as Dow Chemical, Monsanto, Union Carbide, American Cyanamid, Shell Oil and B. F. Goodrich. Many of the companies had been involved in toxic waste and water pollution enforcement cases with the EPA (*Boston Globe*, September 23, 1983, p. 3).

tration had justified the cuts in part on the basis of increased delegation of environmental programs to the states). Congress reduced the size of the cuts, but they remained substantial. Between the end of 1980 and early 1983, nearly 3,000 staff positions had been cut (from 11,407 in fiscal 1981).[97] Facing the political backlash to environmental deregulation in 1983 and the election year of 1984, the administration finally approved a budget increase for the agency to $1.14 billion, which, even in nonadjusted terms, still stood in sharp contrast to the last Carter budget of $1.35 billion (fiscal 1981). In real spending power, the fiscal 1984 budget represented a cut of about one-third from the 1981 funding.[98]

In combination with the attendant organizational confusion, turnover among professional staff, and widespread loss of morale at the agency in the early 1980s,[99] these cuts necessarily affected the toxic water pollution program. The consequences were delay and dilution, but far from total defeat for the program. The momentum behind the regulation of toxic water pollution, however retarded, was maintained by the widely perceived risks of the problem and by the restraining influence of the courts on attempts to curtail its regulation.

There is little doubt that the new deregulatory philosophy in the Executive Branch weakened the toxics program. Additional delay was occasioned not only by the deepened shortage of agency resources, as a number of EPA officials themselves noted publicly,[100] but also by the increased caution brought to the agency's science and engineering professionals by the executive order and by the antireg-

---

[97] See, e.g., U.S. House of Representatives (1983: 17, 25–32); BNA, "Preliminary Proposal for Fiscal 1983 Included Major EPA Budget, Personnel Cuts," *BNA Environment Reporter – Current Developments* 12 (1981), pp. 675–6, 697–703; Baldwin (1983).

[98] *The New York Times*, July 14, 1984; *Boston Globe*, December 9, 1983.

[99] See, e.g., U.S. House of Representatives (1983); Tolchin and Tolchin (1983).

[100] It ultimately proved impolitic for the agency to claim inadequate resources with its own leadership calling for budget cuts. A few months after petitioning the federal district court in Washington for relaxation of the deadlines in the modified Flannery Decree, arguing reduced budgets and personnel as justification, the EPA's inspector general issued a report saying that resources were quite adequate, but periodically mismanaged by the Office of Water Regulations and Standards, which had originally argued that resources were insufficient. This internal dispute signaled the political versus professional tensions that gripped the EPA in the early 1980s, as the political leadership argued that greater agency efficiency would clearly cover budget cuts while professional program staff continued to cite resource shortages for regulatory delays. See BNA, "Judge Sets Hearing on EPA Motion to Ease Decree on Toxic Discharges," *BNA Environment Reporter – Current Developments* 12 (1981): 484–5; "Order Sought for EPA to Release Data in Request to Ease Toxic Control Decree," ibid. 12 (1981): 752; "EPA Erred in Citing Budget

ulatory stance of their own superiors at EPA. The toxics regulations would need not only to pass legal muster in the courts of appeals, but also to survive the new, more restrictive cost tests of the Reagan administration. These mounting delays were adding costs to the environment in the form of hundreds of millions of pounds of toxic wastes discharged annually into U.S. waters. For at least some of the key industries involved, such as the organic chemicals industry,[101] not only had advanced BAT limits been postponed but first-stage BPT limits had not even been established by the early 1980s. Instead, EPA and state permit issuers had set discharge limits on a discretionary, case-by-case basis with only modest and highly variable effects on toxic discharges.

The Reagan policies almost certainly reduced the potential effectiveness of toxics regulation by reducing the stringency of controls below achievable levels. Of course, in a political world this must remain a rather contentious proposition, given the incessant divisions over such notions as "achievable" and cost-versus-benefit tradeoffs. But given the historically modest economic effects of EPA regulation of water pollution (see last section), and the record in the early 1980s of the agency's revision of proposed BAT controls on toxics down to less advanced BPT levels, the proposition is a reasonable one. For example, in the case of the leather tanning industry, the agency had proposed BAT standards in 1979 under the Carter administration, only to revise them to BPT in late 1982 "after analysis of the cost and economic impact of the tighter (BAT) controls." Interestingly, investment costs for the industry were estimated at $171 million under the relaxed rule, more than twice the $65 million estimated for the stricter rule in 1979.[102]

But if the Reagan policies had constrained the reach of the water pollution program, the argument here is that the operation of these limits represented differences in degree, rather than in kind, from their operation in previous administrations. Indeed, as I discuss fur-

Cuts in Bid to Delay Effluent Guidelines, Study Says," ibid. 12 (1981): 928–9; "EPA Rulemaking Delays Assailed by Some, Defended by Others at House Panel Hearing," ibid. 12 (1981): 858–9.

[101] See *Organic Chemicals and Plastics and Synthetic Fibers Category Effluent Limitations Guidelines, Pretreatment Standards, and New Source Performance Standards* (Final Rule), 52 Fed. Reg. 42522 (Nov. 5, 1987), at 42526. (Hereafter referenced as OCPSF Final Rule.)

[102] BNA, "EPA Proposes New Standards, Guidelines for Leather Tanning, Finishing Industry," *BNA Environment Reporter – Current Developments* 10 (1979): 562; "Final Rule Eases Effluent Limits for Leather Tanning Industry, EPA Says," ibid. 13 (1982): 1283–4.

ther in Chapter 8, Reagan's Executive Order 12291 had much in common with policies instituted by President Carter in 1978 as he sought to fight inflation by reducing the economic burdens on industry of government regulations. Moreover, delays have characterized every phase of the program, and both environmentalists and industry groups have always challenged EPA regulations as either too lenient or too strict. Instead, what subtly shifted under the Reagan administration were the institutional dynamics shaping environmental policy, the routes of transmission through which public pressures are transformed into legal requirements.

Through much of the Carter administration, industry perceived environmental policy to be in the unsympathetic hands of a troika comprising the EPA leadership, environmental public-interest groups and congressional oversight committees. From the standpoint of business, the best hope for a more or less sympathetic hearing was in the courts, where the uncertainties and complexities of environmental regulations made possible the case that EPA's rulemaking records were insufficient and the regulations built on them therefore too stringent. Such arguments often won. (After 1978, industry also had a more appreciative audience in the White House, although not so much as it would have after 1981.) During the early years of the Reagan administration, the balance of access changed. Business not only had the ear of the White House but found the EPA's leadership much more sensitive to its concerns regarding regulatory costs.

Despite this dramatic shift, a rough parity in the balance between economic and environmental values was maintained by two less politicized forces in policymaking, two with whom industry itself had often been able to more successfully plead its cause in the past: EPA's midlevel technical experts responsible for specifying the details of regulations and the courts. In effect, these consistently served as stabilizing currents under the uncertain, often turbulent tides of ideological politics.

The record of toxics rulemaking in the 1980s indicates that, while many of the regulations were softened short of their potential reach, they nonetheless promised to substantially curtail the discharges of many harmful substances to the extent that they are effectively implemented and enforced. The final toxics regulations for industry categories typically projected 90 to 95 percent reductions in toxic discharges upon full implementation of the rules, and if these eventually prove to be optimistic, the fact of continuing and vigorous in-

232 **6 Controls and constraints**

dustry challenges to several major rules in court suggests they carry nontrivial impacts. In total, the regulatory record indicates that EPA scientists and engineers continued to respond largely to the logics of their professional expertise and values and to the legal mandate of the water pollution law (safeguarded by the courts via the Flannery Decree), if more cautious to shade the rules conservatively in the face of technical and political uncertainty.

The contrast with the enforcement function is telling in this regard. In the early 1980s EPA's leadership eviscerated environmental law enforcement: industry violations were virtually ignored. This was not because enforcement attorneys, who had long taken their professional and legal mandates as seriously as the agency's scientists and engineers did theirs, simply abandoned their commitments and identities in response to strong political messages and threats. Instead, precisely because of the lawyers' professional orientations, it proved necessary for the leadership to entirely disrupt the function through a rapid series of confusing reorganizations having little apparent relation to either efficiency or effectiveness (see Chapter 8). Such options were less available in the case of the Effluent Guidelines Division, primarily because its work continued to be clearly mandated by both the law and the ongoing oversight of the court via the Flannery Decree (whereas substantial discretion had always characterized the enforcement function).

With regard to the courts, the same juridical concern with legal *process* that had ensured a measure of fairness from industry's standpoint also limited the scope of deregulation by safeguarding the *substance* of both the toxics program and regulations rendered in good faith by the EPA. The courts' influence was manifested in a number of decisions between 1979 and 1989.

For example, in his continuing oversight of the toxics program, Judge Flannery (U.S. District Court, District of Columbia) ruled in 1982 against industry arguments that the consent decree impermissibly interfered with EPA discretion to administer the Clean Water Act.[103] In the context of the moment, the alternative ruling surely would have radically reduced the public-interest potential of the toxics program. Flannery ruled that because it insists only on process rather than enforcing any particular content, the decree does not infringe on the agency's discretion; furthermore, the court's ruling

---

[103] *Natural Resources Defense Council, Inc. v. Gorsuch*, C.A. No. 2153–73, et al. See BNA, "Court Rules Toxic Pollutant Settlement Does Not Interfere with EPA Discretion," *BNA Environment Reporter – Current Developments* 12 (1982): 1323–4.

was authorized under the Administrative Procedure Act of 1946 (Sec. 706[1])[104] because EPA's record of toxic water pollutant regulation "can be considered equivalent to administrative action unlawfully withheld." Throughout the key years of the deregulatory 1980s his court kept vigilant watch over the agency's progress in implementing the terms of the decree, permitting some deadline slippage but never retracting the order's basic terms.

Moreover, the courts often rejected industry challenges to key regulatory decisions, including some relating to industry's traditional control over production data. For example, in 1979 the U.S. Court of Appeals for the First Circuit generally upheld regulations for pesticide industry discharges, rejecting the industry's arguments that the rules were based on inadequate scientific methodology and insufficient data.[105] (The regulations were remanded for agency reconsideration of the data underlying two portions of the regulations.) The court ruled that it would not take the role of "superchemist" given the general adequacy of EPA's rulemaking record in this case, limiting its review to the reasonableness of the agency's decisions in light of that record and the legislative mandate of the 1972 and 1977 amendments.

In response to industry complaints that available data were insufficient to support the record, the court's judgment was trenchant: "EPA faces a severe problem in regulating the pesticide industry because a great deal is not known about treatment of pesticide wastewaters and because the industry is very reticent about revealing what it does (or could) know. . . . we will not hear industry complain that EPA used insufficient data when industry was uncooperative in supplying the missing data." While this decision was not controlling for all industry complaints of data insufficiency, even for the pesticides industry for which later BAT regulations were withdrawn in 1986 by the agency for reconsideration,[106] it began to suggest that courts would expect industry to provide the requisite data for rulemaking, with proper agency protection for industry trade secrets. In

[104] 5 U.S.C. 551 (1946). The act and its supporting case law specify the required procedures for administrative rulemaking by agencies of the federal government, including advance notice of proposed rules and opportunities for meaningful participation in rulemaking deliberations by outside parties such as public-interest groups and industry.
[105] *BASF Wyandotte Corp. v. Costle*, 598 F.2d 637 (1st Cir., 1979). See also BNA, "EPA Water Act Regulations for Pesticide Industry Upheld," *BNA Environment Reporter – Current Developments* 9 (1979): 76–7.
[106] BNA, "EPA to Retract, Review Effluent Limits in Response to Suit by Pesticide Industry," *BNA Environment Reporter – Current Developments* 17 (1986): 460.

1983 the courts even determined that the agency was empowered by law to monitor the *internal waste streams* of productive processes for their pollutants, and was not restricted simply to monitoring at the end of the final discharge pipe.[107]

In general, then, even in the deregulatory years of the 1980s, there were institutionalized limits on the government's ability to roll back legal initiatives. From the standpoint of industry, especially perhaps its most powerful entities, the continuing drift of environmental regulation and its attendant uncertainties was some motivation to continue planning for potential future controls. From the standpoint of individual firms it was better to have BAT regulations be defined on the basis of their own more advanced, in-place controls than on those of their competitors. Thus during the 1980s a regulatory dynamic linking law and technology, private production and public process, politics and uncertainty, continued to limit both environmental protection and its undoing. This was no more clear than in the case of the organic chemicals industry, the most complex and toxic of the industries EPA was to regulate.

Postscript: the penultimate regulations[108]

On November 5, 1987, the EPA promulgated its final rule regulating the effluents of the "organic chemicals and plastics and synthetic fibers" industry category.[109] Thus culminated was a regulatory process begun a full decade earlier, when the agency began analyzing the chemical constituents in the industry's process wastewater in 1977. But the final status of the regulations would remain uncertain until the spring of 1989, when a federal court of appeals finally ruled on the inevitable numerous challenges to them.

The industry group comprises approximately 1,000 production facilities, which together manufacture over 25,000 different organic chemicals, plastics, and synthetic fibers. At the larger plants the production processes are varied and complex, they rely on a variety of continuous and batch operations, and the mix of products can

---

[107] See, e.g., *Mobil Oil Corp. v. EPA*, 716 F.2d 1187 (7th Cir., 1983). EPA also took the position that it could set effluent limits on internal waste streams when necessary, although end-of-pipe limits were typically applied in the regulations. See 40 Code of Fed. Reg., Part 122.45[h].

[108] By mid-1989, one set of regulations was yet to be finalized, those for the pesticides industry.

[109] OCPSF Final Rule, at 42522.

change weekly or even daily. As a result of its often highly toxic products, raw materials, and by-products, the industry has historically been the most serious discharger of toxic water pollutants, including an unusually wide variety of organic compounds and metals. The average daily process wastewater discharge per plant is estimated to be 1.31 millions of gallons per day (MGD) for facilities discharging directly into waterways and 0.25 MGD for factories discharging to municipal treatment plants.[110]

The regulations for this industry group had first been proposed in 1983,[111] but were withdrawn by the agency for further consideration after the rules were challenged on a variety of legal and technical grounds by the Chemical Manufacturers Association (CMA), the Natural Resources Defense Council, and the agency's own Science Advisory Board.[112] The industry had steadfastly resisted such regulations well before the agency proposed them, lobbying both the Congress and the Executive Branch for lesser controls than those indicated in the law. For example, in 1981 the CMA urged the Congress to revise the requirements to allow for the possibility that BAT requirements might be set at current BPT levels, to abandon the "ample margin of safety" standards and instead use risk assessment (which would permit certain levels of identifiable risk), to require cost – benefit analysis in establishing regulations, and to release the EPA from the terms of the Flannery Decree.[113] In addition, in 1982 the steel and chemical industries appealed to the Department of Energy in their effort to move the Reagan administration toward BAT waivers. According to Senator Robert Stafford, the Republican chairman of the Senate Environment and Public Works Committee, the two industries had asked the Energy Department to make the case to the new Cabinet Council on Environment and Natural Resources and the White House that "money spent on pollution control equipment will not be available for the

---

[110] OCPSF Final Rule, at 42526.

[111] *Organic Chemicals and Plastics and Synthetic Fibers Category Effluent Limitations Guidelines, Pretreatment Standards, and New Source Performance Standards* (Proposed Regulation), 48 Fed. Reg. 11828 (Mar. 21, 1983). (Hereafter referenced as OCPSF Proposed Regulation.)

[112] See, e.g., BNA, "Industry, Environmentalists Criticize Proposed Organic Chemical Effluent Limits," *BNA Environment Reporter – Current Developments* 13 (1983): 2,104–5; "Science Board Report Brings Changes in Organic Chemicals Effluent Limits Data," ibid 13 (1983): 2,318.

[113] BNA, "CMA to Seek Easing of BAT Requirements During Clean Water Act Renewal Next Year," *BNA Environment Reporter – Current Developments* 12 (1981): 898–9.

development of energy supplies."[114] Significantly, the EPA had been excluded from membership on this new, high-level council, signaling the subordination of environmental protection to resource development and economic considerations at the top of the Reagan administration.

The final rule. Despite the ideological climate in Washington and the deep recession of the early 1980s, the Congress would not roll back its water pollution legislation. Evidence was quickly mounting that large majorities of American citizens were concerned about a broad array of environmental harms and supported increasing controls on polluting activities. With congressional oversight committees responsible for environmental matters feeling that the Executive Branch was undermining their traditional authority and prerogatives, all of the elements for a major political backlash against deregulation were in place, needing only the hint of scandal to unite them (Chapter 8).

Perhaps the conservative political climate in the Executive Branch influenced the withdrawal of the 1983 proposal for the chemical industry. But the record more strongly suggests that the basic reasons for EPA's reconsideration were the more traditional, mundane ones: technical challenges from all sides in a very complex regulatory matter and the concern to build a court review-proof rulemaking record. In this connection, it is significant that upon announcement of the 1983 proposal, estimated to involve some $800 million in annual costs to the industry, even the deregulatory-minded EPA Administrator Burford was compelled to extoll it as "a major step in our continuing efforts to carry out the requirements of the Clean Water Act. The agency recognizes these rules will be costly to industry, but the control of significant amounts of toxic pollutants, as well as conventional pollutants, is vital to safeguarding the public health."[115] By this time, it is worth noting, the political backlash against environmental deregulation was in full swing and, under pressure from the Congress and White House officials concerned with damage control, Burford resigned only days after her statement. Arguably, then, the balance in environmental politics – continuing to favor *increased* government oversight in pollution

---

[114] BNA, "No Need for Major Water Act Changes, Including BAT Waivers, Stafford Says," *BNA Environment Reporter – Current Developments* 13 (1982): 53.

[115] BNA, "Organic Chemicals Effluent Guidelines to Be Proposed Within Two Weeks, EPA Says," *BNA Environment Reporter – Current Developments* 13 (1983): 2029–30.

matters – in good measure shielded the toxics regulations from simple political manipulation and crippling.

The final rule issued in 1987 established BPT limits for conventional pollutants and BAT for sixty-three toxic substances, an unprecedented number, and set pretreatment standards for industrial discharges to municipal treatment plants, as well as standards for new industrial facilities. The toxics limits were based largely on a combination of in-plant and end-of-pipe pollution control technologies that had already been demonstrated by more advanced firms in the industry. The EPA estimated that the BAT limits would reduce the industry's discharge of toxics by 23.6 million pounds per year.[116] In response to the Regulatory Flexibility Act of 1980,[117] the agency determined that the BAT regulations would have disproportionate economic impacts on small plants, and so set BAT equal to BPT for nineteen facilities producing less than 5 million pounds of material annually.[118]

The EPA estimated the annual costs to the industry to comply with the new regulations at approximately $505 million (in 1986 dollars).[119] While the reduction from the estimated cost of the 1983 proposal may reflect some lessening of the regulation's stringency, it is also due at least in part to the agency's apparent earlier overestimation of the toxic pollution loads being discharged by the industry. The final rule was based on the agency's estimation that the industry was discharging some 24.2 million pounds of toxic pollutants annually; in 1983 the EPA estimated that the industry was discharging at least 668 million pounds of toxics.[120] The industry had claimed

[116] OCPSF Final Rule, at 42530.
[117] Pub. L. 96-354, 5 U.S.C. 601 *et seq.* The law requires that EPA assess whether its regulations create disproportionate impacts on small businesses.
[118] OCPSF Final Rule, at 42539, 42551. The agency determined that the BAT regulations would cause full or partial closure at roughly half of the nineteen small plants, and cause substantial adverse impacts at 80 percent of them, compared to a 7 percent closure rate and 13 percent impact rate for direct dischargers as a whole. Upon investigation the agency determined that in making this exception, it would not distinguish between small plants independently operated and those owned by large corporations. The EPA based this decision on industry comments that small plants owned by larger firms are run as independent profit centers, and on its analytic findings that small plants tend to experience similar levels of regulatory impacts regardless of ownership, and "despite the fact that in our closure analysis the weighted average cost of capital assigned to plants owned by medium and large sized firms was from one to two percentage points lower than the weighted average cost of capital assigned to small single plant firms." OCPSF Final Rule, at 42551–42552.
[119] OCPSF Final Rule, at 42550.
[120] OCPSF Final Rule, at 42530; OCPSF Proposed Regulation, at 11837.

that EPA had vastly underrated the effectiveness of its pollution controls in place by the early 1980s,[121] and the agency agreed in its 1987 decision.

It is difficult to assess whether and to what extent the revised estimate was biased by any industry misrepresentations or induced EPA conservatism. But several facts suggest that the new estimate was not wholly without basis. First, the agency based its final estimate on almost ten years' worth of data collection, including in-plant sampling of individual product or process lines, end-of-pipe discharges, and industry surveys. Presumably all of these efforts are subject to manipulation. Nonetheless, it is worth noting that such a wide-ranging effort can produce data justifying greater regulation than desired by industry. Precisely this occurred in one aspect of EPA's final analysis. Whereas the industry had argued that the end-of-pipe discharge data in companies' permit applications generally showed only limited toxic discharges (therefore justifying the industry's claim that BPT was typically adequate to control them), the agency rejected the data and argument because it found that many end-of-pipe discharges were diluted with nonprocess wastewaters, therefore rendering many organic toxics undetectable. The EPA had discovered this through its surveys of industry plants. As a result, it set limits on toxics in many cases detectable only in waste streams internal to the plant. Second, the final rule regulated sixty-three toxic pollutants while the 1983 proposal addressed only forty-six. Finally, while it did not approve of every aspect of the final rules, the Natural Resources Defense Council, long the environmentalist force behind the toxics program, participated in the final 1989 litigation on these regulations largely to defend them from industry challenge; the NRDC considered the rules to be a significant advance against toxic pollution in the industry.[122]

Given the projected economic impact on the industry of the new regulations, the EPA prepared a "regulatory impact analysis" to comply with Executive Order 12291.[123] In addition to the estimated annualized costs of over $500 million, the EPA estimated that the rules would bring significant economic hardships to 8 percent of plants directly discharging wastes into waterways, and cause job

[121] See, e.g., BNA, "Industry, Environmentalists Criticize Proposed Organic Chemical Effluent Limits," *BNA Environment Reporter – Current Developments* 13 (1983): 2104–5.

[122] Interview with Robert Adler, director of Clean Water Program, Natural Resources Defense Council, April 28, 1989.

[123] OCPSF Final Rule, at 42552.

losses of 1,197, or 0.7 percent of total employment in the industry.[124] Against these costs, the agency estimated benefits in three categories. *Nonquantified and nonmonetized benefits* included restoring the integrity of aquatic ecosystems (EPA's comparative risk project had ranked point source discharges as posing relatively high risk to these ecosystems), and reducing the health risks from swimming, eating fish, and drinking water. *Quantified and nonmonetized benefits* included reduced human exposure to volatile organic compounds through inhalation, while *monetized water quality benefits* included estimates of increased water uses for recreational fishing and boating, commercial fishing, irrigation, and intrinsic (nonuse) benefits.

The agency estimated the monetized benefits of improved water quality at between $178 million and $330 million annually (but in 1982 dollars). Adding the health and environmental benefits projected from improved air quality associated with the lessened volatility of the industrial water discharges, the estimated benefits were set at between $189 million and $393 million. Factoring in the nonquantifiable benefits, and noting that the monetized benefits are likely to be underestimated because of the substantial uncertainties regarding the full impacts of toxics on ecosystems, the agency determined that the "aggregate benefits, both monetizable and non-monetizable, exceed or are at least reasonably commensurate with costs."[125] Clearly, the process mandated by the executive order was an uncertain one.

Of law and limits. To be sure, a good deal of uncertainty accompanied the entire regulatory process. Difficult questions regarding the validity and even the possibility of data, socially optimal trade-offs, between disparate sorts of costs and benefits, and the ultimate effectiveness of government controls will continue to bedevil the regulation of this and other industries. But uncertainty is a double-edged sword, and if the volatility of environmental regulation seems to match that of the toxics it purports to address, then it constrains industry just as it limits the reach of law.

On the one hand, in these regulations as in others the EPA limited the definition of "best" pollution control technologies to those already familiar to much of the industry, rather than working to specify even more effective possibilities. The agency even designed

[124] OCPSF Final Rule, at 42551.
[125] OCPSF Final Rule, at 42552.

its regulatory scheme around the industry's prevalent modes of discharge controls, creating two sets of BAT limits depending on the matrix of controls already installed (or preferred). Even more to the point, because technologies to control certain complexes of toxic metals with organic compounds had not yet been demonstrated in the industry, the 1987 regulations did not set limits for them, instead leaving their control to the "best professional judgment" of permit writers working with individual plants, a highly suspect regulatory process at best. In addition, because of insufficient data, the agency did not provide limits for several other of the priority toxic pollutants it is required by law to regulate, reserving the right to later regulate them pending adequate technical data.[126]

On the other hand, it was the very potential of the regulatory process, uncertain as it was in the 1980s, combined with the intrinsic dynamics of technological advance and economic growth (for instance, regarding the financial utility to firms of resource recovery and recycling, as against waste), that contributed to the development by leading chemical companies of the sophisticated internal and external pollution controls that the EPA used to define substantial limits on toxic discharges. Despite the long delays in the toxics program, by 1980 the chemical and allied products industry reported it was investing about $800 million a year in pollution control equipment (for both air and water), and spending almost $2 billion annually on gross operating costs (Hoerger, Beamer, and Hanson, 1983: 93). Although these investments were costly, studies had begun to suggest that the installation of controls had often stimulated process innovations that increased plant efficiencies (by recovering valuable products from wastestreams, for example), even to the point of helping domestic producers remain competitive with foreign manufacturers (Davies, 1983: 56–7; cf., Ashford and Heaton, 1983). (But note that these sorts of offsetting benefits of regulation are not included in the traditional cost–benefit calculations of government.) If the blessings of technology remain mixed, the trends in both environmental despoliation and broad political sensibilities, indeed in economic growth and technological development, seem to have driven at least some leading sectors of industry to greater consideration of the wisdom of controls on discharges.

For industry as for the environment, regulatory uncertainty bears risk. In the absence of effective pollution controls in increasingly

[126] OCPSF Final Rule, at 42543–42544.

toxic environments, public pressure on government for more stringent regulation will intensify, the more so as analytic techniques for measuring and estimating the chronic effects of pollutants on human health and ecosystems improve. And the FWPCA amendments direct the EPA to review the BAT requirements at least annually in pursuit of the goal of zero discharge.[127]

The chemical industry regulations are especially instructive in connection with this sort of regulatory uncertainty. For example, the agency noted that its abilities to regulate toxics had improved during the lengthy period of rulemaking, precisely because analytic methods had become more sensitive.[128] And looking forward, the agency instructed the industry that while under the water law it typically could not require specific control technologies (it could only enforce specific discharge limits, to be reached by any legal method a plant chose), it heavily recommended that companies use the technologies that were the basis for the limits. This was because the recommended technologies had the advantage of minimizing the toxic air pollution often associated with volatile organics in wastewater, and failure to implement these controls would likely subject the plant to costly future controls currently under study by the EPA in the context of the Clean Air Act, the Resource Conservation and Recovery Act, and other laws.[129]

The penultimate court challenge. Despite the industry's considerable input at every phase of this extensive rulemaking, and the greatly reduced cost estimates attached to the final rule as against the 1983 proposal, the industry aggressively challenged the regulations in the federal appellate courts. It was an enormous legal action, one in which twenty-nine separate cases were consolidated into a single action heard by the 5th Circuit in New Orleans. Some of the nation's leading companies challenged the rules, including Union Carbide, DuPont, Monsanto, Dow Chemical, Goodyear Tire and Rubber, Allied-Signal, and W. R. Grace. The companies challenged the rules on some fifty-seven grounds, arguing among other things that EPA had inadequately assessed the cost–benefit issues. The industry repeated its claim that current controls were largely adequate, removing more than 90 percent of toxic pollutants, and that the costs to

---

[127] Pub. L. 92-500, § 304[b]; 33 U.S.C. § 1314[b] (Supp. V 1987).
[128] OCPSF Final Rule, at 42562.
[129] OCPSF Final Rule, at 42561.

industry of the regulations over the next decade could be as high as
$10 billion, twice the agency's estimate. In all, the legal record com-
piled in the case came to 3,000 pages of legal briefs and an administrative record distilled from some 600,000 pages.

In April 1989, the appellate court unanimously rejected all of the
industry's objections and upheld the EPA's rules in a ruling that at
least one major newspaper said had "jolted" the industry.[130] In so
deciding, the court repeated the long tradition of judicial deference
to agency expertise exercised in good faith, even extending such
deference to agency construction of vague statutory language: "We
must reject administrative constructions which are contrary to the
clear Congressional intent. Nevertheless, we accord some deference
to the agency's interpretation of the statute whose enforcement is
entrusted to it if Congressional intention is not pellucid. If, therefore, the statute is susceptible to more than one interpretation, we
must accept that of the E.P.A. if it is reasonable."[131]

According to Robert Adler, director of the NRDC's Clean Water
Program, the court had upheld the most important single set of regulations the EPA had written in the toxics effort. Nonetheless, the
NRDC had objected that the agency had set discharge standards for
new plants at BAT rather than at more advanced controls, and that
it had inadequately considered more stringent recycling requirements. NRDC won this argument, and the court directed the agency
to consider more stringent limits in these particular areas.[132]

Of course, the effectiveness of these rules in practice remains to
be determined. It will depend on the mix of agency diligence in
writing permits, monitoring firms, and enforcing against violations,
on the one hand, and the industry's stance toward compliance on
the other. But in any event, this key rulemaking episode has already
suggested both the limits and the capacities of law in the context of
vital matters of wide public interest.

The impacts of law

The effectiveness of the federal water pollution program can be
measured on a number of different dimensions, from the obvious
considerations of environmental quality to the subtler dimensions of

---

[130] See Stephen Labaton, "Ruling Jolts Chemical Industry: E.P.A. Waste Plan Is Upheld by Court," *The New York Times*, April 8, 1989, p. 33.
[131] Labaton, ibid.
[132] Labaton, ibid.; interview with Robert Adler, June 28, 1989.

citizen confidence in government and general state legitimacy. But the discussions and debates about the effectiveness of environmental controls have traditionally turned on implicit or explicit cost–benefit logic comparing environmental gains with economic costs.

There are a number of problems with this, ranging from severe measurement difficulties to the restrictive philosophical scope of the underlying utilitarian logic itself (cf., Etzioni, 1988). Because the models of economic effects are highly dependent on their underlying assumptions, it is unsurprising that "advocates and opponents of environmental policy have forecast differing economic effects of such policy" (Haveman and Smith, 1978: 189). Nonetheless, the broad indications from a range of impact studies suggest that, to date, the impacts of the federal water pollution program have been only modest, on both the environment and the economy.

Ecological effects

The environmental effects of the federally mandated water pollution controls perfectly reflect the constraints embedded in the law and its implementation by the EPA. In particular, water quality improvements have been noted for such conventional pollutants as biochemical oxygen demand and total suspended solids, but the control of toxic pollution remained intractable into the 1980s. These effects were entirely dependent on the types of pollution and the types of pollution sources the federal government had found it possible to regulate in the near term.

These were, of course, the conventional pollutants discharged from industrial and municipal point dischargers. By the end of 1977, when the first-phase, BPT regulations had been implemented by the majority of industry (but not of municipalities), the Council on Environmental Quality (1977: 200–3) reported fifty examples of U.S. water bodies that had been moved toward or achieved "fishable, swimmable" water quality through the regulatory efforts of government and the compliance efforts of industry. Even Lake Erie, once pronounced ecologically dead and long the symbol of environmental degradation, had begun to regenerate. And in some regions, high rates of compliance with water quality standards were being reported by the 1980s. For example, New York State has reported that 78 percent of its 70,000 miles of rivers and streams now meet federal water pollution standards (National Wildlife Federation,

1988), an impressive figure even allowing for the potential effects of the "politics of optimism" that may shape such government estimates.

There is little doubt that the industrial BPT controls have substantially reduced the discharges of conventional pollutants and thereby improved the nation's water quality. Despite impressive gains in water quality in some regions, however, the national data on the conventional pollutants suggest that the advances have been more modest for the country as a whole. After analyzing the best available nation-wide database on water quality – the U.S. Geological Survey's National Stream Quality Accounting Network[133] – the widely respected Conservation Foundation concluded in its 1982 report that while "some of the worst pollution problems may be abating," nationally "there has been little change in water quality over the past seven years" in terms of conventional pollutants in waterways (Conservation Foundation, 1982: 97). (The conventional pollutants analyzed were dissolved oxygen, fecal coliform bacteria, suspended solids, total dissolved solids, and phosphorus.)

This does not mean that the point source program of pollution controls failed. As the Conservation Foundation report pointed out (1982: 99), the country's gross national product had grown by about 40 percent in real terms since 1970, and the heavily polluting manufacturing sector had expanded at even a higher rate. At worst, EPA's permit program had held the line against conventional water pollution and likely done much better than that in regulating industrial facilities. The most significant weakness in national environmental policy instead lay in its failure to address the *nonpoint* sources of water pollution, such as urban and agricultural runoffs, which contribute large volumes of pollutants – both conventional (animal wastes, sediments) and toxic (pesticides, fertilizers, oils) – annually to the nation's lakes, rivers, streams, and estuaries. These problems continue to confound federal policy, which has yet to identify and implement a rational system of controls.[134]

[133] The USGS network was established in the mid-1970s and by the early 1980s contained over 500 monitoring stations in various river basins and subbasins around the country. While it measured conventional pollutants, it was not capable of detecting most toxic organic chemicals. See the Conservation Foundation report (1982: 96).

[134] The 1987 amendments to the Clean Water Act explicitly addressed the problem of stormwater pollution, for which the EPA had not yet devised a systematic program of controls through permits. The amendments call for stormwater control permits to be issued to industrial facilities and municipalities during the 1990s, and require EPA to submit a study of remaining unregulated stormwater dis-

The control of the serious toxics was an entirely different matter, of course. The regulatory record outlined above indicates that this is a battle whose outcome remains in doubt. For most of the period it appeared that the federal government did not even wish to measure the nature and extent of the problem, as if the knowledge would too loudly announce the policy failure. Not until the 1987 amendments to the FWPCA did the Congress mandate a national study of toxics in U.S. water due to point sources,[135] the results of which were finally reported in the summer of 1989 (Shabecoff, 1989e).

The study, based on state reports to the EPA, identified 595 segments of surface water, averaging 6 to 10 miles each, that were contaminated at levels dangerous to aquatic life by one or more of the 126 toxic substances examined.[136] (The agency said it could not yet estimate the risk to public health from these contaminated lakes and rivers but noted the tendency of toxics to build up in the food chain and concentrate in fish.) The agency also noted that the number of contaminated segments was probably much higher because of the presence of dangerous toxics not measured in the study. In addition, the report identified 240 municipal sources and 627 industrial facilities responsible for the discharges, including metal-finishing and manufacturing plants, pulp and paper mills, petroleum refining plants, and organic chemicals and plastics and synthetics plants.

Given other new data, these estimates, too, are likely far too low. In the first national inventory of total toxic discharges to the environment, based on reports from 17,500 manufacturing plants around the country, the EPA reported in April 1989 that U.S. industry released or disposed of at least 22.5 billion pounds of hazardous substances in 1987, a level the agency called "startling and unacceptably high" (Shabecoff, 1989c). The discharges included *9.7 billion pounds of toxics released into surface waters*, 3.2 billion pounds injected into underground wells, 2.7 billion pounds into landfills,

---

charges and identifying methods to mitigate their water quality impacts. See Water Quality Act of 1987, Pub. L. 100-4, §§ 401, 402[p][1,2], 405; also Garrett (1987). The success of these requirements remains to be seen, of course, but the development of a comprehensive program of such controls will surely strain agency resources and ingenuity.

[135] Pub. L. 100-4, § 304[1].

[136] In all, the study found that some 17,365 segments of surface water in forty-nine states (excluding Arizona, which had not yet reported) and six territories were contaminated by either toxic or conventional pollution, or both. These segments accounted for about 10 percent of the nation's lake and estuary area and river, stream and coastal water mileage, according to the EPA (Shabecoff, 1989e).

and 2.7 billion pounds into the air; an estimated 2.6 billion pounds were sent to waste treatment and disposal facilities.

Taken together, the two reports suggest that the nation's water pollution program, as well as its other environmental programs, had thus far failed to seriously dent the major problems of toxic waste, a fact acknowledged by the agency's assistant administrator for policy and planning when the April results were reported (Shabecoff, 1989c). Combined with the accumulating evidence of high rates of toxic contamination of groundwaters, which provide much of the water for human consumption, the public policy questions remain both large and vexing.

Economic effects

Since Earth Day in 1970 and the legislative initiatives it helped spawn throughout the decade, the dollar expenditures for environmental control by government and industry have come to the hundreds of billions. The figures are impressive, especially given the modest ecological impacts to date (although the proper comparison for the environmental value purchased by these funds is with the theoretical alternative of no controls whatsoever). Despite the large numbers, these expenses have typically had only modest negative effects on the economy and firms. And not only are some of these effects often overestimated, but they present a misleading picture of the macroeconomic outcomes, because they do not include estimates of the economic *benefits* also conferred by regulation.

The studies reported briefly here do not typically provide breakdowns for types of pollution control, typically speaking of the cumulative costs of all environmental regulations (air, water, solid waste). Moreover, I shall largely focus on studies of the effects during the 1970s, the more aggressive period of regulation before the deregulatory-minded Reagan administration took office in 1981. The economic consequences of the toxic water pollution controls remain to be seen, but if past experience is any guide, they too will be modest, although this is not to say inexpensive.

By the latter 1970s, U.S. Department of Commerce reports showed that total national expenditures for pollution control were edging toward $40 billion annually, double the level in 1972. The government portion of the costs ran to between 27 and 29 percent annually (Hoerger et al., 1983: 92). In 1977, the year by which BPT compliance had been achieved by more than 80 percent of industry according to EPA figures, industry spent about $27.5 billion, while all levels of government combined spent about $10 billion. That year some $16.4 billion was spent on water pollution control, and government had a much higher proportion of these expenditures: 42.6 percent, or about $7 billion. This large share was due primarily to government expenditures for municipal treatment plants, which in fact help subsidize the pollution control expenditures of many businesses that discharge their wastes into such facilities. (Additional subsidies to industry were afforded in the form of tax deductions for pollution control investments.)

In the 1972 amendments, the Congress had provided that industries repay the federal government over a thirty-year period for their share of the costs (based on utilization of the facility) involved in constructing new treatment plants, and to pay user fees for their share of the plants' annual operating costs. But the 1977 amendments exempted from cost-sharing plants discharging less than 25,000 gallons per day into a municipal facility, and permitted municipalities to relax pretreatment requirements for industrial toxic discharges if the municipal treatment facility removed "all or any part" of the pollutant (Koch and Leone, 1979: 103). In late 1980, in his last year in office, President Carter signed a law that repealed the cost-sharing provision altogether for plants funded to that point; the new law did, however, prohibit federal funding for construction of additional capacity in municipal plants where industrial discharges exceeded 50,000 gallons per day.[137] In addition, in 1981 a General Accounting Office study found that most municipalities were not charging adequate user fees. Moreover, the evidence, though quite preliminary, suggested that industrial users may often be charged less than residential users: in one example, commercial users were being charged a rate 50 percent lower than residential users.[138]

Subsidies aside, the business expenditures were large in absolute terms and represented a dramatic rise from levels at the beginning of the decade. But as a percent of all industrial capital expenditures, they remained modest, and the percentage was decreasing toward the end of the decade. According to the Department of Commerce, whereas industry had spent 5.8 percent of its capital outlays in 1975 for pollution control, the proportion had declined to 4.5 percent by 1978 (Hoerger et al., 1983: 97). Moreover, Commerce Department

[137] *BNA Environment Reporter – Current Developments* 11 (1980): 927–8.
[138] *BNA Environment Reporter – Current Developments* 12 (1981): 975.

figures showed that investment in pollution controls declined 6 percent in real terms in 1979, and business plans called for a further decline of 2 percent in 1980, controlling for inflation in the price of pollution control equipment.[139]

In projecting business expenses on pollution control, both business and the EPA tended to overestimate the costs. An EPA-commissioned study found such overestimation to be the rule during the key 1974–77 period when several major pollution control requirements were taking effect, including the BPT standards. For example, both the agency and the industry estimated that total capital costs for pollution control in petroleum refining during the period would be $1.4 billion, when the actual expenditure finally came to between $550 and $750 million. For the iron and steel industry, the agency estimated capital costs of $830 million, and the industry estimated them at $1.6 billion; the actual costs were between $470 and $630 million.[140]

The macroeconomic effects of required environmental controls have proven to be significant but not large; moreover, macroeconomic models overstate negative effects because they inadequately weigh benefits attaching to pollution control expenditures (such as employment generated by the new pollution control industries; reduced health care; and reduced property repair costs). A Brookings Institution study estimated that environmental regulations reduced economic output in the mid-1970s by 0.15 percent (U.S. Senate, 1979: 291) while a congressional report found that studies showed environmental laws reducing the annual rate of productivity growth from between 0.1 and 0.25 percent, the latter considered unreliably high. Most studies of capital investment, the report said, attributed only a minor role to environmental regulations.[141]

The estimated inflationary effects of environmental laws during the period were also modest. A study done by Chase Econometrics projected that pollution control policies would add 0.6 percent annually to the national rate of inflation during the 1970–83 period, and that the consumer price index would rise 4.7 percent more over

[139] BNA, "Business Pollution Control Costs Projected at $7.7 Billion During 1980," *BNA Environment Reporter – Current Developments* 11 (1980): 70.
[140] BNA, "Industry Costs for Pollution Controls Less Than Anticipated, EPA Study Shows," *BNA Environment Reporter – Current Developments* 11 (1980): 280; "Costle Says Cost–Benefit Analysis Cannot Replace Social Policy Judgments," ibid. 11 (1980): 927.
[141] BNA, "Productivity Reduced Up To 12 Percent by Environmental, Health, Safety Rules," *BNA Environment Reporter – Current Developments* 11 (1980): 736.

the period than it would have without the controls (Haveman and Smith, 1978: 184). More recent estimates put the annual increase at 0.2 to 0.3 percent.[142] Again, though, the CPI exaggerates the price impact because it inadequately reflects the economic benefits of environmental regulation (Speth, 1978: 26–7).

In terms of microeconomic effects at the level of plants, the major concern has been closures and job losses due to environmental regulation. In 1972 studies commissioned by the EPA with the Commerce Department and the Council on Environmental Quality estimated that pollution controls would force the closing of 200 to 300 "mainly small, older, and marginally efficient factories" between 1972 and 1976, with a consequent loss of between 50,000 and 125,000 jobs (Cameron, 1972: 103).

Again, while not large these estimates proved dramatically overstated. By 1981 EPA's "economic dislocation early warning system," put in place in 1971 to track such effects, reported that since 1971, 153 plants had closed in part as a result of environmental regulation, causing the loss of 32,611 jobs during the decade.[143] Moreover, environmental requirements had *created* roughly 400,000 jobs over the same period in construction and the new pollution control industry,[144] or roughly twelve for each job lost. Indeed, a study by Koch and Leone (1979) suggests the nonobvious consequence that the requirements of the Clean Water Act may even keep some plants open that otherwise would have closed, to the extent that the consequent price rises for their industry's products are sufficiently greater than their increased costs of compliance.

In sum, the economic impacts of the law appear to have been contained well within tolerable limits during the regulatory-minded decade of the 1970s. Moreover, pollution expenditures and impacts tend to be overstated, with the result that the regulations may have been rendered less than socially optimal. In attempting to balance the economic costs and environmental benefits, the law may have sacrificed some of the latter unnecessarily in deference to strongly expressed concerns for the former, particularly in its often cautious regulation of toxics, as earlier described. The jury is still out on this

---

[142] BNA, "Drayton Says Environmental Rules Contribute 16 Times More Jobs Than Lost," *BNA Environment Reporter – Current Developments* 11 (1980): 82–3.

[143] BNA, "EPA's Second Quarter Labor Report Finds No Jobs Loss, Two Threatened Closures," *BNA Environment Reporter – Current Developments* 12 (1981).

[144] BNA, "Drayton Says Environmental Rules Contribute 16 Times More Jobs Than Lost," *BNA Environment Reporter – Current Developments* 11 (1980): 82–3.

question, one that in any case defies measurement given the confluence of economic, technical, and ultimately philosophical questions it entails.

Finally, there remain important questions regarding the distributional effects of the water law's technology-forcing standards. Because they tend to impose equal costs on all firms in an industry, the unit costs of compliance tend to be higher for the smaller facilities often run by smaller companies, placing them at a competitive disadvantage in the market. To the extent that this occurs, it will

result in an allocation of a disproportionate share of the costs of compliance to the smaller firms which contribute relatively less to pollution. Costs of compliance are thus raised relative to benefits. This outcome supports the business case for deregulation vis-à-vis environmental constraint. (Barnett, 1981: 14)

And there is some empirical evidence regarding such distributional effects. For example, one study examined whether legally mandated pollution controls caused industry to divert much of its capital spending from its traditional "productive" capital investments (Feldman and McClain, 1984). The results suggest that diversion of capital due to environmental regulations was quite modest in the seven industries studied, but that generally such diversion was more pronounced in industries (such as foundries) in which the average firm size is smaller.

The EPA began to formally consider the disparate effects of water pollution regulations on small firms after 1980, and in its rule-making during the 1980s sometimes relaxed the requirements for smaller producers, as it did in the chemical industry regulations of 1987. The ultimate effects of these policies remains to be determined.

But such differential impacts may also occur at the enforcement stage of regulation, and in the next chapter I empirically examine this possibility.

CHAPTER 7

Enforcement: the social production
of environmental offenses

To the public mind, enforcement is the centerpiece of regulation, the visible hand of the state reaching into society to correct wrongs, in social regulation wrongs perpetrated against vulnerable groups and entities. As indicated to this point, of course, the success of any regulatory regime depends on far more than the specific enforcement policies of the state. But both symbolically and practically, enforcement is a capstone, a final indicator of the state's seriousness of purpose and a key determinant of the permeability of the barrier between compliance and lawlessness.

The enforcement process is a deeply textured one. At subsurface levels it is an uncertain mix of the professional ambitions of (usually young) litigators, bureaucratic politics and changing priorities, and virtually constant negotiations with a host of recalcitrants. At its apex is the highly publicized and ballyhooed criminal case, in which egregious violators are demonstrably prosecuted (and often condemned) in the courts of law and public opinion. It is the ultimate expression of the state's power, the power to convict and even incarcerate. It is an expression of large symbolic significance, but there always lurks the danger that it is *symbolic only*, that it intends to signify much more to the general populace than to the population of the regulated.

In environmental law, as in social regulation generally, it is rarely used. This suggests either that the regulated voluntarily comply in large numbers, rarely necessitating the use of the state's full force, or that effective enforcement has been stunted in some part by various factors in social organization.

Given the newness of environmental regulation – its very recent effort to remake the assumptive world in commerce regarding the proper relations between production, waste, and the environment –

it is unreasonable to expect full compliance with laws mandating corporate internalization of the social expenses of production, although some companies have made strong efforts at good citizenship in this regard. On the other side of the coin, there is reason to believe that enforcement is constrained by basic limits, just as is the regulatory process that provides its mandate.

The purpose in this chapter is to examine these limits and their potential effects on enforcement. The emphasis is on the ways in which law is limited by the configuration, or structuring, of enforcement itself. While the experience of the early 1980s in particular suggests the vulnerability of law (and its integrity) to the instrumental manipulations of extremist politics, even the best intended, rationally organized structures and processes of enforcement carry unforeseen limits and unintended consequences. In basic respects, these limits and consequences reflect fundamental constraints on Anglo-American law operating in the context of its institutional history, and raise important questions of regulatory efficiency and justice.

To make this case, I first offer an overview of the EPA's enforcement policies as promulgated in Washington, and describe some of the basic constraints on the function; I also present aggregate enforcement data to illustrate something of the agency's practices. The discussion then turns to a more intensive analysis of enforcement in EPA's Region II offices, responsible for one of the most densely populated and highly polluted areas of the country, including New York and New Jersey. This section investigates the region's enforcement policies and practices, and the possibility that its intendedly neutral enforcement apparatus produces systematic bias in targeting offenders.

The period covered by this analysis is the 1970s through the first part of 1978. These included the peak years of EPA enforcement during the Environmental Decade, covering the agency's efforts to enforce the key 1977 deadline for best practicable technology during the relatively aggressive first two years of the Carter administration. After 1978 the administration began to take a more conservative stance toward environmental regulation in the context of a deepening recession combined with growing inflation, a prelude to the radical deregulation visited upon the EPA in the early years of the Reagan administration. In sum, the analysis inspects the state's enforcement of the modern federal water pollution law at its most stringent. Any limits on law's effectiveness under such "optimum" conditions bespeak fundamental constraints in such regulatory enforcement.

Water enforcement at the EPA

Policies and priorities

Like EPA's regulatory policy more generally, its enforcement policy becomes especially salient in the context of always inadequate resources and broad oversight responsibilities. In this context, priorities must be established and discretion becomes central in policy formation. As I have already noted, the 1972 legislation mandated formal enforcement of all violations of the act, at the very least with administrative orders to comply. However, both EPA policy and the courts have pried a good deal of discretion into enforcement practices.[1]

In the early administration of the water act, enforcement was dormant as the agency concentrated its resources on establishing the effluent discharge regulations and issuing discharge permits. By direction of the statute,[2] until the end of 1974 companies applying for permits could not be prosecuted while their applications were pending (unless permit approvals were being delayed by the bad faith of the applicant, including failure to apply for a permit on a timely basis), no matter the degree of pollution being discharged. As it happened, therefore, enforcement was not substantially applied until 1974, but it was especially accelerated in 1975, by which time most major business dischargers were operating under approved permits specifying interim and final limits and compliance schedules for the construction of first-phase, BPT treatment.

Perhaps because enforcement was essentially a theoretical matter during the first months of the agency's administration of the law, EPA's early policy position was essentially literalist with respect to the statute's indication of mandatory sanctions. In the summer of 1973, the agency established guidelines indicating that administra-

[1] See discussion in Chapters 5 and 6. For additional discussions of issues in the enforcement of environmental laws, see, e.g., Ginn (1978), Macbeth (1978), Moorman (1978), Pedersen (1978), Quarles (1978), Taylor (1978), Tennille (1978a: 9–12; 1978b: 20–22), Carter (1980), Brown (1984), and Kuruc (1985).

[2] Pub. L. 92–500, §402[k].

tive orders were the most appropriate sanctions for minor discharge and compliance schedule violations, with more serious actions – referrals to the Justice Department for civil or criminal enforcement – applied to unjustified or continued infractions.[3] However, the policy also recognized the need for EPA regional administrators to set priorities in the context of limited resources.

By spring 1974, however, the agency issued an explicit statement that formal enforcement was to be a discretionary matter, a position later upheld by a federal court of appeals in *Sierra Club v. Train*[4] despite the clear indication of mandatory enforcement in the legislative history of the act (see Chapter 5). In a memorandum to the enforcement division, the assistant administrator for enforcement and general counsel, Alan G. Kirk, II, wrote that "(administrative) orders should not be used indiscriminately. Not every minor violation warrants an order. Some may be so insignificant as to warrant no action, e.g., report was filed two days late, construction began a day or two behind schedule. Other violations may be better handled by a cautionary letter, e.g., effluent limits for a reporting period are slightly higher than allowed, report is two weeks late." The memorandum did not rest this judgment on inadequate resources; instead, the *credibility* of the new enforcement effort was underscored: "It is *crucial* that the permits be credible. This means that we do not want 'nitpicking' enforcement. . . . Above all, use your head. Ask yourself whether a good, environmentally sympathetic federal district court judge would be impressed that the enforcement action you are taking seems reasonable on the facts."[5]

With respect to court actions, the policy indicated that civil penalties should be sought where the violation was serious (e.g., continuing) and within the control of the management, and where the expected fine would deter further violation. The agency did not have to show negligence to bring these actions, as the statute imposes absolute liability "in the interests of establishing the highest possible standard of care on the permittee." Finally, the policy held criminal cases to be appropriate only in situations of willful or negligent misconduct, such as may be indicated by continuing

---

[3] EPA Headquarters, "Guidelines for Water Enforcement," July 31, 1973.
[4] 557 F.2d 485 (5th Cir. 1977).
[5] EPA Headquarters Enforcement Memorandum, "Compliance Monitoring, Administrative Orders, and Court Actions Under Section 309 of the Federal Water Pollution Control Act Amendments of 1972," March 20, 1974; emphasis in the original.

violations and failure to respond to earlier enforcement efforts. The memorandum noted that criminal prosecutions were already being used in the case of companies' failure to apply for discharge permits.

In basic respects, this enforcement logic continued in force throughout the 1970s, periodically updated and reinforced in later policy statements such as the 1977 *Enforcement Management System Guide,* which attempted to more systematically specify the discretionary uses of enforcement, and the 1978 civil penalty policy designed to ensure that violators did not benefit economically from their noncompliance (by scaling monetary penalties to the company's financial savings from failing to implement the often costly pollution controls), to force firms to internalize the social costs of production, and to compensate the public for harm to the environment or to public health.[6]

The two principal goals of the enforcement program were to bring violating firms into compliance, and in particular to ensure compliance with the July 1977 deadline for compliance with BPT regulations, and to maintain the integrity of the law (hence, of the agency). This latter purpose was essential to the EPA, given the agency's institutional youth and the novelty of the mandate it was attempting to enforce on the private sector.

Indeed, the EPA gave this matter of legal integrity a primary place in its enforcement policy for the 1977 deadline, which it clearly was concerned to enforce, certainly to demonstrate its own effectiveness to Congress, the public, and the regulated. In enforcement policy guidance issued in June 1977, the agency directed that enforcement attorneys select cases for civil and criminal referrals on the basis of three criteria (in descending order of importance): (1) harm to human health associated with the noncompliance; (2) bad faith on the part of the company; and (3) the impact on the environment of the offending discharges and the

---

[6] EPA Headquarters, "Civil Penalty Policy," April 11, 1978. The policy was quite detailed. Among other matters, it stipulated that while business firms could substitute "environmentally beneficial expenditures" for civil penalties, there should be no tax advantage accruing to firms using this option. That is, the substitute expenditures should be sufficiently larger than the minimum civil penalty such that the after-tax cost to the firm was not less than the original penalty. The policy also stipulated that penalties could be reduced or postponed if the violator could demonstrate financial inability to pay. However, the agency took the position that "no such concession may be made with respect to the cost of coming into compliance" with the law. That is, compliance with the facility's permit was not to be a negotiable item in the enforcement process.

length of time required to obtain compliance.[7] For these deadline violators, the guidance indicated that the agency should request at least three judicial remedies upon referral to the Justice Department: substantial civil penalties for noncompliance, a court-imposed order to comply, and the provision of more severe penalties if the company violated the court-ordered schedule. But criminal prosecutions of firms "should be considered in those schedule violation cases *where the authority of the agency has been intentionally and deliberately flouted,* and in other cases as appropriate" (emphasis added).

For companies proving that despite their good faith efforts they could not meet the 1977 deadline, the EPA again administratively amended the statute by issuing what it called Enforcement Compliance Schedule Letters establishing new compliance deadlines for achieving BPT discharge limits.[8] The Congress accepted the need for such enforcement discretion and formally endorsed this option in the 1977 amendments to the water law, permitting extensions in good faith cases up to April 1, 1979.[9]

In addition, referrals to Justice recommending the criminal prosecution of individuals were recommended "only where the evidence demonstrates that intentional corporate noncompliance with the law is the result of an informed policy decision made by such corporate officials." Not surprisingly, given this burden of proof, such individual prosecutions have been very rare; indeed, corporate criminal prosecutions have generally been rare under the provisions of the 1972 amendments, as later discussed.

Finally, the top priorities established for enforcement action were major dischargers (defined rather vaguely by EPA as industrial facilities having "large" discharges "and / or a high potential to violate applicable water quality standards")[10] and violators of compliance schedules for construction of waste control facilities.[11] These were selected because their control would net the greatest reduction in water pollution: the major polluters are the most environmentally

---

[7] EPA Headquarters Enforcement Memorandum, "Setting Priorities for Enforcement Actions Concerning July 1, 1977 Violations," June 3, 1977.

[8] EPA Headquarters Enforcement Memorandum, "Procedures for Issuance of Enforcement Compliance Schedule Letters," June 3, 1976.

[9] Pub. L. 95–217; see 33 U.S.C. 1251 *et seq.* (1982 ed.), § 1319[a][5][B].

[10] EPA Headquarters Policy, "Definition of Terms Used with the Permit Compliance System," 1978.

[11] EPA Headquarters Enforcement Memorandum, "Development of Policies and Procedures for NPDES Program," December 17, 1975.

threatening, while delayed construction can indefinitely prolong high pollution levels. As indicated later in the chapter, compliance schedule violations indeed disproportionately drew the agency's stronger sanctioning responses in Region II, reflecting agency policy recommending administrative orders or court action for such offenses.[12] Pollution discharge violations tended to be treated much more leniently, for both major and "minor" dischargers.

In sum, the EPA had formulated an enforcement policy emphasizing criteria for formal sanctioning that were, prima facie, reasonable. Among the agency's major institutional concerns was to establish legitimacy and credibility on two vital fronts: with polluting companies and with the judiciary. "Nitpicking" enforcement of minor infractions could undermine the agency's purposes in both constituencies. In any event such discretionary enforcement procedures characterize law generally, and they do not necessarily represent undue tendencies toward leniency in the regulatory context.

Nonetheless, the regulatory framework presented by the 1972 amendments met with a number of constraints, limits that were inscribed both in the terms of the statute and in traditional processes of legal controls.

The limits of enforcement

Despite the sense of urgency the Congress displayed in the 1972 law, implementation was unwieldy, encumbered and slowed by the sheer weight of the regulatory workload and the highly technical demands involved in much of the rulemaking. It was predictable, therefore, that enforcement would not proceed as efficiently as the law prescribed. Moreover, the institutional logics embedded in the government's enforcement apparatus often frustrated aggressive enforcement against even serious infractions. The clear intent of the statute was again administratively amended, with the consequence of some diminution of regulatory effectiveness.

Enforcement delays. Delays in mounting a full enforcement effort followed every stage of EPA's implementation of the 1972 amendment. Given the huge effort involved the agency was unable to issue permits to all industrial facilities by the December 1974 deadline specified in the statute. So while enforcement was theoretically to

[12] EPA Headquarters Enforcement Memorandum, "Enforcement of Compliance Schedule Violations," May 28, 1975.

commence for all dischargers no later than the first day of January 1975, the agency could not prosecute polluters who had applied for permits in time but were still awaiting administrative action on them.

Even to approximate the regulatory schedule outlined in the law, the EPA found it necessary to write interim industry discharge regulations for many industries, and to issue discharge permits initially on these rather than on regulations finally developed. In the interim regulations, the agency stipulated that should the final regulations differ significantly from those on which permits had been based, it would consider all petitions for permit modification to reflect new (possibly relaxed) discharge limits. Because of the uncertainty entailed, and the equity and fairness issues involved, the agency determined that it could not fully enforce such permits if violations occurred. EPA policy was that criminal and civil suits would not be filed against violators with interim permits: "enforcement suits under permits issued pursuant to interim guidelines should not be taken until the final guideline is issued and it has been determined that no change in the permit is necessary as a result of the final regulation."[13] The policy did, however, appear to leave open the possibility of such administrative sanctions as warnings and orders to pressure firms into compliance.

The administrative process by which companies could contest the water pollution limits in their permits was also responsible for considerable enforcement delays in many cases. As I noted in the previous chapter, if dissatisfied with their permit terms firms could apply for an adjudicatory hearing with EPA, a judicial-like proceeding in which the relative merits of the agency's and the company's positions could be weighed. The issues could either be settled through negotiations prior to hearing or go to a full hearing before an administrative law judge.

The delays typically associated with this process were often quite lengthy, not uncommonly taking up to two years and more to resolve. The delays themselves were incentive for firms to attempt to use this technical legal procedure (quite apart from the opportunity to have the permit relaxed in the firm's favor); while under administrative appeal, the contested portions of the permit could not be enforced until the issues were resolved. Because of the high demand

[13] EPA Headquarters Enforcement Memorandum, "Scope of Policy Relating to the Enforcement of Permits Issued Pursuant to Interim Final Guidelines," April 15, 1975.

for such hearings and the complex technical nature of many of the deliberations, numerous firms enjoyed substantial immunity from enforcement for long periods, including immunity from the 1977 BPT deadline in many cases. As noted earlier, the agency itself felt the delays in this process were undermining the nation's cleanup efforts. In addition, the adjudicatory hearing procedure created an additional possibility that the law would not be implemented evenly across industry. More powerfully situated firms were more likely to benefit from this ostensibly neutral legal procedure. (This possibility is the focus of the enforcement analysis in the later sections of the chapter.)

Conflicting logics at law. Full and adequate enforcement of the environmental laws entails the fusing of often distinctive bureaucratic requirements, rationales, and legal logics. This is so because, to mount the law's full force through criminal and civil lawsuits, the federal regulatory agencies typically must refer cases to the Department of Justice, which determines whether to bring a case to court. As suggested in Chapter 2, the working relations between Justice and the EPA are therefore key to the success of the enforcement program, as is the match between the regulatory logic applied and typical decision-making logics used by courts.

Unfortunately for the program, these working relations have long been characterized by a good measure of dispute and lack of effective coordination as seen from both sides of the government's enforcement apparatus. In this case, the several-month delays in the Justice Department's processing of EPA's referrals (let alone the actual prosecution of cases), about which the agency complained to the department in 1976,[14] were among the less serious difficulties limiting the effectiveness of enforcement. Instead, the more serious obstacles were fundamental problems regarding case requirements for prosecution and competing institutional logics for handling offenses.

[14] For example, in early 1976 an EPA Region II memorandum complained that cases referred to the Justice Department for prosecution "languish for over nine months without ever being filed" (EPA Region II Enforcement Memorandum, "Enforcement Techniques," January 26, 1976). Although recognizing that U.S. attorneys were generally overburdened, the agency was especially concerned that in cases of compliance schedule violations such delays would prevent the early establishment of new schedules and the attainment of the 1977 BPT deadline. In 1977 the problem was addressed in a memorandum of understanding between Justice and the EPA (June 13, 1977), which specified that within five months of receipt the department would determine whether or not to file cases referred by the EPA.

By the middle part of 1976, the EPA found that the Justice Department was declining to prosecute in 38 percent of the agency's referrals,[15] leaving the agency to negotiate compliance as best it could with often resistant firms. In part the problem was one of inadequate case preparation by the EPA, a problem both sides recognized and which the EPA attempted to resolve through policy guidance to its enforcement attorneys in 1976. In a July memorandum the enforcement chiefs directed that careful internal review standards be applied before referral of any cases to the Justice Department, and that referred cases be "sufficiently grave" that the agency would itself be willing to file civil prosecutions if Justice declined them.[16] (In fact, the agency has rarely filed such suits on its own behalf in water pollution cases.) But later evidence suggests that the tension regarding quality of referrals has continued to plague enforcement of the federal environmental laws. In the 1980s Justice Department prosecutors were still complaining about the inadequacy of EPA's case preparation. According to one former assistant U.S. attorney, for example:

EPA people . . . don't have the FBI mentality. They are engineers and academics. . . . I had fights with EPA over getting samples analyzed. "We have other kinds of priorities," EPA said. If you do get enforcement going, people stand up and listen, but I was up against an agency that was reluctant and inexperienced in enforcement. There must be some changes in the federal government before there will be substantial progress in the environmental field. (Quoted in DiMento, 1986: 138)

In the context of EPA's typically overburdening regulatory responsibilities, this criticism rings true. There may also be in it some measure of the sort of bureaucratic sniping that occurs when two state agencies share jurisdiction over policy matters. Bureaucracies often jealously guard their respective turfs, rather than coordinate effective strategies to reach policy goals.

To some unknown extent, such dynamics appear to constrain rigorous enforcement of federal environmental laws. At least from the standpoint of some Justice Department prosecutors, the agency refrains from referring some prosecutable cases because the EPA does not wish to share credit for the case with the department; instead, it will jawbone dischargers (or, more rarely, file civil suits) in the attempt to gain compliance so that it will get sole enforcement credit,

[15] EPA Headquarters Enforcement Memorandum, "NPDES Case Referrals to the Department of Justice," July 21, 1976.
[16] Ibid.

and subsequently have a stronger regulatory record to show its superiors and congressional oversight committees when annual budgets are requested (cf., Bequai, 1977). According to the chief assistant U.S. attorney for Los Angeles, for example:

> In fact, many cases by the non-criminal investigative agencies – by that I mean the regulatory agencies – never get presented to the U.S. Attorney's Office. A very significant reason why they don't . . . is because the agency gets no credit for a criminal prosecution. The agency gets credit for a civil action [or other compliance-generating actions] that it can file and that its lawyers can handle, but the agency gets no statistical credit at budget time for a criminal case that has been prosecuted.
>
> The best example is that for the last three years the United States Attorney in Los Angeles . . . has been trying to get the United States government more actively involved in environmental prosecutions. . . . But when the EPA takes a look at a case, very often we never even hear about it. They will handle it either administratively or civilly and they will not bring the U.S. Attorney's Office into it for criminal prosecution.[17]

To the extent that this occurs, enforcement of the environmental laws undercuts its ability to engender timely compliance among violators, and also forgoes the symbolic force of criminal prosecutions that could deter violation by other firms.

One other factor inhibits prosecutions. A principal advantage of the 1972 amendments over previous water pollution control legislation was that they explicitly eliminated the difficult burden of proof of showing environmental harm. Under the new law infractions were to be demonstrated by a simple showing of a violation of a plant's discharge permit, regardless of level of damage, a measure included to encourage the more vigorous enforcement of environmental standards. However, by 1976 the EPA discovered that U.S. attorneys were often declining to file its enforcement cases unless there was evidence of actual environmental damage. Dismayed at this executive "amendment" of the statute, the agency asked the Justice Department to inform all U.S. attorneys "of the correct interpretation of our statutes and the importance of prosecuting our enforcement cases without requiring proof of harm."[18]

[17] Statement of Richard E. Drooyan, chief assistant U.S. attorney, Los Angeles, in *Proceedings of Symposium 87: White Collar/Institutional Crime – Its Measurement and Analysis* (Sacramento: California Department of Justice, Bureau of Criminal Statistics and Special Services, 1988), p. 69.
[18] EPA Headquarters Enforcement Memorandum, regarding correspondence between EPA and the Justice Department on problems in enforcement, December 3, 1976.

The department responded that its official policy recognized that proof of environmental harm was not an essential element in water act prosecutions, and that it did not support U.S. attorneys automatically rejecting referrals from EPA for lack of such proof. However, the department wrote EPA that in its experience, "the only assured way of receiving meaningful relief is a showing by the Government of some adverse effect of the defendant's pollutants, and some courts require it. This is a fact which cannot be ignored." The Department of Justice therefore told EPA that it declined to issue a " 'hard and fast' directive of any sort" to its prosecutors around the country, leaving the "degree of harm" issue a relevant factor in the discretionary decision to prosecute cases.[19]

Thus, a number of institutional logics – organizational and legal – constrained enforcement, particularly the application of the law's ultimate sanction, criminal prosecution. There was also some testimonial indication that the EPA hesitated to prosecute large corporate polluters, other things being equal. In 1978 a seasoned EPA attorney in the Office of Water Enforcement said, "We're afraid to go after [the big corporations]. We prefer to go after the little guys."[20] This tendency can be understood in the context of limited enforcement resources and the agency's bureaucratic need to demonstrate an effective overall enforcement record. Putting a large portion of the agency's limited enforcement resources into a few cases against powerful corporate adversaries that might win in court could be seen as less cost effective – from the standpoint of bureaucratic politics if not from that of the environment – than spending the same resources enforcing the law against smaller violators the agency could more readily expect to bring into compliance in the near term.

In addition, this attorney and others indicated that the agency was suspicious that many states that had chosen to undertake their own enforcement of the 1972 amendments (under EPA's auspices) were not aggressively and evenly enforcing the law's requirements against industry.[21] It was suggested that this relatively lenient approach in many states had to do with their governments' closer ties to or dependence on local corporate citizens. EPA was authorized under the 1972 law to reclaim enforcement programs when state oversight was found to be inadequate, but despite the agency's con-

[19] Ibid.
[20] Conversation (with author), EPA Headquarters, spring 1978.
[21] Interviews at EPA Headquarters, Office of Water Enforcement, spring 1978.

cerns (for example, over Ohio's program in the late 1970s) it has never done so, a not surprising result given its own thin resource base.

Ultimately it is not possible to determine precisely the effects of such constraints on criminal enforcement of the water act; to my knowledge this question has never been empirically examined and would be difficult to assess in any event. Nonetheless, in the aggregate the evidence suggests that criminal prosecutions are infrequently used among the agency's enforcement options; tend to concentrate on quite egregious cases that pose serious threats to the environment, the integrity of the law, or both (illegal dumping of pollutants and filing false reports, for example); and disproportionately focus on the smaller violators rather than large corporate offenders. The conviction and incarceration of individual managers were infrequent as well, despite the arguably high potential for both specific and general deterrence (see, e.g., Carter, 1980).[22] The data analyzed later in this chapter, although limited in terms of number of court cases, suggest these trends as well.

To the extent that such trends are real, they raise questions regarding the law's effectiveness and fairness. It appears that systemic constraints routinely shape the enforcement of the law in ways not intended or expected by its framers.

[22] The evidence on these points is suggestive rather than definitive. For example, in a 1980 review of recent trends in criminal prosecutions under the water act that suggested a possible tendency toward prosecuting managers as well as their firms, Carter (1980: 605–9; cf., DiMento, 1986: 191–203) cited five prominent cases against industry, three of which involved small firms. In *U.S. v. DeRewal et al.* (Crim. No. 77–287, E.D. Pa., 1978), the president and four employees of the DeRewal Chemical Company were convicted of dumping industrial wastes into the Philadelphia sewer system; the president was fined $20,000, sentenced to six months' incarceration, and given four and one-half years' probation. His subordinates each received three years' probation. In *U.S. v. Distler* (Crim. No. 77–00108–01–L [1979]; 671 F.2d 954; 454 U.S. 827), the president of the Kentucky Liquid Recycling Corporation, Donald Distler, was convicted of dumping toxic chemicals into the Louisville sewage system; he was sentenced to two years' imprisonment and given a $50,000 fine. In *U.S. v. Frezzo Brothers, Inc.* (642 F.2d 59; 703 F.2d 62), two brothers who owned a mushroom farming business were convicted of water pollution due to continuing overflows of their manure tank into a local creek. The brothers were fined a total of $50,000 and sentenced to thirty days in jail; the company was fined another $50,000.

In *U.S. v. Olin Corporation* (465 F. Supp. 1120 [1979]), three high-level managers were prosecuted for making false statements to the EPA, while in *U.S. v. Ford Motor Company* (*BNA Environmental Reporter*, Decisions No. 1 [1980]), corporate officials were criminally indicted for misrepresentation and conspirary in connection with the excessive discharge of carbon tetrachloride.

The enforcement record

To provide some sense of the trends during the 1970s in enforcement, Table 7.1 shows the distribution of EPA-administered sanctions under the water act from 1971 through 1977. Shown are the most formal sanctions; excluded are informal enforcement measures such as phone calls to violators and less serious sanctions such as warning letters, which data for Region II show to be one of the most common enforcement tools used by the EPA. These data are largely derived from EPA's own enforcement reports for the early years of the program; curiously, the agency ceased publishing such reports when the Carter administration took office (Brown, 1984: 15), a fact that accounts for the truncation of the table in 1977. The data shown in the table exclude enforcement actions taken by individual states' pollution control authorities under the federal law, and therefore represent only trends in purely federal enforcement.

For the 1971–72 period the table shows sanctions in cases handled under prior legislation, especially the 1956 amendments (conferences, notices of violation) and the Refuse Act permit program that EPA began to establish in the early 1970s prior to the 1972 amendments. There was a significant decline in enforcement activity in 1973, as the agency shifted to processing permit applications under the new amendments and established an enforcement moratorium during the pendancy of the applications.

As more permits were issued containing interim construction and effluent discharge deadlines, more of the EPA's attention turned to enforcement by 1974, as indicated by the great increase in administrative orders to come into compliance. The following year referrals to the Justice Department for civil and criminal prosecutions jumped markedly, as some early industrial permittees had by then established records of recalcitrance. It is to be noted, however, that administrative remedies continued to account for the lion's share of agency enforcement activity. Also in 1975, notices of violation reappeared as an enforcement tool, this time in the form of warnings to selected violators of state-issued permits. If the state authorities administering the federal requirements did not then take adequate enforcement action, the EPA was authorized by the statute to issue sanctions to violators.[23]

---

[23] Pub. L. 92–500, § 309[a][1]; 33 U.S.C. § 1319[a][1].

Table 7.1. *Water enforcement actions initiated by EPA*

	Refuse Act Referrals to Justice		Failure to apply for permits	FWPCA				
	Civil	Criminal		Administrative orders	Notices of violation	Referrals to Justice[a]	Enforcement conferences convened[b]	Total
July 1971–Dec. 1972[c]	106	169	96		143		9	523
1973	11	57		19		9(7)		96
1974	2	22		514		38		576
1975	7[d]			751	100	113		971
1976[e]				863	134	102		1,099
1977				1,035	295	138		1,468

Note: These water enforcement actions were taken largely under the Refuse Act and the 1972 amendments; they do not include oil spill enforcement actions or cases initiated by the Department of Justice. The actions include municipal as well as industrial dischargers. Except where otherwise noted, data were compiled from EPA Enforcement Reports.

[a] Except for the seven criminal referrals in parentheses, the data on which the table is based do not distinguish between criminal and civil referrals.

[b] In addition to the new conferences, a number of older conferences were reconvened or held additional or progress sessions.

[c] Data for this year and a half were taken largely from Davies and Davies (1975: 209); notices of violation are for period December 1970–December 1972. Conference data are for the period December 1970–March 1972, and were taken from the enforcement reports.

[d] Data source did not distinguish between civil and criminal referrals.

[e] Data for 1976 and 1977 taken from EPA paper ("Recent Developments in Federal Water Pollution Enforcement") presented at ALI–ABA Course of Study: Environmental Law, Washington, D.C., February 9–11, 1978.

Table 7.2. *Water enforcement actions, July to December, 1976 and 1977*

	July–December 1977	July–December 1976
Notices of violation	151	70
Administrative orders	392	395
Referrals to Justice	82	40
Totals	625	505

Data taken from EPA paper ("Recent Developments in Federal Water Pollution Enforcement") presented at ALI–ABA Course of Study: Environmental Law, Washington, D.C., February 9–11, 1978.

Thereafter, in 1976 and 1977, the use of all sanctions under the amendments increased as enforcement became a greater priority and the congressionally mandated July 1977 deadline approached. Indeed, Table 7.2 indicates that with the passing of this deadline for firms to have established "best practicable control technology," EPA more than doubled its referrals to Justice over the comparable half-year period a year earlier, underscoring the agency's policy of stronger legal sanctions in cases of violation of the statutory deadline.

These raw figures need to be interpreted in a broader context. In the first place, as implied above, the types of sanctions listed in these agency data were in fact used relatively infrequently by the EPA, and therefore are neither a good measure of total noncompliance nor of the agency's enforcement choices more generally. Instead, as shown in the Region II data later, the agency more typically used warning letters, informal sanctions, and even no sanction at all in the case of many industrial violations of law.

Second, of the 633 major (EPA definition) industrial plants in the United States that did not meet the July 1977 deadline, the EPA planned enforcement action against only 317 of them, or 50 percent (U.S. Environmental Protection Agency, 1977b). Part of the problem was a shortage of enforcement resources (Buglass, 1977), but much of the difference lay in extensions such as those provided by the agency's Enforcement Compliance Schedule Letters (17.3 percent) and significantly by pending adjudicatory hearings (11.3 percent), which agency personnel had recognized as delaying both compliance and enforcement.

Third, despite such delays the agency was by mid-1977 reporting an 84 percent compliance rate among the nation's 4,020 major industrial dischargers (U.S. Environmental Protection Agency, 1977b). Given the resource constraints, tight timetables, and the major shift in environmental law the 1972 act represented, this was not an unimpressive feat. But there remained a question of the *evenness* with which the law was being administered, in both permitting and enforcement. The remainder of this chapter inspects this question closely with an assessment of policy and practice in EPA's Region II.

Compliance and enforcement: a study of EPA's Region II

EPA's Region II, with headquarters in New York City, is responsible for implementing federal pollution control laws in New Jersey, New York, Puerto Rico, and the Virgin Islands. Its jurisdiction covers a heavily industrialized and populated section of the country, one that contains a wide spectrum of industrial activity and that has experienced some of the most serious water pollution problems in the nation. Despite having only two states, Region II had the sixth largest number of private sector wastewater dischargers (2,474) among the EPA's ten regions, but had the second largest number of major industrial dischargers (547), as defined above. New Jersey, which provides the site for the study presented here, is an especially heavily industrialized state, long a national leader in manufacturing and chemical processing facilities. It also has a long history of heavy pollution loads. In addition to its high levels of industrial water pollution, the state has 110 toxic waste sites on the federal government's priority list for cleanup (the "Superfund" list), more than any other state.[24]

As late as 1978 only Region II among the EPA regions had a relatively comprehensive, computerized data file listing key permit requirements and the history of violations and agency sanctions for each permitted facility. As it happened, EPA was rather stronger on data collection than on the systematic organization of regulatory intelligence. Having failed at an effort in the mid-1970s to develop a computer-based, centralized enforcement tracking system at EPA headquarters in Washington, the agency instead began in 1975 to simply collect quarterly noncompliance reports from its ten regional offices and the various states enforcing the water pollution control program under EPA authority. These paper reports were kept in numerous files and could be reviewed periodically to gauge the

[24] Robert Hanley, "New Jersey's Tough Toxic Cleanup Law: Too Harsh?" *The New York Times*, May 15, 1989, p. B1.

consistency and appropriateness of enforcement activity across jurisdictions. But they were naturally much less amenable to the measurement of consistency and enforcement policy over time, or to determining whether a large corporation was compiling long records of noncompliance at its numerous factories around the country (as against isolated problems at specific facilities), a fact relevant to prosecution and sanctioning decisions.

The lack of modern, comprehensive computerized data bases is by itself a substantial impediment to effective and rational enforcement of the law. Not only does it hinder the development of consistent, deterrence-maximizing enforcement, but it also prevents the agency from sending clear signals to the regulated regarding the fairness, firmness, and rationality of its enforcement policies.[25] It is also a problem that continued to characterize the EPA by the mid-1980s (Brown, 1984: 18).

Against this background, Region II's enforcement tracking system was advanced, indeed. For all permitted facilities, it contained information on the permit itself (when issued, whether the plant was under orders to install new pollution control equipment, whether it had been issued to a large volume discharger), violations (effluent, construction schedule, or reporting offenses, often which pollution parameters had been violated, etc.), and sanctioning responses by the agency, including the region's decisions to issue no sanctions for some offenses, a data item rarely found in enforcement files of any sort.

The data analyzed for this study track the regional office's enforcement of the Clean Water Act against industrial polluters in New Jersey from 1973 through early 1978. This selection was driven by my interest in focusing on *direct federal enforcement* of the law, rather than on enforcement as mediated by separate state authori-

---

[25] While conducting my research at EPA headquarters in Washington in 1978, I discussed the lack of a centralized data base with one of the agency's chief data management managers, who explained that the EPA had once tried to establish such a computer file, but when the initial effort failed the project was abandoned. When I obliquely suggested that this "data gap" served some interests better than others, he lowered his gaze to the floor, nodded quietly, then said, "That's all I'll have to say about that." Ultimately I was unable to determine whether he had in mind internal struggles within the agency (for resources), concerns that the agency shouldn't track enforcement too closely for fear that any weaknesses in its policies would be divulged to the public, or the advantages that such a data void might offer some polluters over the long run (e.g., as a consequence of the government's inability to easily determine whether a corporation with many facilities has developed a long record of noncompliance at all of them).

ties to whom EPA had delegated the water pollution program, as in New York State. This is surely a simpler approach than comparing the disparate jurisdictions involved, but also has the merit of concentrating on the federal agency upon which such high expectations had been placed during the 1970s.

In sum, the study investigates the regulatory record compiled by Region II's enforcement officials for 321 industrial facilities discharging wastes into New Jersey's waterways. Of these plants, 117 (36 percent) were classified as major dischargers, the types of facilities the EPA has typically targeted for priority regulatory effort. The remaining 204 plants were classified as minor dischargers.[26]

In the remainder of this chapter, I shall first describe the region's enforcement policy and practices in aggregate terms. Then I present closer analyses of the regulatory records of the sample plants, with interest in the possibility that regulatory law of this type manifests what I refer to as "structural bias," the tendency of ostensibly neutral legal structures to reproduce inequalities in the private sector.

Enforcement policies and practices

As with the general logic of the water law's enforcement described above, the earliest concern of Region II's regulators was to quickly secure industry's compliance with the baseline requirements of permit application and the submission of self-monitoring reports; together these comprised the heart of regulatory effort. Given the heavy regulatory burden and scarce enforcement resources, the law's success depended on a good measure of voluntary compliance

---

[26] The final sample studied herein was purposively selected from the almost 600 private facilities in New Jersey with EPA-issued permits limiting their water pollution discharges. First, the analysis was confined to *manufacturing* plants, those with Standard Industrial Classification codes ranging from 20 to 39, inclusive. Among businesses directly discharging wastes into the nation's waterways, manufacturing facilities constitute the major source of waste and are the focus of regulatory attention. Second, plants that processed their wastes through a municipal (public) treatment works, rather than build their own treatment facilities, were excluded from the study. Such facilities are not directly regulated by EPA pollution control permits; rather, they are regulated indirectly through the permits issued to the municipal treatment works. Third, plants owned by non-American corporations were excluded to avoid potentially extraneous factors, such as those related to international trade. Fourth, some forty plants were dropped from the analysis due to incomplete government regulatory data. Finally, a few plants were dropped for miscellaneous reasons, including ownership change and plant closings.

by industry, which could be best secured by the agency's consistent and firm enforcement against violators.

The enforcement data suggest that the Region was successful in prompting companies to make timely application for discharge permits. Only six enforcement cases for the entire period were found in these data. Assuming this number reasonably approximates the violation rate (it is relatively difficult to hide factory pollution for long periods), part of the reason for the success was EPA's seriousness of purpose: These offenses drew the EPA's most serious penalties, as later illustrated.

By early 1975 the majority of the Region's 124 enforcement actions had been taken for violation of the self-reporting requirements of the law (76 cases; 40 other cases involved companies' failures to meet construction schedules for pollution control facilities, while only 3 enforcement actions were taken for pollution discharge violations).[27] Most of these cases involved late reports, rather than false reporting per se.

Here a few words are in order regarding the self-reporting system, so central is it to enforcement of the water law. The agency requires two kinds of report from industry dischargers. Compliance schedule reports certify companies' progress in meeting their permits' mandatory schedules for installing pollution controls. Discharge monitoring reports, on the other hand, are required to indicate the degree of the plants' compliance with or violation of the various discharge limits contained in the individual permits. The frequency with which these self-reports are required (monthly, quarterly, annually) is specified in the permits, and is determined by the seriousness of the pollution load being discharged. The integrity of the self-reporting system is undergirded by periodic inspections of plants by federal and state authorities.

Inspection resources are scarce, however. The EPA's official policy called for inspection of major dischargers "at least once a year if possible, and of minor permits [facilities with less polluting discharges] on a spot basis."[28] According to an agency official in EPA's Region II office, this goal proved to be "basically impossible" to meet given the limited resources. The enacted policy in the region therefore focused inspection resources on likely "trouble areas"

[27] EPA Region II Memorandum, February 18, 1975: "Water Enforcement Statistics."
[28] EPA Headquarters Enforcement Memorandum, "Compliance Monitoring, Administrative Orders, and Court Actions under Section 309 of the Federal Water Pollution Control Act Amendments of 1972," March 20, 1974.

among the major polluters, in combination with some random inspections.[29]

At one level, enforcement of the reporting requirements was a straightforward affair. Late or incomplete reports themselves constituted violations of the act and were quickly responded to by the EPA (see enforcement data below). But there remains the question of the credibility of the self-reports, the extent to which they accurately measure real rates of violation among regulated firms. The question remains without answer, and I discuss the methodological implications in Appendix A to this chapter. That many firms continue to report numerous infractions even after the EPA has issued orders to comply, for example, suggests that many reports are reasonably accurate. And the government responded to identified cases of false reporting with its stiffest sanctions, including criminal prosecutions under the water amendments and other federal fraud statutes (Carter, 1980: 608–9). Nonetheless, the relation of EPA's enforcement records and true rates of violation necessarily remains uncertain.

In 1975 Region II shifted to a broader enforcement effort for the industrial permits. Noting that most of the staff's energies in 1974 had "been consumed, successively, with the issuance of permits and the handling of Adjudicatory Hearings," the head of the region's water pollution enforcement unit asserted that "it is time for the Water Enforcement Branch to do a little something about water enforcement."[30] The focus in 1975 was on the enforcement of the construction schedule requirements generally, and on the discharge violations of the major polluters. By 1976, when many major dischargers had completed construction of their BPT control facilities, enforcement priorities increasingly turned to violations of the permit pollution discharge limits.[31]

Stretching the law: enforcement options. Region II availed itself of the range of enforcement options suggested by the policy guidance from Washington. The region took the position (as had EPA's Washington headquarters) that not every violation of the law merited the issuance of a formal administrative order to comply,

[29] Interview, EPA Region II, 1978.
[30] EPA Region II Enforcement Memorandum, "Water Enforcement," February 14, 1975.
[31] EPA Headquarters Enforcement Memorandum, "Year-end Report [Water Enforcement]," November 10, 1975.

despite the contradictory indication in the original legislation. Instead, the region used a series of enforcement tools ranging from phone calls and warning letters to administrative orders and referrals to the U.S. Justice Department for civil or criminal prosecution.

Enforcement memoranda in the mid-1970s, for example, indicated the use of warning (or enforcement) letters (sometimes in combination with phone calls) for such violations as exceeding discharge limits or failing to submit required reports on a timely basis. Continued noncompliance with the law was to be met with escalated legal responses, including the formal EPA administrative orders to comply, show cause orders to appear before the agency to explain noncompliance (and thus "show cause" why the agency should not proceed with further legal action), and eventually civil or criminal legal action.[32]

In addition, Region II attempted to create more enforcement options both for mild offenses and for grievous ones. Regional authorities formalized a "no (legal) action" option, in which they would essentially overlook some violations, typically because the infractions were not considered serious (for example, exceeding effluent limitations by only 10–15 percent),[33] the company was making adequate progress toward compliance, aspects of the facility's permit were under appeal, or an existing enforcement case was currently pending. The formalization of these no-action responses is indicated by their inclusion in the computerized compliance records used in this study; thus the possibility that such overlooked offenses favor some businesses over others can be investigated, an unusual opportunity in sociolegal studies dependent on official data.

There is also evidence that Region II's enforcement authorities attempted to create more stringent enforcement options not recognized by EPA headquarters in Washington. In early 1976 the chief of the region's Water Enforcement Branch argued in an internal memorandum that the region should consider instituting its own civil court actions against serious violators, rather than referring such cases to the Department of Justice for the decision of whether to prosecute; the enforcement chief argued that the region should

---

[32] EPA Region II Enforcement Memoranda, "Compliance Monitoring," November 5, 1974; "Water Enforcement Executive Committee [and] Enforcement Responses Available to the Enforcement Division," February 11, 1976.
[33] Interview, EPA Region II, 1979.

not "rule [EPA-initiated court action] out or give up trying to push it," even though the procedure "has been frowned upon by both HQ [Headquarters] and Justice."[34]

Even more notable, the chief suggested that show cause hearings could be used not only to reestablish enforceable compliance plans in cases in which facilities had failed to meet their required compliance schedules, but also to collect monetary penalties for such violations without any court proceedings whatsoever. He noted, "This procedure is not specifically set out in the Statute [the Clean Water Act], nor is it specifically forbidden. I feel any problems can be overcome by styling it a payment of penalty in consideration of not referring to Justice for the imposition of actual civil penalties." His reasoning was that such a procedure would be more effective in promoting compliance with the pollution abatement schedules; the Justice Department had a policy of not creating new, enforceable compliance schedules during court cases in which it sought civil monetary penalties for noncompliance. In an earlier memorandum he had noted that the region was receiving "poor service from our U.S. attorneys. Cases languish for over nine months without ever being filed. . . . Obviously the long delays occasioned by court practice and over burdened U.S. Attorneys make this [Justice Department policy] impossible if we are to even approach compliance with the 1977 date [July 1, 1977 deadline for reaching 'best practicable technology' for pollution abatement]."[35]

Despite this strong rationale, evidence from this research indicates that neither of these novel legal procedures gained formal approval. The data analyzed show no such legal cases by 1978. During the 1970s the Congress was unwilling to sanction the notion of monetary penalties administered for water violations by EPA (rather than by the courts): in amending the Clean Water Act in 1977, the legislature rejected a proposed amendment authorizing such administrative penalties, despite the agency's support for this enforcement option;[36] many members of Congress were persuaded that this option would intrude on the prerogatives of the Justice Department, as would the prospect of large numbers of EPA-initiated civil suits. Thus the water law regulators were left with the more conventional,

[34] EPA Region II Enforcement Memorandum, "Enforcement Procedures," February 11, 1976.
[35] EPA Region II Enforcement Memorandum, "Enforcement Techniques," January 26, 1976.
[36] *Environmental News*, U.S. Environmental Protection Agency, December 29, 1977.

but arguably less efficient and effective, legal measures described before.

Alterations and outcomes. The other legal variable of note in this regulatory scheme, besides violations and sanctions, involves the alteration of a company's permit requirements after the discharge permit has been issued. If a company is able to convince the agency that such alterations are warranted in its case, the legal requirements are brought more into line with the company's ability or willingness to comply with the law.[37] Under such circumstances, one might expect the company to evidence fewer subsequent violations, having relieved something of the original regulatory burden.

As earlier noted, in passing the amendments to the water pollution law in 1972 the Congress – with something of Bernstein's (1955) capture thesis in mind – had been concerned to avoid the behind-closed-doors relaxing of permit requirements that had been originally established in the full light of public participation. Thus only two methods of permit alteration were sanctioned by the terms of the legislation: the often lengthy adjudicatory hearing process, in which newly permitted facilities could challenge all or parts of their permits' legal requirements, and the "modification" process, in which any proposed alterations of either effluent limitations or compliance schedules would be published to provide the opportunity for a public hearing on the matter. However, the agency determined that the modification process would, if applied to every request for permit alteration, strangle the regulatory process in a tangle of red tape. Therefore, EPA used its discretion to create an alternative process of permit "revision," in which permit alterations that did *not* change the final effluent limitations, or substantially extend the final date for compliance with the BPT requirement, could be made by the agency without public participation. Company re-

[37] The financial and technical abilities of any given firm to comply with governmental regulation are often quite difficult to disentangle from its philosophical willingness to comply. Thus questions of the perceived appropriateness of governmental intervention into the economy are interwoven with arguments concerning a company's or industry's very capacity to comply with regulation. Because of private industry's "knowledge advantage" in financial and technical matters often considered proprietary, it is possible to shroud ideological opposition to the fact of regulation itself with arguments couched in the language of feasibility. Since in any case both the fact and *degree* of regulatory intervention are determined by political processes involving questions of power and legitimacy, this private-sector advantage may work against socially efficient and just regulation.

quests to change the final limits or the ultimate compliance date by more than ninety days were to be handled through the formal "modification" process. And according to Region II policy, "Such changes should be resorted to only as a last resort in cases where ample justification exists."[38]

Measured against this stringent policy toward compliance with the 1977 deadline, Region II's record was somewhat mixed. The compliance data for the 321 industrial plants examined in this research show that 18 percent of the facilities had been granted modifications, while the same percentage had been issued the less consequential revisions. But in an interview a Region II official said that many of the modifications were related to changes in the federal pollution control regulations after the permits had been issued.[39] On the basis of these data, then, regulatory slippage appears not to have been extensive, at least by 1978 in the region studied.

An important indicator of the degree of such slippage is the proportion of major dischargers that did not meet the critical July 1, 1977, deadline for compliance with the BPT standard. Nationally EPA data showed that 633 major industrial plants, or 16 percent of the nation's 4,020 major permitted industrial dischargers, did not meet the deadline. The EPA contemplated enforcement actions against only 50 percent of these facilities; the majority of the rest (another 28 percent) saw enforcement delayed due to extensions granted through hearings procedures or the agency's compliance letters.

In contrast to the national data, Region II planned enforcement actions against only 25 of its 112 major industrial facilities that did not meet the statutory deadline, or 22 percent.[40] And the majority of the cases of nonenforcement were accounted for by formally granted extensions. For example, of the 49 cases of nonenforcement involving conventional manufacturing facilities such as those studied in this research (excluding the 38 cases involving electric power utilities companies), 27 (55 percent) were due to extensions related to

---

[38] EPA Region II Enforcement Memorandum, "Compliance Monitoring," November 5, 1974; EPA Region II Memorandum, "Reiteration of 'Modification' and 'Revision' Procedures for NPDES Permits," January 20, 1975; EPA Headquarters Enforcement Memorandum, "Compliance Monitoring, Administrative Orders, and Court Actions under Section 309 of the Federal Water Pollution Control Act Amendments of 1972," March 20, 1974.

[39] Interview, EPA Region II, 1979.

[40] EPA Region II Enforcement Memorandum, "Enforcement of 1977 Deadline Violations Against Major Industrial Polluters," June 2, 1977.

adjudicatory hearings, including 10 cases in which hearings were still pending. (Another 27 percent of the cases were accounted for by the compliance delays of municipal sewage treatment plants, to which some industrial dischargers were to connect their discharges.)

Rather than indicating unusual regulatory leniency, it is likely that the differences between Region II and national data reflect the region's especially heavy concentration of major dischargers, many of whom appealed the terms of their permits through the available avenues. In the end, the region achieved an 80 percent compliance rate for the 1977 deadline, compared with the national rate of 84 percent, a small difference. Nonetheless, an important question remains concerning whether such exceptions and extensions tend to favor some types of firms, in particular those with greater economic power. The remainder of the chapter develops some answers to that question by inspecting the trends in Region II's enforcement data.

Structural bias in regulatory law

The record: an overview

Given the dramatic shift in environmental policy represented by the 1972 water law, it is perhaps not surprising that 70 percent of the sample of 321 industrial plants had committed nonminor violations of the act by 1978.[41] (Nonminor violations include all infractions except effluent discharge violations that were designated as minor in

---

[41] It is instructive to compare these results with those obtained by the Clinard et al. (1979: 93) research, in which only 27 percent of parent manufacturing corporations were found to have been in violation of *any* of the several federal environmental statutes. This impressive difference is due to several factors. First, the Clinard et al. study was necessarily limited to data sources that were national in scope (in order to manage the vast amounts of material involved in researching the enforcement activities of some twenty-five federal agencies), and which therefore did not possess the detail of the regional data analyzed here. Importantly, the earlier study did not include most cases of water pollution violations for which only EPA administrative penalties were issued (warnings and orders), due to their omission from the *EPA Enforcement Report* for the two years studied. (Curiously, the *Report* did contain administrative enforcement activity for violations of the Clean Air Act, which were included in the study; see Clinard et al., 1979: 68.) As it happened, the water violations handled administratively were available in the form of the periodic reports made to EPA Headquarters by the ten regional offices, a fact learned too late in the research process. In contrast, the data used in the present investigation contain even infractions for which no enforcement response was made; such information can typically be retrieved from federal agency sources only by vastly time-consuming research of individual case files.

Second, the present research includes violations for the "lives" of existing discharge permits, typically three to four years, whereas the Clinard et al. study investigated only a two-year period, 1975–6. It might be thought that an additional

the region's data.) Moreover, while almost a third of the facilities had no nonminor infractions of any type, many of these are plants only recently permitted (prior to 1978), or for which no significant new construction was required to meet effluent limits.

Violation rates varied substantially by type of infraction. While half the sample had committed nonminor effluent violations, and 47 percent had violated the self-monitoring, self-reporting requirements at least once, only 14 percent had violated their compliance schedules. Among facilities found to have violated the water law extensively, such variation continued to exist: 14.5 percent of the sample had five or more nonminor effluent violations, while only 0.6 percent had as many compliance schedule infractions and 1.2 percent had five or more reporting offenses.

The high degree of compliance with the construction schedules suggests that EPA was successful in targeting this facet of the regulatory scheme for attention. The agency consistently emphasized the importance of maintaining compliance in this area, and took its stiffest enforcement stance against such violations (as described later). The compliance rate is all the more impressive in view of the often expensive construction requirements made of manufacturing facilities. But some of the increased compliance is due to firms' successful challenges to the conditions imposed by the schedules set in their permits; in such cases the agency modified the requirements, with the result that some firms experienced reduced violations, as illustrated in the findings reported in the next section. In addition, in response to early violations of the construction schedules, the agency established new schedules that the violators agreed to keep. In part at least, this accounts for the result that only a very small proportion of plants repeatedly violated the schedules.[42]

Effluent discharge violations, in contrast, were considerably more

source of difference between the two studies is the inclusion in the present research of many companies much smaller than the *Fortune* 500 corporations examined in the earlier investigation, the assumption being that smaller firms are substantially more likely to violate the often expensive environmental regulations than larger, wealthier corporations. The results of this research do not indicate wide variation in compliance by firms of different size, however. For example, the correlation between firm size and total nonminor violations is a mere .043, although it is worth noting that firm size data were unavailable for 105 of the facilities, presumably including the smallest in the sample studied. My impression from studying the data, however, is that the difference in compliance as between the largest and smallest firms do not account for much of the variation in the two studies' results, although the largest firms do enjoy some advantages in the regulatory process, as discussed later in this chapter.

[42] Only 6 percent of the facilities had two or more compliance schedule violations,

common, both because such offenses can occur on a spot basis even for plants that have maintained their compliance schedules (due to such factors as operator error or carelessness or equipment failure), and because EPA's and Region II's enforcement policy did not aggressively discourage such offenses in the 1970s. Typically, these violations were treated either with no enforcement action or with warning letters. Not uncommonly, a company could receive a number of such responses to these offenses, especially if they did not constitute evidence of systematic noncompliance (bad faith), without incurring more stringent enforcement responses such as formal orders or referrals to the Justice Department for civil or criminal prosecution. It might be argued that a rather more stringent enforcement policy would pay some dividends by improving compliance with discharge limits. A policy, for example, of scaled administrative fines would need to be carefully designed to punish only clear cases of inattention to good pollution-control operating procedures, however, in order to avoid such counterproductive effects as increased misrepresentation in self-monitoring reports.

The findings for reporting offenses are also suggestive of policy effects. While almost half the sample had violated reporting requirements at least once, only 21 percent did so two or more times, and a fractional 1.2 percent committed five or more offenses. This pattern suggests that EPA's policy emphasizing the centrality of self-reporting for the entire regulatory effort was successful in fostering compliance, once the rhythms of the new legal scheme had been established with the regulated. This compliance success, however, has to do with submitting correctly completed reports on time; it does not speak to the degree of honesty in companies' self-reports.

Patterns in sanctioning

Of central interest to this investigation is the pattern of enforcement responses to the various types of violations and companies. Table 7.3 was constructed to provide an initial look at the pattern for Region II.

The first thing of note in these results is that the single most common agency response to these violations is to take no formal action against them; this response occurred in more than 40 percent of the

while 34 percent had two or more nonminor effluent violations and 21 percent had as many reporting offenses.

Table 7.3. *EPA Region II enforcement responses to violation types*

	No action	Warning letters	Administrative orders	Civil/criminal referrals
Total violations	42.5%	40.8%	3.3%	0.6%
	(390)	(374)	(30)	(5)
Nonminor effluent violations	61.5%	17.5%	2.6%	0.4%
	(348)	(99)	(15)	(2)
Reporting violations	12.3%	82.4%	1.5%	0%
	(32)	(215)	(4)	(0)
Compliance schedule violations	10.7%	70.2%	10.7%	1.2%
	(9)	(59)	(9)	(1)
Failure to file for permit	16.7%	16.7%	33.3%	33.3%
	(1)	(1)	(2)	(2)

Note: The percentages often do not add across the rows to equal 100% because of the exclusion of a category of "Other" enforcement responses that include such region actions as placing the case on the docket of the Water Enforcement Executive Committee for hearing, and other pending resolutions. In parentheses are the numbers of cases of violation for which the indicated enforcement reponses were made. Total violation counts in each column are sums of counts for the types of violation listed.

cases. In another 40 percent of the cases, the agency issued formal warning letters for infractions. Notable, too, on the other side of the ledger, is the rarity with which more serious sanctions were administered. Administrative orders were used in only 3.3 percent of the cases, while referrals to the Justice Department were made in only five cases, or less than 1 percent of the time.

The table also shows that agency responses differed significantly by violation type, in ways broadly consistent with the stated enforcement policies discussed above. Most of the no-action determinations[43] are accounted for by the nonminor effluent violations, against which the region took no action fully three-fifths of the time, while issuing warning letters for nearly another fifth of the cases. Agency orders to comply were used in less than 3 percent of the cases, while civil or criminal referrals were made in only two of the more than 460 cases of these discharge violations.

While it may be arguable whether the enacted policy maximized compliance, and the enforcement pattern indicates that "no-action" decisions were made for many nonminor as well as for minor dis-

---

[43] Cases were recorded as receiving no enforcement action if the Region's data directly specified the agency's decision to take no action or if no discernible action was indicated in the report.

charge violations, these results suggest that the region stayed well away from nitpicking enforcement, as EPA enforcement officials had been directed by the agency's top management. The region typically used formal sanctions only in those cases which indicated systematic (bad faith) noncompliance with the effluent limitations. It is also worth noting that the no-action policy may have encouraged more honest self-reports by regulated companies. Were the agency to issue formal sanctions for single or otherwise explainable violations of the discharge limits – sanctions that may rather quickly tend to escalate upon continued violations if the agency is to maintain credibility, given the few enforcement options available – the benefits to misrepresenting true discharge levels increase. Thus here, as in many areas of law, there remains the thorny issue of where to strike the balance between legal forbearance and strict enforcement if public policy is to achieve some socially optimal result. The question finds no simple answers.

The region was much more likely to issue formal sanctions for violation of the reporting requirements so central to enforcement of the law. In more than 80 percent of these cases warning letters were sent to violators, while in only 12 percent of the cases did the enforcement officials take no action. Again, more serious enforcement actions were rare: Only 1.5 percent of these cases of noncompliance were met with administrative orders, while none received criminal or civil disposition, indicating that late or incomplete reports constituted the identified offenses.

For violations of compliance schedules, a different pattern emerges. Again, formal sanctions are typically used, warning letters accounting for 70 percent of the enforcement responses. But for these offenses, considered of highest priority by the agency in terms of ultimate pollution reduction, administrative orders are much more common than for either effluent or reporting violations, accounting for almost 11 percent of sanctions in compliance schedule cases. Again, the agency rarely resorted to criminal or civil penalties; only a single case resulted in such action.

Finally, while there were few such cases in these Region II data, failures to file for water pollution discharge permits were typically met with the most serious sanctions. Two of the six cases were referred to the Justice Department for civil or criminal penalties, while another two resulted in administrative orders. This sanctioning pattern bears a logical relation to the seriousness of these offenses. Not only does nonfiling delay the reduction in pollution levels, but it also flouts the law and the agency's legitimacy.

Table 7.4. *Sanctioning responses by firm size*

	Small firms (125 plants)		Large firms (93 plants)	
Total violations				
No action	27.8%	(84)	56.2%	(169)
Warning letter	53.6%	(162)	25.6%	(77)
Administrative order	4.3%	(13)	1.7%	(5)
Civil/crim. Ref.	1.3%	(4)	0	
Compliance schedule violations				
No action	9.8%	(4)	11.1%	(2)
Warning letter	65.9%	(27)	83.3%	(15)
Administrative order	12.2%	(5)	0	
Civil/crim. Ref.	2.4%	(1)	0	
Nonminor effluent violations				
No action	51.1%	(67)	67.7%	(155)
Warning letter	19.8%	(26)	11.4%	(26)
Administrative order	3.1%	(4)	1.8%	(4)
Civil/crim. Ref.	1.5%	(2)	0	
Reporting violations				
No action	10.2%	(13)	21.2%	(11)
Warning letter	85.8%	(109)	67.3%	(35)
Administrative order	1.6%	(2)	1.9%	(1)
Civil/crim. Ref.	0		0	

Note: Percentages of violations receiving the indicated sanction. The numbers in parentheses represent the number of cases of violation receiving the indicated sanction. The category of "Other" enforcement responses is again omitted, as in Table 7.3.

Beyond the general sanctioning pattern, there lies the question of whether the enforcement responses are differentially distributed by company size, an indicator of business strength or power. Table 7.4 provides a preliminary assessment of this issue. The table compares small companies, defined as those with annual sales of $10 million or less, with the largest firms in the sample, those with annual sales in excess of $1 billion.[44] The two groups of firms are compared for

[44] Firm strength (size), measured in terms of annual sales, was determined through the use of the major business references. For the 143 cases the data base had in common with the earlier Clinard et al. (1979) study, sales values were simply extracted from the file I had earlier created for that investigation. These data had been drawn from the COMPUSTAT data base of Investors Management Science, Inc., made available by the School of Business at the University of Wisconsin–Madison. For the other 178 plants in the present study, the following references

both total violations and for the major types of offense considered separately.

Looking first at the total violations comparisons, the distributions show that the large companies are twice as likely to receive no-action determinations, and conversely half as likely to receive warning letters for infractions, as the small firms. Moreover, the small firms were more than twice as likely to receive administrative orders as the large, and the former received all of the civil or criminal referrals in these data while the large companies experienced none, although as indicated the number of such referrals is small indeed.

A pattern of differential sanctioning tends to hold for the different violation types as well. For compliance schedule violations, the difference lies not so much with the no-action determinations as it does in comparing warnings with the more serious sanctions. For both large and small companies, warning letters were by far the most common response to these offenses. However, in 12 percent of their cases small firms received the more intimidating orders, while none of the large companies' offenses drew such a response. The latter also drew no civil or criminal referrals, although one small company did for violating its compliance schedule.

For nonminor effluent discharge violations, large corporations are again significantly more likely to receive no-action determinations, and less likely to receive formal sanctions of any kind, than are small companies. And as with total violations, the difference in likelihood of formal sanction increases with the stringency of enforce-

were consulted to determine annual sales: Moody's Industrial Manual, Dun & Bradstreet's Million Dollar Directory and Middle Market Directory, and the New Jersey State Industrial Directory.

The result of this process was that annual sales information was available for 216 of the 321 plants included in this research. For the 105 cases for which this information was not available, it is reasonable to assume that the companies are typically significantly smaller than those multimillion-dollar firms for which the annual data are available. Therefore, the small firms discussed in Table 7.4 include twenty plants for which company sales were identified, and the 105 plants for which no data were available in any of the standard references, which generally exclude the smaller outfits.

A final methodological note on the sales variable is in order. The Clinard et al. (1979) study measure of corporate size used for 143 of the cases here, and the supplementary size data used for the rest were slightly different in form. The former had been calculated in terms of *average* annual sales for the five-year period 1971–5. The supplementary data, on the other hand, were single year figures typically extracted from 1977 records. The difference is not serious, however, because the supplementary data were typically for firms significantly smaller than the Wisconsin study companies, which were all *Fortune* 500 industrials.

ment response. In the case of reporting violations, a similar result obtains for the distinction between no-action and warning letters. Here, however, companies in both size groups were equally likely to receive the more serious enforcement responses (administrative orders), which again proved quite uncommon. Finally, not shown are the results for the few cases in which companies failed to file for discharge permits under the Clean Water Act, offenses generally considered very serious by the agency. Of the three such offenses committed by small companies, two received orders while the other was referred to the Justice Department for prosecution. Of the two such offenses committed by large corporations, one received no action and the other a warning letter. Although these numbers are small, the differential sanctioning responses are nonetheless impressive.

It should be noted that the intermediate-size companies, those with annual sales ranging from $10 million to just under $1 billion, do not always fall midway between the two groups considered here in terms of sanctioning experience (see Yeager, 1981: 242). For example, some of the intermediate groupings[45] were more likely than the small companies to receive administrative orders for infractions, and the twenty-five companies in the $500 million to $1 billion category received slightly fewer (26.6 percent) no-action decisions than the smallest companies. Nonetheless, the sanctioning differences remain impressive at the margins. In particular, the smallest companies were more likely than any other grouping to receive the harshest sanctions: civil and criminal referrals. At the other end of the scale, the very largest companies (the billion-dollar-plus firms in Table 7.4) were, in terms of total sanctions, the least likely of all groupings to receive civil or criminal referrals, orders, and warnings, and most likely to receive no-action decisions.

Taken together, these results begin to suggest that sanctioning decisions favor the largest corporations as compared to smaller firms. They suggest that the agency is reluctant to issue formal sanctions, particularly the more serious orders and referrals, to very large companies. Once the EPA begins issuing formal sanctions to a company for ongoing violations of the law, in contrast to the option of bargaining no-action responses to elicit "good faith" efforts at com-

---

[45] The groups examined were the following: $10 million and under ($N$ = 125 plants), $10,000,001 to $300 million ($N$ = 53 plants), $300,000,001 to $500 million ($N$ = 25 plants), $500,000,001 to $1 billion ($N$ = 25 plants), greater than $1 billion ($N$ = 93 plants).

pliance, it tends to commit itself to an escalating course of penalties in the face of continued noncompliance, or to loss of face, clearly an unacceptable outcome.

With respect to the ultimate sanctions, civil and criminal prosecutions brought on the agency's behalf by the Justice Department, the agency faced the constraints of the department's inefficient processing of cases described previously (thus delaying ultimate compliance), and the department's redefinition of legal liability in terms of demonstrable environmental damage rather than simply on the basis of permit violations. The sanctioning results reviewed here suggest an additional constraint on legal action, however: The agency appears reluctant to engage powerful corporations in formal legal action, perhaps because such action may commit the agency's prestige and mission to high-risk encounters in court with opponents whose financial and technical might may combine to frustrate that very mission and prestige. This interpretation is lent support by the witness, noted earlier in the chapter, of the long-time water enforcement attorney at EPA who imputed just such reluctance in enforcement to his agency.

But these results constitute, at best, only a preliminary suggestion of structural bias in social regulation. It remains to investigate the dynamic nature of the regulatory nexus through which bias may operate to reproduce inequality in the private sector. It is to this investigation that the discussion now turns.

A test of the model

Chapter 2 presented a model (Figure 2.1) linking company strength, agency procedures, and violations and sanctions experience, suggesting that the social production of environmental offenses is a joint and systematic effect of the behavior of both law and business. The model proposes that the larger, more powerful firms have both direct and indirect advantages at law over their smaller brethren. The direct advantages have to do, first, with what might be called the regulatory economies of scale by which larger companies can more easily manage expensive regulatory costs and, second, with the proposed reluctance on the part of agency officials to aggressively sanction more powerful adversaries, as just discussed. The indirect advantages involve the larger companies' greater access to technical agency procedures by which firms can generate exceptions to the regulatory requirements imposed on them, thereby bringing the law more into line with their intent or capacity to comply. The argument can be briefly summarized in the form of hypotheses:

1. Larger corporations have fewer violations than smaller companies because of their greater ability to absorb regulatory costs or pass them on.
2. Larger firms receive fewer sanctions than smaller companies, holding violation levels constant, because regulatory agencies seek to avoid legal confrontations with powerful adversaries.
3. Larger companies have disproportionate access to regulatory proceedings, due to their greater technical resources.
4. Because of this greater access, larger firms have fewer violations than companies without such access, by virtue of having their legal requirements altered in their favor, or stayed.
5. Because of this greater access, larger firms also have fewer sanctions for a given level of violation, as the regulatory agency stays enforcement while requirements are being negotiated.

In this investigation, firm strength is measured in terms of a company's annual sales, both because this is a commonly assumed convention (cf., Clinard et al., 1979), and because other indicators of strength (such as market share) are unavailable for large samples. Because annual sales data were not available for smaller companies, only 214 discharging plants are included in these analyses.[46] These plants are owned by firms with annual sales ranging from $325,000 to more than $32 billion, with a mean size of $2.5 billion. Two of every five plants are owned by companies with more than $1 billion in annual sales.

Two types of pollution control violations are separately analyzed here. First, a plant's total number of effluent offenses was calculated, excluding any discharge violations that EPA's record indicated had been of a minor nature (to omit trivial matters unlikely to reflect poor compliance behavior). Second, the empirical tests analyze the number of compliance schedule violations committed by plants. As earlier pointed out, enforcement of the construction schedules was a top priority at the agency. On the other hand, construction requirements mandated costly capital outlays by businesses, which

---

[46] As noted in footnote 44, 216 companies had sales data; however, two of these firms were missing other data central to the analyses conducted here, and thus were dropped from the sample.

therefore had ample incentive to appeal their permit requirements and often fell behind their schedules.

The models analyze two sanctions variables, corresponding to the two violations counts. These are measures of a plant's total number of sanctions for, first, effluent violations and, second, compliance schedule violations. Total sanctions measures are used in the models for two reasons. First, not all violations received sanctions; thus it is important to investigate whether the no-action cases were differentially distributed across the dimension of firm strength. Second, the sanctions used by the agency consisted almost entirely of warnings and orders to comply, with warning letters comprising the lion's share of total sanctions. Therefore the most meaningful distinction for analysis is whether or not an offense was sanctioned at all. (However, I shall also briefly report on some secondary analyses done for the use of administrative orders as sanctions.) Lest it be argued that warnings and orders are trivial sanctions, recall that from the agency's standpoint these formal enforcement responses commit it to a line of action that can quickly lead to more stringent, but also more resource-intensive sanctions if the firm continues to violate the law.

The appellate procedure examined is EPA's formal adjudicatory hearing process, through which companies could most substantially challenge the restrictions contained in their pollution discharge permits. Successfully invoking this process requires the company to marshal substantial legal and technical expertise in defense of its position; therefore the hearing procedure is hypothesized to be more accessible to the larger, richer firms. The advantages of utilizing this procedure are twofold: Significant changes in the firm's favor can be made in permit requirements, and violations of challenged permit conditions cannot be enforced while the hearing is pending, a moratorium that often lasted many months and even years for successful corporate applicants. Thus the ability to mobilize adjudicatory hearings may have a salutary effect on both violations and sanctions experience. As there was typically no information in the available data as to which aspects of their permits companies had challenged, the process was analyzed as such. Plants for which such hearings were either pending or settled were coded as having successfully invoked the process; nonapplicants and those denied hearings comprised the comparison group.[47]

[47] On the question of whether hearings had been requested and granted, in some cases there were apparent discrepancies between the EPA Headquarters listing of adjudicatory hearings requested by industry and the Region II compliance data

Not shown in the theoretical model, but used as control variables throughout the analyses, are four measures logically related to the violations and sanctions experience. Two of these are proxy indicators of the relative stringency of the permit requirements imposed on polluting facilities. The first is simply an indicator of whether or not a plant's permit contained a compliance schedule for the construction of pollution control apparatuses. The absence of such a schedule indicates that a plant needed to make relatively little change in its operations to comply with pollution discharge limits; a required construction schedule, on the other hand, indicates a facility for which compliance required significant effort, often costly. The second indicator is the frequency with which a plant is required to make the self-monitoring compliance reports to the EPA. This frequency reflects the seriousness of the discharge relative to the pollution control requirements imposed. The assumption I make is that the greater the reporting frequency, the greater the stringency of the permit conditions and thus the higher the likelihood of violation. The reporting frequency varied over the categories of monthly, quarterly, semiannually, annually, and no reports required (coded 1, 3, 6, 12, and 13, respectively).

The third control used is the length of time a facility has been under permit requirements (counted in months). Because permits were issued individually as the regulatory program was phased in, some plants had been under permit requirement for several years, while others had been permitted for only a year or less. Other things being equal, the former can be expected to have more reported infractions than the latter. The fourth control simply indicates whether or not the facility is a major discharger of pollutants, as defined previously. Major polluting facilities were targeted for priority regulatory attention by the agency.

The results indicate the importance of these controls. For example, the more frequent offenders were found to be the facilities that are major dischargers, have compliance schedules and more stringent reporting requirements, and that have been under permit longer. Moreover, plants with compliance schedules, more frequent

accounts. With the assistance of EPA personnel, I made efforts to determine the meaning of the ambiguous coding in the regional data. On closer inspection, in most such instances the regional data were found to correspond with the Headquarters listing. In the remaining handful of cases where doubt remained, I used the more detailed Headquarters data. While this routine may have resulted in some measurement error, the small numbers and types of cases involved suggest that it would be of little consequence to the reported results.

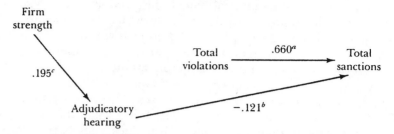

Figure 7.1. Nonminor effluent violations and sanctions: [a]Significant at .001 level; [b]significant at .05 level; [c]significant at .01 level.

reporting requirements, and longer standing permits were signifi-cantly more likely to have had changes (modifications, revisions) in their restrictions, indicating a greater tendency for companies facing more stringent permit requirements to seek exceptions to them.

Finally, a measure of whether or not a plant was operated by a subsidiary or a parent corporation was included to control for any compliance variation due to differences in organizational structures (recall that the corporate size data are for the parent corporations). The results indicate, however, that this variable had no relation to the legal and compliance processes examined below.

Effluent discharge violations. Figure 7.1 depicts the analytic results for pollution discharge violations and the accompanying sanctions. (See Table 7.5, Appendix B, for the full regression equations that pro-duced these results.) The findings indicate that for this type of vio-lation, the advantages of large firm size are only indirect, and act to insulate larger companies from some sanctions but not from a record of pollution offenses. That is, controlling for the number of discharge violations, larger firms are no less likely to be sanctioned by the agency than are smaller companies (unless they have success-fully invoked the formal appellate procedures), and are no less likely to commit infractions in the first place.

That larger firms have no direct advantage over their smaller counterparts in the sanctioning experience suggests that the EPA may typically apply the law in evenhanded fashion in the face of actionable infractions. However, it is important to enter a caveat re-garding such a conclusion. It is altogether possible that any reluc-tance on the part of the agency to legally grapple with more powerful enterprises only manifests itself in connection with the more substantial sanctions, which in these data are heavily outnum-bered by the use of agency warning letters. This might be expected to be true for those sanctioning options for which agency resources are often overmatched by those of large corporations: civil and criminal court cases. And the scant available evidence in this study, reported above, in fact suggests this conclusion: Most court cases were initiated against smaller polluters, a result apparently unrelated to the pollution records of large and small companies.

Other results suggest that bias operates as well in the use of the agency's administrative orders, the most serious sanctions available "in house" to the agency (inasmuch as court cases are referred to the Justice Department for consideration of prosecution). Although these results must be considered only tentative, because of the rather small number of orders issued during the period studied, they indicate that the agency is somewhat less likely to issue orders to larger companies, controlling for total violations records and the relevant permit characteristics discussed above. In general, then, these results support the conclusion that, while the agency is equally likely to respond formally to the violations of larger and smaller polluters, it is relatively less inclined to engage the former in sanctioning processes that can lead to expensive and risky legal confrontations, as discussed in the previous section.

The lack of a direct (negative) relationship between firm size and discharge violations suggests that the incidence of these infractions may be determined less by a company's ability to afford regulatory compliance than by its commitment to the adequate operation and maintenance of pollution abatement technology once in place. If there has been a generalized reluctance on the part of industry to make full compliance with the environmental laws of the 1970s a priority (cf., Yeager, 1986), then the distribution of violations reflecting daily operations may be relatively random across firms.

In contrast to this randomness, the results indicate that larger companies more often successfully invoke the EPA's formal hearing procedure than do the smaller businesses, as hypothesized.[48] This ability to appeal the regulatory conditions applied to companies' facilities provides a degree of insulation from EPA sanctioning, holding the level of violations constant. That is, companies whose pollution control permits were under appeal were not sanctioned by

[48] Because the adjudicatory hearing variable is dichotomous, standard regression techniques may produce distorted results. To test for this possibility, a parallel logit model was estimated for this variable. The results were virtually identical. In particular, firm size (as measured by the natural log of the sales variable) was significantly and positively related to the likelihood of successfully invoking this appellate procedure. The ratio of the logit coefficient (.21) to its standard error was 2.74444.

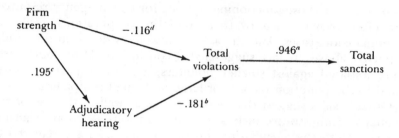

Figure 7.2. Compliance schedule violations and sanctions: ^{a}Significant at .001 level; ^{b}significant at .05 level; ^{c}significant at .01 level; ^{d}significant at .08 level.

the agency for violations of discharge limits that were being legally challenged. The findings suggest, then, that larger firms have an advantage over smaller companies in being able to delay compliance because of their greater access to ostensibly neutral legal procedures. In addition, such access also typically leads to altered permit conditions more in a line with companies' ability or intention to comply.

While the agency policy of nonenforcement during pending appeals is rational from the legal standpoint, the sanctioning moratorium it occasioned grew to troublesome proportions due to the large backlog of cases for appellate hearing. By the end of 1975, for example, the EPA had received more than 1,800 hearing requests from companies nation-wide, of which more than 1,100 were pending,[49] many for periods longer than a year. In New Jersey at the time of data collection for this research, many of the hearings cases were pending and had been so for two to three years or longer. Therefore, the enforcement advantage enjoyed by the larger companies under appeal was substantial in terms of deferred compliance.

Finally, the adjudicatory hearing process was found to be unrelated to companies' violations records. This finding is again related to EPA's regulatory policy in Region II. For companies that had successfully invoked the hearings procedure to challenge the terms of their permits, violations of the originally established pollution limits were recorded in the agency's compliance files but no action was taken against them while the appeal was pending.

Compliance schedule violations. Figure 7.2 illustrates the study's findings for compliance schedule violations and the associated sanctions. As earlier indicated, these offenses involve companies' failure to

[49] EPA Headquarters Memorandum, November 21, 1975.

meet mandated construction schedules for installation of pollution abatement facilities.

These findings contrast interestingly with those for discharge violations. First, as indicated by the much larger coefficient, compliance schedule infractions were substantially more likely to meet with agency sanction than were effluent violations. This again indicates that the EPA was indeed implementing its policy that schedule violations were to be met consistently with formal agency pressure to comply. Unlike its patience with periodic violations of discharge limits, the agency took a more rigorous stance against these offenses because of the centrality of the construction of control facilities to ultimate pollution reduction.

Second, while a firm's economic strength is again found to be unrelated to sanctions (controlling for violations records), larger companies were slightly less likely than smaller businesses to have committed these offenses in the first place. Although the effect of size on compliance is small, it nonetheless suggests that larger companies enjoy some "regulatory economies of scale," and can therefore more easily absorb regulatory demands requiring large expenditures of capital. That they don't enjoy even greater economies of scale may suggest that such economies are more often determined at the plant rather than at the corporate level. Even at large firms, the smaller plants may not enjoy the regulatory advantages of larger plants. (The legal data are necessarily analyzed at the plant level.) Nonetheless, the findings suggest that to some extent – and considering the findings for discharge violations – larger, more powerful companies are able to make a better show of compliance with expensive construction requirements. But they are no more committed to ongoing discharge compliance than smaller firms, perhaps especially given the very low risk of serious sanctions, particularly for the larger corporations.

Third, the results again show that larger firms are more likely than smaller firms to successfully invoke the hearings procedure. And again this invocation results in indirect regulatory advantages for the former, only in this case the advantage takes the form of reduced violations records rather than that of a reduction in sanctioning experience. Inspection of individual case records indicates two explanations. For hearings cases that had been settled, some companies succeeded in having EPA modify the construction schedule requirements so that they were subsequently easier to meet. For those cases in which companies' appeals were still pending, the adjudicatory hearings often had the effect of staying the requirements of the original construction schedules while the terms of these requirements were under negotiation; in effect, the agency treated the contested schedules as nonbinding while under appeal, anticipating a relaxing of them. In the situations of both pending and settled appeals, however, the results are often the same: the ultimate relaxation of regulatory requirements through a legal procedure that is differentially available to firms depending on the level of resources they command.

Conclusion

The findings reported in this chapter carry a number of theoretical, policy, and research implications. In terms of theorizing the relations between law and society, this research indicates that environmental law of this sort systemically both reflects and reproduces the inequality of the social system of which it is part. Technology-forcing standards such as those required under the Clean Water Act tend to be regressive, disproportionately burdening the smaller companies with expensive implementation duties. It is in this sense that large corporations may enjoy regulatory economies of scale to the extent that they are able to amortize compliance costs over larger volumes of production (at least in their larger facilities). Such an advantage is amplified to the extent that oligopolistic corporations are relatively more successful at avoiding price competition in their markets than are the smaller firms, permitting the former higher rates of profit. Whether the agency's consideration more recently of the differential impacts of regulations on firms of various sizes (see previous chapter) will alter this effect remains to be seen.

The process of enforcement itself reproduces economic inequality to the extent that it proves to be more accessible to firms with greater resources for mounting legal challenges to regulation. Because such regulation further strengthens the economic position of the larger firms compared with the smaller companies, it only reproduces the conditions creating structural bias in law.

These conclusions do not amount to a call for deregulation, whether in general or for smaller producers, which are indeed capable of much debilitating pollution. Rather, considerations of ecological and economic well-being, as well as of legal justice, suggest such solutions as progressively structured tax incentives and legal or technical assistance to reduce the inequities otherwise inherent in such regulatory schemes. If both a clean, usable environment and economic health are widely valued social goals, then citizens may well be agreeable to helping underwrite some of the costs of compliance, particularly for the smaller firms, which account for a substantial share of employment and a disproportionate share of industrial innovation in the United States. Survey results on environmental attitudes suggest that citizens are willing to pay for environmental protection; this willingness can only be reinforced by creative legislative proposals designed to equitably share out the costs of such vital protection.

In terms of methodological considerations, the findings indicate that both real and discovered rates of regulatory violation are produced by the systemic nexus linking law and economy; that is, such rates are jointly determined by business and regulatory operations in the context of an historically situated political economy. The result is that researchers need be cautious when relying on official sanctioning data in the study of corporate offenses. To the extent that larger companies are treated more leniently than smaller ones, regulatory data will be systematically distorted. If any sense is to be made of regulatory offense patterns, therefore, it is essential that the nature and degree of such distortion be estimated for the period and place under investigation.

This last point suggests the remaining question in the chapter: the extent to which the findings for the enforcement of the Clean Water Act represent processes also characteristic of other arenas of the social regulation of business. As it happens, there is evidence for such generalization in both historic (see the discussion of the federal Meat Inspection Act of 1906 in Chapter 2) and recent policy differences, and in other sociological research on such regulation.

The differential relation of larger versus smaller businesses to social regulation is nicely illustrated in a recent account of a split in the business community over government-enforced affirmative action hiring goals (Noble, 1986). The largest corporations tend to support the requirement that government contractors achieve hiring goals, while smaller businesses oppose them. According to a spokesperson for the opposition, "One of the reasons you have big business coming out in favor of these regulations is that they have the staff and the industrial relations people to fill out all that paper work. They benefit from the status quo. The small-business man doesn't." Here, again, the greater resources and regulatory economies of scale enjoyed by larger corporations place them in a favored position vis-à-vis law, and in at least two respects: enhanced corporate images as a result of apparent support for socially valued, progressive goals, and the marginal competitive advantages over their smaller competitors due to the differential financial burdens imposed by regulation.

Two recent studies of the enforcement of social regulations also find advantages at law for larger firms. Lynxwiler and his colleagues (1983) found such advantages in their study of the use of enforcement discretion by field inspectors from the federal Office of Surface Mining Reclamation and Enforcement (see also Shover et al., 1986). The study found that larger mining companies, because of their greater resources and technical expertise, were able to more successfully negotiate the nature of violations with the government inspectors, who generally viewed the larger firms as both more cooperative with regulatory expectations (due in part to their ability to negotiate at the highest technical levels with government experts), and more likely than smaller firms to challenge stringent enforcement through legal appeals. One important result was that smaller companies tended to be assessed higher fines than larger corporate violators, because inspectors tended to *interpret* the violations of the former as more serious offenses, quite apart from more objective measures of the harm occasioned by them.

Particularly apposite to this discussion are the conclusions Keith Hawkins (1983, 1984) reached in his intensive investigation of field inspectors attempting to enforce water pollution regulations in Britain. He analyzed the enforcement process as involving an exchange relationship in which forbearance in enforcement is traded for good faith efforts at compliance. In so doing, he identified a number of the law-shaping and limiting processes that have been indicated in my research.

Enforcement forbearance, rather than more stringent policing, results from several processes that constrain law, particularly in the area of social regulation. In the first place, because the regulated behavior is vitally linked to the (re)production of core political economic values, its status is at worst morally ambivalent, with the result that the law itself shares the same characterization (see Chapter 2). In such a context, enforcement agents in the field find it necessary to negotiate compliance rather than stringently enforce it. Second, and relatedly, Hawkins notes the field agents' perception that enforcement must be patient and "reasonable" lest it produce uncooperative attitudes toward compliance on the part of the regulated.

Among other things, the consequent negotiation stance taken by enforcers is believed by them to promote greater honesty by the regulated in reporting instances of pollution (1983: 49–50), a logic also suggested above for EPA's enforcement policies in this country. Finally, the British study correctly points to a more general process in law that produces negotiated rather than enforced compliance: as also indicated in such studies as Bittner's of skid row (1967), where police have regularly recurring relationships with the regulated, enforcement tends to take the form of negotiated compliance rather than of strict prohibition of proscribed behaviors. It is worth adding that this will be all the more the case to the extent that other publics are not involved in the situations of enforcement; in such circumstances legal agents enjoy greater discretion in implementing the law.

Thus Hawkins concludes that "the reality of law is negotiated" (1983: 68) but suggests that this does not necessarily mean that it is emasculated. While the question of which combination of negotiation and enforcement strategies would produce the highest compliance rates remains unanswered in the literature on regulation, his study – like the present investigation – outlines some of the systematic limits to social regulation. Moreover, his analysis similarly suggests that the negotiation process by which law is effectively created is disproportionately advantageous to the larger, more powerful companies. Hawkins notes, for example, that such firms are more likely to be seen by enforcement agents as socially responsible, as generally cooperative regarding the aims of the agency. Among other results, their pollution episodes are more likely to be viewed as accidents than as evidence of recalcitrance.

Although the fines established by the British water law are recognized by enforcement officials as much too small to deter any but the poorest of business offenders, agents sometimes rely on bluffing strategies in which they play on the latters' relative ignorance of enforcement options to induce compliance by threatening more force than is legally available to them. Because such ignorance cannot be equally distributed across types of firms, it is only to be expected that such bluffing is relatively more effective with smaller, technically less sophisticated producers than with their opposites, particularly when the pollution control issues at stake are being hotly contested.[50]

---

[50] Hawkins himself does not make this point. Instead, he suggests that legal bluffing is also useful with the large firms because the contact between enforcement agents

Finally, because compliance negotiations usually go forward as scientific and technical matters (rather than as moral affairs) between regulators and the regulated, firms with the relevant expertise at hand enjoy a regulatory advantage over those without, as implied in the British agents' perceptions of differential cooperativeness as between larger and smaller companies. As importantly, such negotiations tend to exclude the concerns and viewpoints of other publics, so that public-interest victories won at the highly visible legislative stage may be at least partially compromised in the much less visible, often arcane problematics of legal implementation, a result suggested in Chapter 6 for EPA's implementation of the Clean Water Act.

In sum, the limits of law identified in the present research have been similarly indicated in investigations conducted at different levels of analysis (field studies of situational interactions), in different cultural contexts (albeit within the broader context of Western, capitalist political economies with a much shared legal heritage), and in different regulatory areas. The constraints on social regulation range from the reality that private production and profitmaking maintain top priority in capitalist political economies, to the interpretive work done by enforcement agents in the field in the exercise of their discretion. Therefore, state sanctioning leverage is limited to options well short of plant closure – even temporarily, as indicated in the Reserve Mining case in Minnesota – even in the face of major noncompliance. In an effort to maintain even modest levels of accomplishment and credibility, social regulators must essentially bargain enforcement with the regulated. And in so bargaining over what is to be the reality of regulation, law inescapably reflects and reproduces the favored status of major producers.

Appendix A: methodological issues in the study

As with all research, this investigation raises a number of methodological questions, some generic to any research and others specific to this type of sociolegal study. The most salient issues here have to do with the representativeness of the study, the use of aggregate

and companies typically takes place at low levels of the corporate hierarchy, rather far removed from the legal expertise higher up (1983: 62). Nonetheless, it is only reasonable to assume that any deterrence owing to bluffing is *relatively* less effective with more powerful firms, which are more likely to marshal their expertise should regulation begin to appear "unreasonable."

data, the validity of the data, and the often complicated matter of how offenses are to be counted for purposes of analysis.

The representativeness issue involves the question of the extent to which a study's findings can be extrapolated or generalized in the dimensions of time and place. Given the complicated and politically volatile nature of the regulatory enterprise examined here, generalizations, if they are to be made, must be carefully considered and circumscribed. The first question, then, is whether the findings for Region II can be said to adequately represent the EPA's enforcement processes nationally in the case of the Federal Water Pollution Control Act (also known as the Clean Water Act). (Of course, no claim is made that the results represent the enforcement by the many states that enforce the law on delegation of the program to them by EPA.) This, too, is a complicated question, and in fact no straightforward determination is available. But a number of factors help to asymptotically approach an answer.

My interviews at EPA headquarters indicated substantial variation in the ten regional offices of the agency in terms of both enforcement and compliance data systems; indeed, by 1978 the EPA had become concerned enough with such variation that it was attempting to develop policies toward a more uniform national response to water pollution violations, as indicated for example in the preparation of its *Enforcement Management System Guide*. Therefore, easy generalization of findings to the other regions is rather hazardous. Nonetheless, I suggest that Region II's enforcement activities tend to at least represent the modal EPA response around the country, and perhaps to exceed it in terms of the sufficiency of enforcement. This judgment – and it is indeed a judgment – is based on a rather high degree of correspondence between headquarters and the Region's formal policy stances (with the latter at some points challenging the former as insufficient, as noted in the chapter); the more sophisticated compliance data tracking system at this region than at any other, containing even indicators of the region's decisions to take no enforcement action in the case of many violations, all of which suggests greater proficiency in tracking, explaining, and publicly communicating compliance rates; and organizational enforcement structures – such as the Water Enforcement Executive Committee – that appear rationally designed to produce effective and efficient enforcement responses to the degree possible.[51]

[51] The Water Enforcement Executive Committee was established by EPA Region II in early 1976 as it was gearing up for the more concentrated focus on enforcement

The second question involves the representativeness of the time period studied, and again firm conclusions are necessarily elusive. But given the history of environmental regulation by the EPA in the 1970s and 1980s, I propose that the agency's implementation and enforcement of the water law in the period of focus, the middle 1970s, was at least approaching peak levels in terms of the policy goals stated by the Congress. (I suggest this mindful of the long delay in the toxics program, and only note here that EPA enforcement of the law appears to be resurgent at the dawn of the 1990s.) As suggested in the previous chapter, the EPA, fueled by the environmental fervor of the early part of the decade, made significant progress in implementing the various laws with which it was charged. Moreover, the Carter administration took office broadly dedicated to the enforcement of social regulations such as these, as reflected in the appointments made to the leaderships of the regulatory agencies, including the EPA. Nonetheless even by 1978, when these data were collected, the winds of regulatory change had begun to blow over Washington as the Carter administration became increasingly concerned that regulation and the nation's economic health might become contradictory, at least at the margins of both. Therefore, even before the deregulation-minded Reagan administration took office in 1981, there was movement toward more circumspect and cost-conscious regulation of the private sector. Thus the findings reported here represent the tendencies present in rela-

matters earlier described. The committee comprised all the relevant legal and technical units in the regional office responsible for compliance with the law and which could put a matter on the docket for discussion and decision at the committee's monthly meetings. In addition, all enforcement decisions of the committee – whether to issue an EPA order, refer the case to the Justice Department for prosecution, etc. – were docketed for later meetings to follow up on the success of the enforcement response (to determine whether further action was required). In an indicative memo to his enforcement attorneys, the chief of the water enforcement branch both exhorted them to the task and suggested that to this point, perhaps due to the considerable start-up costs of the new program, enforcement had been at best cumbersome, but could now proceed more fruitfully: "I'm counting on you to initiate cases and pursue them. The formalization of procedures will make it easier to get cooperation in moving a case quickly and should cut down on the frustration that saps the initiative of each of us. . . . These procedures are not overly bureaucratic and will serve to get us into *interesting, valuable* cases and away from the bull shit we have been mired in for so long" (EPA Region II Memorandum, February 11, 1976: "Enforcement Procedures – Institution of Cases"; emphasis in original. See also EPA Region II Memorandum, February 11, 1976: "Water Enforcement Executive Committee.") The latter reference likely refers to either the "red tape" of hearings that challenged permits, organizational inefficiencies attendant upon the development of the complex regulatory scheme or, most likely, both.

tively activist state regulation and therefore indicate something of the ultimate limits of such regulatory policies.

The use of aggregate data presents additional methodological considerations. Whereas longitudinal studies assessing regulatory enforcement *over time* can make substantial contributions to both theory and practice, the data in this study were aggregated into total violations and sanctions for the entire period covered. This was done for two reasons. First, as earlier indicated there was a particular logic to the evolution of federal enforcement of the Clean Water Act that, I suggest, accounts for the lion's share of temporal variation in broad enforcement trends. Therefore, such factors as political influences on the agency during this period will be relatively less salient. Second, the computer data base available for this investigation in Region II was progressively structured over time, such that various categories of relevant information were added to the system as enforcement policy itself evolved. For example, the system tracked compliance schedule and reporting violations from the outset (from the dates individual facility permits were issued), added effluent discharge violations for major polluters in early 1976, and for minor dischargers in March 1977. Also in 1977, violations for which the region's officials determined to take no action were added to the data base. Therefore, the parallel logics of enforcement policy and recordkeeping in this case militate against desegregated longitudinal analyses.

Next, these data share with other sets of officially generated violations records the problem of bearing an uncertain relation to true rates, levels, or profiles of lawbreaking. The major question here, then, is whether these data present a systematically biased profile of offense rates and offenders (biased by size of company, for example) that would render the findings spurious. Because of the way the agency's records are generated, and due to the logic of this research, I believe they do not. EPA's compliance monitoring program for the Clean Water Act is based principally on a self-reporting system, supported by periodic inspections that focus on likely "trouble spots" among major polluters. From all indications, such reported violations are faithfully recorded in the Region II computerized files, even those infractions for which the agency decided to issue no sanction at all. Thus bias in the data would arise from systematic differentials in reporting honesty by type of company. While there is no substantial a priori reason to believe that any particular form of distortion exists, the logic of my analysis – that larger, more powerful firms have greater resources with which to negotiate favorable resolutions with government agencies in terms of both regulations and sanctions – suggests that *smaller companies* would perhaps have more to gain by such misrepresentation (cf., Lynxwiler et al., 1983), a result which would run counter to my hypotheses. In any event, my analyses control for violations when investigating sanctioning responses by the agency, and control for such compliance-relevant matters as whether the plants are major polluters, are frequently required to report to the agency, and so on.

Finally, the research faced a salient methodological problem not uncommon to the study of business offenses: that of counting the number of violations an individual firm has committed (cf., Reiss and Biderman, 1980). As it happens, the problem is especially well exemplified by the environmental violations data examined here. Compare, for example, the plant that falls behind in the construction of its pollution control facilities and therefore violates its discharge limits continuously for a period of months, with a company that violates its limits one day due to operator carelessness or equipment malfunction. Other things being equal, the relative damage done to the environment in the two cases is clear; indeed, the Congress appears to have relied on this assumption in structuring civil and criminal monetary penalties for violations of the law: they are to be assessed *per day of violation*. But this straightforward policy solution does not address the analytic question of counting infractions, with all it implies about recidivism, incorrigibility, culpability, and the like.

Moreover, the difficulty is compounded by the way in which Region II tracks violations in its computerized data base. For example, the region lists an effluent discharge violation every time a self-monitoring report from a plant shows one, but individual facilities often have different requirements for the frequency with which they must submit such reports. Therefore, in the case of a six-month continuous violation, it will appear in the data base once for the plant that is required to submit the reports only every half-year, and six times for the plant submitting monthly reports (assuming reporting honesty). In addition, companies were also required to send "notices of noncompliance" to the EPA soon after violations had been discovered at the plant. Because the same infractions could also be reported in the companies' separate periodic self-monitoring reports, they could therefore appear twice in the agency's compliance data base. In short, the information contained in the agency data was often too scanty to distinguish between (1) continuous and discrete offenses and (2) discrete offenses and a single violation recorded twice in the record.

I employed two safeguards in the analysis to help control for these problems. First, I made the decision generally to record only one effluent discharge violation per reporting period, unless the data clearly indicated two distinct offenses (such as an oil spill from a holding tank on site and an illegal discharge of a different substance in the company's regular effluent).[52] Second, the frequency with which companies are required to make self-monitoring compliance reports to the EPA (monthly, quarterly, annually) was used as a control variable in the multivariate analyses to control for bias against the more frequent reporters.

Appendix B: tables showing regression coefficients for models

Table 7.5. *Regression results for nonminor effluent violations and sanctions (N = 214)*

	Dependent variables		
Independent variables	Total sanctions	Total violations	Adjudicatory hearing
Total violations	.66***		
Adjudicatory hearing	−.12*	−.10	
Firm strength	−.10	.02	.20**
Major discharger	−.02	.24***	.15†
Compliance schedule	−.02	−.19**	−.17*
Reporting frequency	.01	−.30***	−.10
Age of permit	.06	.16**	.03
Parent/subsidiary	.01	.09	.12†
Adj. R^2	.43	.38	.17

Note: Standardized regression coefficients are reported.
†$p < .08$. *$p < .05$. **$p < .01$. ***$p < .001$.

[52] In general, the convention of counting only a single infraction per reporting period is conservative, but it is the most accurate count that can be developed from these data. In many cases it was quite clear that the letters of noncompliance and self-monitoring reports referred to violations of the same effluent parameters, suggesting that they were in fact the same offenses.

Table 7.6. *Regression results for compliance schedule violations and sanctions* (N = *214*)

Independent variables	Dependent variables		
	Total sanctions	Total violations	Adjudicatory hearing
Total violations	.95***		
Adjudicatory hearing	.01	−.18*	
Firm strength	−.01	−.12†	.20**
Major discharger	−.02	.07	.15†
Compliance schedule	−.02	−.33***	−.17*
Reporting frequency	−.01	−.13†	−.10
Age of permit	.01	.03	.03
Parent / subsidiary	.01	.09	.12†
Adj. R^2	.91	.17	.17

Note: Standardized regression coefficients are reported.
†$p < .08$.   *$p < .05$.   **$p < .01$.   ***$p < .001$.

CHAPTER 8

Ecology, economy, and the evolution of limits

> What *right* has any citizen of a free country, whatever his foresight
> and shrewdness, to seize on sources of life for his own behoof that
> are the common heritage of all; what *right* has legislature or court
> to help in the seizure; and striking still more deeply, what *right* has
> any generation to wholly consume, much less to waste, those
> sources of life without which children or the children's children
> must starve or freeze?
>
> William John McGee, "The Conservation Bill
> of Rights"

These questions, offered rhetorically, have both a contemporary
ring and unquestioned relevance for matters of ecological policy. In
fact they were first published some 80 years ago by McGee, an advi-
sor to Theodore Roosevelt who was once described as "the scientific
brains" of the early conservation movement in the United States.[1]
In both their timelessness and their construction, these questions
underscore the tension between law and ecology in our political
economy.

The continuing relevance of these questions, of course, testifies to
the limits to fundamental change that are inherent in all complex
social organisms, whether capitalistic or socialistic or some other
variant of large-scale human organization. Indeed, it is as difficult
to imagine the once tightly organized Soviet political economy without its profligate corruption and inefficiencies as it is to conceive
U.S. history without the tensions outlined in this book.[2]

---

[1] McGee served as a member of the Inland Waterways Commission, which he had
conceived as a means of recognizing the interstate interest in natural resources, and
also served on the National Conservation Commission chaired by Gifford Pinchot,
who first labeled McGee the "scientific brains" of the conservation movement (see
McGee, 1987: 19).

[2] For discussions of some of these classic problems in the Soviet Union's political
economy, see Berliner (1957, 1979), Richman (1965), Granick (1967; ch. 7), and
Yeager (1977). As this is being written (1990), Mikhail Gorbachev's attempts in the

But all social systems possess unique histories and therefore uniquely characteristic sets of choices and constraints, themselves interrelated. And McGee's language points to much of what has been characteristic in the dilemmas of state regarding environmental matters in the history of American socioeconomic development. His emphasis on the notion of *right* is a straight derivative from the notion of inalienable rights at the core of U.S. political democracy and legality. Eighty years ago, McGee called for the essential completion of the American Revolution by the "framing of a clearer Bill of Rights," including as "inherent and indefeasible" the "equal Rights of the People [both present and future] in and to resources rendered valuable by their own natural growth and orderly development" (McGee, 1987: 21).

But the concept of right, as framed both legally and philosophically in American history, has often proven to be a double-edged sword in the management of collective affairs. On the one hand, the historical exercise of constitutional freedoms in the structural context of formally free markets and the philosophical context of utilitarianism has produced vast inequities in social and economic life. Against this background, the liberal exercise of right becomes fundamentally precarious, because power differentials shade the likely outcomes in the inevitable, recurring conflicts of legal right. On the other hand, the very same constitutional freedoms in our political culture enable the prospect of meaningful challenge to destabilizing and unjust inequities, the more so as basic notions of right are institutionalized in the apparatuses of state. To the extent that the stability of government relies on its democratic legitimacy, the outcomes at law of instant political struggles, however shaded by inequality, remain themselves rather precarious.

All of this is suggested by the history of American environmental law, which continues to manifest the tensions forged in the interplay of economic, environmental, and political limits. Since the Second World War, environmental law in the United States has been shaped by the struggle between the key property rights that underlie the

Soviet Union to both open public discourse (*glasnost*) and restructure the economy (*perestroika*) have stimulated major political and economic changes not only there but also in the other Eastern Bloc countries. The Berlin Wall has fallen, the Communist party has lost hegemonic control virtually everywhere, and capitalist markets are developing in various sectors. The ultimate outcomes of these rapid and dramatic changes remain uncertain, but the results will help define both the old and new limits of social organization in those nations, and in the evolving international political economy as well.

private system of industrial production and expanding public conceptions of personal rights that have mobilized a wide range of group pressures on the state (cf., Bowles and Gintis, 1986; also Wright, 1987). But just as the democratic state resists instrumental control by society's elites, so too is it a rather uncertain protector of environmental rights. Indeed, the rational legal processes that the state implements to balance economic and environmental rights (and to square its own requirements for revenues and legitimacy) are themselves fundamentally constrained in the context of environmental policymaking.

This is not to imply that the constraints on law as an instrument of progressive social change are immutable. Instead, while fundamentally rooted in the basic structures and processes of political economy – indeed, precisely because of this – the limits of law stand in dynamic relation to those structures and processes, bearing a historically contingent relation to their maintenance. While generally tending to reproduce social structures and relations, law in capitalist democracies is also sensitive to the tensions and instabilities inherent in political economy, especially when these manifest themselves as collective assertions for rights and entitlements that only the state can preserve.

The difficult questions for social theory, and in many respects for social policy as well, have to do with the conditions under which such collective demands will be made, what forms will the demands take, with what response in terms of state structures, processes, and legal decisions, and ultimately with what consequences for future social stability or conflict. In the final analysis, these questions seek the key linkages between the content of individual consciousnesses and the forces of systemic change in whole societies. And they have bedeviled both philosophy and social science since they became apparent.

With this case study of industrial water pollution and law's efforts to contain it, I intend no such grand theorizing. The contingent nature of the relation between the state's legal responses and the complex dynamics of political economy would seem to defy rulelike precision and predictability, save perhaps those of the most abstract sort (which often tend, when rendered, to lose sight of human action amid the structural complexities). This is not to say that such theorizing is either impossible or unimportant; quite the contrary, but it stands beyond the limits of these data and this particular effort, and I do not attempt it here.

Instead, my intent has been to search for evidence of law's limits, and movement in them, in the specific history of the federal government's attempts to control industrial water pollution. As I indicated in Chapter 2, the search has been directed in large part by various arguments in social theory and research, if in the end it constitutes no test of any particular theory. Nonetheless, the record established in this search will, I think, bear the weight of some generalization regarding the relations between regulatory law and society in late twentieth-century American history, and I shall discuss some of these. To the extent that case studies such as this begin to build a stronger foundation for broader theorizing down the line, perhaps even for stronger social policy, then this effort will have been more than amply rewarded.

In the sections to follow, I first review the limits of law as they suggest themselves in this analytic history of water pollution law in the United States, and briefly illustrate something of their dynamism through consideration of regulatory events in the 1980s. The discussion then takes up some of the underlying features in American political economy that constrain the rationality of law's approach to the environment. Finally, I review some of the policy implications of these findings for both the public and private sectors.

The limits of law

The limits of regulatory law are inscribed in all of its aspects, from the terms of legislation to the enforcement against violators. In general, the outer bounds of social regulation are set by the systemic needs of the political economic system of capitalist democracies, which are represented in legal determinations in the form of mandated consideration of the *costs* of controls, both those that may be borne by the private sector and those accruing to the state. In the federal government's efforts at water pollution control, sensitivity to these costs has been greatest in the Executive Branch (regardless of which party has been in power), particularly in the White House. The Congress has been in a more ambivalent position. On the one hand it created the substantial body of social legislation in the 1970s that forced business to internalize a greater proportion of the social costs of production. But on the other hand its regulatory fervor has been constrained by such economic realities as recession (the "stagflation" of the latter 1970s and early 1980s) and increasingly by federal budget deficits that grew dramatically during the 1980s. The key role of the enabling legislation notwithstanding, it is arguably the courts that have most effectively maintained the strength of environmental values against once overriding concerns for private sector costs. From the expansion of legal standing to encompass broad environmental interests in the 1960s, to the concerns for due process and due deference to agency expertise, the courts have ensured not only that environmental regulation would be tested against costs, but also that economic goals would be evaluated against environmental consequences. If the judicial emphasis on procedure over substance limits the types of enforcement cases the agency brings (Chapter 2), ironically it counterbalances this result by safeguarding much of the substance and rigor of environmental regulation.

The concern for the costs of environmental protection at the highest levels of the political system does not surprise, of course. In contrast to the language of absolutist rights spawned by the environmental movement and even institutionalized in statutory decrees such as the Clean Water Act, the federal government has always been in the business of trading off virtually all forms of costs and benefits, in policy areas from health care and education to housing and income supports. And in making these choices, government distributes life chances – quite literally – to its constituents. In general, citizens implicitly endorse this procedure, even if they are often critical of its results and hesitant to say that any price is too high for such state-supplied benefits as equal educational opportunity, the protection of the society's most vulnerable groups (such as children in poverty and the elderly), or environmental protection.

Certainly, the structural and cultural contradictions that pervade the society make difficult any precise, objective definition of the composite public interest, let alone the specification of best ways to achieve it. Citizens in advanced, industrial democracies typically want rewarding and remunerative jobs, levels of consumption representing comfort and convenience (if not conspicuousness), fair opportunities, low inflation, at least adequate defense, and a benevolent government that is neither too intrusive nor too expensive. In their roles as consumers and producers, members of the social classes most favoring increased environmental protection have lifestyles intimately associated with massive waste-generating activities including, for example, the serious environmental problems associated with solid waste, automobiles, and the advances of technology.

It is in the nature of social contradictions to manifest themselves variably under the evolving conditions of group life. And without question, by the latter decades of this century there developed both subjective and objective pressures for major changes in environmental law. So despite the difficulty entailed in precisely specifying the objective difference between policy success and failure, it is nonetheless reasonable to suggest both that the limits of environmental law have shifted substantially in the postwar period and that the law-as-policy continues to be constrained in ways characteristic of the present phase of industrial and political organization.

The history of the FWPCA amendments, or the Clean Water Act, indicates that by the onset of the 1970s a conjuncture of systemic and political (class-related) factors had prepared the way for legal change that swept aside some of the key limits that had long emaciated water pollution control efforts at all levels of government. The forces of institutional centralization, in both polity and economy, shifted the balance of governmental power to the federal level as surely as it concentrated economic power in the hands of fewer, larger, and more distant producers. The rapid economic growth after the 1940s produced a large and potentially powerful middle class increasingly concerned with noneconomic values such as those having to do with evolving conceptions of fundamental human rights. Increasingly, civil, consumer, worker, and environmental groups organized to press the federal government for their rights, motivated by the growing scientific evidence of environmental and human damage being done by distant producers with no local accountability. Citizen alienation from such arrangements was also a factor.

This basic shift in popular values was pressed on a Congress that had ever so slowly increased its stake in national environmental matters, always careful to respect states' rights, which typically translated into states' deference to industry's economic interests when it came to pollution control. This limit remained in place until the voices for change organized in a movement that did not coalesce until after the events of Earth Day, 1970. There was another voice as well, the ambivalent voice of sectors of industry, lead by oligopolistic corporations. Although largely reactive, seeking the rationalization of legal policy in the face of (from business's standpoint) rather frightening pressures for radical change in law, industry nonetheless called on the federal government to take control and ensure a level (and "reasonable") regulatory field of play, part of the underlying logic of centralization. There was a small measure of the active industrial voice in this as well, because some firms and industries had begun to understand at first hand the industrial costs of spoiled environments. Trucking in water for production while sitting at the edge of a useless river gives the lie to notions of free environmental goods. And of course there was the budding pollution control industry with a direct economic stake in substantial legal change.

These were the systemic features ushering in change. There were some historically contingent ones as well, including presidential politics (Nixon versus long-time environmental advocate Muskie) and the role of environmental policy in helping to reestablish something of the federal government's tattered legitimacy and a sense of commonweal during the divisive period of Vietnam.

The result was a significant shift in the limits of law, which in the 1972 amendments (and in other social legislation as well) moved past much of the restraint in notions of states' rights and laissez faire relations between state and economy. Environmental values became institutionalized in the key processes of governmental decision making and eventually in much of business planning and operations, and in science and law as well. The law pressed the internalization of many of the social costs of production, even the costly elimination of such spillover effects of production when they proved hazardous to health and life. Environmental values were made an indispensable part of the calculus of choice in both public and private spheres of action.

But the new regulation of industrial water pollution continued to reflect certain limits that constrained its beneficial reach, in both the environment and the economy. These limits are both systemic (or structural) and instrumental (or political) – the former more enduring, the latter more contingent – and shape the content of law from legislation to enforcement. But even the more enduring constraints on law remain subject to future shifts given the tensions between economic growth and future environmental damage, and other strains in the political economy.

The EPA's water pollution program is systemically constrained by, and to, its dependence on industry-defined technologies. In the 1972 amendments, the Congress had mandated a tripartite regulatory scheme that differentially weighed costs and benefits of environmental controls. For the implementation of first-phase "best practicable technology," or BPT, the law required a kind of cost–benefit test on the regulations so that at least at the margins economic costs did not outweigh benefits. Meanwhile, for the more advanced "best available technology," or BAT, it called for a "cost-sensitive" approach, a vague mandate even less clear in the legislative history than in the statute itself. Finally, for the threatening specter of toxic pollutants, the law was "cost oblivious," urging their complete elimination with no mention of costs whatsoever.[3] The latter standard especially suggested the irrelevance of current industry practices for rulemaking.

But as described in Chapter 6, for toxics too systemic constraints limited controls to those demonstrated and used in industry. In the context of considerable measures of scientific and economic uncertainty, and under the twin pressures to regulate "quickly" while not collapsing important sectors of the economy, this was pragmatic policy. It was also motivated by the EPA's longstanding lack of sufficient funds for research and development; because of increasing fiscal constraint,[4] the agency has been in no position to itself experiment with novel treatment modalities. In the end, the EPA, environmental interest groups, and the courts all endorsed what was in effect an administrative amendment of the law, and the Congress ultimately embraced the logic in the 1977 amendments to the statute.

But this regulatory dependence on industry-demonstrated controls, even when "best" controls can be defined, carries certain costs as well. It tends to constrain environmental cleanup to levels below those that are theoretically achievable within economic constraints and may even raise the aggregate costs of pollution control to the extent that more efficient technologies are not explored. This is suggested in the case of the toxics program, where in some industries more advanced BAT controls were forgone (for lack of demonstration) and the more limited BPT technologies were mandated by

---

[3] The terms are borrowed from Rodgers (1980), who provides a nice discussion of the reasonable applicability of such decision-making logics to health and environmental regulation.

[4] The federal government's deepening fiscal crisis increasingly eroded social welfare and regulatory expenses in the 1980s, despite some nominal increases for the EPA by the middle of the decade. For example, a former EPA assistant administrator estimated that in fiscal 1987 the agency would require $1.8 billion simply to do what it had in 1981; but to implement the newer toxic waste laws in addition, a total budget of $2.8 billion was necessary. But the 1986 budget was only $1.426 billion, reflecting a 4.3 percent cut mandated by the Gramm–Rudman law to reduce the huge budget deficits; the EPA's real purchasing power was at 1976 levels, a year prior to the agency's efforts to regulate toxic water pollution, indeed prior to passage of any of the major toxic pollution laws the agency later inherited. Based on the same deficit constraints, the 1987 budget projected to be as low as $1.212 billion. (See "The Expectations Warp," *Amicus Journal* 7 [Spring 1986]: 2.)

the EPA. In many cases, some toxics were not regulated by the rules at all for lack of demonstrated treatment modalities, leaving the discharges in the uncertain hands of individual permit writers. It is also suggested in the evidence, earlier reviewed, that both the EPA and the regulated industries tend to greatly overestimate the costs of water pollution regulations, suggesting the operation of conservative influences in rulemaking.

Technology-based controls such as those mandated by the 1972 law also tend to be regressive, more costly per unit volume of production for smaller producers, both in the regulatory requirements and in enforcement. They also, as a matter of statutory record, tend to place higher levels of control on new sources, whose constituents are less obvious and vocal in opposition at the time of the law's passage, to that extent heightening barriers to entry and further inhibiting the development of smaller businesses. In combination with other regulatory laws with regressive impacts (including the complex tax codes), environmental law thus reproduces the economic advantages of large, dominant firms and may contribute to further concentration in the economy. The logic of finance capital in the 1980s, with the virtually unprecedented swarm of mergers and hostile takeovers, may have accelerated this tendency. Capital markets were particularly risky for firms with "undervalued" stocks, often those with lower short-term earnings that may result from investments with little or no near term payout, such as large compliance expenditures. There is some vague and general evidence that such tendencies exist.[5] To the extent that this process occurs, it not only raises the aggregate costs of regulation relative to benefits, but also weakens the sector of smaller businesses that disproportionately contributes jobs and innovation to the economy.

[5] Necessarily the evidence is more impressionistic or speculative than it is definitive. But for example, a spokesperson for the Smaller Business Association of New England has suggested that the burdens of social regulation had already contributed to the absorption of smaller businesses by larger firms in the paint and metal plating industries (although no hard evidence was supplied; see the *Boston Globe*, October 26, 1987, p. 30). In the summer of 1989, *The New York Times* (June 19, 1989, p. A1) reported that new EPA regulations to protect groundwater may contribute to vast numbers of closings of small service stations around the country, with particularly noticeable impacts in small towns and rural areas. The regulations require that stations install monitoring devices to detect leaks in gasoline storage tanks and acquire at least $1 million in liability insurance. While industry estimates of future impacts are always suspect, the low profit margins of small service stations, and the drop in their number from 226,000 in 1972 to approximately 112,000 in 1989, combined with the growth of large chains of gasoline retailers, suggest their considerable vulnerability.

These results suggest the need for more farsighted government policies, including programs designed to stimulate and require new pollution control technologies, and that are implemented progressively to protect both the environment and the stability of smaller businesses (see below).

The limits of deregulation

The instrumental limitations on regulatory law are those subject to relatively short-term sways under the political direction of the administration in power. To an important extent, these political decisions are shaped by longer term forces in political economy, such as the evolving structures of national and world markets and deepening fiscal crises due to the nature of contradictory policy demands placed on the state. So the distinction between structural and instrumental limits is more convenient than real. But alternative political ideologies can also shape law, especially in the near term, and this was nowhere more apparent than during the years of the Reagan administration in the 1980s. That recent history is instructive about the dynamic nature of the limits of law.

The nation had never seen anything quite like the Reagan administration's blunt assault on social regulation. It was not simply that the administration self-consciously attempted to undo much of government's responsibilities for social protection in the name of economic health; it was also that in many respects it was an executive assault on the legislative prerogatives of the democratically elected Congress (cf., Tolchin and Tolchin, 1983: chs. 2, 3). The administration's deregulatory policy scapegoated health and environmental regulation for the nation's economic ills, treating them more like discretionary monetary and fiscal policies than enduring national law to be enforced in the vital interest of the common good.

But there is an irony here. For all of its drama, in most fundamental respects the Reagan agenda was not novel; indeed, it was precedented in previous administrations, most notably by a Democratic president who had achieved high marks for his environmentalism by 1978. In essence, the Reagan policies reflected fundamental tendencies and contradictions in state policymaking, particularly the tensions attached to government's dual responsibilities to both capital accumulation and democratic legitimacy. And it was precisely where the administration's policies appeared to radically depart from the more subtle choices of its predecessors that the *limits of deregulation* most manifested themselves.

By 1978 rising inflation rates and the onset of recession were scissoring the economy and beginning to threaten the political support for the Carter administration. Under these pressures, President Carter began to reverse field on his earlier commitments to broad federal protection of health and environmental values, as manifested in his initial appointments to the regulatory agencies, including EPA. His response to the growing "stagflation" in the economy was to restructure Executive Branch decision making on environmental matters in the attempt to inject greater "cost sensitivity" into key regulatory decisions of the agency.[6]

Carter established two new executive groups, the Regulatory Council and the Regulatory Analysis Review Group (RARG), both intended to give the White House greater control over the economic impacts of social regulations. In March 1978, he also promulgated Executive Order 12044,[7] which required that all executive agencies conduct economic analyses of the costs and benefits of all regulations, with the results for all major regulations to be reviewed by RARG; major regulations were defined as those estimated to cost industry more than $100 million annually. RARG, the more powerful of the two new groups, consisted of representatives from most of the cabinet departments (save the State, Defense, and Treasury departments), and top officials from the Office of Management and Budget (OMB), EPA, and the White House Office of Science and Technology Policy. It was headed by an executive committee chaired by Charles L. Schultze, the chairman of the president's Council of Economic Advisers, and most of its analytic review work was done by economists from the Council on Wage and Price Stability. In contrast, the Regulatory Council was largely a research and discussion group comprising top officials from cabinet departments and major regulatory agencies. It was formally intended to improve interagency coordination on regulatory matters and to review the cumulative economic impacts of regulations on industry. Given its secondary status in the reorganization, however, it likely served best

---

[6] This discussion draws largely on materials in Tolchin and Tolchin (1983) and the Bureau of National Affairs *BNA Environment Reporter–Current Developments.* In the latter source, see, for example, "Jellinek Says Regulatory Council Will Not Undercut Environmental Protection" 9 (1978): 1,303–4; "Muskie Subcommittee to Review Role of White House Groups in Setting Rules" 9 (1979): 1,913; "Administration Officials Defend Role in Shaping Environmental Regulations" 9 (1979): 2029–30.
[7] 3 Code of Fed. Reg. 152 (1978).

to coopt some of the proregulatory antagonisms toward the new structures. Indeed, Carter appointed his EPA administrator, Douglas Costle, to head the Regulatory Council.

The reorganization was in line with a presidential tradition that had grown up alongside the boom in social legislation after 1965. In its basic logic it reestablished the earlier efforts in the Nixon and Ford administrations to contain congressionally mandated regulation and its costs through the Quality of Life review process (see Chapter 6). But Carter's was a more explicit formulation requiring that agencies conduct economic studies on the impacts of all major regulations, subject to further review by the president's economists. In this it foreshadowed the ascendancy of economists over legalists in environmental regulation (and social regulation generally) during the Reagan administration.[8]

The extent to which this new process caused regulations to be relaxed is uncertain, although there is evidence for example that it reduced the final national ozone standard from that originally proposed by the EPA. And there were charges in Congress and from environmentalists, including at least one former top EPA official, that the White House was improperly communicating its position to top EPA officials after the close of the public comment period (therefore off the record), and that it was intruding on environmental policy with a position focusing on costs alone rather than on the benefits of regulation as well.[9] These were precisely two of the

---

[8] The Congress also took note of the costs of water pollution controls after several years' experience with the 1972 amendments. In the 1977 amendments to the law, the Congress permitted EPA to set final standards lower than BAT for conventional pollutants such as fecal coliform, suspended solids, oil and grease, and biological oxygen-demanding wastes. For these, the law permitted a "best conventional technology" standard, which could be set higher than BPT levels only when the BCT levels passed two tests: (1) a cost comparison test tied to the costs of pollution removal at municipal treatment plants – the test finally devised by EPA was passed if the cost per pound of pollutant removed in going from BPT to BCT was less than 27 cents in 1976 dollars; (2) an internal industry cost-effectiveness test, which was passed if the same incremental cost per pound was less than 143 percent of the incremental cost per pound associated with achieving BPT in the industry. Final standards for conventional pollutants were set at either BPT or BCT for numerous industry categories and subcategories. The relevant section defining BCT in the 1977 amendments is § 304[b][4], 33 U.S.C. 1314[b][4]. See also *Best Conventional Pollutant Control Technology; Effluent Limitation Guidelines: Proposed Rules*, 47 Fed. Reg. 49176 (October 29, 1982). By one early estimate, the relaxed requirements would save industry as much as $200 million (*Wall Street Journal*, August 9, 1978; *Milwaukee Journal*, August 11, 1978).

[9] See, e.g., BNA, "Administration Officials Defend Role in Shaping Environmental Regulations," *BNA Environment Reporter – Current Developments* 9 (1979): 2029–30.

key charges that would later be made against the Reagan administration's executive policies, both of which raised important legal questions.

The Reagan administration built on the Carter approach from the start, but elevated the White House involvement and concern for costs in regulatory matters. Reagan's Executive Order 12291, issued in February 1981 as one of the president's first substantive acts, required agencies to conduct cost–benefit studies of all proposed regulations and legislation with major impacts on industry (to cost more than $100 million per year; see also discussion in Chapter 6); the studies would then be reviewed by a newly aggressive OMB. The approach differed from Carter's in its greater intrusiveness into agency affairs; Carter had essentially forced a greater cost sensitivity on the agencies, while Reagan insisted on explicit cost–benefit analyses and even had OMB drafting regulations. It also differed in its engagement of off-the-record, closed door meetings between OMB officials and business officials; environmentalists were typically excluded from these conferences. In addition, the OMB monitored agency proposals almost strictly on the basis of its cost concerns, and often simply delayed social regulations (and deterred others) at odds with the administration's antiregulatory philosophy.[10]

In all, the Reagan administration mounted a well-rounded assault on social regulation, perhaps especially environmental law: large budget cuts to the agencies, appointment of a deregulatory-minded cadre of leaders to manage them, and the often successful effort to rein in new health and environmental rules that the White House found too costly to industry. This latter process raised substantial legal questions, never fully resolved. One had to do with the off-the-record, post-public-comment period consultations between White House representatives and top agency executives as final rules were being contemplated. The matter was at least partially resolved in favor of the administration's position (and that of the Carter White House before it) when in 1981 a federal appellate court upheld the legality of such "intraexecutive" contacts between the president's staff and agency officials in *Sierra Club v. Costle*.[11] But a number of legal scholars argued that the Reagan process outran

---

[10] During the 1980 presidential campaign, candidate Reagan had complained that the country was in the hands of "environmental extremists," and blamed inflation in large part on "no-growth" environmental regulations (*New Haven Register*, October 23, 1980).

[11] 657 F.2d 298 (D.C. Cir. 1981).

the limits of this decision (Tolchin and Tolchin, 1983: 68–9), which among other things did not endorse the notion of *secret* meetings between the White House and private parties or agency officials. In addition, a legal analysis prepared by the Congressional Research Service concluded that OMB had exceeded the *Sierra* decision by violating both due process (permitting favored access to some interests for the purpose of influencing regulatory decisions, for instance) and the Administrative Procedure Act (subordinating agencies' expertise to the authority and judgment of the OMB director).

The second legal matter involves the question of the separation of powers and congressional authority to legislate. As earlier discussed, the Clean Water Act specifies a range of cost considerations in the formulation of water pollution rules. For the advanced, BAT standards, the law required only that the agency be cost sensitive rather than cost oblivious. And if such a determination remained rather vague, it was clearly distinguished from the cost–benefit determination specified for the lesser BPT controls (cf., Rodgers, 1980). So in forcing cost–benefit analysis on all major social regulations, the Reagan process arguably exceeded its legal authority with respect to the toxic water pollution rules then being contemplated by the EPA.[12] In effect, it amounted to Executive Branch revision of congressional law. And if the process did not simply vacate all meaningful regulation, as in the case of the toxic rules for the organic chemicals industry (Chapter 6), it likely distorted the lawfully mandated regulation contemplated in the legislation by forcing a new logic and more conservative stance on agency rulemaking.

By 1983 the administration's management of the EPA was itself under rabid political assault, as numerous congressional committees, environmental groups and media outlets uncovered a broad pattern of agency corruption (private agreements with industry that vitiated regulation; secret meetings with industrial lobbyists) and "nonregulation," particularly with respect to the EPA's Superfund program to clean up hazardous waste sites. The administration moved to contain the growing political damage of the scandal through the resignation or removal of virtually all of the EPA's top leadership, including Administrator Anne Burford, while one former top offi-

[12] The Regulatory Flexibility Act of 1980 (Pub. L. No. 96–354, 5 U.S.C. 601 *et seq.* [1980]) required agencies to conduct economic analyses to determine whether social regulations created disproportionate burdens on small firms, as the EPA did in setting toxic discharge rules for the organic chemicals industry (Chapter 6). This is quite different from requiring a generalized cost–benefit assessment for rules, however.

cial was convicted of perjury.[13] To further mitigate the damage, the president immediately appointed William Ruckelshaus to again head the EPA, an environmental moderate who could (and in many respects did) return a modicum of legitimacy to the agency's operations, particularly with respect to reopening the agency to a diversity of voices on environmental issues. (See, e.g., Shabecoff, 1984.)

It was a series of dramatic episodes, to be sure, but it hardly shifted the administration's antiregulatory stance and centralized monitoring of all social regulations. However, the administration's efforts to "deregulate" environmental protection met with less public but arguably more potent limits, in both law and citizen resistance to decontrol. As it happened, this occurred more significantly with respect to water pollution than with any other form of pollution or social regulation, and the process manifested itself in all phases of the regulatory enterprise.

Regulating toxic water pollution. As discussed in Chapter 6, the EPA's toxic water pollution program was delayed and diluted to some extent by the conduct of the administration in the 1980s, including the dramatic cuts in research and development. But the legal structure of the toxics program constrained the agency's manipulation of it. After the Reagan administration took office in 1981, industry leaders and lobbyists, including those in the chemical and iron and steel industries, pressed EPA and Administrator Burford to have the 1976 Flannery Decree vacated or substantially weakened in its requirements for toxic controls (Moffet, 1982: 20–1).

But in the face of Judge Flannery's continued insistence on EPA's adherence to the terms of the statute, Burford determined that her only option was to seek delays in the decree's deadlines, resulting in a series of contradictory agency testimony. In court, the officials pled insufficient resources as reason for delay, while before Congress other EPA spokespersons necessarily asserted that the agency could meet its statutory responsibilities despite the major budget cuts the administration demanded. In any event, delay there was but deregulation there was not. And three years after Burford's resignation, Judge Flannery reasserted the limits of law in another decision from the federal bench: In a 1986 decision concerning rules for underground storage tanks, he determined that the OMB could not

---

[13] For a very nice account of the EPA crisis and what might be called the "politics of scandal," see Szasz (1986b).

delay the issuing of EPA regulations beyond the statutory deadline set by Congress (Shabecoff, 1986).

The example of the toxics rule for the organic chemicals industry indicates that even the assertion of cost–benefit determinations by an administration wholly antagonistic to environmental controls, its arguable illegality aside, need not vitiate regulation. The combination of the Flannery court's oversight and the inherent uncertainties in such economistic determinations produced a rule that promised considerable progress in the control of toxics.

The facts of the toxics program indicate that the courts will insist on administrative compliance with clear congressional directives, at least as to schedules for rulemaking and broad mandates, to the extent that there is a vigorous constituency able to bring the matter to the bench. (The subtleties of law, such as those involving cost factors in regulation, remain somewhat less certainly protected.) Such active constituencies have developed in environmental law with respect to water pollution. Where this has been less true, as in consumer protection and occupational safety law, deregulation is typically more extensive.

The paradoxes of enforcement. Long before the deregulatory efforts at EPA erupted in scandal in 1983, Administrator Burford disorganized and virtually vacated the enforcement function during her first two years at the agency. Ironically, this less publicized process contributed greatly to the environmentalist backlash that soon forced the agency toward a more moderate stance. Even key sectors of industry began to call for a more effective agency.

It would be difficult to design a more effective means of disarming an agency's enforcement apparatus than the process invoked at EPA. The agency first abolished its Office of Enforcement, reassigning attorneys to media-specific areas of EPA; ultimately, headquarters enforcement attorneys were reorganized three times (Brown, 1984: 16–17), disrupting both continuity and concentration. Not surprisingly, law enforcement at the agency virtually collapsed in Burford's first year (see, e.g., U.S. House of Representatives, 1982: 96, 668–71). Compared to the year before she took office, EPA case referrals to the Department of Justice declined 84 percent, from 198 to 31, while cases referred from the agency's regional headquarters to EPA headquarters dropped 78 percent, from 230 to 113. At the same time, the Justice Department filed 78 percent fewer cases (from 175 to 38). Interviews at the agency indicate that there had also been declines in all of its administrative enforcement mechanisms as well, including notices of violation, compliance orders, and inspections. The Reagan administration requested large reductions in the agency's enforcement budget for fiscal 1983, including 30 percent each for the air and water programs.

This early and steep decline in regulation and enforcement drew the immediate attention of environmentalists and the Congress, which held joint hearings by various oversight subcommittees only a year after Burford's appointment, hearings that clearly put the agency and the administration on the defensive (U.S. House of Representatives, 1982).

The subsequent evidence suggests that the agency responded by making a show of enhanced enforcement in the form of increased referrals to Justice for civil and criminal prosecution (Brown, 1984). For example, civil referrals increased from 16 to 95 between the first and second halves of fiscal 1982, and from 111 to 161 between fiscal years 1982 and 1983. Criminal referrals remained rare but showed similar increases (from 20 to 26 from 1982 to 1983), and it was during the first Reagan administration that the EPA was allotted its first substantial complement of criminal investigators (24 plus support personnel). In general this portrait was one not unfamiliar to the political dynamics of regulatory law: The overarching impression is that the "revitalized" enforcement effort was designed largely to deflect increasingly harsh public criticism of the EPA (and the administration) in the face of the upcoming 1984 national elections.

Indicators of this include the fact that referrals remained well below pre-Burford levels and the "strengthened" criminal program remained centralized at the newly politicized EPA headquarters. Even its own regional administrators were disallowed from directing the criminal investigations assigned to their own regions (Brown, 1984: 19). Other indicators were even more telling and suggested some of the paradoxes attached to the politicization of enforcement. In early 1984, after several months at the post, returning Administrator Ruckelshaus angrily chided a gathering of EPA enforcement officials from around the country for inaction and a "lack of serious commitment" to enforcing the nation's environmental laws.[14] Indeed, the enforcement data showed a first quarter (fiscal 1984) decline in both civil (22 to 19) and criminal (23 to 8) referrals from its

[14] See "Ruckelshaus Upbraids Staff on Poor E.P.A. Enforcement," *The New York Times*, January 31, 1984, p. A19; also Brown (1984; 21).

regional offices to EPA headquarters as compared to the same period a year earlier, when Burford headed the agency and it was under heavy congressional investigation.

By 1984 Ruckelshaus faced a now cynical and unsure enforcement staff, not eager to press cases that might place them at political risk with Ruckelshaus's successor (his was an interim appointment) in this highly turbulent but still deregulatory environment (Brown, 1984: 21); even EPA's senior enforcement counsel admitted that perhaps "mixed signals" on enforcement might have sent to the regions.[15] Not surprisingly, given the paralyzed enforcement function, a congressional investigation at about the same time estimated that roughly one-third of large industrial wastewater dischargers were in significant noncompliance with the clean water laws.

This was scarcely the last word on the matter. Stunted federal enforcement and high rates of noncompliance with the water pollution laws generated *private enforcement* at a level not before seen in the history of American regulatory law. For the first time under any regulatory statute, citizens' and environmentalist groups in the early 1980s began to file substantial numbers of enforcement lawsuits against industrial violators of the federal water pollution law, seeking civil penalties and compliance with their discharge permits. Section 505 of the 1972 amendments[16] permits citizen suits against pollutors in the case of governmental nonenforcement of violations, allowing as well the recovery of the costs of litigation. The record of the 1980s suggested the potential efficacy of the procedure; using EPA's own publicly available corporate self-monitoring reports, in most cases citizens succeeded in having corporate defendants settle cases rather than contesting them, sometimes for considerable penalties. Civil penalties of up to $10,000 per day of violation may be assessed under the law.

In the five years prior to 1983, citizens filed a total of only 41 notices to sue and lawsuits under the water law (Fadil, 1985: 34; see also Boyer and Meidinger, 1985). But in 1983, with the evidence of collapse in EPA enforcement and high rates of noncompliance in industry, citizens filed 108 notices and suits, and 87 more in the first four months of 1984 alone. This activity, much of it organized by a coalition of national environmental groups, often working with local groups, began to rival the federal government's own enforcement action: of the 108 actions in 1983, 62 eventuated in actual citizen

[15] "Ruckelshaus Upbraids Staff on Poor E.P.A. Enforcement," ibid.
[16] 33 U.S.C. 1365 (1982)

lawsuits, compared to 77 suits filed by the Justice Department for EPA under the water law during fiscal 1983.

One of the principal environmental groups involved, the Natural Resources Defense Council, reported that with but four staff persons and a budget only 2 percent of EPA's own water enforcement budget, it had mounted more suits against industrial violators in 1984 than had the agency. The NRDC reviewed the self-monitoring reports of more than 1,300 major dischargers in 14 states, and took legal action against the 70 worst offenders. By early 1985 the group reported that it had achieved industry compliance with the law in all 7 cases completed to date. And in 1987, NRDC had won the largest case in the history of citizen prosecution, an out-of-court settlement with the Bethlehem Steel Corporation in which the company agreed to pay a $1.5 million penalty ($1 million to go to a third-party environmental fund, the rest to the U.S. Treasury) and install improved pollution control technology to achieve compliance with its discharge permit. The public-interest law firm had sued the company for illegally discharging thousands of tons of toxic wastes into Chesapeake Bay over the previous decade.[17]

The growth in citizen suits represents a widespread process in environmental law during the 1980s, both a reversal of the long trend toward the centralization of policy and greater citizen involvement in matters of environmental protection. By the end of the decade, there were numerous additional indicators of this process. Membership and donations to national environmental groups had soared since 1981 as evidence of the policy void in Washington spread. Local citizen groups were also forming around the country, to press both government and industry to take action against continuing pollution threats. For example, in 1987 some 600 community groups were in regular contact with the National Toxics Campaign, which offered technical assistance to grass-roots environmental organizations; by mid-1989, that Boston-based organization was listing 1,300 such groups. Citizens groups were both lobbying and suing industry to mitigate environmental threats, from toxic spills to air and water pollution, and were often being aided by anonymous factory workers reporting environmentally threatening conditions inside their plants such as unauthorized or accidental discharges. Even some unions are now pressing for greater environmental restrictions on industry. In one case, the Oil, Chemical and Atomic Workers Union

---

[17] See *NRDC Newsline* 5 (April/May 1987): 1; also correspondence (funds solicitation) from John Adams, NRDC executive director, January 1985.

has pressured regulators for greater controls on the chemical industry, and claimed that its environmental campaign was instrumental in helping to negotiate a new contract with the BASF Corporation in Louisiana after a long labor dispute (Marcus, 1990). And national polls showed steadily increasing public concern about environmental pollution despite two decades of federal law. In 1989, 80 percent of a national *New York Times* poll agreed that "protecting the environment is so important that requirements and standards cannot be too high, and continuing environmental improvements must be made regardless of cost." In the mid-1980s roughly 66 percent had agreed with the statement; in September 1981 only 45 percent had so agreed.[18]

Many state and local governments also increased the pressure on pollution. For example, Massachusetts passed a law permitting the state environmental agency to assess administrative penalties for pollution violations, while New York State began charging industry fees for pollution permits to help pay for enforcement, and California passed new legislation to control toxics (Shabecoff, 1989a).

If the effects of such efforts remain uncertain, and if popular opinions on regulatory priorities are shaped not only by perceptions of environmental threat but also by economic conditions, it is also the case that the uncertainties attached to these developments are often quite fearsome to industry, which tends to prefer the predictability of national regulatory policies. This is all the more the case given the prospect of large liability suits for environmental damage, such as those currently mounting against the Exxon Corporation for the large oil spill from one of its tankers off the pristine coast of Alaska in spring 1989. A year later, Exxon was facing lawsuits by the State of Alaska and more than 150 companies and individuals that, cumulatively, were claiming as much as $1 billion in damages for the spill. And in February 1990, the federal government indicted Exxon on five criminal counts for the Alaskan spill; the criminal case carried the potential of fines in excess of $1 billion against the company.[19]

[18] The *New York Times* reported a case in which an Exxon Corporation employee had leaked an internal memorandum to a local citizens environmental group. The memo had been written by the public relations coordinator at an Exxon refinery, and complained of the community group's access to internal information at the plant. The memo said the group had twice in recent months begun to complain of pollution accidents at the plant even before they had been reported in the refinery's internal communications system. (See Suro, 1989.)

[19] See, e.g., "Exxon Is Indicted by U.S. Grand Jury in Spill at Valdez," *The New York*

Given these multidimensional pressures for environmental protection, it was not surprising that early in the Reagan administration sectors of industry also voiced their concerns about the destabilized EPA under Administrator Burford. For example, the chemical industry's trade journal, *Chemical Week*, complained that, "Normally the sight of a regulatory agency in turmoil is not calculated to bring tears to industry's eyes, but an ineffective Environmental Protection Agency is not what the chemical industry needs."[20] Nor is it surprising that by 1990 major publications were reporting on business's new commitments to environmental protection in the face of a massive public movement that is both widening (nationally and internationally) and deepening.[21]

The limits of rationality

By the time I had been there 15 minutes, my voice started cracking a little, then my eyes, my throat and ears started burning and I couldn't breath.

The words quoted were spoken by EPA toxic-waste specialist Bobbie Lively-Diebold, describing the air pollution inside her office, one of many with such problems at EPA headquarters.[22] The comment bespeaks a deep truth regarding the limits of U.S. environmental policy. Indeed, it is ironic that for all the rationalization of Western industrial societies, and the key roles played by science and technology, forecasting and planning, this area of policy exposes fundamental limits to rationality at all levels of group life, from the state to individual action.

At the level of state governance, there exists what might be termed the "politics of rationality," in which policy choices are made largely on the basis of near term political pressures rather than on that of long-term, comprehensive assessments of environmental needs. Law takes an essentially reactive stance to acute (rather than chronic) social crises to secure a certain political legitimacy, the currency of statehood. In this it mirrors rather perfectly the oft-criticized economic behavior of American industry, which is systemically focused on near term profits at the expense of planning

Times, February 28, 1990, p. A1; "Will Exxon Wriggle Off the Legal Hook?" *Newsweek*, March 5, 1990, p. 39.

[20] Quoted in "Enter, 'Ruck'," *Amicus Journal* 4 (Spring 1983): 2. See also *The Wall Street Journal*, April 7, 1982.

[21] See "Environmentalism: The New Crusade," *Fortune*, February 12, 1990, pp. 44–8, 50, 54–5; "Getting with the Cleanup: Big Business Warms to Environmentalism," *Newsweek*, September 25, 1989, p. 35.

[22] Quoted in *Newsweek*, June 6, 1988.

for longer term stability and growth, this to secure the currency of business: high quarterly profits. The deferral of regulation for the high-risk toxic pollutants under the 1972 amendments is a key example of this regulatory process. Another is the federal government's otherwise inexplicable choice to emphasize rulemaking and enforcement to the neglect of research and monitoring.

At the same time, the logic of rationalized Western problem solving – orderly bureaucratization and ever more narrow specialization – has led to the creation of fractionated bureaucratic approaches to regulation that miss the systemic nature of the problems in their charge. For example, even within the federal EPA there is little coordination between the offices responsible for the various media – air, water, land – a problem exacerbated by the separate statutory authorities that address the pollution problems of each. Because nature doesn't pigeonhole waste in the same way, the solution to one problem can be the difficult occasion of another. One example: What to do with contaminated sludge from waste treatment plants? To bury it risks groundwater pollution, to burn it toxic air pollution. What is the least cost solution, and which risk is best to take, for whom, and how should the costs be distributed?

For water pollution alone, there are at the federal level three major relevant statutes that remain fundamentally uncoordinated: the Clean Water Act, the Safe Drinking Water Act, and the Resource Conservation and Recovery Act. Moreover, other units of government have key responsibilities for water in the United States, including the Interior Department and the Corps of Engineers. Despite the increasing risks of drought such as that experienced widely in the United States during 1988, there is no national water policy to implement. And the decentralization of much of the environmental enforcement effort just described, while having certain advantages in the experience of local control, can contribute little to reasonable, long-term environmental protection.

As a consequence, law perceives only poorly at best the systemic nature of the pollution problem and its connections to political economic structures. The history of environmental regulation reveals a tendency to address first this symptom, then that, and to find itself handcuffed in the face of truly integrative and critical pollution problems such as acid rain (which among other things transforms air pollution into water pollution, over long distances), global warming, and the depletion of the earth's ozone layer.

The "rational" techniques of bureaucratic policymaking further distort the approach of law. Cost–benefit techniques can have the effect of narrowly defining the regulatory problem in economistic terms, obscuring the full range of moral and political dimensions of pollution issues (and also extralegally revising law, as noted earlier). The tendency to reduce all costs and benefits, including human lives, to dollar terms simply reproduces the commodification of values in much of contemporary culture, poorly reflecting the evolving distribution of human sensibilities and survival needs.

This decision-making technology also tends to disenfranchise the popular voice in policy determinations, as it has become the province of technical specialists working in the arcane reaches of science and economics. (Given the great uncertainties attached to the estimates, it is vulnerable to abuse in the hands of deregulatory authorities.) Because of the narrow range of values implied in the techniques, it is imperative that where applied their underlying assumptions be laid bare and the alternatives clarified for public consideration. But elite decision makers may choose instead to obscure the methodological underpinnings of regulatory decisions.

This is because of an ironic consequence of such decision-making technologies as cost–benefit and risk–benefit determinations. They require a great deal of input information (and associated value assumptions), and the outcomes tend to identify winners and losers. Once the losers have been identified, societal notice must somehow be taken of them (Rodgers, 1980: 199, 213). Thus government authorities may not wish to be clear about the decision's rationale. According to a federal appellate judge with long experience in environmental litigation:

Although they do not claim to know the unknowable, [this new guild of experts] have developed techniques for estimating uncertain risks and clarifying value trade-offs. One of the most prominent and respected of these experts recently told me that value analyses should *not* be disclosed. Why? Agency choices, he said, if fully understood, are inevitably tragic and inconsistent. Some citizens must suffer so that others may thrive. Public awareness of these trade-offs would tear society apart. The poor and the weak, lacking political influence, would invariably lose in the resulting struggle. Nor would future generations have a voice. Cynics would ask: "What's posterity ever done for me?" – and the question would go unanswered. (Bazelon, 1981: 214; emphasis in the original)

This argument is, of course, inimical to fundamental notions of fairness, human dignity, and democratic process. Within it, ironically, lies the strongest of arguments for the contrary view favoring knowledgeable citizen participation in such key affairs of state.

The philosophical biases that characterize cost–benefit techniques so deeply and subtly pervade governmental policy in general that even efforts to democratize the process are undercut. For example, in late 1983 the EPA was considering what air pollution controls to require of an ASARCO copper smelting plant in Tacoma. The plant's operations created the highest levels of arsenic in the air in the United States. Faced with uncertainty as to the relation between exposure levels and cancer deaths (children in a school a block from the smelter had four times the normal level of arsenic in their urine), the agency decided to hold public hearings in the city to determine the local view of the appropriate trade-offs. The maximum containment of the pollution, almost zero discharge, would likely close the plant and cost the 630 jobs, while a lesser level of control would leave the lung cancer risk at twice the national average (an estimated two cases per year in Tacoma).[23] It presents itself as a draconian choice, and the key limit here lies in the situation being cast precisely in this way: In the context of national policy options (lack of a national industrial policy, little subsidized research and development in environmental controls, few relocation and dislocation policies), this was the only choice offered the citizenry. Government's view of the pollution problem is thus constrained by the traditional political economic limits on its role in economic relations. It is the same sort of blinkered view of the economy that is projected in such measures of national wealth and income as the gross national product. In the GNP, consumption of national resources such as oil and timber in production processes is treated as an economic gain rather than measured for its possible effects on long-term productivity (as depletion of national wealth). Pollution, too, is measured as an economic asset in the GNP because of spending on pollution control equipment and on higher health care costs due to environmentally caused illnesses (Shabecoff, 1989f).

In environmental matters there is a role for such instrumentalities as risk–benefit and cost–benefit assessments in attempting to sci-

---

[23] Ackerman (1983). EPA did something similar in 1988, when it offered for public comment four alternative proposals for controlling benzene, a widely used chemical known to cause leukemia. Each proposal was associated with a different level of cancer risks to the population – from 1 in 170 over a lifetime to 1 in 1 million – with increasing estimated costs to industry. See Philip Shabecoff, "E.P.A. Asks Comment on 4 Plans to Limit Toxic Benzene Emissions," *The New York Times,* July 21, 1988, p. A16.

entifically determine the relative risks of various options and "reasonable" pollution control levels where the threshold effects of exposure are not severe. But some benefits defy measurement (aesthetic, intergenerational risks and legacies, and so forth), and environmental regulation must encourage honest and open inquiry based on intelligible fact finding and citizen participation, the sort of rationality that honors the virtues of honesty, persuasion, and clarity in civic discourse (see, e.g., Sagoff, 1987).

It is worth noting in this connection that economistic solutions are even inadequate where they have been most strongly advocated: in the use of incentives and taxes instead of punishments to control industrial pollution. As John Braithwaite (1981–2) has so well argued, not only do such approaches fail to register the real moral sentiments entwined in the environmental issue, but they are also inadequate to control pollution associated with high risks of harm (there is great uncertainty regarding the relation between various tax rates and consequent pollution control behavior by firms) and to ensure a fair burden both of pollution loads in the environment and of the costs of control on industry.

The limits of the environment

Unless we change our direction, we are likely to end up where we are headed.

– Chinese proverb

The irrationalities bred into our pollution control policies have not always and everywhere utterly crippled them. But they have typically been constrained to short-term solutions to amenable problems. And so the limits of law have become fearsome in proportion to the potentially catastrophic environmental risks the species now faces worldwide.

Twenty years past the informal birth of environmentalism, the serious problems of environmental deterioration are the continuous stuff of daily journalism: medical waste washing ashore at the nation's beaches, frightening levels of toxic air and water pollution,[24] the contradictions between energy generation and pollution, and extreme dangers of potential global warming (the "greenhouse effect," due to the trapping of industrial gases like carbon dioxide in the atmosphere), and the destruction of the earth's protective ozone layer.

[24] In addition to material already referenced, see, e.g., Shabecoff (1989b).

Indeed, the matters of environmental destruction have become foreign policy and national defense issues, in addition to the long-recognized but still unmanaged energy-related problems. At a major summit meeting between seven major industrial democracies in the summer of 1989, at which President Bush represented the United States, international environmental problems such as global warming dominated much of the agenda, and the conferees agreed in principle on the need for strong and coordinated international action. As pollution problems migrate across international boundaries, sometimes barged as toxic waste to underdeveloped countries for dumping, global population pressures and the push for development in Third World countries also strain the environment. Meanwhile, the United States and Canada continue their uncomfortable standoff regarding the problems of containing acid rain, much of which originates here and deposits across the border. (The Reagan administration continued to call for further study before action, in the face of considerable facts verifying the relevant causal relationships.)

By 1989 as well, serious toxic pollution problems had been uncovered in the nation's nuclear weapons producing facilities, including radioactive leaks, and the Justice Department commenced criminal investigations as nuclear weapon production ceased in many places. Perhaps not so ironically, the same problems were discovered at about the same time in the Soviet Union's nuclear weapons facilities.

With the discovery and verification of each new threat, the nation's environmental consciousness has traversed the continuum of concerns from aesthetics to health and safety to planetary and species survival. The question of whether humankind has made a Faustian bargain with technology remains unanswered.

In the face of urgent environmental threats and the irrationalities of environmental policies, there are no simple solutions. But it is clear that these dilemmas test the legitimacy of rule as greatly as have any other threats to national survival and international peace, and deserve the same sort of consideration problems of that magnitude usually attract. In terms of national policy, environmental protection paradoxically requires both increased coordination and greater sensitivity to citizen concerns and informed participation. We have periodically waged wars on crime, poverty, and other nations, and maintain secretaries of state, defense, commerce, and treasury, to name but a few. In 1989 President Bush appointed a "drug czar" to coordinate heretofore fractured federal efforts to contain the menace of drug abuse. If nothing else, the urgency of environmental protection requires the same high priority such issues as these have attracted: A Cabinet-level secretariat is in order to increase coordination, ensure that environmental matters are given equal footing in all the policy deliberations of government, and give the EPA administrator equal standing with foreign environmental ministers. In January 1990, it was being suggested in both houses of Congress that EPA be made a Cabinet department, a move President George Bush said he would endorse despite his previous opposition to it (Shabecoff, 1990).

At the same time, every effort must be made to spare the EPA from the sort of politicking that derailed much of its potential during the Reagan administration. One possibility is the replacement of the administrator structure with an independent commission, although the relative advantages of each alternative would need to be carefully weighed, given the lessons of regulatory history. In any event, politics will inevitably shape the deliberations of environmental control, given the structured diversity of interests involved and the levels of uncertainty often attached to regulatory options. It is imperative for both democratic legitimacy and responsible rulemaking that fully informed citizen participation be not only encouraged but enabled, such as through enhanced environmental education efforts and stipends for concerned parties that otherwise could not afford participation in agency deliberations.

The nation has long eschewed the formulation of industrial policy, but if the challenge of international competition has failed to spur the development of something like it, then perhaps the environmental self-destruction in which we are engaged might be considered just cause. Such a policy, easier to offer in broad terms than to implement politically, to be sure, would at minimum include programs directed at industrial restructuring and economic dislocations in combination with stringent controls on the discharge of harmful pollutants. For example, to avoid forcing no-win choices on communities such as that which faced many residents of Tacoma, government must endeavor to find ways to eliminate toxic waste without eliminating jobs. One possibility is the creation of a broad-based environmental tax on production (and perhaps some forms of consumption as well) to subsidize all or large parts of high-cost controls in exchange for certain guarantees from the industrial grantee (such as to maintain employment in the community over a period of years). Such a tax should be progressive in both its collection and beneficial uses to protect the national interest in the viability of small and medium-sized companies. This is not a radical departure, for example, from the federal legislation that created EPA's Superfund program to clean up hazardous waste sites.

In addition, the government may sponsor consortiums of regulators, industries, and citizens groups to tackle thorny pollution control problems through research and development efforts. The state and industry have in the past created industry consortiums when it was felt necessary to protect the national interest, such as the 1951 consortium of major oil companies formed by plan of the State Department to negotiate oil concessions with Iran (Clinard and Yeager, 1980: 145–7). The government has been especially sparing over the course of EPA's history in spending for research and development, a policy choice long misguided. By increasing its funding for the effort, and joining the combined interests of environmentalists and industry's scientists and engineers, it is likely that such waste-minimizing technologies as recycling will be established and found to be profitable. But these are not the sorts of projects with large expected near term profits. They therefore require state formation and monitoring, with industry agreement that successfully generated controls will in fact be implemented, largely at industry's expense.

For its part, American industry will need to take a proactive role in the protection of the environment. It will be assisted in this, of course, to the extent that law is consistent rather than fickle. One consequence of the Reagan administration's mishandling of the environment was substantial turbulence in the regulatory environment, leading even elements of industry to call for stabilization. But another likely consequence was the relative devaluation of the environmental protection function in corporate headquarters as the administration sent the message that the government was now hostile to costly regulation. When, on the other hand, the state sends a consistent, sure-handed message that environmental controls are of the utmost priority, and their violation invokes the severest sanctions of the state (to say nothing of large and uncertain liability exposures in tort law), it can only enhance the function and status of corporate environmental management offices.

The nation's industries should by now assume more than a defensive posture on environmental protection. The past twenty years have clearly demonstrated the corporate self-interest in advancing environmental safety, including the potential for enhanced profitability not only through recovery of valuable production materials by recycling, and discovery of new products and markets through novel efforts at pollution control, but also through improved corporate images. The environmental, social, and corporate costs of an unthinkable accident such as the Alaskan oil spill by the Exxon tanker in 1989 are truly immense; from the corporate standpoint, they are immeasurably increased by the additional evidence of poor corporate and industry preparedness.

And to take a not trivial example, managers and workers are citizens as well, and as such have the same environmental sensibilities and worries as most. If, as research in organizational psychology suggests, irresponsible corporate activities take a toll in terms of employee loyalty and commitment, then this should be especially true in the case of environmental crime, as suggested above by the evidence of environmental whistleblowing by concerned employees. Precisely to the extent that the environmental threat is experienced as personal and intimate, and as standing in ever increasing contradiction to fundamental human values, to that extent it will be difficult for workers at all levels of responsibility to ignore their firm's association with it.

It remains unclear, of course, whether the present relations in political economy – at both national and international levels – will permit the necessary adjustments in environmental policy that will be required to sustain and improve life. But the evidence suggests we have scarcely even begun to ask the proper questions. And without the development of a new rationality on this matter, our policies threaten to stand as just so many garden hoses aimed at Dresden.

Bibliography

Ackerman, Jerry. "Jobs and Health: EPA Wants Tacoma to Help Decide What to Do About Arsenic from Plant," *Boston Globe*, November 2, 1983, p. 1.

Albrecht, Stan L. "Pollution vs. Paychecks: The Environmental Problem—Movement and Its Opposition." In A. L. Mauss and J. C. Wolfe (eds.), *This Land of Promises: The Rise and Fall of Social Problems in America*, pp. 397–414. Philadelphia: Lippincott, 1977.

"Environment." In Melvin L. DeFleur (ed.), *Social Problems in American Society*, pp. 536–61. Boston: Houghton Mifflin, 1983.

Alexander, Tom. "It's Time for New Approaches to Pollution Control." *Fortune* (November 1976): 128–31, 230–4.

Alford, Robert R., and Roger Friedland. *Powers of Theory: Capitalism, the State, and Democracy.* New York: Cambridge University Press, 1985.

Allan, Richard H. "Criminal Sanctions Under Federal and State Environmental Statutes." *Ecology Law Quarterly* 14 (1987): 117–59.

American Bar Association. *Report of the Commission to Study the Federal Trade Commission.* Chicago: American Bar Association, 1969.

Anderson, Douglas D. "Who Owns the Regulators?" *Wharton Magazine* 4 (Summer 1980): 14–21.

Asch, Peter, and J. J. Seneca. "Is Collusion Profitable?" *Review of Economics and Statistics* 58 (February 1976): 1–12.

Ashford, Nicholas A., and George R. Heaton. "Regulation and Technological Innovation in the Chemical Industry." *Law and Contemporary Problems* 46 (Summer 1983): 109–58.

Aubert, Vilhelm. "White-Collar Crime and Social Structure." *American Journal of Sociology* 58 (November 1952): 263–71. Reprinted in G. Geis and R. F. Meier (eds.), *White-Collar Crime: Offenses in Business, Politics, and the Professions*, pp. 168–79. New York: Free Press, 1977.

Balbus, Isaac D. "Commodity Form and Legal Form: An Essay on the 'Relative Autonomy' of the Law." *Law and Society Review* 11 (Winter 1977): 571–88.

Baldwin, Deborah. "Playing Politics with Pollution." *Common Cause* 9 (May–June 1983): 15–19.

Ball, Richard A. "Toward a Dialectical Criminology." In M. D. Krohn and

R. L. Akers (eds.), *Crime, Law, and Sanctions*, pp. 11–26. Beverly Hills, Calif.: Sage, 1978.

Bardach, Eugene, and Robert A. Kagan. *Going by the Book: The Problem of Regulatory Unreasonableness.* Philadelphia: Temple University Press, 1982.

Barnett, Harold C. "Wealth, Crime, and Capital Accumulation." *Contemporary Crises* 3 (1979): 171–86.

"Corporate Capitalism, Corporate Crime." *Crime and Delinquency* 27 (January 1981): 4–23.

"Political Environments and the Implementation of Social Regulation: The Case of Superfund Enforcement." Unpublished paper presented to the Eastern Economics Association, Boston, March 13, 1988.

Bazelon, David L. "Science and Uncertainty: A Jurist's View." *Harvard Environmental Law Review* 5 (1981): 209–15.

Becker, Howard S. *Outsiders: Studies in the Sociology of Deviance.* New York: Free Press, 1963.

Beirne, Piers. "Empiricism and the Critique of Marxism on Law and Crime." *Social Problems* 26 (April 1979): 373–84.

Benarde, Melvin A. *Our Precarious Habitat: An Integrated Approach to Understanding Man's Effect on His Environment.* New York: Norton, 1970.

Bequai, August. "White-Collar Plea Bargaining." *Trial Magazine* (July 1977): 38–41.

Berliner, Joseph. *Factory and Manager in the USSR.* Cambridge, Mass.: Harvard University Press, 1957.

"Managerial Incentives and Decisionmaking: A Comparison of the United States and the Soviet Union." In M. Bornstein (ed.), *Comparative Economic Systems: Models and Cases* (4th ed.), pp. 380–411. Homewood, Ill.: Irwin, 1979.

Bernstein, Marver H. *Regulating Business by Independent Commission.* Princeton, N.J.: Princeton University Press, 1955.

Bittner, Egon. "The Police on Skid-Row: A Study of Peace Keeping." *American Sociological Review* 32 (October 1967): 699–715.

Black, Donald. *The Behavior of Law.* New York: Academic Press, 1976.

(ed.). *Toward a General Theory of Social Control, Vol. 1: Fundamentals.* Orlando, Fla.: Academic Press, 1984a.

(ed.). *Toward a General Theory of Social Control, Vol. 2: Selected Problems.* Orlando, Fla.: Academic Press, 1984b.

Blumberg, Abraham S. "The Practice of Law as a Confidence Game: Organizational Cooptation of a Profession." *Law & Society Review* 1 (June 1967): 15–39.

Borrelli, Peter. "Epiphany: Religion, Ethics, and the Environment." *Amicus Journal* 7 (Winter 1986): 34–41.

"Environmentalism at a Crossroads." *Amicus Journal* 9 (Summer 1987): 24–37.

Bowles, Samuel, and Herbert Gintis. *Democracy and Capitalism: Property, Com-*

munity, and the Contradictions of Modern Social Thought. New York: Basic Books, 1986.

Boyer, Barry, and Errol Meidinger. "Privatizing Regulatory Enforcement: A Preliminary Assessment of Citizen Suits Under Federal Environmental Laws." *Buffalo Law Review* 34 (1985): 833–964.

Braithwaite, John. "Inegalitarian Consequences of Egalitarian Reforms to Control Corporate Crime." *Temple Law Quarterly* 53 (1980): 1127–46.

"The Limits of Economism in Controlling Harmful Corporate Conduct." *Law & Society Review* 16 (1981–2): 481–504.

"Enforced Self-regulation: A New Strategy for Corporate Crime Control." *Michigan Law Review* 80 (1982): 1,466–507.

Corporate Crime in the Pharmaceutical Industry. London: Routledge & Kegan Paul, 1984.

To Punish or Persuade: The Enforcement of Coal Mine Safety. Albany: State University of New York Press, 1985.

Brown, Michael A. "EPA Enforcement – Past, Present and Future." *Environmental Forum* 3, no. 1 (1984): 12–22.

Buglass, Ralph. "Water Cleanup Inches Forward." *Environmental Action,* July 2, 1977, p. 7.

Burch, Philip H., Jr. *An Analysis of New Jersey's Water Pollution Control Program.* New Brunswick: Rutgers State University, New Jersey Water Resources Research Institute, 1970.

Bureau of National Affairs. "Special Report: Office of Management and Budget Plays Critical Part in Environmental Policymaking, Faces Little External Review." *BNA Environment Reporter – Current Developments* 7 (1976): 693–7.

"Special Report: Effluent Guidelines Rulemaking Nears End; Litigation, Compliance Extensions Expected." *BNA Environment Reporter – Current Developments* 13 (1983): 1629–31.

"Special Analysis: Clean Water Act Reauthorization, Air Pollution Head the Agenda of Environmental Issues for the 100th Congress." *BNA Environment Reporter – Current Developments* 17 (1987): 1547–57.

Burton, J. F., Jr. "An Economist's Analysis of Sherman Act Criminal Cases." In J. M. Clabault and J. F. Burton, Jr., *Sherman Act Indictments, 1955–1965: A Legal and Economic Analysis,* pp. 103–44. New York: Federal Legal Publications, 1966.

Business Week. "Spending Races to Catch Up to the Need." May 13, 1972, p. 7.

Buttel, Frederick H., and William L. Flinn. "Social Class and Mass Environmental Beliefs: A Reconsideration." *Environment and Behavior* 10 (September 1978): 433–50.

Butterfield, Bruce D. "OSHA Gets Tough with Lift-Slab." *Boston Globe,* August 5, 1987, p. 71.

Bylinsky, Gene. "The Limited War on Water Pollution." In editors of *For-*

tune, *The Environment: A National Mission for the Seventies*, pp. 19–
37. New York: Harper & Row (Perennial Library), 1970a.

"The Long, Littered Path to Clean Air and Water." *Fortune* (October
1970b): 112–15, 133–4.

Calavita, Kitty. "The Demise of the Occupational Safety and Health Administration: A Case Study in Symbolic Action." *Social Problems* 30 (April
1983): 437–48.

Cameron, Juan. "The Trials of Mr. Clean." *Fortune* (April 1972): 102–5,
130–2.

Carson, W. G. "The Institutionalization of Ambiguity: Early British Factory
Acts." In Gilbert Geis and Ezra Stotland (eds.), *White-Collar Crime: Theory and Research*, pp. 142–73. Beverly Hills, Calif: Sage, 1980.

Carter, Richard M. "Federal Enforcement of Individual and Corporate
Criminal Liability for Water Pollution." *Memphis State University Law Review* 10 (1980): 576–611.

Castells, Manuel. *The Economic Crisis and American Society.* Princeton, N.J.:
Princeton University Press, 1980.

Chambliss, William J. "A Sociological Analysis of the Law of Vagrancy." *Social Problems* 11 (Summer 1964): 67–77.

"The State, the Law, and the Definition of Behavior as Criminal or Delinquent." In Daniel Glaser (ed.), *Handbook of Criminology*, pp. 7–43.
Chicago: Rand McNally, 1974.

"The Criminalization of Conduct." In H. Laurence Ross (ed.), *Law and
Deviance*, pp. 45–64. Beverly Hills, Calif.: Sage, 1981.

Chambliss, William J., and Robert Seidman. *Law, Order and Power* (rev. ed.).
Reading, Mass.: Addison-Wesley, 1982.

Chandler, Alfred. "The Adversaries." *Harvard Business Review* 57 (November–December, 1979): 88–92.

Chickering, A. Lawrence. "Regulation: Hopes and Realities." In Chris
Argyris et al., *Regulating Business: The Search for an Optimum*, pp. 219–
27. San Francisco: Institute for Contemporary Studies, 1978.

Clinard, Marshall B. "Criminological Theories of Violations of Wartime
Regulations." *American Sociological Review* 11 (June 1946): 258–70. Re-
printed in G. Geis and R. F. Meier (eds.), *White-Collar Crime: Offenses in
Business, Politics, and the Professions* (rev. ed.), pp. 85–101. New York:
Free Press, 1977.

The Black Market: A Study of White Collar Crime. New York: Holt, Rinehart,
1952.

Corporate Ethics and Crime: The Role of Middle Management. Beverly Hills,
Calif.: Sage, 1983.

Clinard, Marshall B., Peter C. Yeager, Jeanne M. Brissette, David Petrashek,
and Elizabeth Harries. *Illegal Corporate Behavior.* Washington, D.C.: U.S.
Government Printing Office, 1979.

Clinard, Marshall B., and Peter C. Yeager. *Corporate Crime.* New York: Free
Press, 1980.

Coffee, J. C., Jr. "Corporate Crime and Punishment: A Non-Chicago View of the Economics of Criminal Sanctions." *American Criminal Law Review* 17 (1980): 419–71.

"No Soul to Damn–No Body to Kick: An Unscandalized Inquiry into the Problem of Corporate Punishment." *Michigan Law Review* 79 (January 1981): 386–459.

Cohen, Stanley, and Andrew Scull (eds.). *Social Control and the State.* New York: St. Martin's Press, 1983.

Coleman, James William. "Law and Power: The Sherman Antitrust Act and Its Enforcement in the Petroleum Industry." *Social Problems* 32 (1985): 264–74.

"Comment: The EPA's Power to Establish National Effluent Limitations for Existing Water Pollution Sources." *University of Pennsylvania Law Review* 125 (1976): 120–66.

Conklin, John E. *Illegal But Not Criminal: Business Crime in America.* Englewood Cliffs, N.J.: Prentice-Hall, 1977.

Conservation Foundation. "Water Resources." In *State of the Environment 1982*, pp. 89–144. Washington, D.C.: Conservation Foundation.

Council on Environmental Quality. *Environmental Quality: The First Annual Report of the Council on Environmental Quality.* Washington, D.C.: U.S. Government Printing Office, 1970.

Environmental Quality: The Eighth Annual Report of the Council on Environmental Quality. Washington, D.C.: U.S. Government Printing Office, 1977.

Cox, Edward F., Robert C. Fellmeth, and John E. Schultz. *The Nader Report on the Federal Trade Commission.* New York: Baron, 1969.

Cressey, Donald R. "Restraint of Trade, Recidivism, and Delinquent Neighborhoods." In James F. Short, Jr. (ed.), *Delinquency, Crime, and Society,* pp. 209–38. Chicago: University of Chicago Press, 1976.

"Criminological Theory, Social Science, and the Repression of Crime." *Criminology* 16 (August 1978): 171–92.

Cullen, F. T., B. Link, and C. Polanzi. "The Seriousness of Crime Revisited: Have Attitudes Toward White-Collar Crime Changed?" *Criminology* 20 (May 1982): 83–102.

Cullen, F. T., and P. J. Dubeck. "The Myth of Corporate Immunity to Deterrence: Ideology and the Creation of the Invincible Criminal." *Federal Probation* 49 (September 1985): 3–9.

Curran, Daniel J. "Symbolic Solutions for Deadly Dilemmas: An Analysis of Federal Coal Mine Health and Safety Legislation." *International Journal of Health Services* 14 (1984): 5–29.

Davenport, John. "Industry Starts the Big Cleanup." In editors of *Fortune, The Environment: A National Mission for the Seventies,* pp. 39–53. New York: Harper & Row (Perennial Library), 1970.

Davies, J. C., III. "The Effects of Federal Regulation on Chemical Industry Innovation." *Law and Contemporary Problems* 46 (Summer 1983): 41–58.

Davies, J. C., III, and B. S. Davies. *The Politics of Pollution* (2d ed.). Indianapolis, Ind.: Pegasus, 1975.

Diamond, Robert S. "What Business Thinks About Its Environment." In editors of *Fortune, The Environment: A National Mission for the Seventies*, pp. 55–64. New York: Harper & Row (Perennial Library), 1970.

Dickson, David, Gene Frankel, David Johns, and Carol MacLennon. "Regulation." *In These Times*, May 13–19, 1981, p. 13.

DiMento, Joseph F. *Environmental Law and American Business: Dilemmas of Compliance.* New York: Plenum Press, 1986.

Dinitz, Simon. "Nothing Fails Like a Little Success." *Criminology* 16 (August 1978): 225–38.

"Economic Crime." Mimeo, 1979.

Domhoff, G. William. *Who Rules America?* Englewood Cliffs, N.J. Prentice-Hall, 1967.

The Higher Circles: The Governing Class in America. New York: Vintage, 1970.

The Powers That Be: Processes of Ruling Class Domination in America. New York: Vintage, 1978.

Donnelly, Patrick. "The Origins of the Occupational Safety and Health Act of 1970." *Social Problems* 30 (1982): 13–25.

Downs, A. *Inside Bureaucracy.* Boston: Little, Brown, 1967.

Dubos, René. "Man and His Environment: Adaptations and Interactions." In Bertrand de Jouvenel et al., *The Fitness of Man's Environment*, pp. 229–50. New York: Harper & Row, 1968.

Dunlap, Riley E. "The Impact of Political Orientation on Environmental Attitudes and Actions." *Environment and Behavior* 7 (December 1975): 428–54.

Durkheim, Emile. *The Division of Labor in Society.* New York: Free Press, 1933.

Edelman, Murray. *The Symbolic Uses of Politics.* Urbana: University of Illinois Press, 1964.

Erikson, Kai T. "Notes on the Sociology of Deviance." In H. S. Becker (ed.), *The Other Side: Perspectives on Deviance*, pp. 9–21. New York: Free Press, 1964.

Ermann, M. David, and Richard J. Lundman. "Deviant Acts by Complex Organizations: Deviance and Social Control at the Organizational Level of Analysis." *Sociological Quarterly* 19 (Winter 1978): 55–67.

Corporate Deviance. New York: Holt, Rinehart & Winston, 1982a.

(eds.) *Corporate and Governmental Deviance* (rev. ed.). New York: Oxford University Press, 1982b.

Erskine, Hazel. "The Polls: Pollution and Its Costs." *Public Opinion Quarterly* 36 (Spring 1972a): 120–35.

"The Polls: Pollution and Industry." *Public Opinion Quarterly* 36 (Summer 1972b): 263–80.

Esping-Andersen, Gösta, Roger Friedland, and Erik Olin Wright. "Modes of Class Struggle and the Capitalist State." *Kapitalistate* (Summer 1976): 186–220.

Etzioni, Amitai. *The Moral Dimension: Toward a New Economics.* New York: Free Press, 1988.

Evans, Medford. Review of Marshall B. Clinard and Peter C. Yeager, *Corporate Crime* (New York: Free Press, 1980). *American Opinion* (June 1981): 73–6.

Fadil, Adeeb. "Citizen Suits Against Polluters: Picking Up the Pace." *Harvard Environmental Law Review* 9 (1985): 23–82.

Fallows, James M. *The Water Lords.* New York: Grossman, 1971.

Farberman, Harvey A. "A Criminogenic Market Structure: The Automobile Industry." *Sociological Quarterly* 16 (Autumn 1975): 438–57.

Federal Water Quality Administration [U.S. Department of the Interior]. *Clean Water for the 1970s: A Status Report* [June 1970]. Reprinted in U.S. Environmental Protection Agency, *Legal Compilation: Statutes and Legislative History, Executive Orders, Regulations, Guidelines and Reports,* Vol. 7, pp. 3,592–705. Washington, D.C.: U.S. Government Printing Office, 1973.

Feld, Barry C. "The Political Economy of Corporate Regulation: The Structural Origins of White Collar Crime." In J. M. Inverarity, Pat Lauderdale, and Barry C. Feld. *Law and Society: Sociological Perspectives on Criminal Law,* pp. 216–42. Boston: Little, Brown, 1983.

Feldman, Stanley J., and David McClain. "Environmental Regulation and the 'Diversion' of 'Productive' Capital Investment: An Empirical Analysis." Paper presented at the 10th Annual Meeting of the Eastern Economic Association, New York, March 16, 1984.

Fellmeth, Robert. *The Interstate Commerce Omission: The Report on the Interstate Commerce Commission and Transportation.* New York: Grossman, 1970.

Fisse, Brent. "Community Service as a Sanction Against Corporations." *Wisconsin Law Review* (September 1981): 970–1,017.

   "Reconstructing Corporate Criminal Law: Deterrence, Retribution, Fault, and Sanctions." *Southern California Law Review* 56 (1983): 1,141–246.

Fisse, Brent, and John Braithwaite. *The Impact of Publicity on Corporate Offenders.* Albany: State University of New York Press, 1983.

Foucault, Michel. *Discipline and Punish: The Birth of the Prison.* New York: Vintage, 1979.

Fraas, Arthur G. "Benefit–Cost Analysis for Environmental Regulation." In V. Kerry Smith (ed.), *Environmental Policy Under Reagan's Executive Order: The Role of Benefit–Cost Analysis,* pp. 86–98. Chapel Hill: University of North Carolina Press, 1984.

Frank, James, Francis T. Cullen, Lawrence F. Travis III, and John L. Borntrager. "Sanctioning Corporate Crime: How Do Business Executives and the Public Compare?" *American Journal of Criminal Justice* 13 (1989): 139–69.

Freeman, A. Myrick, III. "Air and Water Pollution Policy." In Paul R. Portney (ed.), *Current Issues in U.S. Environmental Policy,* pp. 12–67. Baltimore, Md.: Johns Hopkins University Press, 1978.

Freeman, A. Myrick, III, and Robert H. Haveman. "Clean Rhetoric and Dirty Water." In Walt Anderson (ed.), *Politics and Environment: A Reader in Ecological Crisis* (2d ed.). Pacific Palisades, Calif.: Goodyear Publishing, 1975.

Freitag, Peter J. "The Myth of Corporate Capture: Regulatory Commissions in the United States." *Social Problems* 30 (April 1983): 480–91.

Galbraith, John Kenneth. *The Affluent Society.* Boston: Houghton Mifflin, 1958.

Garrett, Theodore L. "Examination of 1987 Amendments to Clean Water Act Shows Refinement of Existing Programs, Addition of New Ones." *BNA Environment Reporter – Current Developments* 17 (1987): 1,805–9.

Geis, Gilbert. "The Heavy Electrical Equipment Antitrust Cases of 1961." In Marshall Clinard and Richard Quinney (eds.), *Criminal Behavior Systems,* pp. 139–50. New York: Holt, Rinehart & Winston, 1967. Reprinted in G. Geis and R. F. Meier (eds.), *White-Collar Crime: Offenses in Business, Politics, and the Professions,* pp. 117–32. New York: Free Press, 1977.

Geis, Gilbert, and Robert F. Meier. *White-Collar Crime: Offenses in Business, Politics, and the Professions* (rev. ed.). New York: Free Press, 1977.

Geis, Gilbert, and Ezra Stotland (eds.). *White-Collar Crime: Theory and Research.* Beverly Hills, Calif.: Sage, 1980.

Ginn, Bo. "Regulation and Monitoring of Toxic and Hazardous Chemicals Under the Clean Water Act." In American Bar Association, *Environmental Enforcement: Selected Readings Prepared in Conjunction with the Seventh Annual Conference on the Environment,* pp. 16–18. Washington, D.C.: American Bar Association Standing Committee on Environmental Law, 1978.

Glenn, M. K. "The Crime of 'Pollution': The Role of Federal Water Pollution Criminal Sanctions." *American Criminal Law Review* 11 (Summer 1973): 835–82.

Goff, Colin H., and Charles E. Reasons. *Corporate Crime in Canada: A Critical Analysis of Anti-combines Legislation.* Englewood Cliffs, N.J.: Prentice-Hall, 1978.

Goffman, Erving. *Asylums: Essays on the Situation of Mental Patients and Other Inmates.* New York: Doubleday/Anchor Books, 1961.

Gold, David A., Clarence Y. H. Lo, and Erik Olin Wright. "Recent Developments in Marxist Theories of the Capitalist State." *Monthly Review* (October 1975): 29–43; (November 1975): 36–51.

Granick, David. *Soviet Metal-Fabricating and Economic Development.* Madison: University of Wisconsin Press, 1967.

Green, Mark J. *The Closed Enterprise System.* New York: Grossman, 1972.
    (ed.). *The Monopoly Makers: Ralph Nader's Study Group Report on Regulation and Competition.* New York: Grossman, 1973.
Greenberg, David (ed.). *Crime and Capitalism.* Palo Alto, Calif.: Mayfield, 1981.
Gunningham, Neil. *Pollution, Social Interest and the Law.* London: Robertson, 1974.
Hagan, John. "From the Shadow of the Law." *Contemporary Sociology* 12 (January 1983): 35–7.
Halberstam, David. *The Powers That Be.* New York: Knopf, 1979.
Hall, Jerome. *Theft, Law and Society.* Boston: Little, Brown, 1935.
Handler, Joel. *Social Movements and the Legal System: A Theory of Law Reform and Social Change.* New York: Academic, 1978.
Harrison, David, Jr., and Paul R. Portney. "Who Loses from Reform of Environmental Regulation?" In Wesley A. Magat (ed.), *Reform of Environmental Regulation,* pp. 147–79. Cambridge, Mass.: Ballinger, 1982.
Hartung, Frank E. "White-Collar Offenses in the Wholesale Meat Industry in Detroit." *American Journal of Sociology* 56 (July 1950): 25–34. Reprinted in G. Geis and R. F. Meier (eds.), *White-Collar Crime: Offenses in Business, Politics, and the Professions,* pp. 154–63. New York: Free Press, 1977.
Haveman, Robert H. and V. Kerry Smith. "Investment, Inflation, Unemployment, and the Environment." In Paul R. Portney (ed.), *Current Issues in U.S. Environmental Policy,* pp. 164–200. Baltimore, Md.: Johns Hopkins University Press, 1978.
Hawkins, Keith. "Bargain and Bluff: Compliance Strategy and Deterrence in the Enforcement of Regulation." *Law and Policy Quarterly* 5 (1983): 35–73.
    Environment and Enforcement: Regulation and the Social Definition of Pollution. New York: Oxford University Press, 1984.
Herman, Edward S. *Corporate Control, Corporate Power.* Cambridge University Press, 1981.
Hochstedler, Ellen (ed.). *Corporations as Criminals.* Beverly Hills, Calif.: Sage, 1984.
Hoerger, Fred, William H. Beamer, and James S. Hanson. "The Cumulative Impact of Health, Environmental, and Safety Concerns on the Chemical Industry During the Seventies." *Law and Contemporary Problems* 46 (Summer 1983): 59–108.
Holsendolph, Ernest. "States Join the Pollution Battle." *Fortune* (October 1970): 116.
Hopkins, Andrew. "The Anatomy of Corporate Crime." In P. Wilson and J. Braithwaite (eds.), *Two Faces of Deviance,* pp. 214–31. St. Lucia: Queensland University Press, 1978.
    "Controlling Corporate Deviance." *Criminology* 18 (August 1980): 198–214.

Ignatieff, Michael. "State, Civil Society and Total Institutions: A Critique of Recent Social Histories of Punishment." In Stanley Cohen and Andrew Scull (eds.), *Social Control and the State*, pp. 75–105. New York: St. Martin's Press, 1983.

Inverarity, James M., Pat Lauderdale, and Barry C. Feld. *Law and Society: Sociological Perspectives on Criminal Law*. Boston: Little, Brown, 1983.

Johnson, John M., and Jack D. Douglas (eds.). *Crime at the Top: Deviance in Business and the Professions*. Philadelphia: Lippincott, 1978.

Jones, Kelvin. *Law and Economy: The Legal Regulation of Corporate Capital*. New York: Academic Press, 1982.

Jorling, Thomas C. "Common Sense Wisdom: Recollections on the Writing of the Clean Water Act." *Amicus Journal* (Spring 1982): 35–6.

Kelly, B. "Allied Chemical Kept That Kepone Flowing." *Business and Society Review* 21 (Spring 1977): 17–22.

Kennedy, Paul. "The (Relative) Decline of America." *Atlantic Monthly* (August 1987): 29–38.

Kidder, Robert L. *Connecting Law and Society*. Englewood Cliffs, N.J.: Prentice-Hall, 1983.

Koch, C. James, and Robert A. Leone. "The Clean Water Act: Unexpected Impacts on Industry." *Harvard Environmental Law Review* 3 (1979): 84–111.

Kolko, Gabriel. *The Triumph of Conservatism: A Reinterpretation of American History, 1900–1916*. New York: Free Press, 1963.

Railroads and Regulation, 1877–1916. Princeton, N.J.: Princeton University Press, 1965.

Main Currents in Modern American History. New York: Harper & Row, 1976.

Kramer, Ronald C. "Corporate Crime: An Organizational Perspective." In P. Wickman and T. Dailey (eds.), *White-Collar and Economic Crime*. Lexington, Mass.: Heath, 1982.

"Corporate Criminality: The Development of an Idea." In Ellen Hochstedler (ed.), *Corporations as Criminals*, pp. 13–37. Beverly Hills, Calif.: Sage, 1984.

Kriesberg, S. "Decisionmaking Models and the Control of Corporate Crime." *Yale Law Journal* 85 (July 1976): 1,091–129.

Kuruc, Michele. "Putting Polluters in Jail: The Imposition of Criminal Sanctions on Corporate Defendants Under Environmental Statutes." *Land and Water Law Review* 20 (1985): 93–108.

Lake, Laura M. *Environmental Regulation: The Political Effects of Implementation*. New York: Praeger, 1982.

Lane, Robert E. "Why Businessmen Violate the Law." *Journal of Criminal Law, Criminology and Police Science* 44 (July 1953): 151–65. Reprinted in G. Geis and R. F. Meier (eds.), *White-Collar Crime: Offenses in Business, Politics, and the Professions*, pp. 102–16. New York: Free Press, 1977.

Lauderdale, Pat, Harold Grasmick, and John Clark. "Corporate Environments, Corporate Crime, and Deterrence." In M. Krohn and R. Akers (eds.), *Crime, Law, and Sanctions*, pp. 137–58. Beverly Hills, Calif.: Sage, 1979.

Lazarus, Simon. "Halfway up from Liberalism: Regulation and Corporate Power." In Ralph Nader and Mark J. Green (eds.), *Corporate Power in America*, pp. 215–34. New York: Grossman, 1973.

Leonard, William N., and Marvin Glenn Weber. "Automakers and Dealers: A Study of Criminogenic Market Forces." *Law & Society Review* 4 (February 1970): 407–24. Reprinted in G. Geis and R. F. Meier (eds.), *White-Collar Crime: Offenses in Business, Politics, and the Professions*, pp. 133–48. New York: Free Press, 1977.

Lewin, Tamar. "Business and the Law: Effect of Curb on U.S. Cases." *New York Times*, September 20, 1983, p. D2.

Lilley, William, III, and James C. Miller III. "The New 'Social Regulation.' " *Public Interest* (Spring 1977): 49–61.

Lipset, Seymour Martin, and William Schneider. "How's Business? What the Public Thinks." *Public Opinion* (July–August 1978): 41–7.

Luthans, Fred, and Richard M. Hodgetts. *Social Issues in Business: A Text with Current Readings and Cases.* New York: Macmillan, 1976.

Lynxwiler, John, Neal Shover, and Donald A. Clelland. "The Organization and Impact of Inspector Discretion in a Regulatory Bureaucracy." *Social Problems* 30 (April 1983): 425–36.

Macbeth, Angus. "The Need for Flexibility and Variety in Environmental Enforcement." In American Bar Association, *Environmental Enforcement: Selected Readings Prepared in Conjunction with the Seventh Annual Conference on the Environment*, pp. 13–14. Washington, D.C.: American Bar Association Standing Committee on Environmental Law, 1978.

Marcus, Alfred. "Environmental Protection Agency." In J. Q. Wilson (ed.), *The Politics of Regulation*, pp. 267–303. New York: Basic Books, 1980.

Marcus, Frances Frank. "Labor Dispute in Louisiana Ends With Ecological Gain." *The New York Times*, January 3, 1990, p. A16.

Marx, Wesley. *Man and His Environment: Waste.* New York: Harper & Row, 1971.

Maslow, Abraham. *Motivation and Personality.* New York: Harper, 1954.

Mauss, Armand L. *Social Problems as Social Movements.* Philadelphia: Lippincott, 1975.

McCraw, Thomas K. *Prophets of Regulation.* Cambridge, Mass.: Harvard University Press, 1984.

McGarity, Thomas O. "Media-Quality, Technology, and Cost–Benefit Balancing Strategies for Health and Environmental Regulation." *Law and Contemporary Problems* 46 (Summer 1983): 159–233.

McGee, William John. "The Conservation Bill of Rights." *Amicus Journal* 9 (Spring 1987): 19–21. (Excerpts from essay first published in the 1909–10 *Proceedings of the Mississippi Valley Historical Association*.)

Meier, Kenneth J., and John P. Plumlee. "Regulatory Administration and Organizational Rigidity." *Western Political Quarterly* 31 (March 1978): 80–95.

Meier, Robert F. "The Arrested Development of Criminological Theory." *Contemporary Sociology* 9 (May 1980): 374–6.

Melnick, R. Shep. *Regulation and the Courts: The Case of the Clean Air Act.* Washington, D.C.: Brookings Institution, 1983.

Melossi, Dario, and Massimo Pavarini. *The Prison and the Factory: Origins of the Penitentiary System.* London: Macmillan Press, 1981.

Miliband, Ralph. *The State in Capitalist Society.* New York: Basic Books, 1969.

Mills, C. Wright. "The Professional Ideology of Social Pathologists." *American Journal of Sociology* 49 (September 1943): 165–80.

Mitnick, Barry M. *The Political Economy of Regulation: Creating, Designing, and Removing Regulatory Forms.* New York: Columbia University Press, 1980.

Moffett, Toby. "A Case of Duplicity." *Amicus Journal* 3 (Winter 1982): 19–21.

Moorman, James W. "Criminal Enforcement of the Pollution Control Laws." In American Bar Association, *Environmental Enforcement: Selected Readings Prepared in Conjunction with the Seventh Annual Conference on the Environment,* pp. 25–8. Washington, D.C.: American Bar Association Standing Committee on Environmental Law, 1978.

Murphy, Earl Finbar. *Man and His Environment: Law.* New York: Harper & Row, 1971.

Myrdal, Gunnar. *An American Dilemma.* New York: Harper & Row, 1944.

Nader, Ralph, and Mark J. Green (eds.). *Corporate Power in America.* New York: Grossman, 1973.

Nader, Ralph, Mark J. Green, and Joel Seligman. *Taming the Giant Corporation.* New York: Norton, 1976.

National Wildlife Federation. "20th Environmental Quality Index." *National Wildlife* (February–March 1988): 38–46.

Natural Resources Defense Council. *Docket: Summary of Litigation, Administrative Proceedings, and Other Matters Relating to the Protection of the Environment in Which the Natural Resources Defense Council, Inc., Has Taken an Active Role.* New York: NRDC, 1977.

"Water Pollution: Implementation of the Clean Water Act." Unpublished, 1981.

Needleman, Martin L., and Carolyn Needleman. "Organizational Crime: Two Models of Criminogenesis." *Sociological Quarterly* 20 (1979): 517–28.

Newman, Donald J. "White-Collar Crime: An Overview and Analysis." *Law and Contemporary Problems* 23 (Autumn 1958): 228–32. Reprinted in G. Geis and R. F. Meier (eds.), *White-Collar Crime: Offenses in Business, Politics, and the Professions,* pp. 50–64. New York: Free Press, 1977.

Nicolaus, Martin. "The Professional Organization of Sociology: A View from Below." In Robin Blackburn (ed.), *Ideology in Social Science,* pp. 45–60. New York: Vintage, 1973.

Noble, Kenneth B. "Employers Are Split on Affirmative Action Goals." *New York Times,* March 3, 1986, p. B4.

Nonet, Philippe, and Philip Selznick. *Law and Society in Transition: Toward Responsive Law.* New York: Harper & Row, 1978.

Novick, Sheldon. "The Corporate Heart." *Environment* 17 (December 1975): 18–20, 25–31.

O'Connor, James. *The Fiscal Crisis of the State.* New York: St. Martin's Press, 1973.

Offe, Claus. "Class Rule and the Political System: On the Selectiveness of Political Institutions." Unpublished translation of Chapter 3 of *Strukturprobleme des kapitalistischen Staates* (Frankfurt: Suhrkamp, 1972), 1973.

"The Theory of the Capitalist State and the Problem of Policy Formation." In Leon Lindberg, Robert Alford, Colin Crouch, and Claus Offe (eds.), *Stress and Contradiction in Modern Capitalism,* pp. 125–44. Lexington, Mass.: Lexington Books, 1975.

Pearce, Frank. *Crimes of the Powerful.* London: Pluto Press, 1976.

Pederson, William F. "The Mechanics of Environmental Law Enforcement." In American Bar Association, *Environmental Enforcement: Selected Readings Prepared in Conjunction with the Seventh Annual Conference on the Environment,* pp. 14–15. Washington, D.C.: American Bar Association Standing Committee on Environmental Law, 1978.

Perez, Jacob. *Corporate Criminality: A Study of the One Thousand Largest Industrial Corporations in the U.S.A.* Unpublished Ph.D. dissertation, University of Pennsylvania, 1978.

Pfeffer, Jeffrey, and Gerald R. Salancik. *The External Control of Organizations: A Resource Dependence Perspective.* New York: Harper & Row, 1978.

Pfohl, Stephen. *Images of Deviance and Social Control: A Sociological History.* New York: McGraw-Hill, 1985.

Platt, Tony. "Prospects for a Radical Criminology in the USA." In I. Taylor, P. Walton, and J. Young (eds.), *Critical Criminology,* pp. 95–112. London: Routledge & Kegan Paul, 1975.

Plumlee, John P., and Kenneth J. Meier. "Capture and Rigidity in Regulatory Administration: An Empirical Assessment." In J. W. May and A. B. Wildavsky (eds.), *The Policy Cycle,* pp. 215–34. Beverly Hills, Calif.: Sage, 1978.

Poulantzas, Nicos. *Political Power and Social Classes.* London: NLB, 1973.

Przeworski, Adam, and Michael Wallerstein. "The Structure of Class Conflict in Democratic Capitalist Societies." *American Political Science Review* 76 (1982): 215–38.

Quarles, John R., Jr. "Widespread Noncompliance and the Need to Rethink Enforcement." In American Bar Association, *Environmental Enforcement: Selected Readings Prepared in Conjunction with the Seventh Annual Conference on the Environment,* pp. 15–16. Washington, D.C.: American Bar Association Standing Committee on Environmental Law, 1978.

Quinney, Richard. *The Social Reality of Crime.* Boston: Little, Brown, 1970.
  Critique of Legal Order: Crime Control in Capitalist Society. Boston: Little,
  Brown, 1974.
  Criminology (rev. ed.). Boston: Little, Brown, 1979.
Reasons, Charles E., and Colin H. Goff. "Corporate Crime: A Cross-
  national Analysis." In Gilbert Geis and Ezra Stotland (eds.), *White-Collar
  Crime: Theory and Research,* pp. 126–41. Beverly Hills, Calif.: Sage,
  1980.
Reisman, W. Michael. *Folded Lies: Bribery, Crusades, and Reforms.* New York:
  Free Press, 1979.
Reiss, Albert J., Jr., and Albert D. Biderman. *Data Sources on White-Collar
  Law-Breaking.* Washington, D.C.: U.S. Department of Justice, National
  Institute of Justice, 1980.
Reitze, A. W., Jr., and G. L. Reitze. "Buccaneering: Kepone and Allied
  Chemical/Life Science Products Co." *Environment* (March 1976):
  2–5.
Rice, Berkeley. "Water Shocks of the '80s." *Across the Board* (March 1986):
  17–23.
Richman, Barry M. *Soviet Management.* Englewood Cliffs, N.J.: Prentice-
  Hall, 1965.
Ridgeway, James. *The Politics of Ecology.* New York: Dutton, 1970.
Rodgers, William H., Jr. "Benefits, Costs, and Risks: Oversight of Health
  and Environmental Decisionmaking." *Harvard Environmental Law Re-
  view* 4 (1980): 191–226.
Rose-Ackerman, Susan. *Corruption: A Study in Political Economy.* New York:
  Academic Press, 1978.
Rosenbaum, Walter A. *The Politics of Environmental Concern* (2d ed.). New
  York: Praeger, 1977.
Ross, Edward A. "The Criminaloid." *Atlantic Monthly* 99 (January 1907): 44–
  50. Reprinted in G. Geis and R. F. Meier (eds.), *White-Collar Crime: Of-
  fenses in Business, Politics, and the Professions* (rev. ed.), pp. 29–37. New
  York: Free Press, 1977.
Ross, Irwin. "How Lawless Are Big Companies?" *Fortune,* December 1,
  1980, pp. 57–64.
Sabatier, Paul. "Social Movements and Regulatory Agencies: Toward a More
  Adequate – and Less Pessimistic – Theory of 'Clientele Capture.'" *Policy
  Sciences* 6 (1975): 301–42.
Sagoff, Mark. "Where Ickes Went Right *or* Reason and Rationality in Envi-
  ronmental Law." *Ecology Law Quarterly* 14 (1987): 265–323.
Salamon, Lester B., and Gary L. Wamsley. "The Federal Bureaucracy: Re-
  sponsiveness to Whom?" In Leroy N. Rieselbach (ed.), *People vs. Government: The Responsiveness of American Institutions,* pp. 151–88. Bloomington: Indiana University Press, 1975.
Schattschneider, Elmer E. *The Semi-sovereign People: A Realist's View of Democracy in America.* New York: Holt, Rinehart & Winston, 1960.

Scheff, Thomas J. *Being Mentally Ill: A Sociological Theory.* Chicago: Aldine, 1966.

Schneider, Keith. "The Data Gap: What We Don't Know About Chemicals." *Amicus Journal* 6 (Winter 1985): 15–24.

Schoenfeld, A. Clay, Robert F. Meier, and Robert J. Griffin. "Constructing a Social Problem: The Press and the Environment." *Social Problems* 27 (October 1979): 38–56.

Schrager, Laura S., and James F. Short, Jr. "Toward a Sociology of Organizational Crime." *Social Problems* 25 (1978): 407–19.

"How Serious a Crime? Perceptions of Organizational and Common Crimes." In G. Geis and E. Stotland (eds.), *White-Collar Crime: Theory and Research*, pp. 14–31. Beverly Hills, Calif.: Sage, 1980.

Schroeder, Christopher. "Introduction: Federal Regulation of the Chemical Industry." *Law and Contemporary Problems* 46 (Summer 1983): 1–40.

Schwendinger, Herman, and Julia Schwendinger. "Defenders of Order or Guardians of Human Rights." In I. Taylor, P. Walton, and J. Young (eds.), *Critical Criminology*, pp. 113–46. London: Routledge & Kegan Paul, 1975.

Scull, Andrew. *Decarceration.* Englewood Cliffs, N.J.: Prentice-Hall, 1977.

Sellin, Thorsten. *Culture, Conflict and Crime.* New York: Social Science Research Council, 1938.

Sethi, S. Prakash. *Up Against the Corporate Wall* (4th ed.). Englewood Cliffs, N.J.: Prentice-Hall, 1982.

Shabecoff, Philip. "Aprés Ruckelshaus le Deluge?" *The New York Times*, December 3, 1984, p. 88.

"Budget Office Limited on Delays." *The New York Times*, January 30, 1986, p. B9.

"The Environment as Local Jurisdiction." *The New York Times*, January 22, 1989a, p. 9E.

"U.S. Calls Poisoning of Air Far Worse Than Expected and Threat to Public." *The New York Times*, March 23, 1989b, p. B11.

"Industrial Pollution Called Startling." *The New York Times*, April 13, 1989c, p. D21.

"Scientist Says Budget Office Altered His Testimony." *The New York Times*, May 8, 1989d, p. A1.

"U.S. Pinpoints Waterways Polluted by Toxic Chemicals." *The New York Times*, June 14, 1989e, p. A24.

"The Environment." *The New York Times*, June 29, 1989f, p. B7.

"Bush Would Agree to Elevate E.P.A." *The New York Times*, January 22, 1990, p. A1.

Shapiro, Susan. *Wayward Capitalists.* New Haven, Conn.: Yale University Press, 1984.

Shaw, Martin. "The Coming Crisis of Radical Sociology." In Robin Blackburn (ed.), *Ideology in Social Science*, pp. 32–44. New York: Vintage, 1973.

Shover, Neal. "The Criminalization of Corporate Behavior: Federal Surface Coal Mining." In G. Geis and E. Stotland (eds.), *White-Collar Crime: Theory and Research*, pp. 98–125. Beverly Hills, Calif.: Sage, 1980.

Shover, Neal, Donald A. Clelland, and John Lynxwiler. *Enforcement or Negotiation: Constructing a Regulatory Bureaucracy.* Albany: State University of New York Press, 1986.

Simon, D., and D. Eitzen. *Elite Deviance.* Boston: Allyn & Bacon, 1982.

Smith, V. Kerry. "Environmental Policy Making Under Executive Order 12291: An Introduction." In V. Kerry Smith (ed.), *Environmental Policy Under Reagan's Executive Order: The Role of Benefit–Cost Analysis*, pp. 3–40. Chapel Hill: University of North Carolina Press, 1984.

(ed.). *Environmental Policy Under Reagan's Executive Order: The Role of Benefit–Cost Analysis.* Chapel Hill: University of North Carolina Press, 1984.

Snider, D. Laureen. "Revising the Combines Investigation Act: A Study in Corporate Power." In P. J. Brantingham and J. M. Kress (eds.), *Structure, Law, and Power: Essays in the Sociology of Law*, pp. 105–19. Beverly Hills, Calif.: Sage, 1979.

Sonnenfeld, Jeffrey, and Paul R. Lawrence. "Why Do Companies Succumb to Price Fixing?" *Harvard Business Review* (July–August 1978): 145–57.

Speth, Gus. "A Small Price to Pay: Inflation and Environmental Controls." *Environment* 20 (October 1978): 25–8.

Spitzer, Steven. "The Rationalization of Crime Control in Capitalist Society." In Stanley Cohen and Andrew Scull (eds.), *Social Control and the State*, pp. 312–33. New York: St. Martin's Press, 1983.

(ed.). *Research in Law, Deviance and Social Control, Vol. 8.* Greenwich, Conn.: JAI Press, 1986.

(ed.). *Research in Law, Deviance and Social Control, Vol. 9.* Greenwich, Conn.: JAI Press, 1987.

Staw, Barry M., and Eugene Szwajkowski. "The Scarcity–Munificence Component of Organizational Environments and the Commission of Illegal Acts." *Administrative Science Quarterly* 20 (September 1975): 345–54.

Steck, Henry J. "Private Influence on Environmental Policy: The Case of the National Industrial Pollution Control Council." *Environmental Law* 5 (1975): 241–81.

Stone, Christopher D. *Where the Law Ends: The Social Control of Corporate Behavior.* New York: Harper & Row, 1975.

"A Slap on the Wrist for the Kepone Mob." *Business and Society Review* 22 (Summer 1977): 4–11.

Sudnow, David. "Normal Crimes: Sociological Features of the Penal Code." *Social Problems* 12 (Winter 1965): 255–70.

Suro, Roberto. "Grass-Roots Groups Show Power Battling Pollution Close to Home." *The New York Times*, July 2, 1989, p. 1.

Sutherland, Edwin H. "Is 'White Collar Crime' Crime?" *American Sociological Review* 10 (April 1945): 132–9.

White Collar Crime. New York: Holt, 1949.

Sutherland, Edwin H., and Donald R. Cressey. *Principles of Criminology* (5th ed.). Philadelphia: Lippincott, 1955.

Sutton, Adam C., and Ronald Wild. "Corporate Crime and Social Structure." In P. Wilson and J. Braithwaite (eds.), *Two Faces of Deviance*. St. Lucia: Queensland University Press, 1978.

Szasz, Andrew. "Industrial Resistance to Occupational Safety and Health Legislation: 1971–1981." *Social Problems* 32 (1984): 103–16.

"Corporations, Organized Crime, and the Disposal of Hazardous Waste: An Examination of the Making of a Criminogenic Regulatory Structure." *Criminology* 24 (February 1986a): 1–28.

"The Process and Significance of Political Scandals: A Comparison of Watergate and the 'Sewergate' Episode at the Environmental Protection Agency." *Social Problems* 33 (February 1986b): 202–17.

Szwajkowski, Eugene. "Organizational Illegality: Theoretical Integration and Illustrative Application." *Academy of Management Review* 10 (1985): 558–67.

Taylor, Ian, Paul Walton, and Jock Young. *The New Criminology: For a Social Theory of Deviance*. New York: Harper & Row, 1973.

(eds.). *Critical Criminology*. London: Routledge & Kegan Paul, 1975.

Taylor, Joel S. "Civil Penalties in Environmental Enforcement." In American Bar Association, *Environmental Enforcement: Selected Readings Prepared in Conjunction with the Seventh Annual Conference on the Environment*, pp. 22–4. Washington, D.C.: American Bar Association Standing Committee on Environmental Law, 1978.

Tennille, Norton F., Jr. "Federal Water Pollution Control Act Enforcement from the Discharger's Perspective: The Uses and Abuses of Discretion." *Environmental Law Reporter* 7 (1977): 50091–9.

"Environmental Enforcement in a Discretion-Based Regulatory System." In American Bar Association, *Environmental Enforcement: Selected Readings Prepared in Conjunction with the Seventh Annual Conference on the Environment*, pp. 9–12. Washington, D.C.: American Bar Association Standing Committee on Environmental Law, 1978a.

"Criminal Prosecution of Individuals: A New Trend in Federal Environmental Enforcement?" In American Bar Association, *Environmental Enforcement: Selected Readings Prepared in Conjunction with the Seventh Annual Conference on the Environment*, pp. 20–2. Washington, D.C.: American Bar Association Standing Committee on Environmental Law, 1978b.

Therborn, Göran. *What Does the Ruling Class Do When It Rules?* New York: Schocken Books, 1978.

Thorelli, Hans B. *The Federal Antitrust Policy*. Baltimore, Md.: Johns Hopkins University Press, 1954.

Tillman, Robert, and Carol A. B. Warren. "A Political Economy of Deviance: The State and Social Control." *Contemporary Sociology* 13 (July 1984): 412–14.

Tolchin, Susan J., and Martin Tolchin. *Dismantling America: The Rush to Deregulate*. Boston: Houghton Mifflin, 1983.

Tripp, James T. B. "Tensions and Conflicts in Federal Pollution Control and Water Resource Policy." *Harvard Journal on Legislation* 14 (February 1977): 225–80.

Turner, James S. *The Chemical Feast: The Report on the Food and Drug Administration*. New York: Grossman, 1970.

Turner, Tom. "The Legal Eagles." *Amicus Journal* 10 (Winter 1988): 25–37.

U.S. Department of the Army. "Permits for Work and Structures in, and for Discharges or Deposits into Navigable Waters" (4th printing). Washington, D.C.: Corps of Engineers, 1972. Mimeo.

U.S. Environmental Protection Agency. *A Progress Report: December 1970–June 1972*. Washington, D.C.: U.S. Government Printing Office, November 1972.

EPA Enforcement: Two Years of Progress – December 1972 to November 1974. Washington, D.C.: U.S. Environmental Protection Agency, 1975.

No Small Task: Establishing National Effluent Limitations Guidelines and Standards. Washington, D.C.: U.S. Environmental Protection Agency, June 1976a.

EPA Enforcement: A Progress Report – December 1974 to December 1975. Washington, D.C.: U.S. Environmental Protection Agency, 1976b.

EPA Enforcement: A Progress Report – 1976. Washington, D.C.: U.S. Environmental Protection Agency, January 1977a.

"Summary Statistics on Anticipated Violations of the July 1, 1977 Statutory Deadline." Washington, D.C.: Office of Water Enforcement, 1977b. Mimeo.

U.S. House of Representatives. *Federal Regulation and Regulatory Reform*. Report by the Subcommittee on Oversight and Investigations of the Committee on Interstate and Foreign Commerce. Washington, D.C.: U.S. Government Printing Office, October 1976.

To Amend and Extend Authorizations for the Federal Water Pollution Control Act. Hearings before the Subcommittee on Water Resources of the Committee on Public Works and Transportation, March 1, 2, 3, 4, 1977; Serial no. 95–5. Washington, D.C.: U.S. Government Printing Office, 1977a.

Implementation of the Federal Water Pollution Control Act: Summary of Hearings on the Regulation and Monitoring of Toxic and Hazardous Chemicals Under the Federal Water Pollution Control Act (P.L. 92–500), July 19, 20, 21, 28, 29, 1977. Report prepared by the Environment and Natural Resources Policy Division of the Congressional Research Service, Library of Congress, for the Committee on Public Works and Transportation, Serial no. 95–25. Washington, D.C.: U.S. Government Printing Office, September 1977b.

Case Law Under the Federal Water Pollution Control Act Amendments of 1972. Report prepared by the American Law Division of the Congressional Research Service, Library of Congress, for the Committee on Public

Works and Transportation, Serial no. 95–35. Washington, D.C.: U.S. Government Printing Office, November 1977c.

EPA Enforcement and Administration of Superfund. Hearings before the Subcommittee on Oversight and Investigations of the Committee on Energy and Commerce, November 16, 18, 1981, and April 2, 1982; Serial no. 97–123. Washington, D.C.: U.S. Government Printing Office, 1982.

EPA Oversight: One-Year Review. Joint Hearings before Certain Subcommittees of the Committee on Government Operations, the Committee on Energy and Commerce, and the Committee on Science and Technology, July 21 and 22, 1982; Serial no. 97–199 (Committee on Energy and Commerce), Serial no. 168 (Committee on Science and Technology). Washington, D.C.: U.S. Government Printing Office, 1983.

U.S. Senate. *A Legislative History of the Water Pollution Control Act Amendments of 1972,* vol. 1. Prepared by the Environmental Policy Division of the Congressional Research Service, Library of Congress, for the Committee on Public Works, Serial No. 93–1. Washington, D.C.: U.S. Government Printing Office, January 1973.

The Clean Water Act: Showing Changes Made by the 1977 Amendments. Committee on Environment and Public Works, Serial No. 95–12. Washington, D.C.: U.S. Government Printing Office, December 1977a.

Study on Federal Regulation. Committee on Governmental Affairs, Vols. 1–6. Washington, D.C.: U.S. Government Printing Office, 1977b.

Environmental Protection Affairs of the Ninety-Fifth Congress. Report prepared by the Environment and Natural Resources Policy Division of the Congressional Research Service, Library of Congress, for the Committee on Environment and Public Works, Serial no. 96–5. Washington, D.C.: U.S. Government Printing Office, May 1979.

Vaughan, Diane. *Controlling Unlawful Organizational Behavior.* Chicago: University of Chicago Press, 1983.

Vogel, David. "Why Businessmen Distrust Their State: The Political Consciousness of American Corporate Executives." *British Journal of Political Science* 8 (January 1978): 45–78.

Vold, George. *Theoretical Criminology.* New York: Oxford University Press, 1958.

Weaver, Paul H. "Regulation, Social Policy, and Class Conflict." In Chris Argyris et al., *Regulating Business: The Search for an Optimum.* San Francisco: Institute for Contemporary Studies, 1978.

Weaver, Suzanne. *Decision to Prosecute: Organization and Public Policy in the Antitrust Division.* Cambridge, Mass.: MIT Press, 1977.

Weidenbaum, Murray L. *The Future of Business Regulation: Private Action and Public Demand.* New York: AMACOM, 1979.

Weinstein, James. *The Decline of Socialism in America, 1912–1925.* New York: Monthly Review Press, 1967.

Wenner, L. M. *Enforcement of Water Pollution Control Laws in the United States.* Ph.D. dissertation, University of Wisconsin–Madison, 1972.

"Federal Water Pollution Control Statutes in Theory and Practice." *Environmental Law* (Winter 1974): 251–93.

One Environment Under Law: A Public Policy Dilemma. Pacific Palisades, Calif.: Goodyear Publishing, 1976.

The Environmental Decade in Court. Bloomington: Indiana University Press, 1982.

Wheeler, Stanton, David Weisburd, and Nancy Bode. "Sentencing the White-Collar Offender: Rhetoric and Reality." *American Sociological Review* 47 (1982): 641–59.

Wickman, P., and T. Dailey (eds.). *White-Collar and Economic Crime.* Lexington, Mass.: Heath, 1982.

Wilson, James Q. "The Politics of Regulation." In J. Q. Wilson (ed.), *The Politics of Regulation.* New York: Basic Books, 1980.

Wolfgang, Marvin. "Crime and Punishment." *New York Times,* March 2, 1980, p. E21.

Wright, Erik Olin. "Alternative Perspectives in the Marxist Theory of Accumulation and Crisis." In J. Schwartz (ed.), *The Subtle Anatomy of Capitalism,* pp. 195–231. Pacific Palisades, Calif.: Goodyear Publishing, 1977.

"Towards a Post-Marxist Radical Social Theory: A Review Essay on Samuel Bowles and Herbert Gintis, *Democracy and Capitalism.*" *Contemporary Sociology* 16 (September 1987): 748–53.

Yeager, Peter C. "Structural Strain Toward Deviance in Soviet Firms: With Comparisons to the American Case." Mimeo, 1977.

The Politics of Corporate Social Control: The Federal Response to Industrial Water Pollution. Ph.D. dissertation, University of Wisconsin–Madison, 1981.

"The Limits of Law: On Chambliss & Seidman's *Law, Order and Power.*" *American Bar Foundation Research Journal* 1983 (Fall 1983): 974–84.

"Analyzing Corporate Offenses: Progress and Prospects." In James E. Post (ed.), *Research in Corporate Social Performance and Policy,* Vol. 8, pp. 93–120. Greenwich, Conn.: JAI Press, 1986.

Yeager, Peter C., and Marshall B. Clinard. "Regulating Corporate Behavior: A Case Study." In P. J. Brantingham and J. M. Kress (eds.), *Structure, Law, and Power: Essays in the Sociology of Law,* pp. 62–82. Beverly Hills, Calif.: Sage, 1979.

Zwick, David, and Marcy Benstock. *Water Wasteland.* New York: Grossman, 1971.

Index

353

law in, 21; constraints on pollution
control, 129; distribution of life
chances in, 19–20; economic growth
as principal value in, 83; and
economic growth/water pollution
trade-off, 55–6, 57; emphasis on
private-sector creation of wealth/jobs,
70; and implementation of law, 176;
larger aggregates of wealth influence
in, 61–2; and legal change, 16; limits
of, 174; limits of law in, 305, 306,
309, 312; negotiation of law in, 42;
nexus linking regulated companies
and legal administration, 10, 11; place
of environmental controls in, 65; policy implications of, 2, 87, 117; regulation and, 141n12, 213; regulatory
logic in, 226–34; tension between law
and ecology in, 303–6; uncertainties
in, 217, 223; values in, 103; and water
pollution control, 121
political ideology, effect on law, 312
politics: of circulation, 160; of complexity, 164–5; and enforcement, 319–20;
of environmental protection, 65, 74,
82, 110–11; and environmental rights,
131; in EPA regulations, 205; ideological, 231; and law, 7, 8, 131–47, 252;
logics of, 226–34; of optimism, 244;
of pollution, 14; of production, 160;
of rationality, 323–4; of regulation,
226–34; and regulation of toxics,
216–42; and regulatory agencies, 39;
and state authority, 23; of symbolism,
59–83, 145, 146–7; of uncertainty,
217, 234; of water, 51–83; and water
pollution legislation, 171–2, 188
pollutants, 101, 113–14, 314n8; inventory of, 125–6; regulation of, 177;
types of, and water pollution control,
243–4; see also toxic pollutants
polluters: resistance to control of, 63–4;
subsidization of, 88–9, 182; suits
against, 107–8, 120–1 (see also civil/
criminal cases); see also major
dischargers
pollution, vii–viii, 4, 85; economic
growth and, 132; in GNP, 326; legal
efforts to contain, 53–9; as necessary
evil, 62; production and consumption
and, 85–6, 109–10; right to, 152; systemic, 59–60; see also industrial pollution; water pollution
pollution control, 60, 104; costs of, 86,
246–8; early efforts at, 53–9; ecologi-

cal effects of, 243–6; economic effects
of, 142–3, 153–4, 156–7, 168–70,
172–3, 246–50; federal government
and, 87, 182; industry efforts at, 96–
8; as public right, 15–16; rationalization of, 203; technology-forcing, 167,
240; see also standards; technology
pollution control industry, 96, 248, 249,
309
pollution control law, 120; indictments
of, 149–50; inequitable impacts of,
213–15 (see also large corporations
advantages of)
pollution control policy, 114, 115–16,
119n39, 124, 128–9; centralization of,
117–18; irrationalities in, 327; to
1970, 51–83
polychlorinated biphenyls (PCBs), 223
Poor Law Commission (Great Britain),
57
pork barrel politics, 147, 166n51
power, centralization of, 98, 99
power relations, 31, 44; in implementation of law, 6–7, 176
"practicability" standard, 69, 70
Presidential Task Force on Regulatory
Relief, 228
press, role in environment as social
movement, 105n23
pretreatment standards, 167, 179–80,
237, 247
price fixing, 8, 26, 36
private accumulation, 40n17, 44–5, 46
private enforcement, 320–2
private production, 296; primacy of,
40–1
private sector, 13; creation of wealth/
jobs, 70; influence on law, 10; need
for regulation, 48; regulation in
reproduction of inequality in, 284–
92; regulatory agencies' dependency
on, 40
private victims, challenging pollution in
court, 60, 61–2
privatization, 26
procedural law, 35–6
Procter & Gamble (Co.), 137
product safety laws, 8, 10, 45
production, 109; and consumption, 85–
6; environmental tax on (proposed),
329–30; organic chemicals industry,
234–5; private, 40–1, 296
production data: industry control over,
233–4; organic chemicals industry,
238

social regulation, 15, 22, 24–5, 227–8, 251; bounds of, in capitalist democracies, 306–7; burden of, 311n5; in Carter administration, 313; constraints on, 296; contradictions and, 46–7; critical perspective on, 20–47; effectiveness of, 188; enforcement of, 298; failure of, 30; firm size and, 293–4; industry response to, 209–10; Quality of Life reviews, 204; Reagan administration assault on, 312, 315–17; structural model of, 47–8; systematic limits of, 295

social relations, 11n11, 23, 27; consensually endorsed, 18; contradictory logic in, 84–5; limits of law institutionalized in, ix; rationalization of, 25, 40

social structure: and environmental values, 98–110; state and, 22–3

social welfare spending, 22, 23

Stafford, Robert, 235

stagflation, 306, 313

Standard Oil (Co.), 26, 27

standards: media-quality, 198, 202; for new facilities, 214–15; pollution control, 153, 162; pretreatment, 167, 179–80, 237, 247; technology-forcing, 151–3, 155, 167, 194–6, 250, 292; toxics, 218n74; *see also* state standards; technology-based standards; water quality standards

standards setting: and enforcement, 193; government/industry cooperation in, 71–2

standing to sue, 111–13, 120; *see also* legal standing, expansion of

Stans, Maurice, 136–7, 141

state: business needs from, 212–15; centralization of social control functions, 25; complexity of, 171n59; control of elite interests by, 18–19; dependence on economic growth in private sector, 32–3, 75, 124–6, 174; interventionist, 45; politicization of, 46; role of, 17–19; and social structure, 21, 22–3; theories of, 21–2

state authority, fragmentation of, 34–6

state–economy relation, 3, 25–6, 48, 49; institutional, 70–1, 81–2; and limits of regulatory law, 31; model of (in regulation), 13

state governments: and environmental protection, 322; and pollution control, 60–3, 68, 69, 70, 72, 73–4, 79, 81, 87, 88–9

state-issued permits, 207–8, 264; EPA veto of, 167–8

state law(s), 27, 28, 29, 113n33; water pollution control, 60–1, 62, 63–4

state power, concentration of, 34–5

state standards, 79–80, 81–3, 141

states, 60, 126, 228–9; enforcement, 262–3; federal deference to, 127, 161; primary regulatory role of, 133; water standards, 121

states' rights, 63, 66, 72, 76, 81, 82, 153, 181, 308, 309

steel industry, 235

Stein, Murray, 73, 76

Stone, Christopher, 99

Storm King Mountain, 111–12

stormwater control permits, 244n134

structural bias, 47–8; in regulatory law, 269, 276–92

structural model: of social regulation, 47–8; test of, 284–92

structuralist theory, ix–x, 22–4

Student Council on Pollution and the Environment, 132–3

Sudbury River, vii

"sunshine" legislation, 33

Superfund program, 316, 330

Supreme Court (U.S.), 27, 35, 112, 113–14, 119, 120, 170, 183n8, 196–7

Sutherland, Edwin, 7–8, 64; *White Collar Crime*, 3–4

symbolism: politics of, 59–83

taconite waste, 93–5

Taft, Robert A., 66

tax, environmental (proposed), 329–30

Tax Reform Act of 1969, 90

technocratic legitimacy, 35

technological innovation, constrained by technology-based standards, 202, 210–12, 213, 214–16, 239–40, 241, 310–12

technology, 147, 177, 328; effects of, 216–17; focus on existing, 215–16, 220; generating social change, 106n25; limits of, 222–34; logics of, 223–6; need for new, 312; pollution control, 12, 151–3, 155, 158–60, 240, 312; risk in new, 216–17; and toxics regulation, 222–3

technology-based standards: as constraint on technological innovation, 202, 210–12, 213, 214–16, 239–